FEMINIST SOCIAL PSYCHOLOGIES

International perspectives

Edited by
SUE WILKINSON

OPEN UNIVERSITY PRESS
Buckingham · Philadelphia

Open University Press
Celtic Court
22 Ballmoor
Buckingham
MK18 1XW

and
1900 Frost Road, Suite 101
Bristol, PA 19007, USA

First Published 1996

A catalogue record of this book is available from the British Library

ISBN 0 335 19354 4 (pbk)   0 335 19355 2 (hbk)

Library of Congress Cataloging-in-Publication Data

Feminist social psychologies : international perspectives / edited by Sue
  Wilkinson.
      p.   cm.
    Includes bibliographical references and index.
    ISBN 0-335-19354-4 (pbk)   ISBN 0-335-19355-2 (hbk)
    1. Feminist psychology.   2. Social psychology.   3. Women—
Psychology.   4. Psychoanalysis and feminism.   5. Feminism.
I. Wilkinson, Sue.
BF201.4.F46   1996
305.42—dc20   96-8815
                                                                                    CIP

Typeset by Type Study, Scarborough, North Yorkshire
Printed in Great Britain by Biddles Limited, Guildford and Kings Lynn

FEMINIST SOCIAL PSYCHOLOGIES

UNIVERSITY OF
WOLVERHAMPTON
KNOWLEDGE • INNOVATION • ENTERPRISE

UNIVERSITY OF
WOLVERHAMPTON
Harrison Learning Centre

Title: SPSS for psychologists : a guide to data
analysis using SPSS for Windows : (
ID: 7622529926

Title: SPSS for psychologists : a guide to data
analysis using SPSS for Windows : (
ID: 7622529942

Title: Feminist social psychologies : international
perspectives
ID: 7620973326

Title: introduction to Wittgenstein's Tractatus
ID: 7620197551

Total items: 4
11/05/2008 14:28

Thank You for using Self Service.
Please keep your receipt.

Overdue books are fined at 40p per day for
1 week loans, 10p per day for long loans.

To John, as promised

Contents

Feminist critique of scien...
Modern / = Masters/ Metaperspe...

Notes on contributors

JUDI ADDELSTON obtained her doctorate in social/personality psychology from the City University of New York Graduate Center in 1996. Her research interests focus on the social construction of gender, masculinities, women's studies, intergroup relations and prejudice, with an emphasis on the development and performance of masculinities in educational settings. She is now working with an elite independent all-male high school investigating the construction of a masculinity privileged by race and class. Additionally, she is preparing a college textbook on the psychology of prejudice. Judi is currently a Visiting Assistant Professor of Psychology and Women's Studies at Rollins College in Winter Park, Florida.

NANCY J. CHODOROW is Professor of Sociology at the University of California, Berkeley. Her books include *The Reproduction of Mothering* (University of California Press, 1978) and *Feminism and Psychoanalytic Theory* (Yale University Press, 1989).

JUNE CRAWFORD is currently a research consultant to the National Centre in HIV Social Research, Australia. Until 1994 she was an Associate Professor in the School of Behavioural Sciences, Macquarie University, New South Wales. Her research interests include women and HIV, feminism and psychology, and memory and emotions. As well as publishing a number of papers in these areas she co-authored *Emotion and Gender: Constructing Meaning from Memory* (Sage, 1992) and *Sustaining Safe Sex: Gay Communities Respond to AIDS* (Falmer, 1993).

JILL J. CROWLEY is a PhD student in social psychology and feminist theory at the University of California, Davis. Her research focuses on the social-cognitive processes through which individuals translate and critically evaluate mass-marketed, culturally produced, ideal images. Specifically, she investigates the ways in which individuals use these images to form impressions of themselves and others. Her approach is informed by theory from various disciplines, including critical film, cultural, and women's studies. She is interested in locating a space for a feminist psychology which is able to challenge and transform conventional disciplines while moving within and between them.

KATHY DAVIS is a Senior Lecturer in Women's Studies at Utrecht University, the Netherlands. She is the author of *Reshaping the Female Body* (Routledge, 1995) and co-editor of several books on gender, power and discourse.

ALICE H. EAGLY is a Professor of Psychology at Northwestern University. She has also held faculty positions at Purdue University, University of Massachusetts at Amherst, and Michigan State University. Her research interests encompass comparisons of female and male social behaviour, gender stereotypes, and various topics in attitude theory and research. She is the author of *Sex Differences in Social Behavior: A Social Role Interpretation* (1987), *The Psychology of Attitudes* (with Shelly Chaiken, 1993), and numerous articles and chapters.

OLIVA M. ESPIN is Professor of Women's Studies at San Diego State University, San Diego, California, and has published widely on issues of identity, sexuality, ethnicity and mental health, especially in relation to Latina lesbians and refugees. Her recent books include *Refugee Women and Their Mental Health: Shattered Societies, Shattered Lives* (co-edited with Ellen Cole and Esther Rothblum) and *Power, Culture and Tradition: The Lives of Latina Healers in Urban Centers in The United States*.

MICHELLE FINE is Professor of Psychology at the City University of New York Graduate Center and the Senior Consultant at the Philadelphia Schools Collaborative. Her recent publications include *Chartering Urban School Reform: Reflections on Public High Schools in the Midst of Change* (1994), *Beyond Silenced Voices: Class, Race and Gender in American Schools* (1992), *Disruptive Voices: The Transgressive Possibilities of Feminist Research* (1992) and *Framing Dropouts: Notes on the Politics of an Urban High School* (1991).

NICOLA GAVEY is a Lecturer in Psychology at the University of Auckland, New Zealand. Her research interests include discourses of sexuality, sexual violence and abuse, and the uses of postmodernism in feminist research.

CAROL GILLIGAN is Professor of Education in the Human Development and

Psychology Department, Harvard Graduate School of Education. Her books include *In a Different Voice: Psychological Theory and Women's Development* (Harvard University Press, 1982) and (with Lyn Mikel Brown) *Meeting at the Crossroads: Women's Psychology and Girl's Development* (Harvard University Press, 1992).

SUSAN KIPPAX is Director of the National Centre in HIV Social Research, Australia. She is a social psychologist at Macquarie University, New South Wales. In the past few years her research work has been focused on the social aspects of HIV prevention and on issues related to sex, gender and emotion. She has published a number of papers on sexuality, as well as a book, *Sustaining Safe Sex: Gay Communities Respond to AIDS* (Falmer, 1993). In 1992 she co-authored *Emotion and Gender: Constructing Meaning from Memories* (Sage, 1992).

CELIA KITZINGER is Director of Women's Studies in the Department of Social Sciences at Loughborough University. Her books include *The Social Construction of Lesbianism* (Sage, 1987) and (with Rachel Perkins) *Changing Our Minds: Lesbian Feminism and Psychology* (New York University Press and Onlywomen Press, 1993). She has edited several books jointly with Sue Wilkinson, including *Heterosexuality* (Sage, 1993) and *Representing the Other* (Sage, 1996), both of them *Feminism & Psychology* Readers.

CHARLENE Y. SENN is currently an Assistant Professor in the Department of Psychology at the University of Windsor, Ontario. Her research interests are primarily in the field of violence against women. She is currently working on a random sample mail survey investigating men's coercive and non-coercive behaviours in dating relationships and a small qualitative study of women's experiences of delayed memory recovery following child sexual abuse.

KELLY SHAW-BARNES is a graduate student in social psychology at Purdue University. She received a BA in psychology at Knox College and an MS at Purdue University. Her research interests include attitudes and social values.

STEPHANIE A. SHIELDS is Professor of Psychology and Director of the Pro Femina Resarch Consortium at the University of California, Davis. She works at the interface of gender theory and the psychology of emotion and focuses on the relationship between emotion consciousness (i.e. 'felt' or experienced emotion) and emotion as a cultural construct. She is deeply interested in the ways in which feminist critiques of social science can inform innovative application and interpretation of conventional empirical methods. She wants her work to contribute to feminist transformation of what experimental social psychology investigates and how its products are deployed in society. As this book goes to press, she is preparing to move to Penn State University as Professor of Women's Studies.

NIAMH STEPHENSON is undertaking a PhD on the topic of women and conversation, in the School of Behavioural Sciences, Macquarie University, New South Wales. She also works as a research officer at the National Centre in HIV Social Research, Macquarie University.

AMY M. SULLIVAN is a research consultant and doctoral candidate in Human Development and Psychology at the Graduate School of Education, Harvard University.

JILL McLEAN TAYLOR is Assistant Professor of Education and Human Services at Simmons College, Boston, Massachusetts, where she also teaches women's studies. She is also co-ordinator of the Comer Project of school reform, working with Boston public schools.

RHODA K. UNGER is Professor of Psychology and Director of the all-college honours programme at Montclair State University. She has a PhD from Harvard University in experimental psychology. She is a past president of Division 35 of APA and the first recipient of its Carolyn Wood Sherif award. Her recent work includes a second edition (co-authored with Mary Crawford) of *Women and Gender: A Feminist Psychology* (McGraw-Hill, 1996).

VALERIE WALKERDINE is Professor of the Psychology of Communication at Goldsmiths College, University of London. She is currently undertaking research on class and transition to womanhood for the ESRC and is writing a book, provisionally entitled *Towards a Psychology of Survival*. Her latest book is *Daddy's Girl: Young Girls and Popular Culture* (Macmillan, 1996).

SUE WILKINSON is a Senior Lecturer in Social Psychology in the Department of Social Sciences at Loughborough University. She is the founding and current editor of the international journal *Feminism & Psychology*, and was a founding member and first elected chair of the BPS Psychology of Women Section. Her books include: *Feminist Social Psychology* and (with Celia Kitzinger) *Heterosexuality, Women and Health, Feminism and Discourse*, and *Representing the Other*.

Acknowledgements

As with my 1986 volume, *Feminist Social Psychology*, my thanks go first to the contributors to this book, all of whom revised their contributions with exemplary speed and grace, so that it could be published in 1996, in order to mark ten years of development in the field. I'm pleased and delighted that this has been possible – and appreciative both of the work involved and of the feminist commitment it represents.

I would also like to thank the staff at Open University Press (Jacinta Evans, Joan Malherbe, Sue Hadden, Maureen Cox and Anita West) for their efficient handling of the publishing process.

Appreciation goes, too, to my colleagues at Loughborough University for making the Department of Social Sciences such a stimulating environment in which to work – and one in which the possibility of debate is ever-present.

Formal acknowledgement is due to: Yale University Press and Polity Press for permission to reprint, as Chapter 1, a slightly edited version of 'Seventies Questions for Thirties Women: Gender and Generation in a Study of Early Women Psychoanalysts', which originally appeared in 1989 as Chapter 10 of Nancy J. Chodorow's *Feminism and Psychoanalytic Theory*; also to Sage Publications Ltd for permission to reprint, as Chapter 4, Oliva M. Espin's article '"Race", Racism and Sexuality in the Life Narratives of Immigrant Women', which originally appeared in 1995 in *Feminism & Psychology: An International Journal* 5(2): 223–38.

Finally, thanks to Celia Kitzinger for her enthusiasm and support for this project – and for sharing my interest in feminist social psychologies, as well as so much else.

Feminist social psychologies: A decade of development

SUE WILKINSON

Ten years ago, I edited a collection entitled *Feminist Social Psychology: Developing Theory and Practice* (Wilkinson, 1986). That book became a 'landmark' text, often cited as marking the beginning of feminist social psychology in Britain. It was also seen as offering useful working definitions of the nature and scope of the field, together with examples of feminist social psychology in practice. Now, a decade on, the field has grown and developed very substantially. It is much more varied and sophisticated in its range of theories and methods; it has attained much greater institutional representation; it has many more publishing outlets; and it has become a truly international academic enterprise. These developments have also enabled feminist social psychology to become more influential both within the academy and beyond it. It is now creating change within mainstream psychology; it is a key contributor to multidisciplinary women's studies; and it is clearly part of the broader feminist struggle to dismantle social inequalities and to improve the conditions of women's lives.

This volume reflects the academic standing and influence of feminist social psychology today, providing a showcase for the richness and diversity of contemporary research in the field. It includes contributions from leading feminist social psychologists in Britain, continental Europe, North America and Australasia. The contributing authors utilize a variety of theoretical frameworks – ranging from empiricism through social constructionism to psychoanalysis – to bring a feminist analysis to a range of key topics for women, among them sexual violence, racism, pornography, femininity and beauty, emotion, social class, and anti-lesbianism.

They also demonstrate the use of a broad range of qualitative and quantitative methods in feminist research. Feminist social psychology is not a unified field with a single 'politically correct' line – rather, it offers a potentially dazzling variety of approaches. Indeed, the field can now more appropriately be called 'feminist social psycholog*ies*'.

This collection offers an ideal introduction to feminist social psychologies. In effect, it maps out the field today. While (of course) not claiming to include every theoretical approach or every possible method, it none the less represents the range of key traditions and techniques. It was very difficult to select whose work to include in the book. The work of many excellent feminist social psychologists is excluded simply for reasons of space. When I put together *Feminist Social Psychology* ten years ago, the task was relatively circumscribed, particularly as my contributors were limited to Britain alone. However, the field has now burgeoned on both sides of the Atlantic, as well as elsewhere in the world, and this book is a much more ambitious project than its predecessor, in attempting to represent feminist social psychologies internationally. I have opted for a diversity of theories and methods, with some attempt to represent a range of nationalities and also individuals at different stages of their careers. Perhaps inevitably, contributors from the USA predominate – both because of the long history of feminist organizing within and beyond the American Psychological Association and because of the sheer number of feminist social psychologists in the USA. Most of the authors whose work is included here are internationally recognized for their contributions; the remainder represent emergent traditions and/or look set to become future leaders in the field. It is perhaps indicative of the maturity of the field in the 1990s that so many theoretically and practically incompatible approaches can coexist. This book, while not attempting to adjudicate between different approaches or methods, highlights some of the lines of tension between them, encouraging explicit debate amongst feminists regarding the implications and utility of the particular traditions within which we work.

In the remainder of this editorial overview, I will first provide a brief introduction to the field of feminist social psychologies. Then, I will highlight some of the main ways in which the field has developed over the last decade, particularly in Britain. Finally, I will contextualize the chapters in this collection in terms of their contributions to the field.

Introducing the field

'Feminist social psychologies' are social psychological theories and practices which are explicitly informed by the political goals of the feminist movement. 'Feminism' embraces a plurality of definitions and viewpoints, but these different versions of feminism share two common themes (Unger and Crawford, 1992: 8–9). First, feminism places a high value on women, considering us as worthy of study in our own right, not just in comparison with men. Second, feminism recognizes the need for social change on behalf of women – feminist social psychologies are avowedly political.

The terms 'feminist (social) psychology' and 'psychology of women' are sometimes used interchangeably, particularly in North American psychology (see, for example, Worrell, 1990). It is true that much of the research conducted under the banner of 'psychology of women' is explicitly or implicitly feminist in intent, although it does not use that label. This has arisen because of mainstream psychology's opposition to any kind of overt politics. Mainstream psychology has polarized 'science' (pure, objective scholarship) against 'politics' (ideologically biased advocacy), and has actively resisted the development of feminist social psychologies with their clear political basis (Unger, 1982; Wilkinson, 1989). So, in order to be able to engage with the mainstream of the discipline (rather than simply be dismissed by it), social psychologists doing feminist work have sometimes made strategic use of the label 'psychology of women' as a less politically contentious euphemism (see Mednick, 1978; Wilkinson, 1990).

However, many psychologists researching 'women' or 'women's issues', with no interest in or commitment to feminism whatsoever, identify themselves as working within the field of 'psychology of women'. A large part of this field is rigidly conventional in its support for the status quo. Much of 'psychology of women' challenges neither the institutions and practices of psychology nor the dominant conceptions of women which the discipline constructs and promotes. It does not engage with the damage psychology has done to many women's lives, nor does it struggle to end psychology's continuing oppressions.

Those who call themselves 'feminist social psychologists' often set out explicitly to differentiate themselves from the anodyne and acceptable face of 'psychology of women'. We use the term 'feminist' specifically to highlight the political aspects of our work. Feminist social psychologies challenge the discipline of psychology for its inadequate and damaging theories about women, and for its failure to see power relations as central to social life.

Feminist social psychologies are distinguished by their insistence upon exposing and challenging the operation of male power in psychology:

> psychology's theories often exclude women, or distort our experience – by assimilating it to male norms or man-made stereotypes, or by regarding 'women' as a unitary category, to be understood only in comparison with the unitary category 'men'. . . . Similarly,

psychology [screens out] . . . the existence and operation of social and structural inequalities between and within social groups (power differentials are written out).

(Wilkinson, 1991a: 7–8)

Feminist social psychologies also look beyond the confines of psychology as an academic discipline, addressing the power it has in shaping everyday understandings and in producing real, material effects in the world. They emphasize how psychology obscures the social and structural operation of male power by concentrating its analysis on people as individuals – and they point to the dangers of this individualism:

> Feminist [social] psychologists have also been critical of the harm that psychology (and the popularization of psychological ideas) has wrought in women's lives: primarily (but not exclusively) through the location of responsibility – and also pathology – within the individual, to the total neglect of social and political oppression.

(Wilkinson, 1991a: 8)

Perhaps most important, according to feminist social psychologist Michelle Fine (1992: viii), is that feminist social psychologies are a form of 'social change strategy'. They aim to end the social and political oppression of women.

Psychology's central assertion has been that women are inferior to men. According to pioneering feminist social psychologist Naomi Weisstein, writing in 1968, women are characterized by psychology as:

> inconsistent, emotionally unstable, lacking in a strong conscience or superego, weaker, 'nurturant' rather than productive, 'intuitive' rather than intelligent, and, if they are at all 'normal', suited to the home and the family. In short, the list adds up to a typical minority group stereotype of inferiority. . . .

(Weisstein, 1993: 207)

All apparent 'differences' between women and men are characterized by psychology as 'inferiorities', except where women's differences equip us so naturally to excel in our roles as wives and mothers. From the beginnings of psychology onwards, this characterization of women as inferior has been used to confine women to the kitchen, the bedroom and the nursery. It has also been used (historically) to deny women access to education and to professional careers; and (more recently) to 'explain' and justify our limited successes within these spheres.

So, for example, the 'founding fathers' of psychology around the turn of the century (such as James M. Cattell, G. Stanley Hall, Edward Thorndike, E. B. Titchener) all drew on the new science of evolution – including the view that women are less highly evolved and possess only primitive mental abilities – to support their arguments that women should be excluded from high academic rank and from professional organizations (Bohan, 1992: 34). According to these psychologists (particularly Hall), education could threaten women's fertility, because the brain would compete with the uterus for blood and energy, leading – in 'the mental woman' – to uterine atrophy and shrivelled, non-lactating breasts (Ehrenreich and English, 1979: 125–31).

Today, discrimination against women in the professions is still justified in some contemporary writing with reference to psychological 'findings'. Take, for example, the work of Dr Glenn Wilson, a Fellow of the British Psychological Society, who says that the reason why 95% of bank managers, company directors, judges and university professors in Britain are men is that men are 'more competitive' and because 'dominance is a personality characteristic determined by male hormones' (Wilson, 1994: 62, 63). The psychological research which enables Wilson to make these claims is derived in part from the psychometric testing industries which are particularly implicated in providing 'scientific' evidence of women's inadequacies: for example, women lack mathematical ability (Benbow and Stanley, 1980), are less good at spatial tasks than men (Masters and Sanders, 1993) and suffer from impaired performance on visual spatial tasks during parts of the menstrual cycle (Hampson, 1990). Even if women are considered to have the ability to perform well in professional jobs, we have personality defects – in particular 'low self-esteem' (Lenney, 1977) or 'lack of assertiveness' (Alberti, 1977) – which impede our performance.

Central to psychology's success in perpetuating oppression is its individualism. By locating 'causes' and 'cures' within individuals, and by ignoring or minimizing the social context, psychology obscures the mechanisms of oppression. The whole field of sex differences, in particular, exhibits a relentless focus on the individual and the internal at the expense of external circumstances and social systems. In giving precedence to individual and interpersonal explanations, mainstream psychology 'explains' and justifies the structural oppression of women.

Feminist social psychologists have their origins in the work of feminists in psychology at the turn of the century – for example, Helen Thompson Wooley (1910: 340), who described mainstream psychological research on sex differences as characterized by 'flagrant personal bias, logic martyred in the cause of supporting a prejudice . . . [and] sentimental rot and drivel'. More than half a century later, as second-wave feminism gathered momentum in the 1970s, feminists launched clear and direct challenges to psychology as a discipline. In one of the most commonly cited early critiques, dating from 1968, Naomi Weisstein (1993: 197) asserted that: 'Psychology has nothing to say about what women are really like, what they need and what they want . . . because psychology does not know'. Other feminist social psychologists have characterized the discipline as 'a psychology against women' (Henley, 1974: 20), which has 'distorted facts, omitted problems, and perpetuated pseudoscientific data relevant to women' (Parlee, 1975: 124).

Since the 1970s, feminists have developed a wide range of different approaches, both within and against psychology. In the early days of feminist social psychologies, we wrote largely for *non-feminist* readers – attacking the theories and implicit political commitments of mainstream psychology. In my 1986 book, I was also concerned to explain and justify the development of a feminist social psychology to traditionalists:

> a feminist perspective is important not just for feminist researchers, but for *all* research in social psychology – and indeed in social science more generally. [It] may be regarded as having far reaching implications regarding changes in research practice. Not only does it strengthen and develop the now well established critique of positivist science, it provides a deeper and more extensive question- ing both of the form and function of research, and of specific theories and research techniques. Out of this questioning comes both an active development of traditional ways of doing research and a committed exploration of alternative modes of investigation.
> (Wilkinson, 1986: 6)

While it remains true that mainstream psychology would benefit from a sustained critical engagement with feminism (see Wilkinson, 1991b), feminist researchers no longer feel routinely obliged to defend their work in terms of its value to the mainstream – rather, we have moved 'from critique to reconstruction' (Wilkinson, 1991a), and are developing our own agendas as feminists. Now, feminist social psychologists are equally likely to write for *feminist* readers with whose theories and politics they disagree. Contemporary feminist social psychologies are characterized as much by debate *within* the field as by debate between feminist and mainstream psychology. The field embraces a rich variety of incompatible – and at times conflicting – theoretical traditions, methodological approaches, and types of activism.

A decade of development

When I edited *Feminist Social Psychology* in 1986, the field was barely established in Britain. Compared with the USA, it had only a handful of practitioners, engaged in a limited range of research; it was largely unknown within mainstream psychology; and it had no institutional representation. Here, I highlight some of the main structural changes which, during the past decade, have enabled the evolution of the field into its present, much more influential, position – and which have provided the platform for its theoretical and methodological development.

First, there is now a formal grouping to represent the field within our national academic and professional organization, the British Psychological Society (BPS). The BPS 'Psychology of Women' Section – see Wilkinson and Burns (1990) for discussion of this name, strategically chosen to parallel the 'Psychology of Women' Division of the American Psychological Association, APA Division 35 – is explicitly dedicated to the pursuit of academic and professional advances in the field. This institutional recognition was only achieved after a two-year struggle (an experience shared by women organizing in psychology in at least five English-speaking countries: the UK, USA, Canada, Australia and New Zealand), and after the then unprecedented move of first being rejected by the BPS Council – for details see Wilkinson (1990). The eventual formation of the BPS 'Psychology of Women' Section was a significant milestone for the development of feminist social psychologies.

In its early days, the Section was subject to unusual scrutiny from the BPS, and had to overcome a range of obstacles to its effective operation (Wilkinson, 1991c). Later, there was a split within the Section over the proposed (and unsuccessful) formation of a 'Psychology of Lesbianism' Section (Comely et al., 1992; Sayers, 1992; Beloff, 1993; Kitzinger, this volume). Now, there are signs that the 'Psychology of Women' Section's political efficacy is being limited by co-option and exhaustion (Wilkinson, 1996a). Despite these external and internal problems, however, the Section is vital as a professional marker for the field, and serves some very important functions. It provides a forum for debate and development within the field of feminist psychology; it offers a crucial lifeline for many individual women within a deeply hostile discipline; and it acts as a catalyst for raising the general awareness of women's issues and creating change more broadly within mainstream psychology. It is popular, particularly among young women just entering the discipline (women constitute nearly 80% of the undergraduate psychology population in Britain; see Morris et al., 1990), and its membership continues to grow.

Britain also parallels the USA in having a – more explicitly – feminist organization outside its national psychological organization. Originally called 'Women in Psychology', this organization acted as a pressure group for the formation of the BPS 'Psychology of Women' Section and has always been overtly political – in much the same way as the Association of Women in Psychology (AWP) was influential in the creation of APA Division 35 and sees itself as a model of 'feminism-in-action' (Tiefer, quoted in Parlee, 1991: 42). Recently reconstituted as the 'Alliance of Women in Psychology', the British group also has a membership which explicitly includes users and survivors of psychology (Burman, 1996). Although quite small, it benefits from exchanges with feminist organizations outside psychology and with other radical movements (e.g. Psychology, Politics, Resistance; Survivors Speak Out).

The second important structural change of the past ten years has been the foundation of the (British-based) international journal, *Feminism & Psychology*. The journal was deliberately established independent of any formal organizational affiliation in order to allow 'a broader and more creative exploration of a conjunction of feminism and psychology which puts feminism first' (Wilkinson, 1991a: 6). Members of the founding editorial group had been involved in the struggles to form a BPS Section, and were only too aware of the costs and compromises, as well as the benefits, of institutional recognition. We were also determined to move the field on 'from critique to reconstruction', and to reaffirm its central, political goal – as the journal's inaugural editorial states:

> The primary commitment of *Feminism & Psychology* is to feminism: we choose to give priority to setting our own agendas and developing our own work, with the primary objective of social change, rather than being primarily accountable to psychology. . . . this does not mean that we will not speak to psychology, or cease the struggle to reconcile it with feminism, or abandon hope of any significant disciplinary change. It is simply that we choose to give our main energies to feminism in order to develop a stronger, clearer voice and to pursue the social and political change that is so badly needed.
>
> (Wilkinson, 1991a: 16)

It was clear from its inception, then, that *Feminism & Psychology* was to be very different from other journals often seen as defining the field: *Psychology of Women Quarterly*, the official journal of APA Division 35, and *Sex Roles*, the relatively mainstream journal representing a sub-field which 'seems to focus more on content than approach' (Wilkinson, 1986: 3).

Now in its sixth volume of publication, *Feminism & Psychology* has substantially broadened the definition of feminist (social) psychologies. Committed both to pluralism and to cutting-edge critical analysis and debate *between* feminists, the journal has played a leading role in the intellectual growth and development of the field. For example, it has turned the critical spotlight on competing feminist perspectives within traditional areas of psychological study, such as 'sex differences' (Kitzinger, 1994); and it has opened up new areas for analysis, often in conjunction with feminist work outside the disciplinary confines of psychology, such as 'representing the Other' (Wilkinson, 1996b; 1996c). It has begun to deconstruct hegemonic identities, such as 'masculinity' (Wetherell and Griffin, 1991; Griffin and Wetherell, 1992), 'heterosexuality' (Kitzinger *et al.*, 1992), and 'whiteness' (Wong, 1994); and insisted, in common with contemporary feminist theory more generally, that the very category of 'woman' is not unitary, but multiple, diverse and fragmented (Bhavnani and Haraway, 1994).

At the same time, however, the journal has maintained a strong focus on the many different ways in which women continue to be oppressed – by, for example, sexism and heterosexism (Gavey, 1992; Schacht and Atchison, 1993); racism (Bhavnani and Phoenix, 1994); classism (Walkerdine, 1996); ageism (Griffin, 1992); anti-Semitism (Burman, 1994); disablism (Appleby, 1992; Marks, 1996) – and on psychology's continued complicity in that oppression. It has highlighted the misogynistic diagnostic categories of North American psychiatry (Caplan and Gans, 1991; Caplan et al., 1992); the 'scientific' evidence of women's inadequacies provided by the psychometric testing industry – used, for example, to justify continued sex discrimination in the workplace (Hollway, 1991); and the woman-blaming messages of the pop-psych, self-help manuals which offer 'revolution from within' if only we can overcome the purported defects of our psyches (Sethna, 1992; Schilling and Fuehrer, 1993).

Finally, the journal has insisted that in seeking to develop feminist theory and practice in the 1990s, we need to build on the insights (and mistakes) of our feminist foremothers. Their valuable work is too often lost to us, for as Dale Spender (1982: 13) argues:

> These women and their ideas constitute a political threat and they are censored. By this means women are 'kept in the dark', with the result that every generation must begin virtually at the beginning, and start again to forge the meanings of women's existence in a patriarchal world, so that . . . every fifty years women have to reinvent the wheel.

Not only are the pioneering feminist theories of the late nineteenth and early twentieth centuries ignored or dismissed as too historically specific by contemporary feminists (Spender, 1982), but also the analyses of second-wave feminism are regarded by many young women today as outdated or irrelevant to their concerns (see Frith, 1994). This constitutes, as Phyllis Chesler (quoted in Wilkinson, 1994a: 264) says, a 'means of dishonouring the warriors who came before'. It also means constantly having to go over the same ground, the same debates, the same dead ends – instead of being able to move forward, benefiting from the efforts of our predecessors. With so many young women now entering psychology, and choosing to enrol on 'psychology of women' courses, in particular, the journal wanted to make available, as a resource, 'classic' articles by feminist social psychologists, whose work might otherwise remain unknown to this new generation; we also wanted to reappraise these classics in terms of their continuing relevance for feminist social psychologies today. To date, Feminism & Psychology has reprinted, along with contemporary commentaries, Naomi Weisstein's 1968 paper 'Psychology Constructs the Female' (Kitzinger, 1993; Weisstein, 1993); extracts from Phyllis Chesler's (1972) *Women and Madness* (Wilkinson, 1994b); and Nancy Datan's 1986 paper 'Corpses, Lepers and Menstruating Women' (Datan, 1995; Unger, 1995). Reappraisals of the work of Carolyn Sherif and of Nancy Chodorow are also in preparation.

Feminist social psychologies today

The intellectual philosophy and political commitment which inspired the founding of *Feminism & Psychology* also informs this volume. While the contributors to this book are united in their endorsement of feminism's overarching project of social change on behalf of women, they reveal major disagreements over the most appropriate and effective strategies for achieving such change. In selecting the contributions, I have been concerned not only to demonstrate the plurality of feminist social psychologies on offer today, but also explicitly to juxtapose incompatible – and occasionally conflicting – theoretical and methodological approaches, in order to stimulate critical analysis and debate about their implications and utility for the feminist political project.

The volume is divided (as was its predecessor, *Feminist Social Psychology*) into two parts. The chapters in the first part focus most strongly on developing feminist theory (although, of course, they also demonstrate the use of particular methods within specific research contexts). The chapters in the second part focus most strongly on interrogating the utility of particular research methods for the feminist project (although, of course, they also contribute to feminist theory in substantive arenas). I will highlight briefly the distinctive contribution of each, locating it within the field of feminist social psychologies.

Chapter 1, by Nancy Chodorow, looks at what we can learn from the lives and work of our feminist foremothers – here specifically second-generation women psychoanalysts. She shows how, in the 1930s, gender was apparently not afforded the significance that she (as a 1970s feminist) anticipated: her interviewees did not reflexively apply their theories of femininity to their own lives. Since her highly influential (1978) book, *The Reproduction of Mothering*, Chodorow has been a leading thinker in psychoanalytic feminism, spanning the disciplines of sociology and social psychology – here she reflects on the importance of context in our feminist work. The chapter is a fascinating illustration of the social, cultural and historical specificity of 1930s and 1970s feminist theory, enriched by Chodorow's 1990s commentary.

Chapter 2 is by Nicola Gavey, and represents a new generation of critical feminist scholarship in New Zealand. Using the framework of poststructuralist, discursive psychology, explicitly informed by radical feminist theory, Gavey examines the sexual violence and abuse perpetrated in the name of heterosexuality. She argues that 'in documenting and theorizing accounts of heterosexual experiences that are not about the eroticization of women's passivity and powerlessness we can make a discursive intervention into the discursive/material possibilities for gendered sexual violence'.

A discursive analysis of power inequities, here in relation to debates about 'difference' and 'sameness', is also central to Chapter 3, by Michelle Fine and Judi Addelston. In turning a feminist spotlight on the practices of a public, all male, military-like college, and an elite private law school admitting 40 per cent women annually, Fine and Addelston eschew traditional psychology's individualism in favour of a structural analysis of women's disadvantage. Cautioning us to resist the 'seductive detour' into explanations based only on 'difference' or only on 'sameness', they demonstrate how institutionalized power depends on the deployment of *both* kinds of discourse. The chapter is underpinned by the authors' strong commitment to feminist political activism, seen also in Michelle Fine's (1992) important book *Disruptive Voices*.

Chapter 4, by Oliva Espin, draws on the fast-growing tradition of narrative analysis to examine the lives of immigrant/refugee women in North America. Well known for her leading role in APA Division 44 (the division devoted to the psychological study of lesbian and gay issues), and for her extensive writings on Latina lesbians, Espin here looks at women's disparate adaptations to migration. She illustrates, in particular, the – literal and metaphorical – importance of 'border' and 'boundary' crossings in the construction of racialized national and sexual identities.

Kathy Davis (Chapter 5) also utilizes a biographical approach – in this case to examine issues of femininity, beauty and identity raised by cosmetic surgery. In common with Gavey and Walkerdine, Davis takes a postmodern perspective, and her contribution is broadly illustrative of a type of feminist social psychology which draws on European (particularly Foucauldian) critical social theory. On the basis of narrative interviews, Davis argues that women who seek cosmetic surgery are not 'cultural dopes' of the 'feminine beauty system', but, rather, show an extraordinary determination to become 'ordinary'. In this way, undergoing cosmetic surgery can be viewed as exercising a form of power, via a literal reconstruction of 'self'.

'The Token Lesbian Chapter', by Celia Kitzinger (Chapter 6), turns the critical spotlight on feminist psychology itself. A contributor to the 1986 volume *Feminist Social Psychology* (Kitzinger, 1986), and author of several influential books (including *The Social Construction of Lesbianism*, 1987) is internationally recognized both as a radical lesbian feminist and as an outspoken critic of psychology. Here, she exposes the continuing heterosexism of feminist psychology (in common with that of the feminist movement more generally) and looks at the ways in which it has prevented the autonomous development of specifically lesbian theory.

Valerie Walkerdine (Chapter 7) returns us to psychoanalysis, here located within the framework of poststructuralism. This perspective has been important in critical theory in Britain since the publication of the influential *Changing the Subject* (Henriques *et al.*, 1984). Valerie Walkerdine also contributed to *Feminist Social Psychology* (Walkerdine, 1986) and is well known for her work on the social regulation of women and children, particularly in relation to social class (see, for example, Walkerdine, 1996). Like Celia Kitzinger, she uses her chapter to castigate feminism – in this case for its failure to theorize the lives of working-class women, except through models of pathologization. Here, she documents some of the specificities of working-class femininity and oppression in relation to a group of educated working-class women.

The book's second part begins with a chapter on epistemology and empiricism by Rhoda Unger (Chapter 8). Unger, who is internationally known and respected for her work – not least as a key figure in APA Division 35 and AWP, and co-author of one of the most wide-ranging, scholarly and influential textbooks in the field (Unger and Crawford, 1992) – makes the case for the continuing use of empirical methods in feminist research as 'one of the most powerful tools at our disposal'. She provides a research autobiography to show how her belief that 'epistemological evidence might be more persuasive than theory' has shaped the kind of feminist research that characterizes her career, and argues for the study of the effects of 'personal epistemology' upon the way people think about themselves, other people and the world.

Chapter 9 is co-authored by three feminist social psychologists from Australia: Niamh Stephenson, Susan Kippax and June Crawford. They demonstrate the use of the method of 'memory work' (first developed by European social theorist Frigga Haug) in studying moral dilemmas and the construction of self, extending their research group's earlier use of this method in examining *Emotion and Gender* (Crawford *et al.*, 1992). Explicitly differentiating this method from those associated with the Harvard Project on Women's Psychology and Girls' Development (described in Chapter 12), Stephenson *et al.* locate themselves within the tradition of discursive psychology also exemplified, in particular, by Nicola Gavey (Chapter 2).

Charlene Senn (Chapter 10) illustrates the use of a primarily quantitative method within a social constructionist framework – a popular combination in feminist social psychology. As another representative of a new generation of feminist scholarship, Senn's approach nevertheless acknowledges a particular debt to Celia Kitzinger's original chapter in *Feminist Social Psychology* (Kitzinger, 1986). Here, Q-methodology is used to study women's views and experiences of pornography, and Senn argues its value – as the culmination of her own 'methodological passage' – in terms of its 'very powerful interpretations of women's experiences' and the extent to which it was 'personally rewarding' in comparison with experimental methods.

Like Rhoda Unger, Stephanie Shields and Jill Crowley (Chapter 11) explicitly acknowledge that 'how we do research does not exist independently of who we are as individuals and the values we hold'. Working within the feminist empiricist tradition of 'doing better science' (although, like Unger, Shields has also offered constructionist analyses, most notably of the situation of early feminist psychologists: see, for example, Shields, 1975), they go on to show how questionnaires and rating scales can be useful in feminist research. They use these tools as part of a multi-method approach; to refine the research question; and as a deliberate strategy to disrupt the research frame (and, thereby, the researcher's own subjective investment in the enquiry).

Chapter 12 is co-authored by three feminist social psychologists working as part of the Harvard Project on Women's Psychology and Girls' Development: Jill Taylor, Carol Gilligan and Amy Sullivan. This project represents one of the most influential strands of feminist social psychology today (see, for example, Gilligan, 1982; Brown and Gilligan, 1992; Taylor *et al.*, 1995; also the commentaries in Wilkinson, 1994c). Taylor *et al.* describe as central to their work the development of a 'voice-centred, relational method' as 'a way of attending to difference . . . using a guided method for listening to interview narrative'. They also document the analysis and interpretation of interview narratives within a 'diverse interpretive community', particularly in relation to the difference of 'race' and ethnicity.

Finally, Kelly Shaw-Barnes and Alice Eagly (Chapter 13) look at the value of meta-analysis for feminist research in social psychology, focusing on the traditional research area of sex differences and similarities. Meta-analysis is a technique for quantitative synthesis of research findings, allowing the researcher to draw conclusions that validly represent and summarize the findings of a large research literature. Shaw-Barnes and Eagly argue that this knowledge can then be used to influence public policy in areas where women have traditionally been disadvantaged. While theoretically incompatible with analyses of sex differences as discursive constructions (see, for example, Fine and Addelston, Chapter 3), this kind of approach has none the less been a powerful and influential contributor to the empiricist tradition of feminist social psychology (see, for example, Eagly, 1987; 1990; Eagly and Wood, 1991; also the commentaries in Kitzinger, 1994).

Taken together, these 13 chapters illustrate the richness and vitality of feminist social psychologies today. They provide both a compelling challenge to mainstream psychology's traditional characterization of women as inferior, and evidence of a new maturity and confidence within the field of feminist psychology which allows us to see our diversity as strength, and to debate amongst ourselves the particular advantages and disadvantages of our differing theoretical, methodological and political strategies. The contributors to this book would probably all agree, however, to 'support, celebrate and actively engage in the feminist struggle', and would want to endorse my invitation to 'all who share these goals and values to join us as we strive to develop that special blend of passion, rigour and responsibility that is so quintessentially feminism' (Wilkinson, 1991a: 16).

References

Alberti, R. E. (ed.) (1977) *Assertiveness: Innovations, Applications, Issues*. San Luis Obispo, CA: Impact.

Appleby, Yvon (1992) 'Disability and "compulsory heterosexuality"', *Feminism & Psychology: An International Journal*, 2(3): 502–5.

Beloff, Halla (1993) 'Progress on the BPS psychology of lesbianism front', *Feminism & Psychology: An International Journal*, 3(2): 282–3.

Benbow, C. P. and Stanley, J. C. (1980) 'Sex differences in mathematical ability: Fact or artifact?', *Science*, 210: 1262–4.

Bhavnani, Kum-Kum and Phoenix, Ann (eds) (1994) 'Shifting identities shifting racisms': A Special Issue of *Feminism & Psychology: An International Journal*, 4(1).

Bhavnani, Kum-Kum and Haraway, Donna (1994) 'Shifting the subject: A conversation between Kum-Kum Bhavnani and Donna Haraway, 12 April 1993, Santa Cruz, California', *Feminism & Psychology: An International Journal*, 4(1): 19–39.

Bohan, Janis S. (1992) 'Prologue: Re-viewing psychology, re-placing women – an end searching for a means', in Janis S. Bohan (ed.), *Seldom Seen, Rarely Heard: Women's Place in Psychology*. Boulder, CO: Westview Press, pp. 9–53.

Brown, Lyn Mikel and Gilligan, Carol (1992) *Meeting at the Crossroads: Women's Psychology and Girls' Development*. Cambridge, MA: Harvard University Press.

Burman, Erica (1994) 'Experience, identities and alliances: Jewish feminism and feminist psychology', *Feminism & Psychology: An International Journal*, 4(1): 155–78.

Burman, Erica (1996) 'Introduction: Contexts, contests and interventions', in Erica Burman, Pam Alldred, Catherine Bewley, Brenda Goldberg, Colleen Heenan, Deborah Marks, Jane Marshall, Karen Taylor, Robina Ullah and Sam Warner, *Challenging Women: Psychology's Exclusions, Feminist Possibilities*. Buckingham: Open University Press.

Caplan, Paula J. and Gans, Maureen (1991) 'Is there empirical justification for the category of "Self-Defeating Personality Disorder"?', *Feminism & Psychology: An International Journal*, 1(2): 263–78.

Caplan, Paula J., McCurdy-Myers, Joan and Gans, Maureen (1992) 'Should "Premenstrual Syndrome" be called a psychiatric abnormality?', *Feminism & Psychology: An International Journal*, 2(1): 27–44.

Chesler, Phyllis (1972) *Women and Madness*. Garden City, NY: Doubleday. (Second edition published 1989, San Diego, CA: Harcourt Brace Jovanovich.)

Chodorow, Nancy (1978) *The Reproduction of Mothering*. Berkeley, CA: University of California Press.

Comely, Louise, Kitzinger, Celia, Perkins, Rachel and Wilkinson, Sue (1992) 'Lesbian psychology in Britain: Back into the closet?', *Feminism & Psychology: An International Journal*, 2(2): 265–8.

Crawford, June, Kippax, Susan, Onyx, Jenny and Gault, Una (1992) *Emotion and Gender: Constructing Meaning from Memory*. London: Sage.

Datan, Nancy (1995) 'Corpses, lepers and menstruating women: Tradition, transition and the sociology of knowledge', *Feminism & Psychology: An International Journal*, 5(4): 449–59. (First published 1986.)

Eagly, Alice H. (1987) *Sex Differences in Social Behaviour: A Social-role Interpretation*. Hillsdale, NJ: Erlbaum.

Eagly, Alice H. (1990) 'On the advantages of reporting sex comparisons', *American Psychologist*, 45: 560–2.

Eagly, Alice H. and Wood, W. (1991) 'Explaining sex differences in social behaviour: A Meta-analytic Perspective', *Personality and Social Psychology Bulletin*, 17: 306–15.

Ehrenreich, Barbara and English, Deidre (1979) *For Her Own Good: 150 Years of the Experts' Advice to Women*. London: Pluto.

Fine, Michelle (1992) *Disruptive Voices: The Possibilities of Feminist Research*. Ann Arbor, MI: The University of Michigan Press.

Frith, Hannah (1994) 'Turning us off', *Feminism & Psychology: An International Journal*, 4(2):315–16.

Gavey, Nicola (1992) 'Technologies and effects of heterosexual coercion', *Feminism & Psychology: An International Journal*, 2(3): 325–51.

Gilligan, Carol (1982) *In a Different Voice: Psychological Theory and Women's Development*. Cambridge, MA: Harvard University Press.

Griffin, Christine (1992) 'Fear of a black (and working-class) planet: Young women and the racialization of reproductive politics', *Feminism & Psychology: An International Journal*, 2(3): 491–4.

Griffin, Christine and Wetherell, Margaret (eds) (1992) Open Forum: 'Feminist psychology and the study of men and masculinity – Part II: Politics and practices', *Feminism & Psychology: An International Journal*, 2(2): 133–68.

Hampson, E. (1990) 'Variations in sex-related cognitive abilities across the menstrual cycle', *Brain and Cognition*, 14: 26–43.

Henley, Nancy (1974) 'Resources for the study of psychology and women', *R.T.: Journal of Radical Therapy*, 4: 20–1.

Henriques, Julian, Hollway, Wendy, Urwin, Cathy, Venn, Couze and Walkerdine, Valerie (1984) *Changing the Subject: Psychology, Social Regulation and Subjectivity*. London: Methuen.

Hollway, Wendy (1991) 'The psychologization of feminism or the feminization of psychology', *Feminism & Psychology: An International Journal*, 1(1): 29–37.

Kitzinger, Celia (1986) 'Introducing and developing Q as a feminist methodology:

A study of accounts of lesbianism', in Sue Wilkinson (ed.), *Feminist Social Psychology: Developing Theory and Practice*. Milton Keynes: Open University Press, pp. 151–72.

Kitzinger, Celia (1987) *The Social Construction of Lesbianism*. London: Sage.

Kitzinger, Celia (ed.) (1993) Special Feature: '"Psychology constructs the female": A Reappraisal', *Feminism & Psychology: An International Journal*, 3(2): 189–245.

Kitzinger, Celia (ed.) (1994) Special Feature: 'Should psychologists study sex differences?', *Feminism & Psychology: An International Journal*, 4(4): 501–46.

Kitzinger, Celia, Wilkinson, Sue and Perkins, Rachel (eds) (1992) 'Heterosexuality': A Special Issue of *Feminism & Psychology: An International Journal*, 2(3).

Lenney, E. (1977) 'Women's self-confidence in achievement-related settings', *Psychological Bulletin*, 84: 1–13.

Marks, Deborah (1996) 'Able-bodied dilemmas in teaching disability studies', *Feminism & Psychology: An International Journal*, 6(1): 69–73.

Masters, M. S. and Sanders, B. (1993) 'Is the gender difference in mental rotation disappearing?', *Behavior Genetics*, 23: 337–41.

Mednick, Martha T. S. (1978) 'Now we are four: What should we be when we grow up?', *Psychology of Women Quarterly*, 3: 123–38.

Morris, Peter E., Holloway, Julie and Noble, Julie (1990) 'Gender representation within the BPS', *The Psychologist*, 3(9): 408–11.

Parlee, Mary Brown (1975) 'Review essay: Psychology', *Signs*, 1: 119–38.

Parlee, Mary Brown (1991) 'Happy birth-day to *Feminism & Psychology*', *Feminism & Psychology: An International Journal*, 1(1): 39–48.

Sayers, Janet (1992) 'A POWS reply', *Feminism & Psychology: An International Journal*, 2(2): 269–70.

Schacht, S. P. and Atchison, Patricia H. (1993) 'Heterosexual instrumentalism: Past and future directions', *Feminism & Psychology: An International Journal*, 3(1): 37–53.

Schilling, Karen M. and Fuehrer, Ann (1993) 'The politics of women's self-help books', *Feminism & Psychology: An International Journal*, 3(3): 418–22.

Sethna, Christabelle (1992) 'Accepting "total and complete responsibility": New age, neo-feminist violence against women', *Feminism & Psychology: An International Journal*, 2(1): 113–19.

Shields, Stephanie A. (1975) 'Functionalism, Darwinism and the psychology of women: A study in social myth', *American Psychologist*, 30: 739–54.

Spender, Dale (1982) *Women of Ideas and What Men Have Done to Them*. London: Pandora.

Taylor, Jill McLean, Gilligan, Carol and Sullivan, Amy (1995) *Between Voice and Silence: Women and Girls, Race and Relationship*. Cambridge, MA: Harvard University Press.

Unger, Rhoda K. (1982) 'Advocacy versus scholarship revisited: Issues in the psychology of women', *Psychology of Women Quarterly*, 7(1): 5–17.

Unger, Rhoda K. (ed.) (1995) Special Feature: 'From the heart and the mind: Nancy Datan', *Feminism & Psychology: An International Journal*, 5(4): 441–93.

Unger, Rhoda K. and Crawford, Mary (1992) *Women and Gender: A Feminist Psychology*. New York: McGraw-Hill. (Second edition published 1996.)

Walkerdine, Valerie (1986) 'Post-structuralist theory and everyday social practices: The family and the school', in Sue Wilkinson (ed.), *Feminist Social Psychology: Developing Theory and Practice*. Milton Keynes: Open University Press, pp. 57–76.

Walkerdine, Valerie (ed.) (1996) 'Social class': A Special Issue of *Feminism & Psychology: An International Journal*, 6(3).

Weisstein, Naomi (1993) 'Psychology constructs the female; or, the fantasy life of the male psychologist (with some attention to the fantasies of his friends, the male biologist and the male anthropologist)', *Feminism & Psychology: An International Journal*, 3(2): 195–210. (First published 1968.)

Wetherell, Margaret and Griffin, Christine (eds) (1991) Open Forum: 'Feminist psychology and the study of men and masculinity – Part I: Assumptions and perspectives', *Feminism & Psychology: An International Journal*, 1(3): 361–91.

Wilkinson, Sue (ed.) (1986) *Feminist Social Psychology: Developing Theory and Practice*. Milton Keynes: Open University Press.

Wilkinson, Sue (1989) 'The impact of feminist research: Issues of legitimacy', *Philosophical Psychology*, 2(3): 261–9.

Wilkinson, Sue (1990) 'Women's organisations in psychology: Institutional constraints on disciplinary change', *Australian Psychologist*, 25(3): 256–69.

Wilkinson, Sue (1991a) '*Feminism & Psychology*: From critique to reconstruction', *Feminism & Psychology: An International Journal*, 1(1): 5–18.

Wilkinson, Sue (1991b) 'Why psychology (badly) needs feminism', in Jane Aaron and Sylvia Walby (eds), *Out of the Margins: Women's Studies in the Nineties*. London: Falmer Press, pp. 191–203.

Wilkinson, Sue (1991c) 'Institutional power and historical hegemony: A reply to Williams (1991)', *Australian Psychologist*, 26(3): 206–8.

Wilkinson, Sue (1994a) 'Phyllis Chesler: "Amazon warrior" – Then and now', *Feminism & Psychology: An International Journal*, 4(2): 261–7.

Wilkinson, Sue (ed.) (1994b) Special Feature: '*Women and Madness*: A Reappraisal', *Feminism & Psychology: An International Journal*, 4(2): 261–306.

Wilkinson, Sue (ed.) (1994c) Special Feature: 'Critical connections: The Harvard project on women's psychology and girls' development', *Feminism & Psychology: An International Journal*, 4(3): 343–424.

Wilkinson, Sue (1996a) 'Still seeking transformation: Feminist challenges to psychology', in Liz Stanley (ed.), *Borderlands: Feminisms in the Academy*. London: Sage.

Wilkinson, Sue (ed.) (1996b) Special Feature: 'Representing the Other – Part One', *Feminism & Psychology: An International Journal*, 6(1): 43–91.

Wilkinson, Sue (ed.) (1996c) Special Feature: 'Representing the Other – Part Two', *Feminism & Psychology: An International Journal*, 6(2): 167–216.

Wilkinson, Sue and Burns, Jan (1990) 'Women organizing within psychology: Two accounts', in Erica Burman (ed.), *Feminists and Psychological Practice*. London: Sage, pp. 141–51.

Wilson, Glenn (1994) 'Biology, sex roles and work', in Caroline Quest (ed.), *Liberating Women . . . From Modern Feminism*. London: Institute of Economic Affairs, Health and Welfare Unit, pp. 59–71.

Wooley, Helen Thompson (1910) 'Psychological literature: A review of the recent literature on the psychology of sex', *Psychological Bulletin*, 7: 335–42.

Wong, L. Mun (1994) 'Dis(s)-secting and dis(s)-closing "whiteness": Two tales about psychology', *Feminism & Psychology: An International Journal*, 4(1): 133–53.

Worrell, Judith (1990) 'Feminist frameworks: Retrospect and prospect', *Psychology of Women Quarterly*, 14(1): 1–5.

PART I

Developing theory . . .

—————• 1

Seventies questions for thirties women: Some nineties reflections

—————• NANCY J. CHODOROW

In 'Seventies Questions for Thirties Women: Gender and Generation in a Study of Early Women Psychoanalysts' (Chodorow, 1989), I reflected on a methodological dilemma with which I was confronted. I had sought out and interviewed second-generation women analysts – those trained between the 1920s and the mid-1940s – because I had been impressed with the prominence and eminence of women in this field, beginning at least in the 1920s. Without, really, much methodological justification, I decided to pursue my questions through interviews, thinking that, somehow, a set of brief life histories would provide answers to what were, really, structural and historical questions. Also, it must of course be admitted, I was curious about these women: I wanted to meet and talk with them.

When I began my research in 1980, feminists had not paid much attention to methodology. Both Sherif (1977), a psychologist, and Smith (1974; 1977), a sociologist, had noted that objectivist, positivist, natural science models of research and knowledge tended to sit more naturally with men and to occlude women's perspective. Reinharz's (1979) argument for experiential analysis did not, in its first edition, tie its argument to feminism at all. Oakley's classic, 'Interviewing Women: a Contradiction in Terms', appeared in 1981. By the mid-1980s, when I presented 'Seventies Questions' at a professional meeting, I was able to draw from these sources as well as a few beginning ventures into what we now know as feminist epistemology and methodology (Bowles and Duelli Klein, 1983; Krieger, 1985) which, more assertively, argued that qualitative and reflexive methodologies might be more appropriate to feminist inquiry.[1]

With a 1990s lens, we can, I think, see in this paper both a reflection and a foretelling of issues that have now become central to much feminist research. We are now acutely aware of the various axes and the multiplicities of identity within which women create their lives, so that we no longer expect gender always to be salient. We expect subjectivity to be shifting, situated and contextual. We reflect in complex ways about the researcher's subjectivity, 'bifurcation of consciousness' (Smith, 1974) or 'outsider within' status (Collins, 1986), and we assume that feminists bring personal interests to the study of 'great women'. By contrast, when I submitted this methodological paper – with its fundamental attention to the researcher-researched relationship – to a feminist journal, it was rejected. According to reviewers, I did not begin from the demographic characteristics of my 'sample', and I described a circuitous routing through my own consciousness and expectations when I should have focused in a more straightforward informational manner on my interviewees' responses.

In the ten years since my first presentation of 'Seventies Questions', feminist methodology has become a field in its own right (see, for example, Harding, 1987; Bordo and Jagger, 1989; Personal Narratives Group, 1989; Nielson, 1990; Fonow and Cook, 1991; Gluck and Patai, 1991; Reinharz, 1992; Alcoff and Potter, 1993; *Frontiers* 1993; Franz and Stewart, 1994). Life history, oral history, personal narratives, narratives of identity, and the study of women's lives have become central to much feminist research. Several writers have recently articulated the exact dilemma that 'Seventies Questions' addresses (see especially Borland 1991 and Zavella 1993). In what follows, I describe my own early attempt to contribute to this literature.

One of the earliest articulated and still most important goals of feminist scholarship has been to allow women's voices to be heard.[2] We have been aware of ways in which dominant ideologies have shaped our discourse and understandings so that women have had to see things from male perspectives or have had their own, perhaps less articulated, perspective ignored or silenced. Because of this goal, feminist scholars have often chosen to employ qualitative and reflexive methods, which, traditionally, allow the subjects of inquiry to speak and make subjects' perceptions and understandings central. These scholars argue that we need to recognize and articulate women's double consciousness, the 'disjunction between experience and the forms in which experience is socially expressed' (Smith, 1977: 135). Feminists, finally, argue that feminist research must address the researcher's own subjectivity and the relation between her and her research subjects.

Here, I consider a problem I found in attempting to follow these feminist methodological principles. I trace my own discovery of my dilemma and the process I went through in attempting to resolve it. When a researcher wants to respect the voices of other women and is concerned about a history of dissolving differences into a hegemonic unity, she runs into problems when the voices she wants to respect seem not to recognize the central categories in her research. I confronted just such a problem as I sought answers to questions about gender consciousness in interviews with early women psychoanalysts. I discovered that, from the point of view of a 1970s feminist hypersensitive to gender (i.e., myself), second-generation analysts were relatively gender-blind, or unattuned to gender, regarding both their role in the profession and their profession's theory. I was thus faced with two kinds of questions. First, how can and should we conceptualize the gender consciousness of women for whom gender itself does not seem like a salient category? Second, does the discovery that the very topic of inquiry is not salient to research subjects raise problems for feminist methodological principles and qualitative and reflexive methodologies that privilege the perspective and voice of the subject? If we impose categories on women that are not otherwise important to them, we imply that we have more access to truth – an epistemological privilege that they lack. We undercut the very commitment to women's subjectivity that motivated our research in the first place. A tension arose between the feminist injunction to let women's voices be heard and the feminist injunction to analyse the social and cultural relations of gender and the problems of gender identity.[3]

My attempts to resolve this epistemological dilemma went through several stages. I had come to the study – as, I believe, do many feminists who study women's lives, and particularly the lives of notable women in their field (see, for example, Ascher et al., 1984; Hornstein, 1994; Stewart, 1994; and many biographies of women by women) – with what I self-mockingly called 'unresolved positive transference' to my research subjects. They were somewhat idealized grand old women and foremothers. Lurking in my preconscious was probably a romanticized image of the reproduction of professional mothering. I had images of the half dozen women – Grete Bibring, Florence Clothier, Helene Deutsch, Eleanor Pavenstedt, Eveoleen Rexford, and Helen Tartakoff – who had sat on the dais at a symposium I attended on early psychoanalysis in New England. I thought of Anna Freud, Dorothy Burlingham, Jeanne Lampl-de Groot, Helene Deutsch, Grete Bibring, Marianne Kris, Annie Reich, and other women in the idealized culture of Viennese psychoanalysis described in much psychoanalytic history; of Karen Horney, Melanie Klein, and their followers making their individual and powerful ways against the psychoanalytic mainstream; of Marie Bonaparte, Ruth Mack Brunswick, Lampl-de Groot, Deutsch and others discussing the psychology of women with Freud. I knew less of the Americans and English who became members of the second generation but soon found that there were many of these as well. I wanted such women to hold views like my own, and I was dismayed to find that they did not think gender had been important in their professional lives.[4] Given these findings, I also was not sure how to proceed with my research.

My second strategy, having reluctantly given up idealization, was, not surprisingly, to move to its opposite – to consider that my interviewees were (mentally to accuse them of being) gender-blind (on the psychological links between mother-blame and maternal idealization, see Chodorow and Contratto, 1982). I began to search for the cognitive and emotional functions that such gender blindness served. This was easy. As a feminist sociologist drawing upon interpretive traditions – like psychoanalysis, Marxism, structuralism, and functionalism – that claim to reveal underlying meanings or patterns or to demonstrate the significance of particular forms of consciousness for the maintenance of social structure, identity, or hegemony, I was used to thinking in terms of false consciousness, rationalization, denial, defence, and hidden latent meanings.

My suspicion of an analysis that can dismiss women's subjectivity as false consciousness led me, finally, to relativize and expand my understanding of my own gender consciousness and of the varieties of gender consciousness and female self-understanding available to women of different eras and milieux. Drawing on a basic premise of the sociology of knowledge and on the feminist methodological injunction that we pay particular attention to the relationship of researcher to researched, I came to see that my own ideas and identity, as well as those of my interview subjects, were rooted in our different social and cultural conditions. Differences in women's interpretations of a situation may be understood not only in terms of more familiar structural categories like class and race but also historically, culturally and generationally. I came to recognize that rather than being gender-blind, the second-generation women analysts had different forms of gender consciousness than I and experienced a different salience of gender as a social category and aspect of professional identity. Gender salience became a central concept in my research.[5]

As I noted earlier, I began my research in 1980, and I spent about two years interviewing second-generation women psychoanalysts.[6] My research questions grew out of several observations. Unlike most male-dominant professions, psychoanalysis seemed to have been extraordinarily open to women. It counted a fair proportion of women in its ranks and recognized many of these women as significant, eminent and even great.[7] I wanted to know how such a situation had come about and what the experiences of women were in this field that seemed to have facilitated rather than impeded their participation. I wanted to ask these women the kinds of questions that we often want to know about women in the professions – about friendships, colleagueship, mentors, the gendered tone of professional culture, family and career. Given that I began psychoanalytic training in the mid-1980s, I now also assume that I had less conscious desires simply to know what it was like to be a woman psychoanalyst.

Studying women psychoanalysts posed a particularly interesting problem concerning the role of culture and consciousness in the creation of gender relations, and vice versa. As is well known, psychologies of gender and sexuality are central to professional knowledge and practice in psychoanalysis. Prevalent cultural conceptions, especially feminist critiques, of psychoanalysis might have led to the expectation that psychoanalysis would have been particularly *in*hospitable to women, a field in which women would not want to participate.[8] Classical psycho-analysis held sexist and even misogynist views of women's lives: in this view, women's lives are dominated by penis envy, and women are naturally passive. Their career achievement is a substitute for or ex-pression of unresolved penis envy. In the psychological and cultural translation of psychoanalytic theories of child development, women must stay at home full-time with their children during these children's early years or risk serious consequences. I wondered how this field, with a radically dichotomous understanding of male and female personality and capacities, could have admitted both as presumably equal prac-titioners, and how the early women practitioners reconciled a theory that seems to devalue them with their own self-esteem, life situation and practice. I wished to know how and whether they related their lives as women, wives and mothers to psychoanalytic theory, whether the issue of penis envy was salient for them, and what they made of the feminist challenge to psychoanalysis. My study, then, though ostensibly about structural and historical conditions of psychoanalytic practice, also called out for an investigation of women practitioners' consciousness in relation to the field's theories.

Gender consciousness among early women psychoanalysts

From the beginning, my interviewees did not conform to my expec-tations. I was studying women in the professions, but throughout my interviews, I found that their gender, and that of colleagues, had simply not been significant professionally to the women I was studying. Even noticing women analysts as women was striking. As one European said:

> I don't understand your problem. Why is it so peculiar that women?
> . . . there are many professional women in the world; why
> shouldn't they be analysts too?

When I pointed to my observation that there were proportionately more women than in other fields, she responded with the example of Marie Curie and her daughter. I demurred.

Not so many, you think? But there are many male analysts too.

As an American trained in Vienna more bluntly put it:

> You interest me in your question about were there women, what did
> the women do? I don't know, what did the women eat? Where did
> the. . . I just took it as a matter of course . . . The thing that struck *me*
> the most and was hardest for *me* was doing all this in German,
> seeing as I didn't know German.

Some interviewees, when specifically asked, could notice the relative
prominence of women in the field of psychoanalysis and speculate about
the reasons for this. One British analyst, asked about the impact of
women analysts on the field, pointed out that because so many of the
leading analysts were women, the impact *had* to be big. Their impact,
however, was because they were important individuals, not because they
were women. I asked her:

> Did it make a difference that so many of the leading analysts were
> women? What if it had all been men?

She answered:

> I don't know. I find it difficult to *lump* together women, you know. I
> can think of *special* women; it would have been different without
> *them*. But women, when you *lump* them into a *whole*, I don't know.

She followed this answer with an association to Winnicott's 'immense
identification with mothers', as if further to emphasize that the analyst's
gender was irrelevant.

I asked an American analyst whether relations among women analysts
were different from those among men – feminist theories about women's
personal relationships as well as studies of women in the professions
would predict an affirmative answer. She responded:

> I think we were all analysts. We kept pretty much to talking about
> things of that sort . . . I don't think of them any different.

The British analyst who didn't lump women together went back and
forth, reflecting a typical pattern among interviewees. When I asked why
there were so many women, she suggested that psychoanalysis was:

> a passive sort of thing. Lots of men are too assertive and active. It is
> difficult for the *ordinary* sort of male to do a lot of sitting all day in a
> passive analysis, sit still all day . . . that sort of receptiveness is
> easier for women, don't you think? But then again one thinks of how
> bossy some of the women are – they're not very receptive. You
> know, bisexuality is very real to me. I could never get around the fact

that a lot of the women are very masculine. So how can one generalize?

In contrast to these women, other interviewees disagreed with my basic premise. 'I didn't know there were so many; I don't see anything so many about it', said one Viennese-trained American, echoing many of her colleagues. Upon reflection, she added:

I guess it was the period when women were getting involved, but I never thought of it so much. The feminine part, I didn't know anything about feminist movements, feminist activity. I never even thought of such a thing. Because it seemed to me pretty easy as a woman to do what you wanted.

Thus, they did not think of their own professional histories in terms of being women; they did what they did because they wanted to do it. Women analysts as a category did not seem to exist. Some, when I asked about women analysts in general, had no associations, emphasized that they simply did not think and never had thought of their colleagues that way, or laughingly, almost scornfully, claimed that of course the men and women were different: women are women; men are men. To emphasize my point, I might note that their major teachers – their training analyst, their two supervisors, the people who first interviewed them when they applied for training – were all women. They responded, as one Viennese put it:

I took it as a matter of course. It didn't matter, and I didn't notice. Look, training was so easy going; people were consumed by our interests in psychoanalysis.

There were a few areas where some interviewees perceived gender differences in professional experience. A very few had noticed discriminatory treatment or patterns in the ways men and women psychoanalysts conducted themselves, related to the profession and to each other, and so forth. Many stressed discrimination in medical school and medical school admissions and contrasted this with the favourable situation in psychoanalysis. Two noted areas of inequity in the arena of formal leadership, where there was a tendency not to have female psychoanalytic society officers proportional to their numbers in the field.[9] A few talked of the general societal discrimination against women. One Kleinian spoke of her relief when men came into the Kleinian ranks:

one did feel uneasy [when the women were dominant] whereas previously one didn't feel . . . uneasy if there was a predominance of men.

This woman attributed some of this unease to the content of Melanie Klein's theories – their centring on the mother and her breast.

In keeping with the position that there are natural gender differences – that women are women and men are men – many women analysts could see the influence of gender in the analytic situation itself.[10] They talked of a different transference towards women, claiming that women more easily elicit a mother transference and the expression of pre-Oedipal issues, and they noted the fact that women analysts are particularly good for patients with certain kinds of problems. Several interviewees remarked that women analysts were more maternal, more open, warmer, less threatening, or 'gifted'. One said 'more of us have a feeling for the unconscious, maybe', and another suggested that it was easier to confide in a woman. Still others noted that women had made major contributions to our understanding of children. One claimed, without specifying how, that women were just special and different. Yet one suggested that another reason for the low professional salience of gender among women analysts was precisely this same transference. Transference, she claimed, does not respect gender boundaries: 'In a complete analysis, the analyst is experienced as father, mother, monster, anything.' A few, indicating identification with women, pointed to the fact that they didn't engage in mother-blaming in their developmental theories. In the analytic situation, then, gender was relevant and interviewees expected that they would be experienced, at least some of the time, as women. Otherwise gender was not particularly significant to their professional life.

I found it hard to understand how the early women psychoanalysts could be seemingly so unattuned to gender, when their field seemed to make a theory of gender central (this dilemma was very much like Borland, 1991, whose interviewee claimed that her account – a story beginning from how women of her generation were expected to act and about male–female and father–daughter relations – was not about gender, and Zavella, 1993, whose Mexican-American interviewees told ethnicity-laden stories but did not accept the Chicana label that was central to Zavella's own ethnic identity). To a 1970s feminist, it was incomprehensible that one could be a psychoanalyst without much noticing the theory of femininity. Concepts of context and salience again helped: for the most part, early women psychoanalysts were more interested clinically in individual women than they were in the 'theory of femininity' writ large. Clinically, some women might be narcissistic, some passive, and others might express penis envy, but these were matters for individual interpretation.[11]

Nevertheless, when pressed, most interviewees could reflect on the theory, and a few were quite critical:

> We strongly have the feeling that it's nonsense to think that every woman thinks she has a terrible lot and then finally makes the best of it, the way Freud really presents it,

said one European, who then went on to defend psychoanalysis by pointing to the many recent revaluations and revisions of the theory. Interviewees were more likely, however, to modulate their criticism or to defend only part of the theory. They argued that penis envy is a developmental stage rather than a major determinant of women's lives, that anyone can see that little girls envy the penis just as boys have castration anxiety, or that boys have womb envy just as girls have penis envy. 'Envy is a human quality', said one. Some claimed that Helene Deutsch, a leading defender and extender of Freudian gender orthodoxy, just wanted to please Freud or personally disliked women. One woman, trained in New York when Karen Horney and Clara Thompson, both dissidents against the Freudian theory of femininity, were still members of the New York Society, claimed that she and her friends held the 'secret theory' that penis envy was socially derived. Others emphasized alternate aspects of female psychology. Kestenberg, for instance, modified the theory of libidinal development, holding that an 'inner-genital' phase precedes the phallic phase in *both* girls and boys and is the early libidinal origin of parentalism. Kleinians opposed Freud's phallocentrism with, in one interviewee's phrase, Klein's 'mammocentrism', or focused on women's internal organs, internal organ integrity and the role of feelings about internal organs in conflicts about reproduction and motherhood.[12]

Second-generation women analysts employed another strategy to address the Freudian devaluation of women. They split their concept of the personal, familial side of femininity and women's lives into the areas of sexuality and maternality. By making this separation, they could valorize femininity in terms of maternal interests and could even conceptualize psychoanalysis itself as a womanly endeavour and understand their own professional practice to grow out of women's empathy and maternality. They could pay not too much attention to the sexual theories. In these latter areas, Freudian theory may be misguided, as it emphasizes inevitable penis envy, passivity and masochism, but the area of women's lives addressed in these invidious ways is reduced. Moreover, for several, it was more significant that Freud affirmed women as desiring sexual beings rather than sex objects. This affirmation was part of what attracted them to psychoanalysis.

Interviewees' assessment of the Freudian theory of femininity must be seen in the context of a firm belief in gender difference, and such a belief also affected early women psychoanalysts' reactions to the contemporary feminist challenge. Most saw themselves to some degree as critical of contemporary feminists, who in their view disparage women's maternality and the child's need for its mother and want to get rid of men. In this view, feminists deny basic physiological sex differences, 'going without bras as if they don't have breasts'. My interviewees often attributed feminist denial of gender difference to a deep-seated fear on feminists' part that women are in fact inferior: feminists have ourselves not got past the early penis envy stage, where only presence or absence of maleness matters, to a true genital stage where the sexes are different but equal:

> I don't quite agree with the feminist ideas that the theory is discriminating. Again, there is after all a reality of difference, and I think many of these, you know, ultra-feminists are more, feeling themselves really inferior, and have to fight it that way. . . . I don't see that one is inferior because one has no penis.

Between the two, then – on the one hand Freud's theory with its perhaps problematic notion of penis envy but its firm assertion of gender difference, and on the other a perceived denial of any sexual difference – interviewees were more comfortable ignoring or modifying what they saw as the biologically, psychologically and clinically more accurate former than accepting what they took to be the fundamentally flawed basic assumptions of the latter.

Seventies questions for thirties women

Problems in differential attunement to gender were particularly acute when I asked what I came to call seventies questions for thirties women. These questions were developed in order to elicit reflections, not upon women's role in the profession nor upon the theory of femininity, but upon the relationship of interviewees' own self-understanding as women to their understanding of psychoanalytic theory. Had one affected the other? Had one led them to try and change the other? This set of questions also asked interviewees to address directly the feminist critique of psychoanalytic theory in relation to their own obvious professional success and active public careers. I wanted to know not only what they thought about the theory of femininity, penis envy, and so forth, but whether they thought about this theory *in relation to* their own identities as women. I found that although some interviewees criticized the theory of femininity, they almost never arrived at their conclusions by measuring the theory against their own lives.

I seem to have been intuitively clued into the problematic nature of these questions: even in my original interview schedule, they are quite lengthy and seem to require a lot of explanation. When I asked them, they were always extraordinarily convoluted and almost incomprehensible in their recursive reflexivity. The following example comes from the end of one of my first interviews. It is evident that I knew that such a question would not work. I said:

> One of the things that people always ask me because, you know, I'm a product of this recent women's movement and a feminist, and yet obviously very committed to psychoanalytic theories and studies, how do you reconcile being, you know, a feminist and believing or thinking that this theory – which ranges from anywhere from, you know, it's male-centered or it's sexist or misogynist or phallocentric, I mean people use a lot of different terms–and I'm wondering whether in your history as an analyst or when you were in training – I don't mean the sort of accusations, although I'm interested in that too–but did that come up for you or for other women? Did you think of yourselves, I mean the issue of the theory of femininity in relation to yourselves, was that something you talked about or did it come up?

These 'seventies questions' were asked in the 1970s of any feminist who was passionate about psychoanalytic theory, or even any feminist who was undergoing analysis or in analytic therapy, and such suspicions are still widely articulated among feminists. I had certainly been challenged many times in just such terms. But my interviewees had neither thought of these issues nor did they seem relevant to most of them when I asked. They did not see themselves in relation to psychoanalytic theory or vice versa:

> You know, it wasn't something that was more, much more central for me than many other questions, perhaps even less important.

I asked an American:

> As you were bringing up your children and also being in training, did the kinds of theories about femininity you were learning, or about motherhood, seem to be compatible?

She responded:

> No, they didn't seem to conflict. Because I took such pleasure in my children. . . . I had these two really strong interests, getting an analytic background, . . . and also my fascination by my children. But I was never bothered in a theoretical sort of way. I can see it from the point of view of patients. I never bothered myself.

I asked one of the first theorists of female and pre-Oedipal development:

> Do you think that the fact of your being a woman influenced what you chose to work on in psychoanalysis?

She answered:

> No, not because I was a woman, but because I was an analyst, and I learned from my patients. [She did go on to concede that for the *very*

early period in life women may have more understanding because of their experiences as mothers. *Maybe.*]

The psychoanalytic theory of femininity, then, was relevant to patients, but not to practitioners' selves.[13] One European interviewee had been articulate about the low feminine self-esteem which she had felt since early childhood. This low self-esteem provided one personal reason why she went into analysis and analytic training. I asked if the psychoanalytic theory of femininity contributed to her understanding of this low self-esteem or to her sense of how she ought to be feminine. At first she did not understand my question. I repeated and rephrased it:

> Do you think, when you started learning about the psychoanalytic theory of femininity, did that increase your sense, or did that affect your sense, of whether you were feminine or not?
> No, it didn't go through my brain, no.

I asked another if she thought at all about the psychology of women while she was in training. Our interchange was typical:

> NJC: Did you think about it in relation to yourself, or did women think about it in relation to themselves?
> I: Uh uh . . . It doesn't figure at all. [I reformulated my question, again using myself as an example of someone who had had such thoughts.] Those didn't surface, at least as far as I was concerned. The mother part did because I felt I was missing something, as I told you before.
> NJC: But you didn't think it was harmful to your child not to have . . . ?
> I: Well, I didn't think it was the greatest thing in the whole world, but I also didn't . . . I felt I was giving enough prime time to offset it. I don't think he always felt that way. [She went on to say that she spent as much time with him as did 'full-time mothers', who went off to social activities.] So I didn't feel guilty on that score. I just felt deprived that *I* didn't have as much time with him as *I*'d like to have. But otherwise I didn't. I don't think this women's issue came up until really . . .

It is important to remember what kinds of women gave these responses. The second-generation psychoanalysts were in no way docile, passive, unthoughtful women. Some opposed parental wishes in becoming professionals; many, depending on country of origin, were part of the earliest wave of women to enter the university. As psychoanalysts, they identified themselves with and participated in what was felt to be a small, highly embattled avant-garde radical movement, and many thought of themselves as unconventional and as cultural radicals. They were often involved politically, as anti-fascists, social democrats or communists. Compliance, then, does not explain their beliefs and claims.

Interviewees themselves began to develop an answer, as they pointed implicitly and explicitly to their own historical and social situation – a historical and social situation that I, ironically, had to be dragged into considering. Near the end of her interview, I asked the woman who said 'what did the women eat?' if her mother had worked.

> Did my mother work! Now you make me see the difference between men and women . . . I can't imagine my mother working . . . I can't imagine any woman working, of our acquaintanceship.

I had finally come up with a question that situated things historically *for her*. The more sociologically minded themselves commented on my questions as historically grounded. When I asked one about the relation between her consciousness as a woman, wife, or mother and the analytic theories she was learning, she did not answer directly. Instead, she responded:

> Well, I think you have to keep in mind that these theories became attacked, under attack, at a time when I'd way already passed my participation in the analytic world.

Another said:

> I don't think those issues were as important then as they are now.

Context and consciousness

By following interviewees' responses, then, I also found some answers to my perplexity. As my interviewees first noted, structural-organizational, historical, and cultural aspects of their lives situate and explain the consciousness I found. The context of their psychoanalytic training is in the first instance relevant to women psychoanalysts' accounts. According to one, non-clinical training consisted in reading and rereading *The Interpretation of Dreams* along with the case histories and the works on technique. These works do not give theoretical prominence to gender or to gender-specific sexuality, and these latter topics were not much discussed or thought about. The theory of femininity was simply not a salient part of their training.[14]

We know that there were written debates about the theory of femininity in the 1920s and early 1930s, when some of my interviewees were in training and beginning to practice, and these debates to a contemporary reader seem quite passionate. It may well be, as Fliegel (1982) claims, that these early debates suffered a sort of repression by the collective consciousness of the field. But it is not clear that they were central to most psychoanalysts. Moreover, as I noted earlier, it is quite clear that on many of the issues that concern 1970s feminists, all protagonists would have been on the same side: all believed in sex differences and recognized the developmental importance, if not over-arching determinism, of penis envy.[15] More important, most analysts of both sexes felt themselves actively engaged in other struggles that were more important to them – in cultural and medical struggle, controversy and debate about Freud's theories of the unconscious, and his claims for the existence of infantile sexuality. In these debates, they were certainly on Freud's side.

Professional and personal experience also seem to have helped keep the early women psychoanalysts from personally reflective notice of Freud's theory of femininity. The extent of real discrimination or invidious differential treatment against early women practitioners in the field cannot be definitively measured. In later years there clearly was some differential treatment, both in terms of access to certain kinds of positions and in terms of male attitudes to at least some female practitioners. My own interviews with men produced memories of being the only man in the Anna Freud Seminar in Vienna or at the Putnam Center in Boston and of the powerful women whose presence dominated the Boston, Washington and London societies. Men referred to the 'lovely women' who were active in psychoanalytic affairs, to the Kleinian 'phalanx of women who all wore black' and to the 'Boston matriarchy'.[16] But women clearly received substantial recognition. Male analysts I spoke with also respected women, referred patients to them, thought they were as good or better as practitioners. As the field developed, moreover, male analysts had themselves often had women of an earlier generation as training analysts and retained a positive transference to them. Equally important, the early women analysts did not perceive much discrimi-nation, but felt that they were treated without regard to gender.

Cohort features of their life cycle and of beliefs about femininity also seem to have shaped the consciousness of early women practitioners. Modally, they married in their early to mid-thirties and had children in their mid- to late thirties; even those who seemed the most domestic members of psychoanalytic couples did not marry until at least their late twenties. Thus, their careers were already established by the time they were confronted by the demands of motherhood. Of greater cultural significance than I had anticipated, women of this cohort were not confronting a post-World War II feminine mystique version of psycho-analytic theory. The Europeans all assumed they would have careers. As one European put it: 'we were told you *have* to be independent'.[17] People asked her after she had emigrated why she was not married: 'such a question would have been unthinkable in Vienna'. Several Europeans pointed to the sexism which shocked them upon arrival in the United

States and claimed that they did not notice the phallocentrism of the theory until they were in the context of a sexist culture that kept women in the home. American interviewees, though more aware of the practical conflicts of family and career (as one said, 'the Americans were a more domesticated brood'), were nevertheless also of the 1890–1910 birth cohort that married late and had few children. For many of these women, moreover, becoming a psychoanalyst and doctor was often so foreign to their origins that it could not even be compared to the cult of domesticity.

The early women psychoanalysts did have a concept of femininity and the female life cycle, but it was one that implicitly or explicitly included work and career. Even Freud (1933: 135) had said that the psychoanalytic theory of femininity only describes 'women in so far as their nature is determined by their sexual function', acknowledging that 'an individual woman may be a human being in other respects as well'. Judith Kestenberg, who began to develop her reformulation of the theory of femininity in the 1950s, extends the theorizing of these 'other respects', in a way that I think reflects the conceptions of other women analysts of the 1930s generation. There were, for these women, 'three faces of femininity', motherhood, eroticism, and career or intellectual development (Kestenberg, 1980c). In Kestenberg's account, each of these faces draws on different aspects of drives, unconscious processes, object relations and developmental phase, but *all* are part of a full female life.

Partly because of class background and partly because of European background, almost none (and the few who did were not themselves mothers) operated under the assumption often attributed to their theories that children need 24-hour maternal care. As one put it, it was 'a very American phenomenon that women should be home full-time'. Many did not have children, and most were quite accepting of this option for those contemporary women who have chosen it.[18] Those who did have children all talked of the competing claims of their different roles and said that they had cut back on work when their children were small. 'I had a husband, two houses, and two children, so I never really fulfilled my destiny', said one American who nevertheless had a private practice, wrote two books, and was a training and supervising analyst at a major institute. As another put it,

> You have a feeling now, well, should I be there or should I be there? I mean I'm having fun with my child, but should I be reading a book? And you read the book and you wonder what they're doing now.

About professional women with children, she said:

> They're enriched intellectually by what they do, and they're enriched emotionally by the little person upstairs.

But, she concluded, 'one doesn't have to be too ambitious, I think'. Mothers did tend to express *their own* regrets – for *their* sake rather than that of their children – that they could not spend more time with their children, and one claimed that she had to work and would have liked to be a full-time mother. A few felt that their children had been affected by not enough maternal care, but others were quite comfortable with afternoons or a couple of hours' contact a day with their children.

Interviews made clear just how historically specific good-enough mothering is. One interviewee talked about her great delight in domesticity and her children and said that she 'did a good deal of the childrearing'. She claimed that 'the high point of the day [was] the time I spent with the children'. I asked whether that was a couple of hours in the evening, and she said 'It would be about that'. A younger analyst who had trained in the feminine mystique 1950s talked about asking a very busy and eminent older woman analyst when this older woman had had time to crochet a series of little table cloths used for entertaining. This woman had answered, 'When I was with the children'. As the younger woman, who had had to contend as she was in training with American 1950s cultural theories of mothering, interpreted this, 'being with the children' seemed comfortably to have consisted for the older woman in visits to the nursery where she sat on a chair and crocheted.[19] Several second-generation women had long separations from children, one when she was able to emigrate to the United States and left her son for six months with her husband until she was settled, another upon arrival sending her German-speaking children off to the country for the summer, ostensibly so they could get fresh air. Another, ready to give up her analysis in Zurich because her small son was living with his father and grandmother several hours away, was told by her analyst to stick with it and just go visit her son when she couldn't stand to be away from him any longer.[20]

The second-generation women analysts, then, were not gender-blind or unattuned to gender. Low gender salience did not characterize all aspects of their lives. Rather, their cultural conception of gender and sense of gender identity were culturally and historically specific. As products of their era, they split their interpretations of public and domestic gender. As European social democrats and socialists, as products of the American women's colleges or of Bloomsbury, as cultural radicals, they believed in women's right to work and to lead creatively fulfilling lives. As post-World War I Middle Europeans, they often knew that they had to work: the former Austro-Hungarian Empire was devastated; the Weimar monetary system collapsed in the early 1920s; their own once substantial families might be currently needy, and millions of men of their generation had been killed, so that marriage was by no means a certain future. If they were feminist, it was as participants in socialist or social democratic politics that argued for women's rights to equality in the public sphere, where, unlike in the domestic sphere, there was no reason for difference. As one interviewee put it:

You see the sociological side of it in the patriarchal societies, of course, and that I am against: Why should a woman who works not have the same payment and the same status as the man? But otherwise, it is very good to be a woman. And a mother.

Another agreed that feminists have a point about sexual inequality but claimed that over her lifetime, she had been more preoccupied with social democratic politics, anti-fascism, economic inequality and social legislation. She expressed agreement with Friedan's 'second-stage feminism', which wanted to resuscitate concern for preservation of the family and family values:

We've done sort of the rough job, and the Pankhurst-like things, you know, but now we have to get down to what are the *real* issues for women. And I am more inner-directed, and more interested in the internal issues.

She spoke of the 'complexity' of the 'inner conflicts' and 'inner tasks', which include such things as how to reconcile career and family. Another said:

I'm not the right person really, because at my time it was absolutely taken for granted that a woman is as good as a man, can do as much, has an absolute free choice.

There were, she recognized, still some inequalities in the higher echelons of power and status to work out, but she and her cohort had believed that with the achievement of social democracy these would be taken care of as well. She concluded, with rueful hindsight: 'Instead of that, Hitler came'.

Even as they believed in sex similarity and equality in the public sphere, second-generation analysts believed passionately (and in keeping with their commitments to psychoanalytic theory) in natural differences in the domestic sphere. Women psychoanalysts did not think that they were challenging basic notions of women's nature: their move away from tradition was in the public – professional, economic, political – realm. They did not feel the need to transform or uproot the domestic sexual division of spheres. They continued to take major responsibility for child and home care and for entertaining (particular second-generation women psychoanalysts were well-known as party givers), and they believed that women have special nurturant capacities. For example, the woman for whom it had been 'absolutely taken for granted that a woman is as good as a man' worried about why women had been put into inferior positions over the millennia, but she disagreed strongly with 1970s feminist advocacy of shared parenting. Men, she claimed, do not have the right body configuration and are not cuddly enough to take care of infants. In her own career, the only time gender was relevant was when she had children. In remarkably clear reflection of the notion that what differentiates women is their family and sexual role, another said:

> Being a woman was fully satisfied by having a very good husband and two children. My psychoanalytic interests emerged out of my literary concerns.

Low gender salience, then, did not characterize *all* aspects of women psychoanalysts' lives or identity. Participation in an exciting professional movement as equals and notions of socialist comradeship and cultural avant-gardism characterized their experience of work and societal gender relations, while women's natural role as mothers and (equal but different) wives characterized their experience of home roles. They assumed a division of labour in the home, assumed women's natural maternality, and assumed innate, and desirable, gender personality differences.

Their views, then, were in sharp contrast to the 1970s feminist challenge to the domestic division of labour and to notions of innate gender differences. However, it should be noted that these views are in equally sharp contrast to the belief that innate differences between women and men or women's natural domestic location entail that women should not be in the public world of work and politics. The early women psychoanalysts' firm sense of gender difference did not feel like a life restriction that required 24-hour mothering or women's dependence on men. This division of conceptions of gender into public and domestic aspects provides a first step in answering questions about how early women analysts dealt with the psychoanalytic theory of femininity in relation to their own professional success: this theory applies to the domestic side of women's lives.

A further, more abstract, meta-feature of second-generation women analysts' gender consciousness is equally important. The 1970s women's movement began with the slogan that the personal is political. For the students and scholars in this movement, this also meant that the personal was theoretical and, conversely, that the theoretical had to be validated by the personal. In sharp contrast, as I describe above, it had not *occurred* to most of my interviewees to think of the theoretical as personal: their personal life and their personal analysis were personal; their reading and evaluation of theory was as professional practitioners. When an interviewee, reflecting historically, claimed that 'these theories became under attack' after she had 'passed her participation in the analytic world', she did not mean to imply that she had never thought about them. She in fact *had* thought about the issue of penis envy and its cultural determination at that earlier time, but she rightly saw *my* question, which related these issues to her own life, as a product of the contemporary debate where the personal is theoretical and vice versa. Such thoughts 'go through one's brain' when they are in the cultural air. In the deepest sense, self-reflection here seems culturally shaped and delimited, even for practitioners in a field that invites and insists upon self-reflection.

Readers who have commented on this paper have been extremely puzzled by this claim that my interviewees did not think of the theoretical as personal. They have assumed, not unreasonably, that the process of psychoanalysis is mainly about rerendering the personal via psychoanalytic theory. But until very recently, and still for most practitioners, the culture of psychoanalysis has maintained a firm separation between practitioner and patient, so that clinical examples are given only in terms of patients, and never in terms of the self. One has a personal analysis, but one applies the theory to those one treats.

Seventies questions about psychoanalytic theory are a particular instance of a cultural and historical discourse, not self-evident and automatic. These questions arise under two conditions. First, the theory must seem dissonant with one's own identity. Second – and helping to condition and evoke the first – the theory must be a subject of historically situated cultural discourse. For the early women psychoanalysts, the psychoanalytic theory of femininity felt largely consonant with their identity, and it was not a subject of cultural or psychoanalytic discourse or debate. They did not experience the theory to constrain *them*, and it is unclear if they imposed it in negative ways on their patients. One told of a miserable woman painter with a 2-year-old who was staying at home full-time with her child:

> I said why don't you paint *and* be a mother? And I never saw her again after I made that suggestion.[21]

We can understand what I considered the second-generation women analysts' low gender salience not only in terms of the internal structure of their gender consciousness – emphasizing natural difference and public-sphere equality – but also in relation to other aspects of social location and self-categorization. Cultural and historical setting served further to make early women psychoanalysts, from the viewpoint of 1970s feminism, relatively unattuned to gender in some aspects of their lives. Cynthia Epstein (1970) early argued that social categorizations that cross gender lines can minimize the salience of gender in women's lives (such a claim has become widespread and almost definitional of 1990s feminism). Following this line of reasoning, the gender identity of second-generation women analysts demonstrates the situatedness and multiplicity of possible identities. For many of the Europeans I interviewed, it is not surprising that Jewishness was a much more salient self-categorization than gender, and this was also a characteristic shared with men. Participation in psychoanalytic families and couples, in a psychoanalytic social world, and in the radical social movement that was psychoanalysis, being a lay analyst in medical psychoanalytic America, socialist youth movement membership, and participation in other avant-garde movements or social groups like Bloomsbury also created identities, all held in common with some male psychoanalysts, that modulated the salience of gender identity.

Interviewees could see this in relation to both selves and others. 'She probably felt handicapped by being Polish and Jewish, but not as a woman', said one about another, who said that it had also been much harder for her to be Jewish than to be a woman. This woman described the anti-Semitism that drove her from her native country to anti-Semitic Germany, where students demonstrated against her and she was almost ousted from the university for being Jewish. The issue of being non-medical dominated the entire interview of another woman, an American who was probably the first child analyst in New York and who had trained in Vienna and through independently gained supervision (such informal training was common in the 1920s). This woman was never made a regular member of the New York Psychoanalytic Society and spent her long professional career with special visiting privileges. Another, whose father was a card-playing partner of Freud and whose husband also became a prominent analyst, was first cousins with another woman analyst and related to yet another, both also married to analysts. For all these women, structural characteristics not linked to gender were more personally and culturally salient than was their gender.

Portraying self and other: generation

My interviewees had different forms of gender consciousness and experienced a different salience of gender as a social category and aspect of professional identity than second-wave feminist professionals like myself (including those in their own field).[22] They interpret and interpreted their situation differently than we, imaginatively placed within it, might do, leading us to wonder at their ability to reduce what to us seem such striking instances of contradiction and cognitive dissonance. Of course, my interviews draw upon retrospective accounts – and accounts of considerably distant experience – so we cannot be certain that interviewees describe how they really felt at the time. And we also know that psychoanalysis as a field has not always been kind to its internal dissidents: interviewees may have had practical motives for their ways of experiencing and interpreting the situation. Resolving contradiction and ambiguity, faulty memory and instrumental motives for avoiding punishment for dissent may all have contributed to the accounts I found.

However, I believe it is methodologically sounder and empirically more illuminating to assume that interviewees' accounts document how they in fact consciously feel and felt. Taking such a position, moreover, proved generative, because it enabled me to see how cultural and historical processes, as well as social situation, make certain conceptualizations and not others more probable. At the same time, this position also reflexively problematized and relativized my own expectations and understandings. Gender emphasis on the one hand, and the relative downplay of gender issues on the other, are not only objectively determined by a structural situation. They are also subjective features of identity and culture. Like other 1970s feminists, I needed to learn that feminist analysis could focus on subjects who minimized the importance of gender and on situations of low gender salience.

To return to myself as a historically situated 1970s feminist researcher: in our time (both the 1970s time of my identity in this essay and the 1990s time in which I am updating it) the existence of unconscious mental phenomena and childhood sexuality is widely accepted, and the theory of femininity has been a major contested arena both within the field and without. I therefore noticed a lack of attention to this theory. Similarly, as a feminist, I was attuned to comparative historical statistics on women in the professions, as well as to the less measurable question of the comparative prominence of women in other fields, when I thought that women seemed so prominent in psychoanalysis. As a researcher from without, I noted that even in fields like anthropology and child development, percentages were never as high, and practitioners did not find it easy to obtain regularized high-status institutional positions. My few interviewees who 'don't see so many about it' trained when participation was growing from about 20 per cent to 30–40 per cent women, depending on location, and when one-third of psychoanalytic trainees might be women. Comparatively, these figures are high, but from the point of view of practitioners, women remained a distinct minority. In the United States in particular, membership figures for women declined beginning in the 1950s. By 1980 they were much lower than in many other professions.[23]

On the other side, comparative statistics also help us to understand interviewees' putative false consciousness. We can point to the theory of femininity, to sexist remarks by colleagues, to how some were passed over for positions. But it is hard to argue that something was radically wrong and that they should have noticed, when with some accuracy we can probably characterize their professional lives as a huge advance over the lives of women of the previous generation as well as greatly advantaged compared to most women of their own generation. It may not be false consciousness or denial in such a situation not to focus on the remaining arenas of discrimination or difference. Rather than denying gender stratification in their profession, they may have been justifiably conscious of the extent of gender equality within it.

There is also an ironic reversal in the generation gap that I have labelled seventies questions for thirties women. The gender consciousness and apparent gender unattunedness of my interviewees were not only different than mine; they were the reverse of my own. Feminists, even as we want to eliminate gender inequality, hierarchy and difference, expect to find gender salient in most social settings and in psychological life. In our effort to demonstrate the importance of social and cultural relations of gender and of gender identity – to put women in the centre – we have begun from the assumption that gender is always a salient feature of social and psychological life, and we have not developed theoretical approaches that emphasize sex similarities over six differences. As Atkinson (1982) aptly put it, feminist ethnographers do best understanding societies with extreme male domination and practices that 'fairly scream out for' feminist critique. They do less well with societies exhibiting low gender salience. Psychological commentators also note overreporting of studies that find gender differences and underreporting of those that do not.

But *low* gender salience characterized the women analysts' interpretation of their lives and their situation as psychoanalysts – characterized *their* cultural meaning system. And, it seems at least to some extent, low gender salience characterized their objective professional situation as well. This contrasted strikingly with my own situation and with the assumptions of contemporary gender theory. At the same time, feminist sociologists hold a *psychological* theory that downgrades or eliminates notions of innate or desirable sex differences. A psychological theory of innate and desirable sex difference is precisely what women psychoanalysts held.

Feminist researchers have had to learn to be especially careful about our own normative patterns of gender consciousness and gender blindness, and my study, I believe, was an early instance of such learning. In my study, the situation was compounded. My interviewees were not the disadvantaged, silenced women of colour, class or sexual orientation that white, heterosexual middle-class professionals have been admonished not to subsume under a monolithic feminist hegemony. They were long-time, leading professionals in an important field. We were, moreover, in parallel situations. My interviewees and I were in fields that centre on issues of gender and that attribute underlying meanings and causes to stated beliefs. Just as feminists are liable to impute false consciousness or denial to women who do not see our gendered truth, so psychoanalysts are liable to impute to feminists denial, fixation or regression.

Even as it illuminates in a straightforward way women's voices and women's subjectivity, my research points to a productive tension in feminist research. In the most consistently phenomenological qualitative methods, the researcher privileges research subjects' understandings. The feminist methodological imperative to let women's voices be heard and women's consciousness be expressed leads to a similar position. But feminists also ask structural or organizational questions, which grow from our concerns with gender inequality, asymmetry, or difference and not necessarily from subjects' understandings. Thus, even as my structural and organizational conclusions draw upon why my inter- viewees told me, my questions often did not have much significance for them. We had, in fact, basically opposed interpretations of the import- ance of gender in different settings, and perhaps in social life more generally.

Gender as a feature of professional life and knowledge was minimized by the particular way that the women analysts interpreted gender – as relevant in the domestic sphere but not the public; by the fact that social characteristics not linked to gender were personally and culturally salient to them; and by their interpretation of the psychoanalytic theory of femininity – as not to be evaluated in relation to their own lives and as not as important as the theory of the unconscious. Low gender salience characterized my interviewees' interpretation of their professional lives. As I have described it, this variable and situated quality of gender came to me in a forceful way, as I was talking to interviewees. The pervasiveness to me of gender as a social, psychological and cultural category simply did not resonate with their own life experiences. I began to realize how much my own perceptual and analytic categories had been shaped by my coming of age in the women's movement and my immersion in feminist theory. Only with this recognition, that the salience and meaning of gender were products of one's time and place, could I come to understand gender within the fabric of my interviewees' lives.

As I was pondering this dilemma, some feminist theorists had begun to argue for situating gender as a relational and relative category both in itself and in relation to the social and cultural whole (see, for example, Rosaldo, 1980). The methodological requirements that we let women's voices be heard, and that we examine our own relationship to our research subjects, and the theoretical concept of gender salience, enable us to do this, to go beyond conceptualizing gender in absolute terms. They guide us to look at gender as a situated phenomenon, both in itself, as it can be more or less salient in different arenas or at different times of life, and in relation to other aspects of social and cultural categorization and identity. Social, historical and cultural context – in the case of the second-generation women analysts a social situation of low gender salience and a relative lack of feminist politics, or a politics that assumed natural differences between the sexes; in my case a social, professional and political situation that stressed high gender salience – served to create what I considered to be normative patterns of gender blindness in early women psychoanalysts, and what I came to see as normative patterns of hypersensitivity to gender in contemporary feminists like myself. At the same time, variations in the organization of gender and in gender as a social and structural category are, partially, reciprocally created by these situated personal and cultural interpretations. An examination of interpretations of gender and of the dialogue between those with different interpretations informs our understanding of the social, historical and cultural context that these interpretations help to produce and that also help to produce them.

Notes

1 The earliest version of this paper was presented at the 1984 Meetings of the American Sociological Association.

2 I am grateful to the Russell Sage Foundation and the National Endowment for the Humanities for support for the research upon which this paper is based. I also acknowledge support from the Center for Advanced Study in the Behavioral Sciences, the University of California, Santa Cruz, and the Institute of Personality Assessment and Research, University of California, Berkeley. Rose Laub Coser, Annette Lawson, Shulamit Reinharz, Judith Stacey, Avril Thorne and Barrie Thorne provided helpful comments and suggestions. In what follows, I have edited and clarified my account and added some appropriate references, but I have left my argument essentially as it was published in 1989. Occasionally, parenthetical remarks reflect back from the 1990s.

3 Compare Borland, who entitles her article, '"That's Not What I Said": Interpretive Conflict in Oral Narrative Research'. Borland notes: 'on the one hand, we seek to empower the women we work with by revaluing their perspectives, their lives and their art in a world that has systematically ignored or trivialized women's culture. On the other, we hold an explicitly political vision of the structural conditions that lead to particular social behaviors, a vision that our field collaborators, many of whom do not consider themselves feminists, may not recognize as valid. . . . What should we do when women disagree?' (Borland, 1991: 64).

4 For insightful discussion of the felt threat of differences among women, see Flax (1978), Krieger (1983), Miner and Longino (1987), and Ascher et al. (1984). Daniels (1983) makes a related point concerning the relations between the field researcher and her informants.

5 Zavella faced a similar dilemma, not about gender identity but about Chicana identity. As she puts it: 'It was only in retrospect, when I came to understand how Mexican American women informants from New Mexico constructed their ethnic identity in very different ways, that I realized I needed to deconstruct and problematize my own sense of Chicana feminism so that I could "see" the nuances of ethnic identity among my informants' (Zavella, 1993: 57). For an early suggestion that we pay attention to situations of gender salience, see Thorne (1978). For more recent discussions, see Thorne (1990; 1993) and Deaux and Major (1990).

6 My sample was, to put it mildly, opportunistic – I talked to those who would see me in areas where several potential interviewees were clustered throughout the United States, in Great Britain and in the Netherlands. Of 80 scheduled interviews, 44 were with second-generation women psychoanalysts, the oldest born in 1894, the youngest in 1918, and most born between 1900 and 1910. Eighteen were with men of the same generations. Interviewees were, in the USA, members (or affiliates) of institutes connected to the American Psychoanalytic Association; in Britain, members of the three branches of the British Psychoanalytic Society – Contemporary Freudian (followers of Anna Freud), Kleinian and Independent (broadly, those associated with object-relations theory). They were lay and medical and were born, trained and practiced (in a variety of combinations of mobility characteristic of their analytic generation) in the United States, England, Austria, Germany, Hungary, Czechoslovakia, the Netherlands, and elsewhere. About two-thirds of the women (and all the men) had married, and about one-half had children. Ten interviewees were sons, daughters, and one granddaughter of second-generation women; eight of these are themselves practising analysts or therapists. Six others were analysts in their fifties, trained around the mid-1950s, who had close relationships with particular second-generation women or were particularly knowledgeable about the history of psychoanalysis. Two, finally, were women married to men of the early generation who participated in the interviews with their husbands. In addition, at the time and since, I treated the research somewhat ethnographically, talking informally over the years with historians, analysts, relatives of early women analysts, staff of various analytic institutes, and so forth.

Although it is not the subject of this paper, I should note that, just as I seem to have found myself in a methodological dilemma later noted by several feminist researchers, I also seem to have picked a topic waiting to be found. Since I began my research, there has emerged a veritable industry of biographies, autobiographies, or studies of early women psychoanalysts.

7 I discuss and document these observations in Chodorow (1986; 1991).

8 Appignanesi and Forrester (1992) seem to have been motivated by similar observations.

9 On this see Chodorow (1986).

10 Gender in the analytic situation has been a subject of interest since women first entered the field. Study of the transference toward women played a central role in the development of the psychology of femininity (see Freud, 1931), and the modal transference situation was seen as woman patient and man analyst (Freud, 1915). In recent times gender in the transference has been a subject of lively debate.

11 As a clinician, I now more easily understand their point. In recent writings (Chodorow, 1994; 1995), I have also argued for the individuality and personal construction of gendered subjectivity, and I have become more attuned to the complex relations between psychoanalytic theory (about anything) and clinical understanding.

12 See, for example, Kestenberg (1968; 1980a; 1980b; and other writings); Klein (1928; and other writings), and Langer (1952).

13 There is a classic exception to this claim. Horney not only criticized Freud's

theory of femininity, she did so by appealing to her own experience: 'I, as a woman, ask in amazement, and what about motherhood?' (1926: 60).

14 *Bloomsbury/Freud: The Letters of James and Alix Strachey 1924–1925* (Meisel and Kendrick, 1985) provides one first-hand account of reactions to the theory of femininity. One gets a sense of irreverence and amusement on the part of the Stracheys and those around them, a playful attitude toward sexual theory and little sense that it must be seriously challenged. Alix, discussing Klein's theory of the female Oedipus complex and the girl's fear of castration, writes: 'Tho' many are puzzled as to how this threat can affect the little girl, who has nowt to castrate' (1985: 152). James later writes to Alix about a meeting of the British Psychoanalytic Society 'devoted exclusively to a question raised by Bryan upon whether some kind of excitation of the clitoris was not after all essential before a female could have an orgasm. . . . The discussion was rather heated; but went round & round. And the extraordinary thing was that no one seemed to know what an orgasm was. Mrs. Riviere asserted flatly that there was a vaginal orgasm & a clitoris orgasm. . . . But the gentlemen of the party seemed not to agree with this' (1985: 196).

In my own psychoanalytic training, undertaken in the mid-1980s, it was also the case that we did not discuss the psychology of gender except briefly in one or two courses on development. I believe that this has changed by now (the mid-1990s), and that more training programmes offer courses on the psychology of women (although not yet on the psychology of men).

15 Karen Horney, it must be remembered, held a biological theory of natural femininity, although her biological theory disagreed with Freud's, and although her early writings were also sensitive to cultural discrimination against women and to the unconscious childhood components in the Freudian views of women. See Horney (1967).

16 For further discussion of the issue of equal treatment, see Chodorow (1986). For a later generation of analysts, see Schuker (1985). For at least one example of an early man's attitude to some women, see *Bloomsbury/Freud* (Meisel and Kendrick, 1985), in which James Strachey repeatedly disparages as a group the women child analysts in London.

17 I discuss further the economic and historical situation of second-generation women analysts in Chodorow (1991).

18 Still, both mothers and non-mothers did not accept what they saw as women having children and then virtually never parenting. In this context they expressed (what I myself would now consider to be prescient) concern about how the demanding professions of today prevent women from taking pleasure in their children, because they have no time to spend with them. And they particularly faulted the organization of training and practice in their own specialties, medicine and psychiatry: these fields argue for the importance of extensive maternal care, but, by refusing (at the time of my interviews) part-time options and leaves, make it impossible for women residents and interns to mother.

19 In Vienna, where being a governess was a respectable women's profession, some younger analysts in training and nursery school teachers studying with Anna Freud took care of more established analysts' children.

20 See also Deutsch (1973), who describes leaving her son with his father in

Vienna for several months while she pursued analysis and further training in Berlin. For a related instance, concerning marriage rather than children, see *Bloomsbury/Freud* (Meisel and Kendrick, 1985), in which Alix Strachey reiterates the necessity of remaining apart from James for the sake of her personal analysis. I emphasize that I use these examples not to criticize the early women analysts for inadequate mothering or for maternal deprivation on a daily or long-term basis. My point is to stress the contrast between their behaviour and sense of appropriate maternal care and subsequent psychoanalytically inspired views that every child needs full-time maternal care for the first several years. I also stress that mothers expressed regret about cases of longer separation, and that some of these were thought necessary because of refugee status and the stress of emigration.

21 See also Webster (1985), who argues that the evidence we have from Helene Deutsch's published case accounts indicates that, rather than imposing her theories about women's biologically inevitable passivity, masochism and narcissism on women patients, Deutsch worked hard to overcome these qualities both in these patients and in herself.

22 Schuker (1985) suggests that women of the current generation may be very much influenced by expectations about appropriate feminine behaviour and feminine role norms, and that traditional and conformist gender-role pressures on them may well be greater than on women in other fields. My own observations support this.

23 It seems now, in 1995, that a majority of psychoanalytic candidates, at least in the United States, are women.

References

Alcoff, Linda and Potter, E. (1993) *Feminist Epistemologies*. New York: Routledge.

Appignanesi, Lisa and Forrester, J. (1992) *Freud's Women*. New York: Basic.

Ascher, Carol, DeSalvo, L. and Ruddick, S. (1984) *Between Women*. Boston: Beacon.

Atkinson, Jane (1982) 'Anthropology' review essay, *Signs*, 8: 236–58.

Bordo, Susan and Jagger, A. (1989) *Gender/Body/Knowledge*. New Brunswick, NJ: Rutgers University Press.

Borland, Katherine (1991) '"That's not what I said": Interpretive conflict in oral narrative research', in Sherna Gluck and D. Patai, *Women's Words*. New York: Routledge, pp. 63–76.

Bowles, Gloria and Duelli Klein, Renate (eds) (1983) *Theories of Women's Studies*. London: Routledge & Kegan Paul.

Chodorow, Nancy J. (1986) 'Varieties of leadership among early women psychoanalysts', in Leah Dickstein and Carol Nadelson (eds), *Women Physicians in Leadership Roles*. Washington, D.C.: American Psychiatric Press, pp. 45–54.

Chodorow, Nancy J. (1989) 'Seventies questions for thirties women: Gender and generation in a study of early women psychoanalysts', in *Feminism and Psychoanalytic Theory*. New Haven, CT: Yale University Press, and Cambridge: Polity, pp. 199–218.

Chodorow, Nancy J. (1991) 'Where have all the eminent women psycho-analysts gone? Like the bubbles in champagne, they rose to the top and disappeared', in Judith R. Blau and Norman Goodman (eds), *Social Roles and Social Institutions: Essays in Honor of Rose Laub Coser*. Boulder, CO: Westview Press, pp. 167–94.

Chodorow, Nancy J. (1994) *Femininities, Masculinities, Sexualities: Freud and Beyond*. Lexington, KY: University Press of Kentucky, and London: Free Association Books.

Chodorow, Nancy J. (1995) 'Gender as a personal and cultural construction', *Signs*, 20: 516–44.

Chodorow, Nancy J. and Contratto, Susan (1982) 'The fantasy of the perfect mother', in *Feminism and Psychoanalytic Theory* (1989). New Haven, CT: Yale University Press, and Cambridge: Polity.

Collins, Patricia Hill (1986) 'Learning from the outsider within: The sociological significance of black feminist thought', *Social Problems*, 33: s14–s32.

Daniels, Arlene Kaplan (1983) 'Self-deception and self-discovery in fieldwork', *Qualitative Sociology*, 6: 195–214.

Deaux, Kay and Major, Brenda (1990) 'A social-psychological model of gender', in Deborah Rhode (ed.), *Theoretical Perspectives on Gender Difference*. New Haven, CT: Yale University Press, pp. 89–99.

Deutsch, Helene (1973) *Confrontations with Myself*. New York: Norton.

Epstein, Cynthia (1970) *Woman's Place: Options and Limits in Professional Careers*. Berkeley and Los Angeles: University of California Press.

Flax, Jane (1978) 'The conflict between nurturance and autonomy in mother–daughter relationships and within feminism', *Feminist Studies*, 4: 171–91.

Fleigel, Zenia Odes (1982) 'Half a century later: Current status of Freud's controversial views on women', *Psychoanalytic Review*, 69: 7–27.

Fonow, Mary and Cook, J. (1991) *Beyond Methodology*. Bloomington, IN: Indiana University Press.

Franz, Carol and Stewart, A. (1994) *Women Creating Lives*. Boulder, CO: Westview Press.

Freud, Sigmund (1915) 'Observations on Transference Love (Further Recommendations on the Technique of Psychoanalysis III)', in *Standard Edition of the Complete Psychological Works*, Vol. XII. London: Hogarth Press, pp. 157–71.

Freud, Sigmund (1931) 'Female sexuality', in *Standard Edition of the Complete Psychological Works*, Vol. XXI. London: Hogarth Press, pp. 223–43.

Freud, Sigmund (1933) 'Femininity', in *New Introductory Lectures, Standard Edition of the Complete Psychological Works*, Vol. XXII. London: Hogarth Press.

Frontiers (1993) Special Issue: 'Feminist dilemmas in field work', *Frontiers: A Journal of Women's Studies*, 13(3).

Gluck, Sherna and Patai, D. (1991) *Women's Words*. New York: Routledge.

Harding, Sandra (1987) *Feminism and Methodology*. Bloomington, IN: Indiana University Press.

Horney, Karen (1967) *Feminine Psychology*. New York: Norton.

Hornstein, Gail (1994) 'The ethics of ambiguity: Feminists writing women's lives', in Carol Franz and A. Stewart, *Women Creating Lives*. Boulder, CO: Westview Press, pp. 51–68.

Kestenberg, Judith (1968) 'Outside and inside, male and female', *Journal of the American Psychoanalytic Association*, 16: 457–520.

Kestenberg, Judith (1980a) 'The inner-genital phase', in D. Mendel (ed.), *Early Feminine Development: Contemporary Psychoanalytic Views*. New York: Spectrum.

Kestenberg, Judith (1980b) 'Maternity and paternity in the developmental context', *Psychiatric Clinics of North America*, 3: 61–79.

Kestenberg, Judith (1980c) 'The three faces of femininity', *Psychoanalytic Review*, 67: 313–35.

Klein, Melanie (1928) 'Early stages of the Oedipus conflict', in *Love, Guilt and Reparation* (1975). New York: Delta.

Krieger, Susan (1983) *The Mirror Dance*. Philadelphia: Temple.

Krieger, Susan (1985) 'Beyond subjectivity: The use of the self in social science', in *Social Science and the Self* (1991). New Brunswick, NJ: Rutgers University Press, pp. 165–83.

Langer, Marie (1952) *Motherhood and Sexuality* (1992). New York: Guilford.

Meisel, Perry and Kendrick, Walter (eds) (1985) *Bloomsbury/Freud: The Letters of James and Alix Strachey 1924–1925*. New York: Basic.

Miner, Valerie and Longino, Helen (eds) (1987) *Competition*. New York: The Feminist Press.

Nielson, Joyce (1990) *Feminist Research Methods*. Boulder, CO: Westview Press.

Oakley, Ann (1981) 'Interviewing women: A contradiction in terms', in Helen Roberts (ed.), *Doing Feminist Research*. London: Routledge & Kegan Paul, pp. 30–61.

Personal Narratives Group (1989) *Interpreting Women's Lives*. Bloomington, IN: Indiana University Press.

Reinharz, Shulamit (1979) *On Becoming a Social Scientist: From Survey Research and Participant Observation to Experiential Analysis* (1984). New Brunswick, NJ: Transaction Books.

Reinharz, Shulamit (1992) *Feminist Methods in Social Research*. New York and Oxford: Oxford University Press.

Rosaldo, Michelle Z. (1980) 'The use and abuse of anthropology for cross-cultural understanding', *Signs*, 5: 389–417.

Schuker, Eleanor (1985) 'Creative productivity in women analysts', *Journal of the American Academy of Psychoanalysis*, 13: 51–75.

Sherif, Carolyn (1977) 'Bias in psychology', in Julia Sherman and Evelyn T. Beck (eds), *The Prism of Sex*. Madison: Wisconsin University Press.

Smith, Dorothy (1974) 'Women's perspective as a radical critique of sociology', in Sandra Harding (ed.) (1987), *Feminism and Methodology*. Bloomington: Indiana University Press.

Smith, Dorothy (1977) 'A sociology for women', in Julia Sherman and Evelyn T. Beck (eds), *The Prism of Sex*. Madison: Wisconsin University Press.

Stewart, Abigail (1994) 'Toward a feminist strategy for studying women's lives', in Carol Franz and A. Stewart, *Women Creating Lives*. Boulder, CO: Westview Press, pp. 11–35.

Thorne, Barrie (1978) 'Gender . . . how is it best conceptualized?', in Laurel Richardson and Verta Taylor (eds) (1983), *Feminist Frontiers*. Reading, MA: Addison-Wesley, pp. 61–3.

Thorne, Barrie (1990) 'Children and gender: Constructions of difference', in Deborah Rhode (ed.), *Theoretical Perspectives on Gender Difference*. New Haven, CT: Yale University Press, pp. 100–13.

Thorne, Barrie (1993) *Gender Play*. New Brunswick, NJ: Rutgers University Press.

Webster, Brenda (1985) 'Helene Deutsch: A new look', *Signs*, 10: 553–71.

Zavella, Patricia (1993) 'Feminist insider dilemmas: Constructing ethnic identity with "Chicana" informants', *Frontiers*, 13: 53–76.

—————• 2

Women's desire and sexual violence discourse

—————• NICOLA GAVEY

In 1987, I embarked upon uncharted doctoral research, knowing only that I wanted to study 'acquaintance rape'. At this time in New Zealand, the whole concept of acquaintance rape – or date rape – was virtually unheard of. I remember a conversation I had with a friend at the time, during which I tried to explain what my research would be about. I said I was interested in those situations where a man was pressuring a woman to have sex with him, where she did not want to and unambivalently said 'no', but he went ahead anyway and they had sexual intercourse that was unwanted by her. I still remember my friend looking a bit blank and unimpressed and saying 'But that's what happens all the time', as if to remind me that that's just the way things are. I was simultaneously deflated and intrigued. Perhaps my new-found interest was an irrelevant tangent, bearing no relation to 'real rape' (see Estrich, 1987). But, on the other hand, what our conversation implied was that the boundary between coercive and normal heterosexuality is blurred. With some reluctance I realized it would be impossible to study date rape, or marital rape, or rape within any heterosexual relationship, without also critically studying normative heterosexual practice.

It later became clear that my friend's matter-of-fact assertion about the nature of heterosexual sex resonated with an important strand of radical feminist theory on rape. This theory emphasizes the close connection between (heterosexual) rape and normative heterosexual sex and, in doing so, deconstructs what has been a common-sense dichotomy between rape and sex. Proponents of this particular feminist view of rape, perhaps most eloquently expressed by Catharine MacKinnon (1983;

1987a; 1987b; but see also Weis and Borges, 1973; Medea and Thompson, 1974; Russell, 1975; 1982; 1984; Clark and Lewis, 1977; Jackson, 1978; Plaza, 1981; Berger and Searles, 1985; Kelly, 1987; 1988), claim that heterosexual sex is imbued with a gendered dominance–submission dynamic and that much violence is contained within it as a matter of course. Rape, radical feminists have suggested, is just an extreme expression of male-aggressive and female-passive positions which are normative within heterosexual practice. This analysis of (hetero)sexual violence builds on and reinforces radical and lesbian critiques of the institution and practice of (compulsory) heterosexuality (see, for example, Jackson, 1978; Rich, 1980; MacKinnon, 1983; Dworkin, 1987; Jeffreys, 1990; Wilkinson and Kitzinger, 1993).

In this approach to sexual violence, male sexuality has been portrayed as predatory, insatiable and aggressive. For example, Catharine MacKinnon (1987a: 70, 75) has written that 'sexuality equals heterosexuality equals the sexuality of (male) dominance and (female) submission', and that 'violation, conventionally through penetration and intercourse, defines the paradigmatic sexual encounter'. Andrea Dworkin argued that pornography 'reveals that male pleasure is inextricably tied to victimizing, hurting, exploiting'; and that 'dominance in the male system is pleasure' (Dworkin, 1981, cited in MacKinnon, 1987a: 77). She has also stated that 'the hatred of women is a source of sexual pleasure for men in its own right . . . [and] intercourse appears to be the expression of that contempt' (Dworkin, 1987: 163–4); and that 'intercourse is the pure, sterile, formal expression of men's contempt for women'. The corollary of this representation of male heterosexual practice as violation and domination is an (implicit, at least) representation of female sexuality as vulnerable and submissive: Heterosexual women's powerlessness and victimization are foregrounded.

During the course of my doctoral research, I became particularly interested in highlighting the existence of forms of coercion which are commonplace and seemingly 'natural' within the realm of normative heterosexual sex (Gavey, 1989; 1990; 1992). Repeatedly in women's accounts the point at which consensual heterosexual sex ended and sexual coercion began was not always clear. Furthermore, several women reported experiences which seemed to me like clear cases of rape or sexual aggression, but which they were reluctant to label as such – thus implicitly accepting them to be within the realm of ordinary heterosexual practice. It wasn't difficult for me to be convinced of the value of this deconstructive radical feminist understanding of heterosexuality and rape, and I still find it the most convincing explanatory framework for making sense of rape within heterosexual relationships. However, while deconstructing the dichotomy between rape and sex, this analysis rests upon another dichotomy which may itself turn out to be problematic: the gendered dominance–submission binary of heterosexual relations, which holds that men are sexually dominant and women are sexually submissive. This binary is closely related to the active–passive dichotomy in heterosexuality: that is, men are normatively represented as sexual actors, in charge of heterosexual relations, while women are represented as relatively passive partners. I am now concerned with beginning to problematize the reproduction of this gendered binary of sexual dominance–submission within our feminist discourse. Although I will discuss feminist representations of heterosexuality, the purpose of my project here is not to contribute to recent debates about heterosexuality and feminism. Rather, my purpose is to argue that a discursive intervention into our representations of heterosexualized male and female subjectivities is necessary for feminist politics concerned with ending rape and heterosexual coercion.

In this chapter I will first briefly discuss my previous work on rape and sexual coercion, which further highlights the close relationship between sexual coercion and normative heterosexuality. I will then return to the question of women's desire and agency in heterosexual relationships, as they relate to radical feminist sexual violence discourse. Finally, I will discuss two women's accounts of particular heterosexual experiences as a way of highlighting some of the complex and diverse ways women experience heterosexual relations. My contention is that in documenting and theorizing accounts of heterosexual experiences that are not about the eroticization of women's passivity and powerlessness we can make a discursive intervention into the discursive/material possibilities for gendered sexual violence.

Rape and sexual coercion

Rape is far more common than was previously imagined (see, for example, Russell, 1984; Koss *et al.*, 1987), and heterosexual coercion of some form is an experience common to most women, one which occurs most often within heterosexual relationships (Gavey, 1990; 1991a; 1991b).

I have found Michel Foucault's ideas on sexuality and 'disciplinary' power to be useful in attempting to understand how heterosexual coercion occurs, and, in particular, how sometimes women can feel they have no choice but to submit to have sex against their will in the absence of force or the threat of force. According to Foucault (1981), 'sexuality' is neither a natural nor neutral entity, but a collection of practices, feelings, behaviours and forms of identity that has historically come to be specified as sexuality. Furthermore, Foucault's analysis of the relationship between sex and power shifts attention away from the notion that sexuality has been 'repressed' to the idea that sexuality is socially produced and constituted. Foucault's (1979) work on power suggests that it is 'inherently neither positive nor negative' (de Lauretis, 1987: 16), and that it is not just a unitary force that only operates from the top down, as we understand 'sovereign' power to be. Rather, power is also diffuse, multiple, and relatively subtle, infused throughout social practices and discourse. This 'disciplinary power' is *productive* and *constitutive*. Through processes of normalization and regulation, disciplinary power operates to produce particular meanings, forms of desire, behaviours, and so on. Out of Foucault's work arises the notion of social 'technologies' which construct and reproduce practices in, and come to constitute our experiences of, our personal/social/cultural world. When these Foucauldian ideas are supplemented with an understanding of the different ways in which power infuses sexuality for women and men (see, for example, de Lauretis, 1987), then they become useful for making sense of women's experiences of heterosexual coercion.

As an effect of disciplinary power or 'technologies of heterosexual coercion', women may be induced to engage in sex with men irrespective of their own sexual desires. Dominant discourses on heterosexuality provide subject positions for women which are relatively passive and which prescribe compliance with and submission to male initiatives or demands irrespective of women's desire (Gavey, 1990; 1992). It should be noted that although Foucault makes a sharp distinction between power (which acts upon free subjects) and force or domination, this distinction is not so clear in understanding the effects of power and domination in the form of male coercion and violence towards women (Deveaux, 1994). As my research showed, although a woman may be theoretically free to resist the operations of power that persuade and oblige her to submit to unwanted acts, she does not always see or feel this freedom. From the accounts women have given me of their experiences of forced, unwanted, or unsatisfactory sex with men, I have identified a number of cultural supports for sexual coercion (Gavey, 1992). For instance, (1) there is a powerful heterosexual narrative which prescribes the inevitability of a penetrative culmination to any 'natural' heterosexual interaction; (2) there is also the absence or limitation of any discourse of women's self-determination and rights within the heterosexual interaction, which may be manifest in women not having any way of saying 'no'; (3) there is the lack of meaning in the notion of consent because of the restraints around not consenting (as Catharine MacKinnon, 1987b: 95, noted, 'If "no" can be taken as "yes", how free can "yes" be?'); (4) there is the power of factors such as pragmatism, a woman's fear of becoming or being seen as abnormal in some way (e.g., uptight, crazy, cold, frigid); (5) and there is the discursive construction of feminine nurturance which may lead women to have sex with men when they do not desire it for themselves.

All of these processes can be seen as part of a heterosexual institution in which men's supposed sexual wants and pleasures are powerfully foregrounded and hegemonic, and women's sexual desire is relatively uncharted territory. Recent debates within feminism have revived critical discussion of women's desires for and pleasures in heterosex (see, for example, Kitzinger, 1994; Hollway, 1995; Jackson, 1995a). While this debate is long overdue for its own sake, it is also critically important to developing praxis in relation to rape and sexual coercion prevention. If the success of technologies of heterosexual coercion relies, in part, on the effective construction of women as passive and submissive sexual subjects, then other positions for women's sexual subjectivities need to be explored.

The missing discourse of desire

Feminist critiques of heterosexuality have problematized women's heterosexual desire and pleasure (see, for example, Jeffreys, 1990; Kitzinger, 1994). For example, Sheila Jeffreys (1990: 299) has argued that 'heterosexual desire is eroticized power difference'; and she says that 'It is difficult to imagine what shape a woman's desire for a man would take in the absence of eroticized power difference since it is precisely this [i.e., men's greater power] which provides the excitement of heterosexuality today' (Jeffreys, 1990: 316). It is clear that Jeffreys' assumptions about what women find exciting about heterosexual sex echo and reproduce dominant traditional constructions of heterosexual women as the contented objects of male desire.

Within feminist discourses of sexual violence, the concept of women's desire has had quite understandably no explicit place. Implicitly, the radical feminist approach discussed earlier reinstates a familiar cultural representation of women as the relatively passive objects of active male sexual desire, who respond to and regulate its expression:

> Thus, ironically, on the real character of heterosexual eroticism, radical feminism and the dominant culture have been in fairly good agreement. Both represent sexual relations between male and female as relations between master and mastered, predator and prey, and, in the bluntest of representations, sadist and masochist. Both portray man's eroticism as bound up with aggression and conquest, and women's eroticism with a passive yielding in front of man's desire.
>
> (Cocks, 1989: 146)

Historically, feminist action was concerned with drawing attention to the social problem of rape and producing new understandings of rape which undermined the woman-blaming accounts of rape causation which were dominant until the 1970s. This oppositional strategy led feminist accounts to accept and reproduce a gendered dominance–submission binary. I am concerned that an unintended effect of such feminist portrayals of heterosexuality and rape is perhaps the production of a regulatory discourse which unwittingly colludes with technologies of heterosexual coercion. If men are always positioned as sexually preoccupied, insatiable, and aggressively 'driven' to getting their sexual 'needs' met, then heterosexual women remain positioned as passive objects of these desires, able only to be 'responsive', uninterested, or asexual. According to Michelle Fine (1988: 36–7):

> the language of victimization and its underlying concerns – 'Say No,' put a brake on his sexuality, don't encourage – ultimately deny young women the right to control their own sexuality by providing no access to a legitimate position of sexual subjectivity.

Conceptualized as passive, submissive sexual subjects, heterosexual women are discursively positioned so that we are perhaps inevitably vulnerable to heterosexual coercion. Our only position and power within heterosexual relations is in responding to, regulating, or limiting male sexual expression. The possibilities for disruption, resistance, and change in this portrayal are quite limited.

Much feminist social science research on sexual victimization has *imposed* a victim status on women who report certain sorts of experiences judged by the researcher to meet the definition of sexual victimization (particularly Koss, 1985; but see also Russell, 1982; 1984; Gavey, 1991a; 1991b). There have been very good scientific and political reasons for doing this. For instance, rape prevalence was previously underestimated, partly due to underreporting as a consequence of the acceptance of rape myths by many women. Because common-sense definitions of rape are extremely narrow and lay judgements about what is 'real' rape are determined by legally irrelevant factors, past estimates of rape prevalence were ridiculously low. Martha Burt (1983: 25; see also Burt and Estep, 1981) has emphasized the importance of claiming the status of victim, because 'a person who is recognized, legitimated, as a victim is recognized as someone who has received a wrong, who has been treated unfairly and unjustly'. From this perspective, emphasizing that women who are forced to have sexual intercourse against their will are victims of sexual assault or rape is a positive political act. It is one that is likely to validate the experiences of women who have felt abused and harmed, but who, without access to a concept of date rape, for example, may have felt confused, isolated, and have blamed themselves for what happened. This sort of reconceptualization has been a part of successful feminist political action against male sexual violence, and is extremely important for supporting and empowering women who have experienced it.

However, our dilemma as feminists is how simultaneously to recognize, to make sense of and to fight against the violence and abuse perpetrated by men against women, and yet not to develop a theory which implies that we see women as inevitably victims of this violence and abuse. Pop 'postfeminist' protests about this same point have faltered on an either/or logic, whereby in their desire to promote women as strong and agentic, they are left desperate to refuse the possibility of women being victimized by men in the absence of overt violence (see, for example, Roiphe, 1993). Roiphe's (1993) will not to see and hear accumulating evidence of women's experiences of date rape and sexual coercion is so strong that her message lacks credibility.

I celebrate feminist political action which names and protests the problem of rape and sexual violence within heterosexual relationships. Yet in taking action to promote a clear and strong anti-rape position, it is difficult not to contribute inadvertently to the cultural representation (and arguably the construction) of women as passive objects of men's violence. The solution is not to pretend sexual violence doesn't exist in the hope that it will go away! Women *are* victims of male violence, and at times in history when there has been silence about this the problem hasn't disappeared. Therefore, we need simultaneously to continue to challenge directly the victimization of women and to disrupt the discursive construction of women as passive sexual objects and ready-made victims. One way we can do this is by documenting, celebrating and theorizing women's successful resistance, whether it be lesbian resistance to compulsory heterosexuality or heterosexual women's avoidance of date rape. In promoting competing discourses about women's agency, independence and strength we can contribute in a different, but equally important, way to the prevention of heterosexual rape and abuse (see also Marcus, 1992; and Jones, 1994). These strategies are less obviously related to the goal of rape prevention, but the aim is the same.

In the next section, I make a small beginning to this promotion of diverse ways of understanding women's heterosexual experience that may disrupt but not deny our assumptions about women's vulnerability to sexual coercion.

Two women's experiences of heterosexual sex

Here, I consider the examples of two women I interviewed in the context of a study about sexual coercion (Gavey, 1990; 1992). In this small study, I talked with six women about their experiences of unwanted and forced sex with men. These women were selected because they had expressed an interest in my research on unwanted sex and everyday forms of sexual coercion, and not because they had had any particular sorts of experiences. The two women whose reports I will discuss here both gave powerful, almost chilling, accounts of having been coerced into having sex with men against their will (not reported here). Although I had neither developed a particular interest in the concepts of desire or sexual agency, nor considered their potential relevance to sexual violence at the time I interviewed these women, in both cases we ended up talking about sexual desire, power and pleasure. At the time I regarded these parts of the interviews as almost irrelevant tangents. What follows is a beginning attempt to make sense of some of these two women's competing and contradictory experiences of heterosexual sex in relation to notions of coercion, desire and power.

Both of these women discussed experiences of having been positioned within traditional androcentric versions of a heterosexual narrative, which scripted their unwilling passivity, compliance and submission to a man's desires. Each, however, also spoke about sexual experiences with men which contravened this narrative, and in which they found sexual desire, pleasure and power. In both of these cases, however, the women's desires and pleasures were not associated with an eroticization of their own passivity and relative powerlessness, as both traditional and radical feminist accounts would predict. Neither are they utopian narratives of egalitarian sex that I am advocating as a heterosexual ideal. Instead, these accounts are presented as examples of other stories that can be told about how women can experience heterosexual sex in ways that are disruptive of our taken-for-granted expectations.

Marilyn

Marilyn[1] was a middle-class, professional, pakeha[2] woman, 28 years old when I interviewed her. She was married to a professional man of a similar age, and she had had a number of heterosexual relationships before this. She described a loving, egalitarian and comfortable relationship with her husband. However, she felt no sexual desire for him. In fact, her feelings of revulsion towards sex with him were a threat to the continuation of their relationship. In talking about this relationship, she said: 'I don't feel any sexual desire at all'; 'I hate penetration'; 'male orgasm makes me feel sick. It makes me feel really physically ill'; 'I can't *bear* the fact that he wants to have an orgasm'; 'when something sexual happens, I feel like my body's being taken over, or I start to feel like I just want to put some sort of skin on or something like that . . . I feel a bit sort of invaded'; 'The thought of him as a sexual person turns me off'; 'I don't like the feeling of him wanting to have sex with me'. Marilyn's use of the language of invasion suggests she experienced sexual relations with her husband as the passive recipient of his actions. This is not entirely inconsistent with a traditional discourse about how women do experience sexual intercourse, but in traditional discourse women would usually be expected to tolerate, if not enjoy, their experience. Marilyn's constitution as a sexual subject was obviously complex. To the extent that she was very worried that her negative feelings about sex were 'a bit odd', her experience was partly constituted through dominant discourses about women and heterosexual pleasure – that is, her experience did not fit with what she thought was normal, therefore it was problematic and might suggest that she was abnormal. However, the fact that she did not find sex with her husband tolerable, let alone pleasurable, obviously implies that she was not umproblematically positioned within traditional discourse on heterosexuality.

It also emerged during our conversation that Marilyn had recently had some of the best sexual experiences of her life, during a time when she was separated from her husband, with another man. She said of this other man: 'He was actually a student [at the institution in which she worked], and he is much younger than me [he was 22], and for some bizarre reason I had this real sort of sexual desire, and I don't know why'. She went on to say:

> With Chris, this student at work, I don't really have to prove anything at all to him. It's like, I don't want him to particularly love me to bits, because I don't. Because that would just, you know, be a real pain. Being with him doesn't give me any sort of status to anybody at all . . . In fact, you know, he's 22 and he's a bit physically disabled, and so it's like, I mean I want to say it's like I'm doing him a favour, but I don't feel like that, I don't feel that sort of hard about it. But it is like, you know, I don't have to prove anything by the fact that I'm with him. It was really good, and so I can sort of just be free to have it or not have it, you know.

Marilyn's account can be read as presenting some problems for the version of heterosexuality and heterosexual desire portrayed in some radical feminist discourse (for example, Jeffreys, 1990). Her sexual desire and pleasure involved neither Jeffreys' (1990) ideal of eroticized mutuality and equality nor the eroticization of male dominance and her own submission and powerlessness. Indeed, there were various ways in which she was arguably more powerful than Chris. For instance, she was in a position of professional authority over him in the institution in which she worked, she was quite a bit older than him, and he was slightly disabled, which may have increased his vulnerability in relation to Marilyn. It was only in a relationship which had nothing to do with love and commitment, and where she was not in a less powerful position than her male partner, that 'for the first time in my life I could actually understand why people wanted to have sex'.

The experience Marilyn describes calls into question the accuracy of some of our taken-for-granted assumptions about what women can enjoy in heterosexual sex. For example, while the traditional pattern of women having relationships with men who are usually regarded as more powerful than or at least as powerful as they are in terms of certain indicators of interpersonal and social power (such as age, occupational status, economic power) is consistent with women having eroticized their own powerlessness *vis-à-vis* men, these relationships may arise from other (not specifically sexual) sorts of desire and may fulfil other needs. Furthermore, while male power is institutionalized within heterosexual relationships, it is not always possible to appreciate how power works in a relationship on the basis of gender alone. Male dominance can be mediated (and arguably diffused in particular cases) by other factors which may include all sorts of complex and subtle characteristics in addition to class, race and ethnicity. Therefore, we cannot simply assume that we know how power operates in any given relationship solely on the basis of what we can observe; and we cannot assume that it is unidirectional and static. It is possible to imagine that some women who enjoy sex with particularly powerful men find excitement in the power they experience through his vulnerability and neediness, rather than their own submissiveness. Jeffreys (1990) argues that any eroticized power difference is 'heterosexual desire', and that it can be recreated in lesbian relationships, and is common in gay male relationships, as well as in heterosexual relationships. But when it is women's power (and perhaps transient dominance) that is eroticized in a heterosexual encounter, it has complex possible meanings which may be disruptive to our usual understandings of heterosexuality. I expect there are few feminists who accept this can occur, who would be willing to argue simply that it is a straightforward reversal of male power and dominance (see also Bijlmer, 1993). I do not raise this point in an attempt to 'rehabilitate heterosexuality' (cf. Kitzinger and Wilkinson, 1994), because there is little evidence that heterosexual relationships characterized by true equality and/or relations of power which favour women are very common. However, the possibility that some women enjoy heterosexual sex where they feel powerful and in control is a discursive/material space in need of further exploration. The articulation of such stories makes available a new range of subject positions for heterosexual women which provide opportunities for resistance to some forms of heterosexual coercion.

Another interesting feature of Marilyn's experience is its disjunction from traditional discursive constructions of women's sexuality as predominantly concerned with love and intimacy. Although the concept of romantic love has recently been critically interrogated within feminist literature (see, for example, Jackson, 1995b), the taken-for-granted conflation of women's sexuality with love has rarely been subjected to any empirical investigation, or critical questioning, other than by sexual libertarians and sado-masochists. Marilyn described how, in her experiences, sex, intimacy and love were not synonymous:

> The situation now is that I live with Rick, and I want to live here and be with him, but I don't want to have sex with him. And Chris, who I see quite a lot because he's at work, I wouldn't want to live with him or have that with him, but I do have that sort of sexual feeling towards him.

Lee

Lee was a middle-class, professional, pakeha woman, 33 years old when I interviewed her. She had been married previously, and had also had other sexual relationships with men, but was now living with a male partner who was older than herself and who worked in business. We had discussed at length a previous heterosexual relationship, in which she had regularly engaged in unwanted sex. At a time when she was having a secret 'affair' with this man, sexual intercourse became inevitable on the occasions they met, because of the power of an unstated coital imperative. Their meetings required a considerable degree of planning and effort to execute, so it did not seem possible to her to say to him when they met, 'I'm sorry, actually, I just wanted a cuddle and a cup of tea' (Gavey, 1992: 333). She said she felt that on making a 'phone call or the decision to meet somewhere you've given your tacit agreement that you'll have sex' (which, for her at the time, meant intercourse). At other times, she submitted to sex with him because it was easier than continuing to resist all night, and it meant she was more likely to get some sleep (Gavey, 1992).

Although not as negative about sexual intercourse as Marilyn, Lee was nevertheless indifferent about it: 'I don't think I ever really rejected it particularly, it was just a bit of a nothing – couldn't really understand why people would want to do it'. We also discussed sexual desire and excitement. In Lee's case, this existed within her current relationship. For her, part of the excitement lay in the fact that

> we've worked out these wonderful and everchanging ways of sexually relating. It's never the same and I think that is because we've allowed ourselves to do unordinary things. We've allowed ourselves to move beyond common-sense ideas about what it is that people do in their bedrooms.

Specifically, for Lee and her partner, this involved 'being able to enter as well as being able to be entered. And that makes a big difference.' She said: 'I suppose it's a little bit like there's this vulnerability about him.

There's this part that's vulnerable, that I can love and protect, because potentially I can exploit'. By engaging in particular sexual practices, that is, entering her male partner's body, normative discourses of gendered heterosexuality were disrupted. Indeed, she said about 'coitus', '[now] I can understand why it's exciting for men!'. So, in contrast to Jeffreys' (1990: 316) contention that women only desire sex with men because they have eroticized their own powerlessness, Lee's heterosexual desire and pleasure derived from power she experienced through enacting penetration. This did not simply involve a gender reversal of a fixed power difference, however, because both Lee and her partner assumed positions of power and vulnerability through their shifting sexual roles.

Concluding remarks

Marilyn and Lee had both experienced heterosexual coercion and powerlessness within heterosexual relationships. They had also experienced heterosexual desire which was not characterized by a stereotypical eroticization of their own powerlessness. They had been victims, but they were not always victims. In fact, they had both reported positive sexual experiences which seemed to involve some degree of eroticization of their own power in the situation or the relationship more generally.

Catharine MacKinnon (1987a: 74) has warned us about the naivety of questions such as 'how do women negotiate sexual pleasures?':[3]

As if women under male supremacy have power to; as if 'negotiation' is a form of freedom; as if pleasure and how to get it, rather than dominance and how to end it, is the 'overall' issue sexuality presents feminism.

'Maybe we do just need a good fuck', she provocatively continued. Indeed, it would be simplistic and foolish to imagine that, by merely asserting the right to explore and articulate female sexual desire and pleasure, women's experiences of heterosexism and heterosexual coercion would disappear. Women face threats of punishment of various forms (including violence) for asserting sexual agency and/or autonomy. Furthermore, a Foucauldian analysis reminds us that sexual desire is not essential or unproblematic but that it is itself deeply inscribed by gender/power relations and, similarly, that sexual pleasure is 'both fundamentally gendered, and inequitably assigned' (Wilton, n.d.: 13), making it a 'profoundly problematic' concept for women (Wilton, n.d.: 12). Nevertheless, if our feminist analyses only reinstate a discourse of heterosexuality as inevitably about male dominance and female submission, then we are arguably complicit in reproducing the particular traditional cultural constructions of passive female sexuality and aggressive male sexuality which so neatly script the roles for male sexual violence against women. The answer is not to deny male dominance and the pervasiveness of women's sexual victimization, but to disrupt this analysis at the same time as we use it, by highlighting, promoting and theorizing competing discourses which offer positions of resistance for women. An important part of this strategy should be the articulation of women's (hetero)sexual desire, agency and power. When we expect heterosexual women to be active, desiring and powerful sexual subjects, it will not be so easy to confuse rape and heterosexual coercion with ordinary sex with men. I would argue that the discursive intervention of articulating and promoting such subject positions for women will gradually make these ways of being seem more possible and desirable to some, if not all, women and men who engage in heterosexual sex. The more we move towards these conditions of possibility, the easier it will be for my friend, as well as police, judges and juries, to determine that a man is committing rape if he has sex with his unwilling and non-consenting girlfriend.

Acknowledgements

The research discussed here was partly supported by grants from the Auckland University Research Committee and the Health Research Council of New Zealand. An earlier version of this paper was presented at the Fourth International Conference on Language and Social Psychology, Santa Barbara, California, USA, 18–23 August 1991.

I would like to thank Chris Atmore for helpful comments on an earlier draft, and Sue Wilkinson for helpful editorial assistance.

Notes

1 Names and potentially identifying details have been changed to protect anonymity.
2 New Zealander of European descent.
3 This question was posed in 1992 by Carole Vance in the *Diary* of the Barnard Conference on sexuality (see MacKinnon, 1987a).

References

Berger, Ronald J. and Searles, Patricia (1985) 'Victim–offender interaction in rape: Victimological, Situational, and Feminist Perspectives', *Women's Studies Quarterly*, 13: 9–15.
Bijlmer, Sabine (1993) 'Women's sexual desires'. Unpublished Master's thesis, University of Auckland.
Burt, Martha R. (1983) 'A conceptual framework for victimological research', *Victimology: An International Journal*, 8: 261–8.

Burt, Martha R. and Estep, Rhoda E. (1981) 'Who is a victim? Definitional problems in sexual victimization', *Victimology: An International Journal*, 6: 15–28.

Clark, Lorenne and Lewis, Debra (1977) *Rape: The Price of Coercive Sexuality*. Toronto: The Women's Press.

Cocks, Joan (1989) *The Oppositional Imagination: Feminism, Critique, and Political Theory*. London and New York: Routledge.

de Lauretis, Teresa (1987) *Technologies of Gender: Essays on Theory, Film, and Fiction*. Bloomington and Indianapolis: Indiana University Press.

Deveaux, Monique (1994) 'Feminism and empowerment: A critical reading of Foucault', *Feminist Studies*, 20: 223–47.

Dworkin, Andrea (1987) *Intercourse*. London: Arrow.

Estrich, Susan (1987) *Real Rape*. Cambridge, MA: Harvard University Press.

Fine, Michelle (1988) 'Sexuality, schooling, and adolescent females: The missing discourse of desire', *Harvard Educational Review*, 58: 29–53.

Foucault, Michel (1979) *Discipline and Punish: The Birth of the Prison* (trans. Alan Sheridan). London: Penguin. (Original work published in 1975.)

Foucault, Michel (1981) *The History of Sexuality. Volume 1: An Introduction* (trans. Robert Hurley). Harmondsworth: Penguin. (Original work published in 1976.)

Gavey, Nicola (1989) 'Feminist poststructuralism and discourse analysis: Contributions to feminist psychology', *Psychology of Women Quarterly*, 13: 459–75.

Gavey, Nicola (1990) 'Rape and sexual coercion within heterosexual relationships: An intersection of psychological, feminist, and postmodern inquiries'. Unpublished PhD thesis, University of Auckland, New Zealand.

Gavey, Nicola (1991a) 'Sexual victimization prevalence among New Zealand University students', *Journal of Consulting and Clinical Psychology*, 59: 464–6.

Gavey, Nicola J. (1991b) 'Sexual victimization among Auckland University students: How much and who does it?', *New Zealand Journal of Psychology*, 20: 63–70.

Gavey, Nicola (1992) 'Technologies and effects of heterosexual coercion', *Feminism & Psychology*, 2: 325–51.

Hollway, Wendy (1995) 'Feminist discourses and women's heterosexual desire', in Sue Wilkinson and Celia Kitzinger (eds), *Feminism and Discourse: Psychological Perspectives*. London: Sage, pp. 86–105.

Jackson, Stevi (1978) 'The social context of rape: Sexual scripts and motivation', *Women's Studies International Quarterly*, 1: 27–38.

Jackson, Stevi (1995a) 'Gender and heterosexuality: A materialist feminist analysis', in Mary Maynard and June Purvis (eds), *(Hetero)sexual Politics*. London: Taylor & Francis, pp. 11–25.

Jackson, Stevi (1995b) 'Women and heterosexual love: Complicity, resistance and change', in Lynne Pearce and Jackie Stacey (eds), *Romance Revisited*. London: Lawrence & Wishart.

Jeffreys, Sheila (1990) *Anticlimax: A Feminist Perspective on the Sexual Revolution*. London: The Women's Press.

Jones, Alison (1994) 'Pedagogy, desire and sexual harassment in the university'. Unpublished lecture for Harassment Awareness Week on Campus, University of Auckland.

Kelly, Liz (1987) 'The continuum of sexual violence', in J. Hanmer and M. Maynard (eds), *Women, Violence and Social Control*. Basingstoke and London: Macmillan Press, pp. 44–60.

Kelly, Liz (1988) 'How women define their experiences of violence', in Kersti Yllo and Michele Bograd (eds), *Feminist Perspectives on Wife Abuse*. Newbury Park, CA: Sage, pp. 114–32.

Kitzinger, Celia (1994) 'Problematizing pleasure: Radical feminist deconstructions of sexuality and power', in H. Lorraine Radtke and Henderikus J. Stam (eds), *Power/Gender: Social Relations in Theory and Practice*. London: Sage, pp. 194–209.

Kitzinger, Celia and Wilkinson, Sue (1994) 'Virgins and queers: Rehabilitating heterosexuality?', *Gender & Society*, 8: 444–63.

Koss, Mary P. (1985) 'The hidden rape victim: Personality, attitudinal, and situational characteristics', *Psychology of Women Quarterly*, 9: 193–212.

Koss, Mary P., Gidycz, Christine A. and Wisniewski, Nadine (1987) 'The scope of rape: Incidence and prevalence of sexual aggression and victimization in a national sample of higher education students', *Journal of Consulting and Clinical Psychology*, 55: 162–70.

MacKinnon, Catharine A. (1983) 'Feminism, Marxism, method, and the state: Towards feminist jurisprudence', *Signs: Journal of Women in Culture and Society*, 8: 635–58.

MacKinnon, Catharine A. (1987a) 'A feminist/political approach: "Pleasure under patriarchy"', in James H. Geer and William T. O'Donohue (eds), *Theories of Human Sexuality*. New York: Plenum Press, pp. 65–90.

MacKinnon, Catharine A. (1987b) *Feminism Unmodified: Discourses on Life and Law*. Cambridge, MA and London: Harvard University Press.

Marcus, Sharon (1992) 'Fighting bodies, fighting words: A theory and politics of rape prevention', in Judith Butler and Joan W. Scott (eds), *Feminists Theorize the Political*. New York: Routledge, pp. 385–403.

Medea, Andra and Thompson, Kathleen (1974) *Against Rape*. New York: Farrar, Straus, & Giroux.

Plaza, Monique (1981) 'Our damages and their compensation. Rape: The will not to know of Michel Foucault', *Feminist Issues*, 1: 25–35.

Rich, Adrienne (1980) 'Compulsory Heterosexuality and Lesbian Existence', *Signs: Journal of Women in Culture and Society*, 5: 631–60.

Roiphe, Katie (1993) *The Morning After: Sex, Fear, and Feminism*. London: Hamish Hamilton.

Russell, Diana E. H. (1975) *The Politics of Rape: The Victim's Perspective*. New York: Stein and Day.

Russell, Diana E. H. (1982) *Rape in Marriage*. New York: Macmillan.

Russell, Diana E. H. (1984) *Sexual Exploitation: Rape, Child Sexual Abuse, and Workplace Harassment*. Beverly Hills, CA: Sage.

Weis, Kurt and Borges, Sandra S. (1973) 'Victimology and rape: The case of the legitimate victim', *Issues in Criminology*, 8: 71–115.

Wilkinson, Sue and Kitzinger, Celia (eds) (1993) *Heterosexuality: A 'Feminism & Psychology' Reader*. London: Sage.

Wilton, Tamsin (n.d.) 'Feminism and the erotics of health promotion'. Unpublished manuscript, Bristol Polytechnic (now University of the West of England).

—————• 3

Containing questions of gender and power: The discursive limits of 'sameness' and 'difference'

—————• MICHELLE FINE AND JUDI ADDELSTON

> In structure and function human beings are still as they were in the beginning. 'Male and female He created them.' It is a patent and deep-lying fact that these fundamental anatomical and physiological differences affect the whole psychic organization. They create the differences in personality between men and women, and personality is the predominating factor in delinquent careers . . .
>
> (*State v. Heitzman*, 105 Kan. 139, 146–47, 181 P. 630, 634, 1919; cited in Rhode, 1990).

Arguments for discrimination and segregation have typically been cast in a biological discourse of gender/race, where difference means deficit. In response, many of us have engaged in defensive combat with such arguments, demanding rights or access for women because we are, after all, basically the 'same' beneath the drapery of *our* bodies, and the armor of *their* discrimination.

Across the USA and elsewhere, second-wave feminists have, indeed, successfully agitated through this line of argument to secure institutional access, opening previously locked doors to education, employment and even private clubs, ranging from Rotary Club International, to the United States Jaycees, police and fire departments, all-male public high schools and colleges. Girls and women of all colours now stand inside the halls in which we were never supposed to trespass.

Access, however, has been achieved within a narrow band of success. Acquired through a discourse of sameness, 'access' has been granted, disproportionately, to elite white women. Once inside these institutions that now represent themselves as 'diverse', these women find them/ ourselves confronting, and often colluding in the denial of, gendered, raced and classed structures of power and privilege. For gender, race or class, access without structural transformation has degenerated into a liberal sop to keep institutions as is, and still 'diversify'. While most white women and women and men of colour linger outside the doors, those 'on the inside' sit at the bottom of hierarchies we presumably 'chose' to climb. Such access is not hollow, but it is severely flawed. And, as you will see, psychology has been the ideological handmaiden of structural strategies deployed to justify both the exclusion of women from all-male institutions, and the inclusion of women into untransformed, hierarchical settings.

Moving targets

The exclusion of women of all colours has historically been argued through a discourse of the biological, as narrated above in *State v. Heitzman*, 1919. The biological, of recent years, has been yoked, perhaps 'advanced', to the psychological. That is, ironically or not, feminist psychology has been appropriated to 'prove' the existence and endurance of psychological and developmental gender 'differences' sufficient to justify women's exclusion from all-male institutions. Consider the following excerpt from a document written by two academics in this decade (1992), in defence of the exclusion of women from The Citadel, an all-male military-like public college in South Carolina, USA:

The intellectual development across the sexes, even at this age has implications. The evidence of greater specialization in the two hemispheres of the brain on the part of males suggests that men will dichotomize their learnings through the various channels more. This may, in a coeducational setting, lead males to close off some of their participation and thus do less well academically. . . . Also relevant is the fact that frontal lobe development in males lags at this age. Hartlage and Telzrow . . . write: 'Adolescence in many cases marks the emergence of abilities typically attributed to the maturation of the front lobes. Although the frontal lobe is usually not fully mature until late adolescence, and often not until age 21 in boys, its maturation is associated with behavioral changes concerning judgment, planning and realistic assessment of risks and consequences of given behavior'. . . . This comment provides the basis for the development of both a more highly structured regimen and a more confrontational experience for the male.

Carol Gilligan has explored the moral development and moral reasoning across the sexes. Her research has led her to conclude that women and men have different perspectives on moral issues. . . . The implications here are twofold: on the one hand, single gender education can be a most effective medium to assist males to confirm this identity and to look at the strengths and limitations of their perspective; on the other hand, it will be important to include within the experiences (but outside the program) interactions with women to enhance awareness and sensitivity to the richness of both perspectives.

(Mahan and Mahan, 1992: 5)

As this statement testifies, psychological difference has been invented and then appropriated to justify exclusion, and to occlude questions of gendered power.

Demands for access are, in contrast, typically cast within a discourse of sameness (see Hare-Mustin and Marecek, 1990). Feminism's relentless press for access to institutions that have historically been the exclusive domain of, and site for advantaging, while elite males, has been voiced in drag. The robes of sameness and equality testify, 'We can do it. Just like the men.' Subtext: you don't have to change anything for us to fit in (see, for example, Milkman, 1986; Yoder, 1989).

Arguments about exclusion and access swing together within a suspiciously narrow discursive range of difference and sameness. Questions of structural power remain well beyond reach; the 'standard' of white maleness unchallenged. We begin to question whether arguments of difference and sameness are indeed so different (Minow, 1990). As Rachel Hare-Mustin has written: 'Difference is, after all, only an aspect of sameness' (in Hare-Mustin and Marecek, 1990).

On the face of it, these two positions, difference and sameness, appear to be in opposition. But in recent history, arguments about difference and sameness have both been exploited towards the same end – to exclude women and people of colour from elite institutions and to obfuscate questions of structural inequities organized through gender, race and class. As Chandra Mohanty (1994: 146) has written:

The central issue, then, is not one of merely *acknowledging* difference; rather the more difficult question concerns the kind of difference that is acknowledged and engaged. Difference seen as benign variation (diversity), for instance, rather than as conflict, struggle, or the threat of disruption, bypasses power as well as history to suggest a harmonious, empty pluralism.

We find ourselves worrying about constructions of 'difference' and 'sameness', as they have been the psychological rationales for both exclusion and access to untransformed institutions. We are persuaded, instead, by Joan Scott who writes:

> When equality and difference are paired dichotomously, they structure an impossible choice. If one opts for equality, one is forced to accept the notion that difference is antithetical to it. If one opts for difference, one admits that equality is unattainable. . . . Feminists cannot give up 'difference;' it has been our most creative analytic tool. We cannot give up equality, at least as long as we want to speak to the principles and values of our political system. But it makes no sense for the feminist movement to let its arguments be forced into preexisting categories and its political disputes to be characterized by a dichotomy we did not invent.
>
> (Scott, 1992: 142)

Questions of institutional *disadvantage* and *power* are masked by 'difference', and muzzled within those of deliberate exclusion and contexts of liberal access. These, then, are the very questions that frame this chapter. While the contested borders which constitute exclusion and access in our two research sites are marked by gender, this analysis should inform critical theory on gender as well as racial, sexual and class formations (Omi and Winant, 1986). Here we analyse the ideological and material forces that shape institutional life when women of all colours are out and in, and we investigate how the bodies and voices of those excluded from without and those alienated from within are crafted to justify exclusion and/or access.

We recognize that we are treading on dangerous territory of feminist and civil rights jurisprudence, activism and theory. In these days of affirmative action backlash, we are pressing the limits of a legal strategy – access – that is both worn and fragile, but also is hardly accomplished. This chapter must be read not as a retreat from, but as a demand for, deep access; a critical analysis of power inequities buried inside debates about 'difference' and 'sameness'. We pry open this opposition because we believe it obscures and protects institutional arrangements of privilege and stratification, sedimented through currently available layers of gender, race, class, sexuality and disability.

Our data derive from two research projects located within quite distinct educational institutions. The site for studying exclusion is The Citadel, a South Carolina based, public, all-male military-style college that was, at the time of writing, being sued by four women for equal access.[1] The site for studying access is the University of Pennsylvania Law School, an elite, private law school to which women now enjoy substantial access, constituting over 40% of the incoming class annually. Theoretically we are interested in how institutions of exclusion and access produce *ideologies* to justify their borders and internal hierarchies, and how individual men and women narrate their *identities* within (and outside) these institutions.

These two cases create an occasion, an analytic wedge, through which we can see and examine the bodies and voices that lie within settings of policed exclusion and settings of surveilled access (Foucault, 1979). We take it to be the case that in both circumstances, institutions are desperate to conceal and secure their external boundaries and their internal hierarchies.

This chapter spills out of the delights and frustrations of one of the authors (MF) as an expert witness, tossed between litigious arguments of difference and sameness, in lawsuits for gender and race integration. Testifying to get white girls/women and boys and girls of colour into schools, workplaces and other settings in which we have been un-welcome, she finds herself unable to interrupt the litigious volley of 'difference' and 'sameness' in order to argue for access *and* institutional transformation. Likewise, this chapter comes out of the intrigue and annoyance of the other author (JA) with the ideological mantra of biological differences she heard at her visits to The Citadel, voiced by white males whose identities were precariously shaped by, and hinging on, the exclusion of women.

On exclusion: 'A discourse of difference'

The role of public educational institutions in fostering the social good is an old Jeffersonian ideal of levelling the field and letting the cream rise to the top. The Citadel is one such institution that claims this ideal as its own. Its mission is

> to educate male undergraduates as members of the South Carolina Corps of Cadets and to prepare them for post-graduate positions of leadership through academic programs of recognized excellence supported by the best features of a disciplined military environ-ment. . . . The purpose of the cadet system at The Citadel is to develop and graduate the whole man. During four years, The Citadel system matures, refines a young man's character. This finely balanced process is called the whole man concept. During four years, cadets will develop academically, physically, militarily and spiritually.
>
> (The Citadel 1992–3: 19, 22)

Located in Charleston, South Carolina, with a 150-year-old tradition, The Citadel is viewed as one of the most prestigious colleges in the South, ranked sixth in academic reputation among regional colleges in the South.

The Citadel relies on the politics of exclusion to maintain its reputation of academic excellence. It manufactures, at once, discourses of *difference* (between women and men) and *sameness* (among predominantly white, presumably heterosexual men) to support institutionalized discrimination within its walls and perpetuate social injustice beyond its gates. Resting comfortably on the couch of tradition, The Citadel adamantly wishes to remain a woman-free space to protect its power, privilege and educational objective. Called by a faculty member 'one of the last bastions of true masculinity left in the United States', The Citadel wields its sword of exclusive practice to protect it from transformation. By claiming to benefit the social good through its traditions, the school begs the questions 'whose tradition?', 'for whose collective good?', and 'why?'.

> The idea is we have created something virtually perfect, something that creates a whole man, a real man, and there are only certain people who can do this and those people who can't do this are less of a man than you are and you have got to become part of this group. . . . It was either that or be a wimp, a fag, a woman. Those are your choices. Get the ring or be a woman and that is the way it is presented to you every day. . . . They set up a system by excluding others and making other people feel inferior.
>
> (Vergnolle, 1993)

In the spring of 1993, one of the authors (JA) travelled to The Citadel with a colleague to investigate institutional claims for remaining an all-male school, and to talk with students, faculty and staff about the lawsuit currently facing the school. A young high-school student, Shannon Richie Faulkner, had applied to The Citadel and been accepted. Shannon self-consciously omitted any reference to gender on her application, and asked that her teachers and counsellors do the same in their letters of recommendation. Upon discovering her gender, The Citadel revoked her acceptance and she, with the American Civil Liberties Union, subsequently sued the school for sex discrimination. How does a public institution, in the 1990s, defend discrimination?

Institutional support for discrimination relies fundamentally on the discourse of difference. One administrator explains: 'God has made men and women different.' This rationale was enough for him to justify the exclusion of women at the school. Likewise, the sociologist David Reisman testified in the Virginia Military Institute (VMI) case (a case directly analogous to The Citadel lawsuit and currently being heard by the US Supreme Court):

> I think that if women were admitted to VMI the whole program would collapse. I cannot imagine . . . , given the executive qualities we were talking about earlier with reference to Carol Gilligan's work

and my own parallel work, that women would, for example, treat rats as rats are treated now at VMI. They simply wouldn't. Women would not go through the shaving of the head, the other reductions of previous attributes. They can't shed their gender. They can't shed their physical attributes.

(Reisman, 1991: 193)

Physically, women are thought to be unable and unwilling to handle the rigours of the paramilitary style and fourth class system of The Citadel. Psychologically, too, The Citadel has (mis)appropriated years of feminist psychological research on gender differences to justify the exclusion of women. A report by Citadel faculty members Aline Mahan and Thomas Mahan cites Carol Gilligan (1982) and Kay Deaux (1985) on the 'different ways women and men behave and learn' as reasons for maintaining a 'woman-free' environment. Cadets, Mahan and Mahan (1993: 3) argue, must develop in 'freedom . . . away from the mother-dominant home . . . and safe from female reaction'. They continue: 'There is also basis in the data reported by McClelland to speculate that some of the diminishing signs of leadership development can be attributed to the then recent shift of Ivy College from an all male to a coeducational institution'. The weakness of women seems to be hauntingly contagious.

Too weak and vulnerable for admission, women swell, grow strong and irresistible, once in the classroom. One faculty member claimed that the 'introduction [of] females in the classroom [would] distract the cadets because they are lusty' (Rembert, 1993: 87). Similar institutions (such as Annapolis and West Point) which have begun admitting women were described by the cadets as 'weakened' by them.

To illustrate the ways in which women are seen simultaneously as weak incompetents to be dismissed and as powerful objects to be controlled, we need only look at how men refer to those cadets who do not perform to expectations. Ronald Vergnolle, a graduate of The Citadel, testified that to insult a cadet, others call him 'a fag, a woman . . . a sally, or a skirt' (Vergnolle, 1993: 70, 80). At The Citadel, 'you spend your entire career . . . connoting women with negativism. When you screw up, you are a woman' (Vergnolle, 1993: 81). 'Every time I did anything wrong at The Citadel someone made a point of telling me that I was, with expletives, a woman, you're weak, why don't you go to a woman's school, you belong in a woman's school. What is the matter, are you having your period? Why can't you do the push ups? Are you a woman? Why don't we go get a skirt for you?' (Vergnolle, 1993: 84). In this way, the construction of the 'whole man', of heteromasculinity, is secured through the derogation of outgroups – that is, women and gay men.

Ideologies of gendered difference patrol the borders of this institution, justifying exclusion. But on the inside, a discourse of sameness among men is embodied in the barracks, the uniform and the Ring. The barracks are seen as private spaces to the cadets. There are no locks on the doors to the rooms and the cadets frequently go to and from the showers nude or semi-nude. There are also informal ceremonies in the barracks that require nudity, such as the birthday ceremony; one cadet told us that for a cadet's birthday, his friends tie him naked to a chair and place him in the middle of the foyer of the barracks. They cover him with boot polish, tar and feather him, and circle around him while ridiculing him. As in fraternities (Sanday, 1990), this sadistic homosociality creates a sense of ingroup solidarity, sameness and superiority to Others.

Likewise, the uniform homogenizes the cadets towards an internal sameness and a 'subordinate self'. All cadets wear the same grey uniform which, I (JA) was told by an administrator, creates a sense of equality and solidarity, a greying of race in an institution composed of only 7 per cent blacks. Reisman (1991: 79) concurs, with some irony, that race is e-raced by deindividuation and democratic access to social abuse: 'In its egalitarian spirit, blacks are treated just as badly as everyone else, and they can't interpret this as racism because everybody is treated badly'. The 1977 and 1982 Citadel yearbooks depict cadets dressed in Ku Klux Klan attire, and in one case, portray the lynching of a black cadet. In two separate incidents in 1987, a black student was awakened in the middle of the night by several other cadets in white hoods who left a burning paper cross in his room. He brought charges against them; they were not expelled, but reprimanded, and he resigned a few days after the incident. In 1992, a black cadet awoke to find a noose above his head, allegedly placed there by several white cadets after he refused to sing Dixie for them in the showers the previous day. Race is an occasion, unlike sex, where the institution may promote 'access', but the sabre of racism cuts deeply into some of these sons of the South. Difference within is dangerous, monitored and 'whited out'.

The Ring is the final embodiment of a shared hegemonic masculinity at The Citadel. To see the Ring inside or outside the gates of The Citadel indicates another 'whole man'. The Ring becomes the symbol of hegemonic masculinity and ingroup pride. Indeed, women are not allowed even to try it on. When I (JA) asked one cadet if I could see his Ring, he let me hold it, but said that I could not try it on as that 'would bring bad luck'.

With a bevy of contradictory claims, The Citadel makes the point that women – as weak or as overpowering – will distract the cadets. Cadets need a male-only environment. However, women are omnipresent on the Citadel campus – in body and in ideology. About 10 per cent of the faculty are women. One woman professor said that the cadets often call her a 'feminazi'. Women are on the staff as secretaries (predominantly white) and kitchen staff (predominantly black). Girlfriends, the sexual partners of the cadets, who are predominantly women at the College of

Charleston, can be found plentifully on the grounds. Most of the women students are night students and they have access to the sports facilities and the library. And there are the women who are idealized – the mothers, who are rarely on campus but are imported periodically as icons. Yet women, at the same time, are seen as evil, omnipresent, hovering, titillating and humiliating. One female professor explained:

> The Citadel fosters a cult of swashbuckling macho which released the students to do – some of the students to do bad things, like torturing to death a female racoon while yelling, 'Kill the bitch,' which desensitizes them to living in a world in which women need their rights . . .
>
> (Bishop, 1993: 46)

At The Citadel, the only category of woman not present is the woman who is an equal peer. This is a crucial feature of how prejudice and discrimination are reproduced at The Citadel. Research demonstrates that equal status contact is an integral part of a comprehensive programme to ameliorate prejudice (Katz and Taylor, 1988). The importing of women as icons of contempt strengthens the borders of masculinity which The Citadel infuses into the cadets.

Why, then, would students of any sex want to join such an institution? For the young men who do go, the answer lies in Southern tradition, academic and career opportunities, and elitism. For the young women who wish to go, they may not go to ensure their manhood, but they would certainly wish to participate in an elite Southern tradition, and accrue all the benefits derived from such an experience. One professor told us that '75 per cent of Chief Executive Officers in Charleston are Citadel graduates'; that 'wearing The Ring gives these boys employment for life via the old boys network'; that 'the young women at the College of Charleston flock to the cadets like bees to pollen' as the cadets are considered 'a prize' who will be economically secure; and that wearing the Ring 'gains one entrance into the best clubs and social networks'. A guidance counsellor remarked that '30 per cent of Citadel graduates go on to illustrious careers in the armed forces'. Given all these life advantages, it seems reasonable to assume that any young person might want to go, even ambivalently, to The Citadel.

Within this infrastructure of exclusion and elitism, however, resistance can be found. Individual cadets, particularly those of colour, if alone, would often voice support for the inclusion of women. The faculty voted, by a substantial majority, to enrol women. Indeed, some individual faculty members were gutsy enough to take on the administration, during the lawsuit. Note a letter written by history professor Jane Bishop, sent in protest when the College eliminated the veterans programme rather than admit women to it:

I know that keeping women out of day classrooms is a major value of yours and the Board's. But is it such a supreme value that, to future it, you will jettison the more fundamental values of support for the services and solidarity of the Corps? Surely not; surely continuing to welcome these deserving men is worth a slightly greater risk of ultimately having to tolerate equally deserving women. Whatever the fate of the women, the barring of the men is morally wrong by The Citadel's own best standards and the school's ideals should be reaffirmed by reversing the decision.

(Bishop, 1993: Defendant's Exhibit 3)

Binary oppositions of overstated difference deceptively define life inside and out of The Citadel. That which is powerful – to be male – is actually incredibly fragile; and that which is weak – to be female – is omnipotent. One faculty member, Professor Rembert, narrates the potential troubles of having young women in class by recalling an incident with a female student:

Well, a coed student from time to time will lean into me and put the point of her breast right on my elbow, put her nipple on me and just sort of lean into me and look very interested. . . . Well, I know what she's doing. . . . She's putting an erogenous zone on me. . . . I think our world knows that the breasts and vagina are the three or two main erogenous zones on the female. The lips, the ears, all that is, too but the mouth, breast and the vagina, the private parts . . . It may mean I'm looking for a good grade from you. . . . I'm putting part of my private body on you to let you know how much I trust you . . .

(Rembert, 1993: 62)

This same faculty member worries about the 'lusty' presence of women distracting young men from their work:

You don't know anything about her. Is she loose? Does she have a boyfriend? Is she uptight? Is she religious? Can she take a joke? Will she talk with me after class? This is a good thing. She smells good. I'm down wind. This is good stuff. I think I'll watch the nape of her neck during class. It sure is pretty, prettier than that guy's next to me. A right nice calf, too. It's good stuff; I like this. Excuse me, sir? Did you call on me? It changes things. They don't do that when another cadet walks in the room, but they will do that when a young woman walks in.

Female presence and female sexuality interrupt the power of men to command the attention of other men. Quoting Professor Rembert again:

Men traditionally have been able to get on fairly well in bonded groups, and the introduction of women alters that. It's like testing the

air pressure on a bicycle tire. You can never – you can never do it
accurately because once you test it, you let out some of the air . . .
(Rembert, 1993: 89)

Deflated tyres; impotence; rivalry with women. Women's absence is
tantalizing. Their presence is terrifying. Women hold men in place, and
knock them out of control. The context at The Citadel is one that creates,
promotes and justifies power inequities between women and men as if
they were 'natural' – biological or psychological – differences. The cadets'
masculinity is fortified by invoking difference. With the case study in
mind, listen to Catherine MacKinnon's (1990: 213) words:

Differences are inequality's post hoc excuse, its conclusory artifact.
They are its outcome presented as its origin, the damage that is
pointed to as the justification for doing the damage after the damage
has been done.

On access: A discourse of 'sameness'

[F]eminists should continue to struggle for women to receive a fair
share of the pie, carcinogenic though it ultimately may be.
(Jaggar, 1990: 253)

Our second 'case' was a rolling collaboration among Lani Guinier,
Michelle Fine, Jane Balin, Ann Bartow and Deborah Satchel (1994),
conducted at the University of Pennsylvania Law School, during the late
1980s and early 1990s. Initially, the research was sparked by Ann
Bartow's interest in gender dynamics within the law school. The study
began as a survey of the full population of 712 students then enrolled in
the Law School, asking about their views of gender and the law school
experience (366 responded, 47.5 per cent female and 52.5 per cent male).
While the detailed results of the survey can be found in Guinier et al.
(1994), below we highlight some of the findings to illustrate how
hegemony, domination and hierarchy operated on the bodies and minds
of elite women and men, studying within an institution that has granted
women substantial access, and equally high levels of alienation, enabled
through a discourse of 'sameness'.

The exchange made through 'sameness' arguments becomes evident.
Women get into a system that privileges few. They can't easily critique
from within, lest they be seen as inadequate. When most women don't
'make it', they have little access to a language of justice. We let you in,
didn't we? Meritocracy creates its own prophylactic against internal
challenge.

The Law School survey

Most simply stated, the survey found that, at least psychologically, men and women law students attended two different law schools. Men and women law students may have attended the 'same' physical school, but they narrate vastly 'different' legal education experiences. In general, the women law students are found to be far more critical of sexism and racism in the broader culture, critical of legal education, of the 'generic he', and of themselves as students than men ($p = 0.05$). Women are three times more likely to express an interest in public interest law than male law students ($p < 0.01$) and far more committed to social issues ($p = 0.05$). Women more often report that men take up a disproportionate share of the public talk in class by asking more questions and volunteering more often, and that men get better reception when they do speak from other students and from faculty (all items $p < 0.05$). While 60 per cent of the men report being 'very comfortable' speaking with professors outside of class, only 40 per cent of women feel the same. Throughout law school, women report significantly higher levels of 'mental health problems' (such as crying, trouble sleeping, seeing a counsellor) than do men.

These survey data, in the aggregate, reveal compelling and consistent evidence to support a gender-based 'differences' argument. Men and women walk through the world of law school, sit in their classes, approach their faculty and process information in very different ways. And yet, when we analysed the data over time, we found that these stark gender differences evaported after the first year of law school. While major and consistent gender differences distinguished first-year women and men, such trends were no longer discernible by the third year. Over the course of their time in law school, women came to express attitudes, beliefs and experiences that mimicked those of first-year men. By their third year, the women sounded more like the third-year men than they did first-year women. 'Difference' was unstable.

Most troubling among these indicators of diminishing differences is the finding that a disproportionate number of first-year women came into law school with commitments to public interest law and a ready fight for social justice, but when they left law school their interest in public interest law had been replaced by galvanized commitments to corporate, bank-ruptcy and tax law. In short, women and men come into law school looking quite 'different' and yet they leave looking very much the 'same'. As we wrote in an earlier paper:

> From the foregoing, one could conclude that women become more 'like men' over time in this particular law school, at least in reported attitudes toward gender, sexism and career goals. One might assume, then, that women's academic performance over time

would also mirror that of men. But . . . a disproportionate number
of women – who move away from an interest in public interest law
or drop their initial social critique – also graduate with significantly
less impressive credentials than their male counterparts.

(Guinier et al., 1994: 1024)

Academic performance data

The survey whetted our theoretical interest in the short shelf life of
gendered 'differences'. Because the survey traced a shift in time from
women's attitudinal 'difference' from men to their 'sameness' as men,
we wanted to know if women's academic performance would also
become more like men's over time. Analysing four cohorts of academic
performance data, we witnessed just the opposite trend. Academically
first-year men and women were the 'same' in terms of initial academic
profiles. Over time, however, a dramatic gender 'difference' emerged.
Drawing on the language of Deborah Rhode, the difference looked a lot
more like *institutional disadvantaging* than a matter of *individual style*.
'Sameness', too, is unstable.

The academic data, drawn from 981 law school students, come from
women and men in the classes of 1990, 1991, 1992 and 1993. An analysis
of incoming statistics, including college grade point average (GPA), rank
in college, Law School Aptitude Test (LSAT) and 'Lonsdorf Index' (a
locally generated weighted index of incoming statistics) revealed no
academic differences between men and women when they enter law
school. Men average 3.49 undergraduate GPA; women 3.52. Men have
an average undergraduate class rank of 78.44; women 80.13. Men's
mean LSAT is 40.98; women's 40.87. Men's mean index is 4.73; women's
4.74.

By the end of the first year, however, women are in a substantially
disadvantaged academic position in the Law School. First- and second-
year men are 1.6 times more likely to be above the median than women.
First-year men are almost three times more likely to be in the top decile
of their class. In the second and third years, men are twice as likely to be
in the top decile of the class. Women and men come to law school with
very similar credentials but, in 'a pattern established firmly in the first
year and maintained thereafter, women receive relatively lower grades,
lower class rank and earn fewer honors' (Guinier *et al.*, 1994: 1028). Due
to their disproportionately low representation in the top decile of the
class, women law students under-receive prestigious positions, and
under-participate in high-status extracurricular activities, including
graduation awards, Law Review membership and board status, and
moot court competitions and board status.

Focus groups

Our academic performance data feed us an even more complicated story than the survey alone. Women come to law school looking 'different' from men with respect to attitudes and experiences, but the 'same' with respect to grades. Women graduate from law school looking 'the same' with respect to attitudes and experience, but 'different' with respect to grades. Neither a difference nor a sameness discourse could suffice. Questions of institutional power, disadvantage and socialization have to be explored. We turned to the students, and began our focus groups.

In the spring of 1991 and 1992, we invited seven groups of law students to help us think through our data. The groups numbered between 10 and 15 in size, and were diverse by gender, race/ethnicity, age and school year. Half of the groups were selected for a particular reason – involvement in Law Review; students of colour; activist students – with the other half more randomly constituted.

The oral narratives reinforce the gendered nature of alienation that respondents offered in their quantitative responses to the survey. The focus group respondents reveal a flood of alienation contained within this presumably equal-access institution.

We were struck by the sheer number of white women, and women and men of colour, who describe deep alienation from law school, and by the equally large group of white men who try to explain away gendered (and raced) findings. Most of the women we interviewed, like those we surveyed, are disturbed by sexist language, biases and treatment by professors and peers. They are particularly troubled that male peers would harass women in class and ridicule their comments. They are even more disturbed that male faculty would simply observe and not inter-vene. As with the survey data, first-year women seem more agitated by – or less used to – this treatment than their third-year counterparts. One woman reports 'a group of frat boys who call you man-hating lesbian or feminist – as though those are bad – if you are too outspoken'. Other women report the hissing, humiliation and gossip they suffered for speaking aloud or 'controversially' in class. These women press the point – where is the accountability of the institution for educating male and female students? Why is this behaviour tolerated and sometimes sanc-tioned by faculty? As another female student says:

Women's sexuality becomes the focus for keeping us in our place. If someone was rumoured to be a woman who speaks too much, she was considered a lesbian. That is, women don't speak partly because our sexuality becomes implicated as soon as we act 'too much like men' for their liking. Now I'm in a room with 120 frat boys, a mass of faces that say nothing when you speak. No feedback from professors. No one cares what you did, and who you were, people hiss, laugh and there is rarely an interruption of that from other students or professors. We need to change class size and how classes are taught so that men and women can speak publicly and not self-consciously in front of others.

Many women describe a disturbing 'loss of self' in the first year, a painful and alienating 'out-of-body experience'. As one first-year woman notes: 'I try to block out the entire experience. I won't take pictures, talk on tapes; I hope to forget this whole thing as soon as I'm gone. I hope to skip that space in time.' In conversation, some women talk about trying to recapture 'forgotten selves', others avoid remembering the scars. Yet men smooth over their difficult memories. Listen to the gendered dynamics in one focus group:

Male student: After my first year I realized that I was making a mountain out of a molehill.

Female student: You're not listening to what M said. She said: 'It entirely shook my faith in myself. I will never recover.' Some of us just sunk deep and deeper in a mire, and just keep sinking lower and lower.

Another female student: That's right. I used to be very driven, competitive. Then I started to realize that all my effort was getting me nowhere. I just stopped trying; just stopped caring. I am scarred for ever.

These women, as the literature on gender and attribution theory might suggest (Deaux and Major, 1987), were more likely than men to make internal attributions for failure, and external attributions for academic success. One explained:

When we get bad grades, we just think we're stupid. You guys get over it! Men suppress their feelings, so it doesn't take a toll. I used to never cry, last year I cried every week. Guys think law school is hard, and we just think we're stupid.

The mental health items on the survey confirm a gendered disadvantaging across the three years of law school. While there were no differences in the use of alcohol or drugs, or fighting, women report more eating disorders, sleeping difficulties, crying and evidence of depression and anxiety than men. Women were more than four times as likely to report seeking professional help for law school concerns as were men: 15.5 per cent of women compared to 3.6 per cent of men. These women pay dearly for their success in terms of political consciousness, commitments to social justice, sense of entitlement, levels of academic performance and mental health.

The first year of law school is designed, intentionally or not, in ways that heighten the likelihood of self-blame, competition and domination. Organized through mandatory bell-shaped grading curves, large lectures taught disproportionately by white male faculty, with explicit limits on student participation, inviting students into adversarial Socratic methods fuelled by fierce academic competition, the structures and pedagogies of the first year could not be better designed to produce a gender-stratified hierarchy.

Becoming gentlemen

Many students told us about a well-known, senior white male law professor who welcomes his first-year students with the following advice: 'To be a good lawyer, behave like a gentleman'.

Many women seemingly do just that. They enter law school as confident and competent, feminist and well credentialed. In their attempts to 'become gentlemen', however, they leave, in the aggregate, depressed, relatively under-credentialed and depoliticized. They have become gentlemen – sort of.

These law school data demonstrate the limits of a discourse of 'sameness' which fundamentally occludes how traditional structures of domination, harassment and alienation organize law school, en-gender disadvantage and force critique, outrage and challenge underground. Organizational access without transformation bears deep and troubling consequences for women's and men's individual identities, for women's collective consciousness and for what is misrepresented as women's individual 'choice' or 'inability' to climb the hierarchy.

As Albert Hirschmann (1970) would argue, women in untransformed 'equal access' settings have three choices – voice, exit or loyalty. In this elite law school, voice was exercised by few. Exit by even fewer. Silence doubled as passive loyalty and active alienation. The price of hegemony – that is, 'becoming gentlemen' – can be tracked in women's depleted academic records, their disadvantaged postgraduate credentials, their conservatized political perspectives and their mental health difficulties. Rarely has there been an opportunity like this one to trace the biography of alienation and hegemony within an institution which proclaims gender and race neutrality but delivers neither – all in the name of access.

Climbing the meritocratic ladder in drag

Nancy Fraser's (1990) essay, 'Rethinking the public sphere: A contribution to the critique of actually existing democracy', helps us make sense of these law school data. We feel confident applying Fraser's writings on the public sphere to this private law school, inasmuch as the school promotes itself as publicly committed, accessible and gender/race-neutral. Yet it bears clearly differential consequences for female and male students and graduates.

The bourgeois public sphere, in Fraser's formulation, represents itself as democratic and accessible but is in fact 'constituted by a number of significant exclusions' (Fraser, 1990: 59). The law school, too, drenched in a liberal discourse of equal access, allows women in, eroding its historic borders and yet simultaneously buttressing its internal hierarchy. Institutional strategies of exclusion and domination seemingly melt once internal strategies of gendered and raced socialization take form. The interior hierarchy, sedimented with race, class and gender, is laminated with a gloss of presumed neutrality. Once women enter these institutions, most collude, cynically or authentically, in a degraded discourse of sameness. They trade their ability to challenge conditions of hierarchy, privilege and disadvantage for a set in class. Struggles over gender (and race) stratification go underground, exchanged for access.

Making sense across cases of exclusion and access

When we put together The Citadel and the Law School data, we see that educational institutions of both exclusion and access work to preserve self-interested hierarchies and to resist invasion by women of all racial/ethnic groups, from outside or from within. Let us take exclusion first. In all-male settings, there is the publicly announced, collective manufacturing of oppositional identities embodied and narrated by white men. As The Citadel data testify, a 'difference' discourse administers a steroid to male identities mounted on the active exclusion and derogation of Others. Institutional exclusion of women of all colours from schools, like the exclusion of men of colour, is not simply illegal; it is dangerous to women on the outside and to men on the inside.

The Citadel data are joined by ample evidence from fraternities, all-male schools and male clubs to suggest that in such contexts men construct and narrate fetishized identities that are precariously premised on oppositional definitions of Self and Other, with Others typically including white women, gays and lesbians, people of colour, and those who 'overlap'. Much evidence suggests that all-male institutions both reproduce and exacerbate already existing inequities, measured in attitudinal academic and economic outcomes. Valerie Lee (1993) studied a large sample of coed, all-male and all-female schools, and writes about sexual harassment in such contexts:

The absence of one sex in single sex classrooms does not ensure that sexism will not occur – in fact, the most serious incidents of sexism we observed were in all boys' classes with male teachers. . . . In some boys' schools, we saw females regarded as sex objects, both in writing in classroom displays and in class discussion. These serious incidents always occurred in all male settings.

(43)

Lee continues, a page later:

[M]y current concern is how we may create and maintain school environments where both males and females flourish. Some single sex schools seem to be such environments, but our research did not indicate that, in general, all male environments were especially healthy ones for adolescents in terms of sex equity.

(44)

Peggy Sanday has documented the violence laced through the collective identities of white fraternity brothers. Sanday (1990: 21) writes:

Cross cultural research demonstrates that whenever men build and give allegiance to a mystical, enduring all male social group, the disparagement of women is, invariably, an important ingredient of the mystical bond, and sexual aggression the means by which the bond is renewed. As long as exclusive male clubs exist in a society that privileges men as a social category, we must recognize that collective sexual aggression provides a ready stage on which some men represent their social privilege and introduce adolescent boys to their future place in the status hierarchy.

Lois Weis (1993) has analysed 'hypermasculinities' of white working-class boys exhibited not in an all-male setting, but in a coed high school within a deindustrializing community. Weis's data force scholars of 'virulent masculinity' to recognize that the oppositional identities of exclusion, documented by Lee and Sanday, are also exercised within coeducational settings. Confirming evidence comes from the American Association of University Women Report (1993), *How Schools Shortchange Girls*. Despite years of feminist work, coed schools continue to produce inequitable outcomes, in terms of academic standing and social harassment, for girls/women compared to boys/men. Given the proliferating evidence of 'gender domination' within coeducational institutions, and the absence of institutional interruptions of this domination, we would argue, as Stephanie Riger (1994) does for the workplace, that the mere inclusion of girls/women into all-male schools has been inadequate to transform institutional culture. Despite the infusion of girls/women, there typically persists a deeply misogynist, institutional climate. While individual boys/men may narrate identities that depart from the collective (for example, men of colour in The Citadel data), the chorus, within contexts of exclusion *and* access, nevertheless invents and punishes 'difference' and Otherness.

In gender- or race-'accessible' institutions, the shift from institutional exclusion to institutional access parallels a shift from domination to hegemony (Gramsci, 1971). Once access is institutionally enabled, the bricks of exclusion are torn down and then recemented into socialization practices towards hierarchy. Once excluded members are 'in', it is easy to see just how thoroughly gender/race-orchestrated these institutions become – in terms of social relations, history, communications between students and faculty, curriculum and pedagogies, networks, legitimated measures of 'success' and student outcomes. 'Becoming gentlemen' is one of the projects of both The Citadel and the Law School. In both cases, the Other is a woman. She is called a 'skirt' or a 'Sally' at The Citadel; 'feminist' or 'lesbian' at the Law School. In both cases, we would argue, harassment of women – as bodies or image – is institutionalized informally and sanctioned formally. The introduction of women does not transform the hegemonic message. The introduction of women may, ironically, only raise the hegemonic voice by an octave.

From individuals to institutions: Beyond difference or sameness

Individual differences are highly visible whereas the shaping power of organizational arrangements is less transparent. . . . Moving from individualistic to organizational explanations permits consideration of new solutions . . .

(Riger, 1994: 28–9)

We wish we could close the chapter on the difference/sameness debate. We believe it is a diversion. Neither a discourse of 'difference' nor one of 'sameness', stripped of analyses of power, will move us forward, for gender-, race- and/or class-based equity. It is as easy to document 'differences', especially before institutional homogenization, as it is to document 'sameness' after institutional homogenization. We have bulky literatures designed to do each of these seemingly oppositional jobs in scholarship and in political rhetoric. We see, however, that both 'difference' and 'sameness' are promiscuous and deceptive discursive strategies. Both deflect our attention away from institutions, domination and radical social change. Feminist social psychology needs to resist the seductive detour into differences *or* sameness, and press on with questions about institutionalized power, disadvantage and transformation.

Note

1 The Citadel as of June 1996, has agreed to 'enthusiastically' admit women after the US Supreme Court ruled that a similar institution, The Virginia Military Institute, could not exclude women.

References

American Association of University Women Report (1993) *How Schools Shortchange Girls*. Washington, DC: AAUW Educational Foundation.

Bishop, J. (1993) Deposition in *Johnson v. Jones*. United State District Court: Charleston Division.

The Citadel (1992–3). *The Guidon*. Charleston, SC.

Deaux, K. (1985) 'Sex and gender', *Annual Review of Psychology*, 36: 49–81.

Deaux, K. and Major, B. (1987) 'Putting gender into context: An interactive model of gender-related behavior', *Psychological Review*, 94: 369–89.

Foucault, M. (1979) *Discipline and Punish: The Birth of the Prison*. New York: Vintage.

Fraser, N. (1990) 'Rethinking the public sphere: A contribution to the critique of actually existing democracy', *Social Text: Theory/Culture/Ideology*, 25/26: 56–80.

Gilligan, C. (1982) *In a Different Voice*. Cambridge, MA: Harvard University Press.

Gramsci, A. (1971) *Selections from Prison Notebooks of Antonio Gramsci* (Q. Hoarse and G. N. Smith). New York: International.

Guinier, L., Fine, M. and Balin, J. with Bartow, A. and Stachel, D. L. (1994) 'Becoming gentlemen: Women's experiences at one Ivy League law school', *University of Pennsylvania Law Review*, 143(1): 1001–82.

Hare-Mustin, R. T. and Marecek, J. (1988) 'The meaning of difference: Gender theory, postmodernism, and psychology', *American Psychologist*, 43: 455–64.

Hare-Mustin, R. T. and Marecek, J. (eds) (1990) *Making a Difference: Psychology and the Construction of Gender*. New Haven, CT: Yale University Press.

Hirschmann, A. O. (1970) *Exit, Voice, and Loyalty: Responses to the Decline in Firms, Organizations, and States*. Cambridge, MA: Harvard University Press.

Jaggar, A. (1990) 'Sexual difference and sexual equality', in D. L. Rhode (ed.), *Theoretical Perspectives on Sexual Difference*. New Haven, CT: Yale University Press, pp. 239–54.

Katz, P. and Taylor, A. (eds) (1988) *Eliminating Racism: Profiles in Controversy*. New York: Plenum Press.

Kitzinger, C. (ed.) (1994) Special Feature: 'Should psychologists study sex differences?', *Feminism & Psychology*, 4(4): 501–46.

Lee, V. (1993) 'Single sex schools', in OERI Report, *Single Sex Schooling: Perspectives from Practice and Research*, Vol. II. Washington DC: Department of Education.

MacKinnon, C. (1990) 'Legal perspectives on sexual difference', in D. L. Rhode (ed.), *Theoretical Perspectives on Sexual Difference*. New Haven, CT: Yale University Press, pp. 213–25.

MacKinnon, C. (1991) 'Difference and dominance: On sex discrimination', in K. Bartlett and R. Kennedy (eds), *Feminism Legal Theory: Readings in Law and Gender*. Boulder, CO: Westview Press, pp. 81–94.

Mahan, A. and Mahan, T. (1993) 'The Citadel: The case for single gender education'. Unpublished manuscript submitted on behalf of the defendants in *Johnson v. Jones*. United States District Court: Charleston Division.

Milkman, R. (1986) 'Women's history and the Sears case', *Feminist Studies*, 12(2): 375–400.

Minow, M. (1990) *Making all the Difference: Inclusion, Exclusion, and American Law*. Ithaca, NY: Cornell University Press.

Mohanty, C. T. (1994) 'On race and voice: Challenges for liberal education in the 1990s', in H. A. Giroux and P. McLaren (eds), *Between Borders: Pedagogy and the Politics of Cultural Studies*. New York: Routledge, pp. 145–66.

Omi, M. and Winant, H. (1986) *Racial Formation in the United States: From the 1960s to the 1980s*. New York: Routledge & Kegan Paul.

Reisman, D. (1991) Deposition in *United States of America v. Commonwealth of Virginia et al*. United States District Court: Roanoke Division.

Rembert (1993) Deposition in *Johnson v. Jones*. United States District Court: Charleston Division.

Rhode, D. (1990) 'Definitions of difference', in D. L. Rhode (ed.), *Theoretical Perspectives on Sexual Difference*. New Haven, CT: Yale University Press, pp. 197–212.

Riger, S. (1994) 'Challenges of success: stages of growth in feminist organizations', *Feminist Studies*, Summer.

Sanday, P. (1990) *Fraternities and Gang Rape*. New York: New York University Press.

Scott, J. (1992) 'Experience', in J. Butler and J. Scott (eds), *Feminists Theorize the Political*. New York: Routledge, pp. 22–40.

Vergnolle, R. (1993) Deposition in *Johnson v. Jones*. United States District Court: Charleston Division.

Weis, Lois (1993) 'White male working class youth: An exploration of relative privilege and loss', in L. Weis and M. Fine (eds) *Beyond Silenced Voices: Class, Race and Gender in United States Schools*. Albany, NY: State University of New York Press.

Yoder, J. (1989) 'Women at West Point: Lessons for token women in male-dominated occupations', in J. Freeman (ed.), *Women: A Feminist Perspective*. Mountain View, CA: Mayfield.

4

'Race', racism, and sexuality in the life narratives of immigrant women[1]

──────• OLIVA M. ESPIN

In March 1994 a new exhibition, *Becoming American Women: Clothing and the Jewish Immigrant Experience, 1880–1920*, opened at the Chicago Historical Society. In the book that accompanies the exhibition, Barbara Schreier (1994), its conceptualizer and curator, recounts her early interest in this study of clothing and acculturation. When she interviewed first- and second-generation immigrants about the years of adjustment to US society, 'everyone had a clothing story' (1994: 2). She concluded that clothing and acculturation mirror each other closely and that 'clothing [is] an identifiable symbol of a changing consciousness' (1994: 5). As she wrote:

> The decision to focus [the exhibition] on women was based on the long-standing relationship women have had with their appearance . . . Issues of dress unified women and framed their experience of life separate from men . . . [E]ven though men considered issues [of clothing], they did not record them with the same iconographic vocabularly as did women. [F]emale immigrants discuss clothing in their memoirs, oral histories, and correspondence as pivotal markers of their journey and remembered objects of desire.
>
> (Schreier, 1994: 8–9)

Referring to a population vastly different in cultural background and immersed in different historical circumstances a century later, Anne Woollett *et al.* (1994) reporting on their research on Asian women's ethnic identity, noted 'frequent associations of dress with ethnic identity' (1994: 124) and observed that

> [w]hile dress is seen as an important aspect of ethnic identity by almost all the women interviewed . . . men's choice of clothing was rarely mentioned in the interviews . . . Clothes would appear to have different significance for women as compared with men, and given that most studies have not focused upon women, may explain why dress is rarely used as a measure of ethnic identity in much of the literature.
>
> (Woollett *et al.*, 1994: 125)

They state that because '[t]he impact of gender on the representations of ethnic identity is not frequently or adequately considered' (1994: 120), aspects of the acculturation process that are expressed through women's clothing choices are usually ignored.

While these authors astutely observe the importance women assign to their clothing and appearance as a statement of their relation to acculturation, they do not question why it is so. Yet we know that women, in Western culture as well as in other cultures, are defined and define themselves through physical appearance. Women are their bodies. Connections and disconnections between mothers and daughters, even without the tensions created by acculturation, are mediated by clothing, fashion, weight and other issues related to appearance (Kaschak, 1992).

Interestingly, the historical period that the Chicago Historical Society exhibition focuses on coincides with a period of intense public preoccupation with young women's sexuality – not coincidentally, a period when large numbers of young immigrant unmarried women living in American cities were gainfully employed (Nathanson, 1991). According to Schreier (1994), the Jewish press admonished young women at the time in lengthy editorials not to use their savings to buy frivolous items of clothing. Similarly, many a family conflict had its source in parental anger with daughters who spent money from their meagre wages buying coveted clothing rather than contributing further to the family's resources. Immigrant women's identity conflicts and identity transformations continue to be expressed in our time through clothing and sexuality. For parents and young women alike, acculturation and sexuality are seen as closely connected (Espin, 1984; 1987b). For parents and young women alike, 'dressing Western' or preserving traditional clothing styles can be grounds for intergenerational conflict.

Obviously, women's preoccupation with clothing and appearance is closely associated with sexuality. (Let me say in parentheses here that heterosexual standards of sexual attractiveness are not the only ones expressed through clothing. Lesbian preoccupation with dress codes, whether the 'politically correct' jeans and sneakers or 'lipstick lesbian' fashion outfits, are an expression of concern with sexual attractiveness. Standards of attractiveness vary among different groups and generations of lesbians but, in any case, clothes and sexual attractiveness are connected for lesbians, too.)

The self-appointed 'guardians of morality and tradition' that are ever-present in immigrant 'communities' are very concerned with women's roles and sexual behaviour. It is no secret that religious leaders are rather preoccupied with women's sexuality. Indeed, the great religions of the world uphold similar principles in so far as the submission of women to men is concerned (see, for example, el Saadawi, 1980). We are witnessing how 'women, their role, and above all their control, have become central to the fundamentalist agenda' (Yuval-Davis, 1992: 278) of Protestants, Catholics, Muslims and others. When immigrant communities are besieged with rejection, racism and scorn, those self-appointed leaders have always found fertile ground from which to control women's sexuality in the name of preserving 'tradition'. Women's subservience is advocated as a type of 'steadying influence'.

It is significant that groups that are transforming their way of life through a vast and deep process of acculturation, focus on preserving 'tradition' almost exclusively through the gender roles and lives of women. Women's roles become the 'bastion' of traditions:

> The 'proper' behaviour of women is used to signify the difference between those who belong to the collectivity and those who do not. Women are also seen as 'cultural carriers' of the collectivity who transmit it to the future generation, and the 'proper' control of women in terms of marriage and divorce ensures that children who are born to those women are not only biologically but also symbolically within the boundaries of the collectivity.
>
> (Yuval-Davis, 1992: 285)

Schreier (1994: 9) tells us that, in the case of Jewish immigrants to the USA at the beginning of the turn of the century, 'contemporary observers did not pay as much attention to male plumage; even when they did, their words lack the moralistic, beseeching, and condemnatory tones with which they addressed women'. Conversely, women resisted domination from both the larger society and their own communities through the use of clothing and other means. The new freedom young immigrant women from diverse ethnic backgrounds acquired from being wage earners, expressed itself through the clothes they wore and through the refusal to accept chaperons and other forms of parental control over their sexuality (Ruiz, 1992).

Although understudied, the role of women in international migration has begun to draw attention from researchers, policy-makers and service providers (see, for example, Andizian *et al.*, 1983; Phizacklea, 1983; Cole *et al.*, 1992; Gabaccia, 1992). However, little is known about experiences of immigrant women considered to be private, such as sexuality.

Referring specifically to women in the Middle East, the Lebanese author Evelyne Accad (1991: 237) asserts that:

> [s]exuality seems to have a revolutionary potential so strong that many political women and men are afriad of it. They prefer, therefore, to dismiss its importance by arguing that it is not as central as other factors, such as economic and political determi- nation . . . [However,] . . . sexuality is much more central to social and political problems . . . than previously thought, and . . . unless a sexual revolution is incorporated into political revolution, there will be no real transformation of social relations.

Not coincidentally, women's clothing has been one of the core issues in the Iranian revolution (Tohidi, 1991).

Indeed, sexuality is not private (Foucault, 1981). This explains why so many cultures and countries try to control and legislate it (Brettell and Sargent, 1993; di Leonardo, 1991). Many immigrant women have experienced restrictions on their sexuality before migration as well as in the context of their communities after migration. And, among political refugees, some may have experienced sexualized torture.

We know that the sexual behaviour of women serves a larger social function beyond the personal. It is used by enemies and friends alike as 'proof' of the moral fibre or decay of nations or other social groups. World-wide, women are enculturated and socialized to embody their sexual desire or lack thereof through their particular culture's ideals of virtue. Women's reproductive capacities are appropriated by the state to establish its control over citizens and territories alike. Thus the social group's expectations are inscribed in women's individual desire and expressed through their sexuality (Jaggar and Bordo, 1989). Historically, warriors have celebrated victories and consoled the frustrations of defeat through the forceful possession of women's bodies: war and rape are deeply connected. The present situation in the former Yugoslavia brings this reality to the forefront in a tragic and dramatic way.

Sexuality may be a universal component of human experience, yet how it is embodied and expressed is not (Laqueur, 1990). As anthropological, historical, and literary studies contend, 'sexuality is culturally variable rather than a timeless, immutable essence' (Parker *et al.*, 1992: 4). Indigenous interpretations of seemingly similar sexual practices (or even what is considered to be sexual or not) are often strikingly different for people in different cultural environments. The study of women's experiences reveals a varied representation of sexual/gender differences among cultures. These cultural constructs inextricably inform the expression of female sexuality. Cultural traditions, colonial and other forms of social oppression, national identity and the vicissitudes of the historical process inform the development and perception of female sexuality. The development of women's sexuality is affected by the eroticization of power differentials and the links between power and sexual violence (see, for example, Valverde, 1985). World-wide definitions of what constitutes appropriate sexual behaviour are strongly influenced by male sexual pleasure. These definitions are justified in the name of prevalent values in a given society, nationalism, religion, morality, health, science, etc. Too often women's expression and experience of their own sexuality are silenced and/or condemned (see, for example, Prieto, 1992; Ruiz, 1992).

The acculturation process opens up different possibilities for women than for men, particularly with reference to gender roles and sexual behaviour (Espin, 1984; 1987a; 1987b; Espin *et al.*, 1990a; 1990b; Goodenow and Espin, 1993). Among immigrant women in the USA who come from traditional societies, sexuality is frequently associated with 'becoming Americanized'. One of the most prevalent myths about American women in other countries is that they are very 'free' with sex. For immigrant parents and the young woman herself, 'to become Americanized' may be equated with becoming sexually promiscuous. Thus, in some cases, during the acculturation process sexuality becomes the focus of the parents' fears and the girls' desires (Espin, 1984). As expressed by Bhavnani and Haraway (1994: 33), '[t]hese young women in their embodiment, are the points of collision of all these powerful forces, including forces of their own'.

Conversely, newly encountered sex-role patterns, combined with greater access to paid employment for women, may create possibilities to live a new lifestyle. This way of life may have been previously unavailable in the home culture. In this scenario, the traditional power structure of the family may be changed (Espin, 1987b). Transmitted through words and silences that pass between women of different generations are values and beliefs about what constitutes appropriate sexual behaviour. These include ideas about pregnancy, male–female relationships, women's reproductive health, and so forth (Marin *et al.*, 1992; 1993). Mothers provide the core of cultural messages for women through what they say about men and other women, and what is allowed and what is forbidden to be a 'good woman' in the culture of origin. These messages continue to be powerful injunctions for first-, second- and even third-generation immigrant women (Espin *et al.*, 1990a).

Not all pressures on immigrant women's sexuality come from inside their own culture. The host society also imposes its own burdens and desires through prejudices and racism. Women immigrants, particularly those who are not white, experience degrees of 'gendered racism' (Essed,

1991; 1994). Although racism may be expressed subtly, the immigrant woman finds herself between the racism of the dominant society and the sexist expectations of her own community. Paraphrasing Nigerian poet and professor 'Molara Ogundipe-Leslie (1993), we could say that immigrant women have several mountains on their back, the two most obvious ones being 'the heritage of tradition' and 'the oppression from outside'. The racism of the dominant society makes the retrenchment into 'tradition' appear to be justifiable, while the rigidities of 'tradition' appear to justify the racist/prejudicial treatment of the dominant society. Paradoxically, the two 'mountains' reinforce and encourage each other. Needless to say, the effect of racism and sexism is not only felt as pressure from the outside, but also becomes internalized, like all forms of oppression are. Women exposed to more direct contact with the dominant society experience the contradictions more dramatically, although perhaps less consciously than those who do not confront the dominant society on a regular basis (see, for example, Essed, 1991; 1994; Gold, 1992). As Essed (1994: 101) argues:

> [F]rom a macro point of view, the massive and systemic repro-
> duction of belief systems which legitimate certain dominant group
> positions, predispose individuals to internalize these ideas,
> whether or not they themselves occupy these dominant positions.
> From a micro point of view, however, individuals do not necessarily
> and unthinkingly accept 'dominant' ideologies. Moreover, the
> cognitive domain of individuals is a fundamental area where new
> and critical knowledge can generate change . . . The study of
> individual motivation and sense-making in the process of resistance
> against confining race and gender boundaries is still, however,
> largely unexplored.

In the last year I have been engaged in a study that seeks to increase knowledge and understanding of sexuality and gender-related issues among immigrant/refugee women. The study is still in its preliminary stages. It focuses on the expression and experience of women's sexuality in different cultures as they are created by disparate social forces. I would like to share some of the preliminary results with you in this chapter. I am collecting narratives from mothers and daughters about their experiences as immigrant women. These narratives are obtained through individual interviews and focus groups.

'The focus group interview is a qualitative research technique used to obtain data about feelings and opinions of small groups of participants about a given problem, experience or other phenomenon (Basch, 1987: 414). The narratives explore immigrant women's understanding of sexuality and their internalization of cultural norms. Their open-ended narratives allow for the expression of thoughts and feelings, while inviting participants to introduce their own themes and concerns. They are a particularly valuable research method when the concepts being explored are 'new territory' for participants and/or researcher (Mishler, 1986; Riessman, 1993). In addition to its value as a research tool (see Denzin, 1989; Josselson and Lieblich, 1993; Riessman, 1993), retelling the life-story, including the migration (particularly if it was motivated by some form of persecution), has been shown to have a healing effect (Aron, 1992). Focus groups provide opportunities for in-depth interviewing of a group concerning a particular topic. This form of in-depth interviewing is effective and economical in terms of both time and money, thus it is a pragmatic approach for any study done with limited funds and limited personnel – in this case, only one researcher. Focus groups follow basic principles of qualitative research and take advantage of the additional information generated by the group interaction. They provide the researcher with the additional flexibility of probing unanticipated areas when initially designing the dicussion questions (see, for example, Morgan, 1988; 1993; Stewart and Shamdasani, 1990; Krueger, 1994).

By the end of the study, focus groups will have been held in a number of cities in the USA – probably San Diego, Chicago and Miami. (Thus far, all data have been collected in San Diego.) Individual narratives will also be collected from immigrant/refugee women in these cities. The choice of these cities has been determined by two factors. One is the possibility of accessing a wider variety of cultures/countries of origin and populations by recruiting prospective participants in three regions of the United States. The three cities chosen for the study have a rich ethnic and racially mixed population of immigrants/refugees. These sites complement one another because they represent geographical and ethnic diversity within the United States and across national origin. The second is pragmatic: personal plans and professional connections facilitate my travel and access to these three cities.

Immigrant/refugee women have been recruited in the chosen cities through personal contacts and friendship pyramiding. They have been asked to participate voluntarily in small groups of five to ten women from the same cultural background (i.e. country, social class, first language). The women recruited so far range in age from early twenties to mid-forties, and they are all college-educated. A few are still in the process of completing their higher education. Women who are first- or second-generation immigrants have participated in these individual interviews and focus groups. These women have been chosen on the basis of their being particularly articulate about the research topic and fluent in both English and the language of origin. The interviews have focused in-depth on respondents' individual life-stories and experiences.

In the focus groups and individual interviews conducted so far, I have explored ways in which women's sexual behaviour signifies the family's

value system; this entails exploring ways in which the struggles surrounding acculturation in immigrant/refugee families centre around
issues of daughters' sexual behaviours and women's sex roles in general.
An important aspect of the focus groups has been to explore the
vocabulary of sex in different languages – specifically, what it is
permissible to say about it. I have explored variations in the speakers'
comfort (or discomfort) when addressing sexuality in the mother tongue
or in English.

The focus groups explore what mothers, as transmitters of cultural
norms, tell (or do not tell) their daughters about what they should (or
should not) do as women. They explore 'protective' behaviours that
silently express prescriptive sexual ideology for women. Generational
differences among women that are usually associated with gender role
differences and sexual behaviour are also discussed. They explore how
generational differences are associated with acculturation and how
differential access to the host culture may circumscribe sexual behaviour.
Younger women talk about how they perceive their mothers' expression
of and comfort with sexuality. Women who are mothers address how
they relate to their daughters concerning sexuality issues. I am giving
primary importance to the messages transmitted between mothers and
daughters concerning sexuality and its related issues.

So far, I have conducted three focus groups and five individual
interviews. Two of the groups have been constituted by native speakers
of the same language (in one case, German; in the other, Spanish). A third
group included women from several different countries. The Spanish
speakers' group was conducted in English and Spanish, the other two
groups were conducted in English.

All focus groups and interviews have been facilitated and conducted by
me. For Spanish-speaking participants, the possibility of conducting the
groups or individual interview in their mother tongue has been offered.
When participants who speak Spanish preferred to be interviewed in
English, their request has been honoured and the request itself will be
considered data. For participants whose first language is not English,
Spanish, or French, careful questioning about vocabulary in their
language and questions about the effect of conducting the interview in
English have been incorporated into the session. In addition to Mexican-
American and German, participants have been Cuban, Korean, South
Asian and Austrian.

Topics discussed in the focus groups and in the individual interviews
cover a wide range of concerns. The issues discussed include menstruation, arranged marriages versus dating, marrying outside one's ethnic
group, sex and violence, lesbianism and bisexuality, sex education in the
schools and at home, mothers' passivity versus active involvement in
their daughters' lives from the point of view of both mothers and

daughters, silences about sex in their families, sex and romance, and sexual behaviour and heterosexual intercourse.

Interviews and focus groups have been taped, transcribed, and analysed following accepted techniques for the analysis of qualitative data (see, for example, Strauss, 1987; Silverman, 1993). The possibility of using a computer package for the analysis of the data is being investigated; the availability of resources and applicability of existing computer packages for data analysis will determine its feasibility.

The study emphasizes the geographical and psychological borders and boundaries crossed in the process of migration. This process is central to the life experiences of women who have migrated from their country of origin. The crossing of borders through migration may provide for women the space and 'permission' to cross boundaries and transform their sexuality and sex roles. For lesbians, an additional border/boundary crossing takes place in relation to the coming-out process. Coming out may have occurred after the migration, as part of the acculturation process or it may have been the motivating force behind the migration. However, for most women, issues of sexuality may not have been part of the conscious decision to migrate.

Through this study, I would like to ascertain the main issues and consequences entailed in crossing both geographical and psychological borders and boundaries for both lesbians and heterosexual women. For example, one of the participants reported the attempts to escape the constraints imposed by society on her lesbianism that inspired and fostered her migration. In other cases, the migration provides the space and permission to come out at a later date, although the awareness of lesbianism may not have been present what the decision to migrate was made.

I am particularly interested in how this internal process develops for lesbian immigrants because obviously their life choices add further dimensions to the process of identity formation (Espin, 1987a). Lesbian immigrants illustrate vividly the notion that 'identity is not one thing for any individual; rather, each individual is both located in, and opts for a number of differing and, at times, conflictual, identities, depending on the social, political, economic and ideological aspects of their situation' (Bhavnani and Phoenix, 1994: 9).

In short, I am exploring how questions of national identity and sexual identity are determined and negotiated for immigrant and refugee women. Throughout, I will highlight two important aspects of these boundary and border crossings: geography/place and language. Both are invaluable and central to understanding immigrant women's experiences in general and sexuality in particular.

Immigrants are preoccupied with 'geography', the place in which events occur. This preoccupation is connected with life events and how they have been and still are being affected by the vicissitudes of place and geography (Espin, 1992; 1994). This phenomenon/preoccupation has two components. First, the vicissitudes of the actual country of origin give that place almost a sense of unreality in spite of its constant psychological presence in the immigrant's life. The other is what I call a preoccupation with 'what could have been'. This translates into ruminations about what life might have been like (and other 'what if's') had the immigrant remained in the country of origin, migrated to a different country of if the immigration had taken place at another life stage.

Bandura's (1982) discussion on the importance of chance encounters in the course of human development addresses the impact that chance has in determining one's life path. For some, chance encounters and other life events are additionally influenced by uncontrollable historical and political events. While all human beings experience life transitions, people who have been subjected to historical dislocations feel more drastic and dramatic crossroads in their lives. The experience of uprootedness and migration is frequently compounded by two factors: one's status as a member of a minority ethnic group in the host country and/or new gender-role patterns that contradict the norms of the home culture.

Even among immigrants who are fluent in English, the first language often remains the language of emotions. Thus, speaking in a second language may 'distance' the immigrant woman from important parts of herself. Conversely, a second language may provide a vehicle to express the inexpressible in the first language (either because the first language does not have the vocabulary, or because the person censors herself from saying certain 'taboo' things in the first language) (Espin, 1984; 1987b). I contend that the language in which messages about sexuality are conveyed and encoded has an impact on the language chosen to express sexual thoughts, feelings and ideas. Among the participants in the study, two apparently contradictory patterns concerning language have emerged. In several cases, after the completion of an interview or group session conducted in English, participants said that they could have expressed themselves and answered my questions and comments more easily had they done so in their first language. However, the same participants felt that, although it would have been easier to use their first language in terms of vocabulary, it was easier to talk about these topics in English. They believed that feelings of shame would have prevented them from addressing these topics in the same depth had they been talking in their first language. Other participants, on the other hand, said that they could not have had this conversation in their first language because they actually did not know the vocabulary for or were not used to talking about sexuality in their native language. These women had migrated at an earlier age, usually before or during early adolescence, and had developed their knowledge of sex while immersed in English. The women who manifested this second pattern explained that they could not conceive of 'making love in their first language', while those in the first case thought they were unable to 'make love in English'.

Is the immigrant woman's preference for English when discussing sexuality – as I have clinically observed and as the participants in this study express – motivated by characteristics of English as a language or is it that a second language offers a vehicle to express thoughts and feelings that cannot be expressed in the first language? Or does the new cultural context, in which English is spoken, allow more expression of the woman's feelings? Acquired in English, these experiences and expressions may become inextricably associated with the language (as happens with professional terminology acquired in a second language).

I would like to devote the rest of this chapter to sharing some of the participants' stories to illustrate the findings thus far. I have chosen two life stories, in some ways very similar and yet quite different, to illustrate two disparate adaptations to migration. (Of course, names and other identifying information have been changed, although significant facts have been preserved.)

Maritza and Olga are both Cuban. Both migrated to the USA during the 1970s, when they were 22 years of age. Olga comes from a middle-class family, Maritza from a poor working-class family. Maritza had come out as a lesbian in Cuba, when she was 14. She had (and still has) considerable artistic talent as a musician and a poet. From a very early age she identified her lesbianism as a consequence of her artistic talent (in Cuba and other Latin American countries there is a widespread association between artists and homosexuality that is more or less accepted). She was rebellious as an adolescent, frequently came home drunk in the middle of the night, and more or less openly displayed her preference for girls. At the age of 22 she decided that staying in Cuba, considering the government's position in relation to homosexuality, was impossible for her. Although she was completely in favour of the Revolution, and precisely because of her connections with it, she masterminded an escape during a trip sponsored by the Cuban government for young artists to Eastern Europe. Her family continues to live in Cuba. Even after all these years, they strongly disagree with her decision to leave the country. In the USA, Maritza refuses to participate in anything to do with gay/lesbian activism and lives a very private life, although she makes no secret about her sexual orientation. Although she still writes poetry and composes music, she decided that 'poems and songs were not going to feed her' and she actively pursued other professional endeavours. The fact that writing in Spanish did not provide her with a significant audience in an English-speaking country and that writing creatively in English was next to impossible for her were not minor factors in her decision to embark on another career. She is now a psychologist and has a fairly successful private practice. Her love relationships, with very few exceptions, have usually been with Spanish-speaking women. She is one of those who 'cannot make love in English'.

Olga left Cuba because of her disagreement with the Revolution. She came to the United States with her family in one of the 'freedom flights' instituted after 1968. Although she was aware of having had feelings for other girls during her childhood and adolescence, those feelings were never acknowledged then, because lesbianism was 'sinful' and she was deeply Catholic. She came out as a lesbian two years after arriving in the United States and was rather torn by the feeling that what she was doing was 'sinful'. On the other hand, she was very much in love with another Cuban woman she had met in Los Angeles, and they both decided to start attending religious services at Dignity, a group of gay Catholics that had just started. Through her involvement in Dignity, Olga started becoming politically active in gay/lesbian issues, mostly inside the lesbian community, and she continues to be so. She is convinced that she would never have come out as a lesbian had she stayed in Cuba, and believes that the process of acculturation to the USA made it possible for her to come out. She has a master's in social work and works in a government agency mostly servicing a Latino population. She remains mostly 'closeted' in the Latino community out of concern about the impact that revelation of her lesbianism could have for her clients and colleagues alike. However, she and her current partner, a Jewish American woman, have decided to have a child, so she is preparing to come out to her colleagues.

For both of these women, their migration clearly offered certain freedoms that foster the development of a lesbian life. Their political, religious and social affiliations with the lesbian community are very different. Their shared experience is the link between migration and sexual self-expression. Both Maritza and Olga are out to their families and don't find any particular conflict with their family members concerning their lesbianism.

A heterosexual perspective is provided by Jazmin, a serious and reflective Korean woman in her mid-thirties, and Sudha, a second-generation Indian woman. Jazmin came to the USA with her family in early adolescence and moved away from her parents a few years later to attend college. She finds sex education in the USA cold and unromantic, while finding her mother's sex explanations, mumbled in Korean, rather irritating. Her mother's position is that men should never be trusted, particularly Korean men – advice that Jazmin has taken rather seriously by never dating Korean men, much to the paradoxical disgust of her mother. Her mother keeps talking to her daughters about not having sex before marriage and never marrying a white man. For this reason, she has not dared introduce her boyfriend to her parents. According to Jazmin, for a Korean woman to date men outside her ethnic group is seen as proof that she is a whore. Recently, while visiting some friends of her family, an old woman turned her back on her for shaming her mother by not being married to a Korean man yet, when she is already old enough to have several children.

Jazmin is keenly aware of the racist stereotype of Asian women as whores and worries about how she is perceived by strangers when she is affectionate in public with her Caucasian boyfriend. She knows that her race is part of her attractiveness for some white men. She finds it hard to believe that race is not always part of sexuality and vice versa. Although she loves her boyfriend, she believes their racial difference gives him additional power in the relationship besides the power he already has in being a man. Because all of Jazmin's lovers have been white men and because she learned about sex in the USA and acquired her vocabulary about sex in English, she believes that she cannot use Korean words when talking about sex. Jazmin believes that her growing up in the USA rather than in Korea has made her more assertive and better able to enjoy sex than both Korean and white American women. She says many Caucasian women who are rather promiscuous in their sexual behaviour, confess in private that they do not enjoy sex. Korean women living in Korea, on the other hand, do not enjoy sex either and frequently feel 'dirty' because of complying with their husbands' sexual demands.

Sudha, on the other hand, could not imagine not dating a man who was not of Indian parentage. In fact, the only reason she has succeeded in convincing her parents to let her date while going to college, rather than arranging a marriage for her, is that she has had only one boyfriend whose parents come from the same social class and region of India as she. In her words, she intends to have a career and not live a life dedicated to a man, like her silent, passive mother. On the other hand, she finds great pleasure in cooking for her boyfriend and taking care of him in a 'traditional way'. Sudha dresses in Western clothes and so does her mother, although her mother would much rather wear a sari. Sudha's father, however, does not permit his wife to wear a sari. He believes saris are too sexually revealing for Western eyes and, besides, it will make his wife look too traditional and this will contradict his professional status and his image as a 'modern' Indian man (never mind that in the process he is behaving like a traditional husband ordering his wife around). Sudha feels a lot of compassion for her mother, and believes that religion has been her only support in all these long years as an immigrant. Her mother's experience is one of the reasons why she will try to avoid an arranged marriage. On the other hand, she believes that arranged marriages are not necessarily bad.

Both Jazmin and Sudha appear to be more openly in conflict about loyalty to their families and cultural traditions while feeling that those same traditions are frustrating and limiting for them as women. They act 'very American' while expressing feeling of alienation in the midst of a racist society. Probably their immersion in North American society at an earlier age than Olga and Maritza plays a part in their greater internal conflict concerning adaptation to this society.

Regardless of their differences, these four women are in agreement about the difficulties of acculturating to American society. The four of them mention encounters with racism. Jazmin and Sudha, in particular, remember being stereotyped by teachers and classmates alike during their high-school years. At the same time, they believe that living in the USA has opened economic opportunities for them and their families and has opened doors for them as women as well.

Talking to them, and to the other women I have interviewed, has been exciting and enlightening. At this point, I am looking forward to the continuation of this study. I hope that it will help me clarify an important aspect of immigrant women's lives.

I also hope (and have already witnessed) that the focus groups and individual interviews can become a tool to encourage participants to get in touch with their own sexuality and their own erotic power. Speaking of the power of the erotic in women's lives, the late poet Audre Lorde (1984: 57), who was also an immigrant, said:

> Our erotic knowledge empowers us, becomes a lens through which we scrutinize all aspects of our existence, forcing us to evaluate those aspects honestly in terms of their relative meaning within our lives. And this is a grave responsibility, projected from within each of us, not to settle for the convenient, the shoddy, the conventionally expected, nor the merely safe.

She warns us that '[i]n order to perpetuate itself, every oppression must corrupt or distort those various sources within the culture of the oppressed that can provide energy for change' (1984: 53). One such source is women's erotic energy. She encourages all 'women . . . to examine the ways in which our world can be truly different' (1984: 55) and to not be afraid of 'the power of the erotic'. 'Once we know the extent to which we are capable of feeling that sense of satisfaction and completion, we can then observe which of our various life endeavors bring us closest to that fullest' (1984: 54) – a necessary endeavour for immigrant women in the essential process of developing our identities and struggling against the racisms we encounter.

Note

1 This article is based on the author's Keynote Address to the *Feminism & Psychology* Day Conference on 'Challenging Racisms', held at the London Women's Centre on 14 May 1994.

References

Accad, E. (1991) 'Sexuality and sexual politics: Conflicts and contradictions for contemporary women in the Middle East', in C. T. Mohanty, A. Russo and L. Torres (eds), *Third World Women and the Politics of Feminism*. Bloomington: Indiana University Press, pp. 237–50.

Andizian, S., Catani, M., Cicourel, A., Dittmar, N., Harper, D., Kudat, A., Morokvasic, M., Oriol, M., Parris, R. G., Streiff, J. and Setland, C. (1983) *Vivir entre dos culturas*. Paris: Serbal/Unesco.

Aron, A. (1992) 'Testimonio, a bridge between psychotherapy and sociotherapy', in E. Cole, O. M. Espin and E. Rothblum (eds), *Refugee Women and Their Mental Health: Shattered Societies, Shattered Lives*. New York: Haworth Press, pp. 173–89.

Bandura, A. (1982) 'The psychology of chance encounters and life paths', *American Psychologist*, 37: 747–55.

Basch, C. E. (1987) 'Focus group interview: An underutilized research technique for improving theory and practice in health education', *Health Education Quarterly*, 14: 411–48.

Bhavnani, K.-K. and Haraway, D. (1994) 'Shifting the subject: A conversation between Kum-Kum Bhavnani and Donna Haraway, 12 April, 1993, Santa Cruz, California', *Feminism & Psychology*, 4(1): 19–39.

Bhavnani, K.-K. and Phoenix, A. (1994) 'Editorial introduction: Shifting identities shifting racisms', *Feminism & Psychology*, 4(1): 5–18.

Brettell, C. B. and Sargent, C. F. (eds) (1993) *Gender in Cross-cultural Perspective*. Englewood Cliffs, NJ: Prentice Hall.

Cole, E., Espin, O. M. and Rothblum, E. (eds) (1992) *Shattered Societies, Shattered Lives: Refugee Women and Their Mental Health*. New York: Haworth Press.

Denzin, N. K. (1989) *Interpretive Biography*. Newbury Park, CA: Sage.

di Leonardo, M. (ed.) (1991) *Gender at the Crossroads of Knowledge: Feminist Anthropology in the Post-modern Era*. Berkeley: University of California Press.

el Saadawi, N. (1980) *The Hidden Face of Eve: Women in the Arab World*. London: Zed Press.

Espin, O. M. (1984) 'Cultural and historical influences on sexuality in Hispanic/Latin women', in C. Vance (ed.), *Pleasure and Danger: Exploring Female Sexuality*. London: Routledge & Kegan Paul.

Espin, O. M. (1987a) 'Issues of identity in the psychology of Latina lesbians', in Boston Lesbian Psychologies Collective (eds), *Lesbian Psychologies: Explorations and Challenges*. Urbana: University of Illinois Press, pp. 35–55.

Espin, O. M. (1987b) 'Psychological impact of migration on Latinas: Implications for psychotherapeutic practice', *Psychology of Women Quarterly*, 11(4): 489–503.

Espin, O. M. (1992) 'Roots Uprooted: The psychological impact of historical/political dislocation', in E. Cole, O. M. Espin and E. Rothblum (eds), *Refugee Women and Their Mental Health: Shattered Societies, Shattered Lives*. New York: Haworth Press, pp. 9–20.

Espin, O. M. (1994) 'Traumatic historical events and adolescent psychosocial development: Letters from V', in C. Franz and A. J. Stewart (eds), *Women Creating Lives: Identities, Resilience, and Resistance*. Boulder, CO: Westview Press, pp. 187–98.

Espin, O. M., Cavanaugh, A., Paydarfar, N. and Wood, R. (1990a) 'Mothers, daughters, and migration: A new look at the psychology of separation'. Paper presented to the Annual Meeting of the Association for Women in Psychology, Tempe, AZ.

Espin, O. M., Stewart, A. J. and Gomez, C. (1990b) 'Letters from V.: Adolescent personality development in socio-historical context', *Journal of Personality*, 58: 347–64.

Essed, P. (1991) *Understanding Everyday Racism*. Newbury Park, CA: Sage.

Essed, P. (1994) 'Contradictory positions, ambivalent perceptions: A case study of a Black woman entrepreneur', *Feminism & Psychology*, 4(1): 99–118.

Foucault, M. (1981) *The History of Sexuality*. Harmondsworth: Penguin.

Gabaccia, D. (ed.) (1992) *Seeking Common Ground: Multidisciplinary Studies of Immigrant Women in the United States*. Westport, CT: Praeger.

Gold, S. J. (1992) *Refugee Communities: A Comparative Field Study*. Newbury Park, CA: Sage.

Goodenow, C. and Espin, O. M. (1993) 'Identity choices in immigrant female adolescents', *Adolescence*, 28: 173–84.

Jaggar, A. and Bordo, S. (eds) (1989) *Gender/Body/Knowledge*. New Brunswick, NJ: Rutgers University Press.

Josselson, R. and Lieblich, A. (eds) (1993) *The Narrative Study of Lives*. Newbury Park, CA: Sage.

Kaschak, E. (1992) *Engendered Lives*. New York: Basic Books.

Krueger, R. A. (1994) *Focus Groups: A Practical Guide for Applied Research* (2nd edn). Thousand Oaks, CA: Sage.

Laqueur, T. (1990) *Making Sex: Body and Gender from the Greeks to Freud*. Cambridge, MA: Harvard University Press.

Lorde, A. (1984) *Sister Outsider*. Freedom, CA: The Crossing Press.

Marin, B. V., Marin, G., Juarez, R. and Sorensen, J. L. (1992) 'Intervention from family members as a strategy for preventing HIV among intravenous drug users', *Journal of Community Psychology*, 20: 90–7.

Marin, B. V., Tschann, J. M., Gomez, C. A. and Kegeles, S. M. (1993) 'Acculturation and gender differences in sexual attitudes and behaviors: Hispanic vs. non-Hispanic white unmarried adults', *American Journal of Public Health*, 83: 1759–61.

Mishler, E. G. (1986) *Research Interviewing: Context and Narrative*. Cambridge, MA: Harvard University Press.

Morgan, D. L. (1988) *Focus Groups as Qualitative Research*. Newbury Park, CA: Sage.

Morgan, D. L. (ed.) (1993) *Successful Focus Groups*. Newbury Park, CA: Sage.

Nathanson, C. A. (1991) *Dangerous Passage: The Social Control of Sexuality in Women's Adolescence*. Philadelphia: Temple University Press.

Ogundipe-Leslie, 'M. (1993) 'African women, culture and another development', in S. M. James and A. P. A. Busia (eds), *Theorizing Black Feminisms*. London: Routledge, pp. 102–17.

Parker, A., Russo, M., Sommer, D. and Yaeger, P. (eds) (1992) *Nationalisms and Sexualities*. New York: Routledge.

Phizacklea, A. (ed.) (1983) *One Way Ticket: Migration and Female Labour*. London: Routledge & Kegan Paul.

Prieto, Y. (1992) 'Cuban women in New Jersey: Gender relations and change', in D. Gabaccia (ed.), *Seeking Common Ground: Multidisciplinary Studies of Immigrant Women in the United States*. Westport, CT: Praeger, pp. 185–202.

Riessman, C. (1993) *Narrative Analysis*. Newbury Park, CA: Sage.

Ruiz, V. L. (1992) 'The flapper and the chaperone: Historical memory among Mexican–American women', in D. Gabaccia (ed.), *Seeking Common Ground: Multidisciplinary Studies of Immigrant Women in the United States*. Westport, CT: Praeger, pp. 141–57.

Schreier, B. A. (1994) *Becoming American Women: Clothing and the Jewish Immigrant Experience, 1880–1920*. Chicago: Chicago Historical Society.

Silverman, D. (1993) *Interpreting Qualitative Data: Methods for Analysing Talk, Text, and Interaction*. London: Sage.

Stewart, D. W. and Shamdasani, P. N. (1990) *Focus Groups: Theory and Practice*. Newbury Park, CA: Sage.

Strauss, A. L. (1987) *Qualitative Analysis for Social Scientists*. Cambridge: Cambridge University Press.

Tohidi, N. (1991) 'Gender and Islamic fundamentalism: Feminist politics in Iran', in C. T. Mohanty, A. Russo and L. Torres (eds), *Third World Women and the Politics of Feminism*. Bloomington: Indiana University Press, pp. 251–70.

Valverde, M. (1985) *Sex, Power, and Pleasure*. Toronto: The Women's Press.

Woollett, A., Marshall, H., Nicholson, P. and Dosanjh, N. (1994) 'Asian women's ethnic identity: The impact of gender and context in the accounts of women bringing up children in East London', *Feminism & Psychology*, 4(1): 119–32.

Yuval-Davis, N. (1992) 'Fundamentalism, multiculturalism and women in Britain', in J. Donald and A. Rattansi (eds), *'Race', Culture and Difference*. London: Sage, pp. 278–91.

5

From objectified body to embodied subject: A biographical approach to cosmetic surgery[1]

KATHY DAVIS

Cosmetic surgery belongs to the growing arsenal of techniques and technologies for body improvement and beautification which are part of the cultural landscape of late modernity. Women, who are numerically and ideologically the primary objects of these practices, have a long tradition of enduring pain 'for the sake of beauty'. From the practices of foot-binding in ancient China to chemical face peeling and collagen-inflated lips in Southern California, women have been prepared to go to great lengths to meet cultural ideals of feminine shape and countenance.

The recent cosmetic surgery craze seems to be just one more expression – albeit a particularly dramatic and dangerous one – of what has been called the feminine 'beauty system' (MacCannell and MacCannell, 1987). This system includes an enormous complex of cultural beauty practices drawn upon by individual women in order to meet the contemporary requirements of feminine appearance. It is one of the central ways that Western femininity is produced and regulated. Symbolically, Woman as sex is idealized as the incarnation of physical beauty, while most ordinary women are rendered 'drab, ugly, loathsome or fearful bodies' (Young, 1990a: 123).

Feminist scholars have tended to cast a critical eye on women's involvement with 'the beauty system' (Wolf, 1991). Originally, beauty was described in terms of suffering and oppression. Women were presented as the victims of beauty norms and of the ideology of feminine inferiority which they sustain. The beauty system was compared to the 'military-industrial complex' and decried as a 'major articulation of capitalist patriarchy' (Bartky, 1990: 39–40). By linking the beauty practices of individual women to the structural constraints of the beauty system, a convincing case was made for treating beauty as an essential ingredient of the social subordination of women – an ideal way to keep women in line by lulling them into believing that they could gain control over their lives through continued vigilance over their bodies.

In recent years, feminist discourses on beauty as oppression have begun to make way for postmodern perspectives which treat beauty in terms of cultural discourses. The body remains a central concern; this time, however, as a text upon which culture writes its meanings. Following Foucault, the female body is portrayed as an 'imaginary site', always available to be inscribed with meanings. It is here that femininity in all her diversity can be constructed – through scientific discourses, medical technologies, the popular media, and everyday common sense. In this framework, routine beauty practices belong to the disciplinary and normalizing regime of body improvement and transformation. They are part and parcel of the production of 'docile bodies' (Foucault, 1980). The postmodern shift in some contemporary forms of feminist theory enables a sensitivity to the multiplicity of meanings surrounding the female body as well as to the insidious workings of power in and through cultural discourses on beauty and femininity.

If feminists have had reason to be sceptical of the more mundane practices of the beauty system, it is not surprising that they are even more critical of the practice of cosmetic surgery. Cosmetic surgery goes beyond the more routine procedures of body improvement and maintenance, such as leg-waxing, make-up and dieting. Along with the pain and costs, it often involves serious side-effects and the not infrequent chance of permanent maiming, should the operation fail to achieve the desired result. With its expanding arsenal of techniques for reshaping and remaking the body, cosmetic surgery seems to be the site *par excellence* for disciplining and normalizing the female body – for, literally, 'cutting women down to size'.

Within feminist scholarship, it is difficult to view the woman who has cosmetic surgery as an agent who – at least to some extent – actively and knowledgeably gives shape to her life, albeit under circumstances which are not of her own making. Whether blinded by consumer capitalism, oppressed by patriarchal ideologies, or inscribed within the discourses of femininity, the woman who opts for the 'surgical fix' marches to the beat of a hegemonic system – a system which polices, constrains and inferiorizes her. If she plays the beauty game, she can only do so as 'cultural dope' (Garfinkel, 1967) – as duped victim of false consciousness or as normalized object of disciplinary regimes.

While I share this critical assessment of the feminine beauty system and the cultural discourses and practices which inferiorize the female body, it is my contention that it is only part of the story. Moreover, in the case of cosmetic surgery, it is a story which may miss the point altogether. It is my contention that considerably more than beauty is at stake when women place their bodies under the surgeon's knife. Understanding why women have cosmetic surgery requires taking a closer look at how women themselves make sense of their decision in the light of their embodied experiences before and after surgery.

This chapter is based on my research on women's narratives about cosmetic surgery (Davis, 1995). Here I begin with the reasons women provide for having their appearance altered surgically. This is followed by an exploration of the process a woman goes through when she has cosmetic surgery. Then, based on an in-depth analysis of one woman's narrative, I show how far-reaching this transformation is. Cosmetic surgery transforms more than a woman's appearance; it transforms her identity as well. In conclusion, I discuss what a narrative approach to cosmetic surgery means for feminist scholarship on women's involvement in the beauty system.

Surgical stories

My inquiry spanned a period of several years. I conducted narrative interviews (see, for example, Sarbin, 1986; Gergen and Gergen, 1988; 1993; Shotter and Gergen, 1989; Stanley, 1990) with women who had already had, or were planning to have, some kind of cosmetic surgery. In some cases, I was able to talk to women both before and after their operation. The interviews were conducted in my home, or the woman's home and, later, in a clinical setting.

I spoke with women who had undergone many kinds of surgery: from a relatively simple ear correction or a breast augmentation to – in the most extreme case – having the whole face reconstructed. My interest being in surgery 'for looks', I did not talk to women who had reconstructive surgery as a result of trauma, illness or a congenital birth defect.

Since the research was conducted in the Netherlands, where cosmetic surgery was – until recently – included in the national health care package, the recipients came from a variety of socioeconomic backgrounds. Some were professional women or academics, others were cashiers or home helps, and some were full-time housewives and mothers. Some were married, some single, some heterosexual, some lesbian. Some were feminists, others were not. They ranged in age from a 17-year-old school girl whose mother took her in for a breast augmentation (a bit like the ritual of buying the first bra) to a successful, middle-aged business woman seeking a face-lift in order to 'fit into the corporate culture'.

These women told me about their history of suffering because of their appearance, how they decided to have their bodies altered surgically, their experiences with the operation itself, and their assessments of the outcome of the surgery. While their stories involved highly varied experiences of embodiment as well as different routes towards deciding to have cosmetic surgery, the act of having their bodies altered surgically invariably constituted a biographical 'turning point' (Denzin, 1989) – a point from which they could look back at the past to make sense of their decision and forward to the future in order to anticipate what it would mean for them. Their stories were organized in such a way that cosmetic surgery could be viewed as an understandable and, indeed, unavoidable course of action in the light of their particular biographical circumstances.

Being ordinary

None of the women I spoke with had cosmetic surgery for the reasons many of us think they do – that is, having their bodies altered so that they could become more beautiful. Indeed, most displayed a noted reluctance to connect their particular problem to beauty and even went to great lengths to assure me that it had nothing to do with a desire to be more beautiful. This point was driven home in different ways.

Some women assured me that they were not particularly interested in how they looked. 'It was never *my* ambition to be Miss World' or '*I* don't have to be some sex bomb' were frequently heard remarks. They would make disparaging comments about other women who were preoccupied with physical attractiveness. For example, a woman who had her breasts 'lifted' after her second pregnancy explained that she found face-lifts ridiculous because 'wrinkles just go along with getting older'. A face-lift candidate, on the other hand, expressed disbelief that any woman could even consider having her breasts augmented: 'Breasts just don't make that much difference; it's not like your face. That's really important.'

Other women acknowledged that beauty did matter to them and that they, too, worried about how they looked ('what woman doesn't?'). They would produce lengthy lists of their own 'beauty problems'. For example, a woman who had a breast augmentation might complain that she had 'never liked the wrinkles on her face' or had always been much too thin ('a real bean pole'). A face-lift candidate would sigh that she 'would give anything for bigger breasts' or 'really hated having such hairy legs'. Others admitted that they would love to have different bodies – bigger breasts, fewer wrinkles, slimmer thighs. However, they would 'never consider cosmetic surgery for something like that'.

For the most part, the women I spoke with insisted that their reasons for having cosmetic surgery were of another order. In their case, one, and only one, part of their body – this nose or these ears, breasts or hips – was perceived as being too different, too abnormal, too out-of-the-ordinary to be endured. They didn't feel 'at home' in their bodies; this particular body part just didn't 'belong' to the rest of their body or to the person they felt they were. As one woman who had a breast reduction explained: 'I know a lot of people think big breasts are sexy, but I'm just not that kind of person. I'm basically a small-breasted type. That's just who I am.' In short, women who have cosmetic surgery want to be ordinary. They were not primarily concerned with becoming more beautiful; they just wanted to be 'like everyone else'.

Ironically, I did not necessarily share these women's conviction that they were physically abnormal or different. Their dissatisfaction had, in fact, little to do with intersubjective standards for acceptable or 'normal' feminine appearance. For example, when I spoke with women who were contemplating having cosmetic surgery, I rarely noticed the 'offending' body part, let alone understood why it required surgical alteration. From their stories, I could not help but notice that they were generally able to acquire jobs, find partners, produce families and, in general, lead fairly ordinary lives despite their problems with their appearance. In other words, their appearance and the circumstances of their lives did not seem noticeably different from those of women who do not have cosmetic surgery.

While women's bodily imperfections were often invisible to me, their pain was not. As they told me about the devastating effects their appearance had on their sexuality, their relationships, their feelings about themselves and their ability to move about in the world, their distress and anguish were utterly convincing. Despite the differences in the specific circumstances which led to a woman's decision to have cosmetic surgery, the experience of suffering was the common feature of their stories. Thus, cosmetic surgery was presented as the only way to alleviate suffering which had passed beyond what any woman should 'normally' have to endure. It was an extra-ordinary solution for an extra-ordinary problem.

Transforming the body, transforming the self

Cosmetic surgery is not the answer to women's problems with their appearance. A new body does not automatically provide a brand new self. Contrary to media promises of an exciting new life in the fast lanes, the women I spoke with described their lives after surgery as still constrained by the mundane problems and worries that were there prior to the surgery. Nevertheless, they indicated that there had been a transformation. This transformation required a long and often painful process of renegotiating their relationship to their bodies as well as their sense of self.

In order to show just how complex and far-reaching this process was, I will now take a look at one narrative in depth. It is the story of a particular woman, whom I shall call Diana. Her narrative – like the narratives of the other women I spoke with – describes what led to the decision to have cosmetic surgery, how she experienced the operation and its outcome, and how she made sense of the events, after the fact. I have selected her case as a particularly good illustration of the transformation involved in the act of having one's appearance altered surgically. There are several reasons for this. To begin with, Diana had the most extreme and extensive operation. Her entire face was reconstructed, requiring several hours under anaesthesia, intensive care, a lengthy hospital stay, and a long and painful recovery period. Moreover, her face was the object of an operation which, literally, made her unrecognizable – to her friends, her family, and even herself.[2] A physical transformation of such magnitude not only requires some getting used to, but presumably also affects in dramatic ways one's sense of who one is. And, finally, Diana was unusually articulate about her motives for having her face altered. She used the interview as an opportunity to reflect on the implications of her experiences for how she felt about her body, her relations with other people, and her sense of self.

Diana's story

Diana is an attractive schoolteacher in her mid-thirties, married, and the mother of a 9-year-old daughter. Her story begins with the statement that she was a perfectly ordinary-looking child until the age of 10, when her teeth suddenly began to protrude. Braces did not help and she became 'super ugly', the object of constant harassment from other children. Throughout her childhood, she suffered feeling different from everyone else. By the time she reached adolescence, she had found ways to compensate for her appearance, however. She was good at making friends, successful at school and 'knew how to make the most of her looks'. Although she remained secretly convinced that she was an outsider – 'the perennial wallflower' – she also believed that she had managed to overcome her problems with her appearance. However, this turned out to be just the proverbial 'calm before the storm'. Diana's conviction that she had finally got her life under control was rudely shattered during her first teaching job. Confronted with the usual problems of disciplining a class, she realized that she had not after all escaped her problems with her appearance. Her students teased her mercilessly about her face and she discovered painfully that she was back at square one. She was devastated at the realization that she was still trapped by how she looked. What she had known all along was confirmed: her body would determine how her life would be. Unable to escape its constraints, she was doomed to a life of misery.

The turning point in Diana's story was a conversation with a friend who had had cosmetic dentistry done on her teeth. After much deliberation, Diana decided to make an appointment with a plastic surgeon. She described her astonishment at seeing photographs of people who had had cosmetic surgery done on their faces. For the first time, she realized that she was not so different, after all. She was no longer the exception, but one among many others. Paradoxically, cosmetic surgery almost seemed like the 'normal' thing to do.

The operation itself was a terrible ordeal and she had to admit that the outcome had been disappointing at first. She did not look nearly as good as she had expected. Nevertheless, she had no regrets about having taken the step. Her primary feeling was relief. As she explained, no one made comments about her looks any more. She had become unnoticeable, invisible. 'That's the main thing. I've got a nice face now. I'm just ordinary.'

Trajectories of suffering

Diana's initial narrative took the form of a trajectory. This concept has been used by social scientists to describe the process of suffering which people with bodily disorders go through as they lose control over their bodies and then, through their bodies, over their lives (Strauss and Glaser, 1970; Riemann and Schütze, 1991). In a narrative about cosmetic surgery, the trajectory begins with the recipient's realization that something is seriously amiss with her body. Gradually, she comes to see her body as different, as uprooted from the mundane world and its normal course of affairs (Riemann and Schütze, 1991: 345). As she discovers that she cannot do anything to alleviate the problem, she is overcome by hopelessness, despair and, finally, resignation. Her body becomes a prison from which there is no escape.

In this context, cosmetic surgery becomes a way to 'interrupt' the trajectory. By having her face remade, the would-be recipient can obtain, like Diana, an acceptable appearance ('just a nice face'). More importantly, however, cosmetic surgery allows her to extricate herself from what has become a downward spiral. It is no wonder, then, that women who have cosmetic surgery describe their experiences with exhilaration or even triumph. As Diana put it: 'It gave me a kick, like, I'll be damned, but I really did it.'

Interrupting the trajectory is only the beginning, however. Cosmetic surgery stories tend to be recycled – that is, told and retold, sometimes as many as five times in a single interview. Just as the narrator has brought her tale to a triumphant end and has announced that she has told 'everything there is to tell', she will often pick up her story once again.

Let us take a look at another, and somewhat different, rendition of Diana's experience with cosmetic surgery.

Biographical work

Diana spent more than half of the interview going back over her initial narrative and unravelling the implications of the operation for her feelings about her body, her sense of self, and her relationships. It turned out that the operation had not provided a panacea for her problems with her appearance, but had generated some new problems as well.

'Having your whole face redone is not like having a breast reduction where no one notices afterwards that you've had anything done.' Diana described going back to work and feeling as though she were 'on stage'. Her students and colleagues kept glancing at her, obviously unsure whether she was the same teacher they had had before the summer break. While most people eventually recognized her by her voice and movements, others walked right past her. She recalled her shock when one of her colleagues entered the staff room at school and looked straight at her, inquiring 'Do you know where I can find Diana?'. The biggest problem, however, was that she had difficulties seeing her face as her own. She recalled looking in the mirror or seeing herself in photographs and thinking: 'This just isn't *me*.'

The transformation in Diana's appearance had unpleasant repercussions in her relationships as well. Her parents and brothers and sisters were disapproving. They complained that she had gone out and got rid of what they considered to be 'the family face'. Rather than supporting her, they were irritated by or critical of her actions. To her dismay, she found that she had become an outsider and had to rethink her own position within her family.

And, finally, Diana had to make sense of her 'new' appearance in terms of her biography. A good example of how she managed this occurred toward the end of the interview. After explaining how she had come to terms with the reactions of friends and family and could now accept her face, she asked me whether I would like to see some photographs. Opening an old album, she proceeded to show me snapshots of herself, taken before the operation: as a little girl swinging in her backyard, playing with girlfriends, or posing with the family at a birthday party. 'See, there I am – I was the cute, petted, youngest child who everyone adored', she explained. She then showed me pictures of herself as a teenager – 'all arms and legs and with those *terrible* teeth'. Suddenly, she looked up and with a big grin announced that it was 'almost as though I am back to the way I was before, back to the beginning'. '*That* face fit me much better than the one I got later.'

Thus, Diana's narrative reduces the history of suffering which was so central to her initial story to little more than an interlude. Cosmetic surgery is now presented as more than a means to interrupt a trajectory of suffering; it has, more generally, restored continuity to her biography.

Cosmetic surgery is an event which divides a woman's life into a before and an after.[3] This necessitates some biographical reconstruction. Women's life histories before surgery need to be integrated with their accounts of their lives after it. This reconstruction process entails going back over the initial narrative and engaging in 'biographical work' – that is, the activity of recalling, rehearsing, interpreting and redefining which accompanies any event that disturbs, disorders or simply alters a person's biography (Riemann and Schütze, 1991: 33–9).

While such biographical reconstructions were an essential ingredient of women's surgical stories, they proved insufficient for making sense of the transformation they experienced. Cosmetic surgery is a dramatic and unsettling action. It therefore requires justification.

Let me return again to Diana.

Justifications and explanations

As we have seen, much of Diana's story was focused on the importance of cosmetic surgery as a means for ending her suffering and reconstructing her biography. She took the perspective of a protagonist who had a long history of feeling different because of her appearance. Cosmetic surgery was defended as a way to become ordinary or 'just a nice face'. However, in other parts of her narrative, Diana took a different stance altogether.

She explained, for example, that she did not find appearance particularly important, after all. It was only relevant in a very 'superficial' way, but had never made any 'real' difference where her friends were concerned. Or, she recalled how people had warned her that the operation might make her a completely different person, but that this was clearly 'ridiculous'. She insisted that in *her* experience the only thing that had 'really' changed was her looks. Or, she went back to the problem of harassment and described her sympathy for the 'irritation' which 'you naturally feel toward people who are deviant in some way'. After all, she felt the same; *she* didn't like the way she had looked before the operation either. Moreover, she had discovered that she could be just as critical as the next person, when all was said and done. 'It's harmless, you know. That's just the way people are.'

In addition to minimizing the centrality of appearance in her own life,

Diana presented herself as someone with 'the usual beauty problems'. 'Hairy legs – now *that's* a problem, let me tell you.' She laughingly regaled me with stories about the indignities of having legs waxed or brave attempts to 'just let it grow'. Having become an ordinary-looking person herself, she became more critical of the practice of cosmetic surgery. For example, she announced that she would 'love to have bigger breasts or a different nose' but 'where do you draw the line?'. There has to be a limit to 'all that manipulation of your body . . . it's not like just taking an aspirin or something'.

By relativizing an action which would otherwise set her apart from other women who are neither as dissatisfied with their appearance as she had been nor as willing to take such drastic measures to alter it, Diana puts the finishing touch on her transformation. She tells how she had, at long last, re-entered the fold and become 'just like everyone else'.

Justifications, like trajectories and biographical work, are an ongoing feature of women's narratives about cosmetic surgery. Narratives are interspersed with argumentative sequences whereby they will often defend their actions one moment, explaining that cosmetic surgery had been necessary in their particular case, only to do an about-face and distance themselves from the practice. It is almost as if an audience of critics is lurking in the sidelines, just waiting to attack. While these reversals seem at first glance to be contradictory, a closer look at their arguments reveals that they are part and parcel of these women's attempts to come to terms with their transformation.

It is not unusual for individuals to arrange debates with themselves, both 'internally' or in conversations, whereby they advocate a particular position one moment, only to take the other side in the next. This may, indeed, be what thinking is all about – the way we make sense of ourselves and the world around us (Billig, 1987; 1991; Billig *et al.*, 1988). Thus, by both advocating cosmetic surgery and also 'taking the other side', women can work through their own ambivalences about an action which is neither self-explanatory nor unproblematic for them. More generally, their justifications display what makes cosmetic surgery both desirable and problematic, necessary and optional, constraint and choice – all in one.

In conclusion, the in-depth analysis of Diana's story shows that cosmetic surgery entails more than the alteration of a woman's appearance. It also involves the ongoing transformation of her sense of self. Cosmetic surgery is, therefore, an intervention in identity.

Negotiating identity

Identity is a contested concept. Most prosaically, it refers to a person's sense of self. However, by identity, I do not mean the empiricist self of social psychology – that is, that unified core of stable traits which is thought to reside in each individual. Nor do I believe in the autonomous (disembodied and disembedded) self of Enlightenment philosophy. On the contrary, I am treating identity here as a process by which an individual discursively constructs a sense of self. Identity entails the ongoing integration of possible perspectives and versions of who an individual is into a coherent and meaningful life history. These possible versions are not idiosyncratic or individual, but part of a cultural web of narratives available to the individual (see, for example, Benhabib, 1992).

Narratives about cosmetic surgery reveal how the surgical transform-ation of the body both constrains and enables a woman to renegotiate her identity. Just how complex the process of negotiating identity can be is illustrated in the way women tell and retell their stories about cosmetic surgery.

Women's initial narratives present their bodies as ugly, abhorrent or deviant and their sense of self as irrevocably disordered. Their experience of embodiment is organized as a trajectory – a vicious circle or downward spiral. Cosmetic surgery emerges as an eminently plausible and, indeed, necessary course of action. This story of self is about *being different*: 'correcting' this is the *raison d'être* of cosmetic surgery.

In retelling the story, women take a metastance, reflecting on what the transformation of their bodies means for who they were before the operation and who they have become after it. Their narratives weave past and present together, thereby integrating their 'new' body into their life histories. This story of self is about *continuity*: the creation of a coherent biography.

In explaining their reasons and doubts about the surgery, they undertake yet another reconstruction. This time, however, the vantage point of critical distance is adopted. Women deconstruct their initial narratives by showing that, when all is said and done, they are no different from anyone else. This story of self is about returning to *life as usual*: the normalizing of the transformation.

Thus, cosmetic surgery does not only represent the constraints and limitations of femininity. It allows some women to renegotiate their relationship to their bodies and, through their bodies, to themselves. In other words, it opens up possibilities for biographical reconstruction and opportunities for women to redefine their sense of self.

In the final part of this chapter, I return to the feminist critique of the feminine beauty system and the tendency to view women who have cosmetic surgery as the 'cultural dopes' of that system. What are the broader implications of a biographical approach for understanding women's involvement in cosmetic surgery, and what does this mean for feminist scholarship on beauty, femininity and the female body?

Embodied subjects?

Cosmetic surgery is a cultural product of late modernity. It can only emerge as a 'solution' to women's problems with their appearance in a culture where the surgical alteration of the body is both readily available and socially acceptable (Bordo, 1993). It requires a culture with an unshakeable conviction in the technological 'fix' – the endless makability and remakability of ourselves through our bodies. It requires a culture with a dualistic conception of body and mind, in which surgery enables us to enact our intention upon our bodies. And, last but not least, it requires a culture where gender/power relations are typically enacted in and through women's bodies – that is, a culture in which women must negotiate their identities *vis-à-vis* their appearance.

In her phenomenology of female body experience, the feminist political theorist Iris Young (1990b) has argued that the 'typical' contradiction of feminine embodiment in Western highly industrialized societies is the tension between the female subject as embodied agent and the female body as object. On the one hand, a woman is the person whose body it is, the subject who enacts her projects and aims through her body. Like men, women experience their bodies as vehicles for enacting their desires or reaching out in the world. On the other hand, women are objectified bodies. In a gendered social order, they are socially defined through their bodies. Under constant critical surveillance by others, women begin to experience their own bodies at a distance. They view themselves as the objects of the intentions and manipulations of others.

Given this tension in women's bodily experience, it is hardly surprising that many women have difficulties feeling at ease, let alone at home, in their bodies. The body is both the site of their entrapment and the vehicle for expressing and controlling who they are. Although the objectification of the female body is part and parcel of the situation of most Western women and accounts for a shared sense of bodily alienation, women are also agents – that is, knowledgeable and active subjects who attempt to overcome their alienation, to act upon the world themselves instead of being acted upon by others. They may not be able to 'transcend' their bodies as the male subject presumably can,[4] but, as subjects, neither can they ever be entirely satisfied with a rendition of themselves as nothing but a body. Women must, therefore, live a contradiction. As Young (1990b: 144) puts it: 'As human she is a free subject who participates in transcendence, but her situation as a woman denies her that subjectivity and transcendence.'

It is in the context of this disempowering tension of feminine embodiment – the objectification of women as 'just bodies' and the desire of the female subject to act upon the world – that cosmetic surgery must be located.

In conclusion, cosmetic surgery is not simply the expression of the cultural constraints of femininity, nor is it a straightforward expression of women's oppression or of the normalization of the female body through the beauty system. Cosmetic surgery can enable some women to alleviate unbearable suffering, reappropriate formerly hated bodies, and re-enter the mundane world of femininity where beauty problems are routine and – at least to some extent – manageable. It is not a magical solution. Nor does it resolve the problems of feminine embodiment, let alone provide the path to liberation. Cosmetic surgery does, however, allow the individual woman to renegotiate her relationship to her body and, in so doing, construct a different sense of self. In a gendered social order where women's possibilities for action are limited, and more often than not ambivalent, cosmetic surgery can, paradoxically, provide an avenue towards becoming an embodied subject rather than remaining an objectified body.

Notes

1 An earlier version of this paper appeared in the Dutch journal, *Comenius* 3 (1995). I would like to thank Willem de Haan, Hans-Jan Kuipers, and Helma Lutz for their helpful comments.
2 Faces are particularly powerful cultural symbols of identity. The face is alternatively regarded as representing who a person really is ('everyone has the face she deserves') or distorting or disguising a person's true character. This mirror/mask dichotomy belongs to Western notions about the relationship between the face and the self (Strauss, 1969; Synnott, 1990).
3 This is the shared cultural format for cosmetic surgery narratives. It can be found in many contexts: for example, in women's narratives, in the slide show accompanying a surgeon's lecture, in the popular press with its stories of surgical successes and failures, or – more implicitly – in women's more routine beauty practices (see, for example, Smith, 1990, who shows how advertisements for make-up 'work' by requiring women indexically to imagine their present bodies before and how they would look following the application of eyeliner).
4 Obviously, men never fully transcend their bodies. The notion of the disembodied masculine subject – the mind without a body – is, like the objectified female body – the body without a mind – a fiction and has been amply criticized in feminist theory (see, for example, Bordo, 1986; Code, 1991).

References

Bartky, Sandra (1990) *Femininity and Domination. Studies in the Phenomenology of Oppression*. New York: Routledge.

Benhabib, Seyla (1992) *Situating the Self. Gender, Community and Postmodernism in Contemporary Ethics*. New York: Routledge.
Billig, Michael (1987) *Arguing and Thinking. A Rhetorical Approach to Social Psychology*. Cambridge: Cambridge University Press.
Billig, Michael (1991) *Ideology and Opinions. Studies in Rhetorical Psychology*. London: Sage Publications.
Billig, Michael, Condor, Susan, Edwards, Derek, Gane, Mike, Middleton, David and Radley, Alan (1988) *Ideological Dilemmas: A Social Psychology of Everyday Thinking*. London: Sage Publications.
Bordo, Susan (1986) 'The Cartesian masculination of thought', *Signs*, 11: 439–56.
Bordo, Susan (1993) *Unbearable Weight. Feminism, Western Culture, and the Body*. Berkeley: University of California Press.
Code, Lorraine (1991) *What Can She Know? Feminist Theory and the Construction of Knowledge*. Ithaca, NY, and London: Cornell University Press.
Davis, Kathy (1995) *Reshaping the Female Body. The Dilemma of Cosmetic Surgery*. New York: Routledge.
Denzin, Norman K. (1989) *Interpretive Biography*. Newbury Park, CA: Sage Publications.
Foucault, Michel (1980) *Power/Knowledge: Selected Interviews & Other Writings, 1972–1977*. New York: Pantheon.
Garfinkel, Harold (1967) *Studies in Ethnomethodology*. Englewood Cliffs, NJ: Prentice Hall, and Cambridge: Polity.
Gergen, Kenneth J. and Gergen, Mary M. (1988) 'Narrative and the self as relationship', in L. Berkowitz (ed.), *Advances in Experimental Social Psychology*, Vol. 21. New York: Academic Press, pp. 17–56.
Gergen, Mary M. and Gergen, Kenneth J. (1993) 'Narratives and the gendered body in popular autobiography', in R. Josselyn and A. Lieblich (eds), *The Narrative Study of Lives*. London: Sage Publications, pp. 190–214.
MacCannell, Dean and MacCannell, Juliet Flower (1987) 'The beauty system', in Nancy Armstrong and Leonard Tennenhouse (eds), *The Ideology of Conduct*. New York: Methuen, pp. 206–38.
Riemann, Gerhard and Schütze, Fritz (1991) '"Trajectory" as a basic theoretical concept for analyzing suffering and disorderly social processes', in D. R. Maines (ed.), *Social Organization and Social Processes. Essays in Honor of Anselm Strauss*. New York: de Gruyter, pp. 333–57.
Sarbin, Theodore (ed.) (1986) *Narrative Psychology*. New York: Praeger.
Shotter, John and Gergen, Kenneth (eds) (1989) *Texts of Identity*. London: Sage Publications.
Smith, Dorothy (1990) *Texts, Facts and Femininity. Exploring the Relations of Ruling*. London: Routledge.
Stanley, Liz (ed.) (1990) *Feminist Praxis. Research, Theory and Epistemology in Feminist Sociology*. London: Routledge.
Strauss, Anselm L. (1969) *Mirrors and Masks. The Search for Identity*. Mill Valley, CA: The Sociology Press.
Strauss, Anselm and Glaser, Barney (1970) *Anguish: The Case Study of a Dying Trajectory*. Mill Valley, CA: The Sociology Press.
Synnott, Anthony (1990) 'Truth and goodness, mirrors and masks. Part II: A sociology of beauty and the face', *British Journal of Sociology*, 41(1): 55–76.

Wolf, Naomi (1991) *The Beauty Myth: How Images of Beauty Are Used Against Women*. New York: William Morrow and Company, Inc.

Young, Iris Marion (1990a) *Justice and the Politics of Difference*. Princeton, NJ: Princeton University Press.

Young, Iris Marion (1990b) *Throwing Like A Girl and Other Essays in Feminist Philosophy and Social Theory*. Bloomington and Indianapolis: Indiana University Press.

6

The token lesbian chapter

CELIA KITZINGER

It is now well over a decade since Adrienne Rich wrote her classic article, 'Compulsory Heterosexuality and Lesbian Existence' (Rich, 1980). This article

> was written in part to challenge the erasure of lesbian existence from so much of scholarly feminist literature, an erasure which I felt (and feel) to be not just antilesbian but antifeminist in its consequences, and to distort the experience of heterosexual women as well. It was not written to widen divisions, but to encourage heterosexual feminists to examine heterosexuality as a political institution which disempowers women – and to change it . . . I wanted, at the very least, for feminists to find it less possible to read, write, or teach from a perspective of unexamined heterocentricity.
>
> (Rich, 1989)

The 'unexamined heterocentricity' of psychology was one of Adrienne Rich's concerns. Of the four books (then just recently published) which prompted her analysis, three have been enormously influential in feminist psychology: Jean Baker Miller's (1976) *Toward a New Psychology of Women*; Dorothy Dinnerstein's (1976) *The Mermaid and the Minotaur* (published in the UK as *The Rocking of the Cradle and the Ruling of the World*); and Nancy Chodorow's (1978) *The Reproduction of Mothering*. (The fourth, Barbara Ehrenreich and Deirdre English's (1978) *For Her Own Good*, is also very widely quoted in feminist psychology.) Adrienne Rich points out that, in these books, female heterosexuality is simply assumed as the natural, taken-for-granted way to be for most women, obscuring the overt and covert violence with which 'compulsory heterosexuality' is forced upon us through (for example) the socialization of women to feel that male sexual 'drive' amounts to a right, the idealization of hetero-sexual romance, rape, pornography, seizure of children from lesbian mothers in the courts, sexual harassment, and the erasure of lesbian existence from history and culture.

Despite the critiques levelled by Adrienne Rich and other lesbian writers (see, for example, Bart, 1977; 1983), feminist psychologists routinely cite the work of Miller, Chodorow and Dinnerstein without any reference to the heterocentrism of these theories (nor, indeed, to their cultural specificity and racist implications – cf. Rich, 1980; Brown, 1990). Although most feminist psychology books index a few pages (at most) on lesbians, few feature 'heterosexuality' (or any variant thereof) in their indices because women's heterosexuality is the assumed, taken-for-granted topic of the remainder of the book (for example – to look through those on my shelves at the moment – Oakley, 1981; Whitelegg *et al.*, 1982; Midgely and Hughes, 1983; Bernay and Cantor, 1986; Matlin, 1987; Phillips, 1987; Walsh, 1987; Williams, 1987; Chaplin, 1988; Doyle and Paludi, 1991; Hyde, 1991; Basow 1992; Kaschak, 1992). Commonly, feminist psychology books confine lesbians to a single chapter (often devoted to sexuality) and ignore us elsewhere in the book, and this is what I mean by 'the token lesbian chapter'. The 'token lesbian' parallels other forms of tokenism to which feminists have drawn attention: the token black woman (cf. Carby, 1987; Watt and Cook, 1991; Bhavnani and Phoenix, 1994a) and the token disabled woman (cf. Begum, 1992). My title is intended as an ironic reminder of the frequency with which lesbian issues are 'added in' to feminist psychology as a nod in the direction of 'inclusiveness' or 'diversity', while feminist psychology as a whole remains resolutely heterosexual.

For example, in Sue Wilkinson's (1986) edited book, *Feminist Social Psychology: Developing Theory and Practice*, there are 11 chapters, of which one reports 'a study of accounts of lesbianism' (Kitzinger, 1986). The presence of this one chapter apparently served to alleviate the need for even a passing reference to lesbians elsewhere in the book, so that its various authors discuss topics such as adolescent identity development (Beckett, 1986), discourses of 'femininity' (Wetherell, 1986), media images of women (Itzin, 1986), and the transition from school to the job market (Griffin, 1986) as though lesbians simply did not exist. The function of the 'token lesbian chapter' is to 'include' lesbians in a carefully defined and contained space such that our 'inclusion' can be pointed to as justification for our systematic exclusion in the book overall.

It is perhaps not too surprising that token lesbianism was common in feminist psychology ten or more years ago: for further examples, see Frieze *et al.* (1978), Hartnett *et al.* (1979), Rohrbaugh (1981), Matlin (1987),

Walsh (1987) and Williams (1987). All of these books either ignore lesbianism altogether (Hartnett *et al.*, 1979), or limit us to a few subsections or chapters with titles like 'Single Women – Lives of Tragedy or Bliss?' (Rohrbaugh, 1981), 'Lesbian Identity' (Williams, 1987), or 'Is Lesbianism a Sickness?' (Walsh, 1987). Lesbianism is almost invariably relegated to those sections of books which deal with love and sex (see, for example, Matlin, 1987), so that there is nothing about lesbian experience in chapters on 'Childhood and Adolescence', 'Later Adulthood', 'Women and Work', 'Pregnancy, Childbirth and Motherhood' and 'Violence against Women' (all chapter headings in Matlin, 1987) – as though lesbians do not grow up and grow old, do not work, or have children, and are never subjected to violence.

It would be nice to think that all this has changed, and that feminist psychology books published in the 1990s are more aware of lesbian issues. Unfortunately, the improvement (if any) still leaves a lot to be desired. So, for example, in Carol Tavris' (1992) *The Mismeasure of Woman* lesbians are not mentioned at all – although lesbians have undeniably borne the brunt of a great deal of psychological 'mismeasurement'. Similarly, lesbians are not even indexed in Colleen Ward's (1995) book on attitudes towards rape – a book which opens with a story about 'May and her boyfriend David'. In Susan Basow's (1992) book, *Gender, Stereotypes and Roles*, lesbians warrant a mention on only 18 of its 359 pages – and nearly one-third of these are in the chapter on 'Comparisons of Sexual Behaviour'. In Sue Llewelyn and Kate Osborne's (1990) *Women's Lives*, lesbians make an appearance on only two of its 258 pages, once in the 'sexuality' chapter, and once in a discussion of bereavement; there is nothing about lesbians in the chapters on growing up, making and breaking relationships, women and work, or motherhood. Precilla Choi and Paula Nicolson's (1994) volume, *Female Sexuality*, deals with les- bianism in a chapter called 'Sexual Orientation in Women', and lesbians are ignored elsewhere in the book, including, for example, in chapters on postnatal sexuality (Alder, 1994) and sexuality and the menopause (Gannon, 1994) both of which use the terms 'sex' and 'intercourse' interchangeably. In particular, lesbianism is virtually never mentioned in chapters dealing with black women or women of colour: all black women are heterosexual and all lesbians are white – as though we are permitted only *one* dimension of deviance from the white, heterosexual norm.

Finally, clinical psychology has been particularly retrograde in dealing with lesbian issues. So, for example, there are only two passing references to lesbians (a sentence each) in *Gender Issues in Clinical Psychology* (Ussher and Nicolson, 1992). In a feature called 'Clinical Psychology Training: Training in Oppression?' (Williams and Watson, 1991), published in the journal *Feminism & Psychology*, anti-lesbianism is nowhere mentioned (see the commentary on this by Perkins, 1991). A year later, in a chapter on 'feminist practice in therapy', these same clinical psychologists state that 'the value of the scholarly and growing literature focusing on therapy and lesbian women . . . needs to be more widely acknowledged' (Watson and Williams, 1992: 229): they do not, however, draw on this literature in writing their chapter. Their statement functions simply as a token reference to an area which the authors seem to perceive as being beyond the scope of 'feminist' therapy *per se*. In sum, lesbianism is reduced to a 'sexual orientation', which is discussed largely in relation to sex, and which is rarely considered in relation to any other aspect of women's lives.

It is still the case, then, that lesbian existence is erased and that 'unexamined heterocentricity' continues to be the norm within much feminist psychology. In making this case, I do not want to deny the merits of many of the books mentioned above, or to obscure the fact that some of the authors and editors I have cited are themselves lesbians. Rather, I want to ask how it is possible that so much innovative, exciting and politically engaged feminist psychology (some of it authored or edited by lesbians) nevertheless reinscribes and perpetuates the erasure of lesbians. Why is it that, despite decades of lesbian activism, feminist psychology is still plagued by the 'token lesbian chapter'?

In exploring the reasons for the persistence of the token lesbian chapter, I will first set this in the context of the historical relationship between lesbian feminism and heterosexual feminism in the women's movement more generally, before moving on to explore the legacy of this relationship in feminist psychology today.

Lavender Herrings and Achilles' Heels: Lesbians in the Women's Movement

In this section, I consider the historical relationship between lesbian feminism and heterosexual feminism in the women's movement as a whole, showing that, because the patriarchal opposition to feminism has relied to a large extent upon 'lesbian baiting', feminism has remained (by and large) wilfully ignorant of lesbian issues; that it has perpetuated the construction of heterosexuality as normality, therefore prioritizing heterosexual women's rights over lesbian rights; and that it has rejected lesbian theory, accusing us of 'diviseness' and 'silencing' especially in relation to attempts to theorize heterosexuality.

From the nineteenth century onwards, accusations of lesbianism have been used to discredit the women's movement. The patriarchal response to feminism included imputing lesbianism to feminist activists, and concurrently pathologizing lesbianism (cf. Jeffreys, 1985; 1990). Lesbian-baiting has always been a favourite ploy in putting down feminists, and its effect is to recast legitimate political demands as expressions of sexual perversion. For example, at the turn of the century, the psychoanalyst Karl Abraham (1907) wrote:

> In some cases, [women's] homosexuality does not break through to consciousness; the repressed wish to be male is here found in a sublimated form in the shape of masculine pursuits of an intellectual and professional character and other allied interests. Such women do not, however, consciously deny their femininity, but usually proclaim that these interests are just as much feminine and masculine ones. They consider that the sex of a person has nothing to do with his or her capacities, especially in the mental field. This type of woman is well represented in the women's movement of today.

Similarly, the sexologist Krafft-Ebing (1965: 34), writing in 1882, described the lesbian in terms that left no doubt about the link between lesbianism and the burgeoning feminist movement of his day. Feminists attempting to avoid stereotypical 'feminine' behaviours, or struggling for women's rights to education, were slotted into his picture of pathology:

> For female employments there is manifested not merely a lack of taste, but often unskilfulness in them. The toilette is neglected and pleasure found in a coarse boyish life. Instead of an inclination for the arts, there is manifested an inclination and taste for the sciences . . . Perfumes and cosmetics are abhorred. The consciousness of being born a woman, and, therefore, of being compelled to renounce the University, with its gay life, and the army, induces painful reflections.

The effect of these accusations of lesbianism was to scare women back into marriage and conformity with fears of abnormality. At no point during first-wave feminism were lesbians able to rely on support from feminist groups. Lesbian feminist Anna Rühling gave a talk in 1904 entitled, 'What Interest Does the Women's Movement Have in a Solution to the Homosexual Problem?'. She said:

> When we consider all the gains that homosexual women have for decades achieved for the Women's Movement, it can only be regarded as astounding that the big and influential organisations of the movement have up to now not raised one finger to secure for their not insignificant number of Uranian [lesbian] members their just rights as far as the state and society are concerned, and they have done nothing – and I mean not a thing – to protect so many of their best known and most devoted pioneers from ridicule and scorn

as they enlightened the broader public about the true nature of Uranianism.

(Rühling, cited in Lauritsen and Thorstad, 1974)

Lesbian-baiting was also a common ploy in the patriarchal response to the second wave of feminism in the late 1960s. But, this time, lesbian feminists explicitly drew attention to the ways in which lesbianism is routinely used to counter feminist demands:

Lesbianism is the word, the label, the condition that holds women in line. When a woman hears this word tossed her way, she knows she is stepping out of line . . . Lesbian is a label invented by the Man to throw at any woman who dares to be his equal, who dares to challenge his prerogatives . . .

(Radicalesbians, 1969)

As Mary (1970) wrote, in a widely circulated leaflet of the time, 'The accusation of being a movement of lesbians will always be powerful if we cannot say "Being a lesbian is good." Nothing short of that will suffice as an answer.' But despite these lesbian-authored analyses of the power of lesbian-baiting to discredit feminists, the feminism of the 1960s and 1970s (like first-wave feminism) was embarrassed by the presence of lesbians, and was prepared neither to fight for lesbian rights nor to consider developing feminist theory and practice from lesbian perspectives.

Many (heterosexual) feminists at the time were, of course, aware of the extent to which accusations of lesbianism served to discredit the women's movement. However, whereas lesbian feminists believed that the most appropriate response to this was to claim lesbianism as a positive identity for women, the women's movement relied instead upon repeated assertions that most feminists were heterosexual. Two lesbians who were involved in both lesbian and feminist activism at the time reported that 'many Feminists and some Lesbian Feminists were telling outsiders that there were no Lesbians in the Women's Movement'. Privately they referred to Lesbians as 'The Achilles Heel' of the movement' (Abbott and Love, 1972: 107–8, 110). Implicit in this phrase is the recognition, by feminists, of the power of lesbian-baiting in defining the feminist agenda.

At about the same time, Betty Freidan described lesbians as the 'lavender herring', meaning that lesbian issues were a distraction from the real business of liberating women. She spoke out publicly against lesbians at meetings of the (US) National Organization of Women (NOW), accused the New York Chapter of NOW of being run by lesbians, and was reported in the press as saying that lesbians were infiltrating the organization as part of a CIA plot to discredit feminism. Lesbian feminist novelist Rita Mae Brown, who had joined the NOW in 1969, resigned a year or so later, saying 'Lesbianism is the one word which gives the New York NOW executive committee a collective heart attack' (quoted in Abbott and Love, 1972: 112).

Not surprisingly, many lesbians involved in second-wave feminist campaigns were angered by feminism's refusal to address lesbian concerns. Although lesbians were at the forefront of many feminist campaigns (including those most likely to benefit heterosexual women, such as demanding child care for women at the worksite, founding battered women's shelters and advocating legal abortion), as soon as these campaigns achieved any success lesbians were often asked to keep quiet about their lesbianism:

> Once the grassroots organizing phase is over, lesbians are often fired or pressured to quit, or else they leave in protest. The first paid director is often a heterosexual woman and lesbian issues are omitted from the organization's publicity in order not to offend the media or potential granting agencies. When lesbians have stayed in these organizations, they have kept quiet about their own needs so as not to offend the membership or else because they believe that that organisation's goals are more pressing or legitimate than those of lesbians.
>
> (Rothblum, 1992: 273)

Reflecting on the extent to which lesbian feminists have subordinated lesbian agendas to those of heterosexual feminists, JoAnn Loulan says:

> We've always been co-opted into the feminist movement. I mean, when was the last time you knew a lesbian who needed an abortion? Gimme a break! . . . Why are we fighting for straight women's rights to fuck men and have abortions? I feel like we've been the wives to the feminist movement . . . When are we going to fight for ourselves? . . . We run the women's centres and the battered women's shelters and the foundations, and we don't come out and we don't kiss in front of their fund-raisers . . . I said to the organizers of the abortion march, 'Why should I support you?' And they said, 'This is to do with women's right to choose.' And I said, 'What does it have to do with lesbians?' And they said, 'Lesbians get the trickle-down effect.' And I said, 'Show me. Show me the trickle. I want to see one law that has a thing to do with lesbians. I have a right to take birth control? Thank you, I have my own form of birth control that won't give me cancer.'
>
> (Hall *et al.*, 1992: 13–14)

In response to feminism's refusal to engage with lesbian issues, many lesbian feminists kept quiet and continued to work with heterosexual feminists. Others joined the mixed lesbian and gay movement, focusing on their oppression as (female) homosexuals, rather than as (lesbian) women. Yet others separated from the mainstream women's liberation movement and set up lesbian-focused groups like Radicalesbians, Gutter Dyke Collective, Lesbian Menace and The Furies. Although heterosexual feminists had made clear their refusal to address lesbian issues as a central part of feminist politics, as soon as lesbians created groups separate from them, these lesbians were accused of being 'divisive'. Divisiveness is an accusation routinely levelled at lesbians who express a desire for an autonomous movement (Claudie *et al.*, 1981:473). As lesbian theorist Charlotte Bunch (1975) has written:

> It is not lesbianism (women's ties to women) but heterosexuality (women's ties to men), and thus men themselves, which divides women politically, and personally. This is the 'divisiveness' of the lesbian issue to the women's movement. We won't get beyond it by demanding that lesbians retreat, politics in hand, back into the closet.

Whereas women involved in the mainstream of the women's liberation movement tended to downplay the existence of lesbianism, and to emphasize the ways in which they were attempting to reform and improve heterosexuality, these splinter groups (composed predominantly of lesbians) developed far-reaching critiques of heterosexuality *per se*. Although many heterosexual feminists responded with fear and defensiveness, the critiques which emerged from such groups generally tried to include *all* women in the struggle against heterosexuality as an institution:

> We are less concerned with whether each woman personally becomes a lesbian than with the destruction of heterosexuality as a crucial part of male supremacy. Lesbians have been the quickest to see the challenge to heterosexuality as necessary to feminism's survival. However, straight feminists are not precluded from examining and fighting against heterosexuality as an ideology and institution that oppresses us all. The problem is that few have done so.
>
> (Myron and Bunch, 1975:12)

For heterosexual feminists the suggestion that they might analyse and struggle against heterosexuality as an institution causes excruciating difficulties if only because, as Tamsin Wilton (1995) points out, it is difficult for the majority of women in heterosexual relationships to enter wholeheartedly into a critique of patriarchal relations of power which implicates *their* men. Probably, as Carol Anne Douglas (1990:167) says, *no* critique of heterosexuality, however politely worded (and of course, they were not all politely worded) would be acceptable to most heterosexual feminists.

It is important to remember, though, that the so-called 'lesbian–heterosexual' split was not so much a split between women of different sexual identities, as between those with different politics:

> It was a lesbian/lesbian split, with radical feminist lesbians on one side insisting that lesbianism was necessary for the feminist revolution, and socialist feminist lesbians on the other worrying about being too threatening to heterosexual women, often referred to as 'most women', or 'the women out there' . . . (Thompson, 1993: 395; see also Alderson, 1981)

Lesbians (and, to a lesser extent, heterosexual women) took up – and continue to take up – positions on both sides of the divide. The debate is about the extent to which lesbianism is an identity worth organizing around politically (as opposed to being simply a sexual preference or choice of lifestyles); and about the extent to which it is possible to create specifically *lesbian* theories and politics (as opposed to purportedly generic 'women's'). It is not simply an argument about whether or not all women should be lesbians – although it has often been seen as such, and this has certainly been *part* of it (cf. Onlywomen Press, 1981). It is also an analysis of the meanings of lesbianism and heterosexuality under patriarchy.

Although, by the mid-1970s, feminists were optimistically describing the 'lesbian–straight split' as history, some lesbians also warned that unless we learned from it, we would be doomed to repeat it (cf. Bunch, 1975). And, indeed, it surfaced again in the 1980s in the UK with the publication of the Leeds Revolutionary Feminist paper on 'the case against heterosexuality', and the responses to it (Onlywomen Press, 1981), and again in the 1990s – and specifically in relation to psychology – with the publication of *Heterosexuality: A 'Feminism & Psychology' Reader* (Wilkinson and Kitzinger, 1993a).

In sum, the continuing persistence of 'the token lesbian chapter' in feminist psychology is in part the legacy of broader problems within feminism as a whole. First, feminism has remained ignorant of lesbian issues and lesbian oppression. Second, it perpetuates the construction of heterosexuality as 'normal' for women, such that lesbian rights come to be viewed as a damaging diversion from generic (heterosexual) women's rights. Third, mainstream feminism has reacted with anger to any attempts to *theorize* heterosexuality, or to develop feminist theory and practice from lesbian perspectives. I will now explore the ways in which these problems continue to play themselves out in feminist psychology today.

The privilege of ignorance

As recently as the mid-1990s, the author of a *Lesbian Studies* primer reports: 'My experience has been that most heterosexual feminists remain in wilful ignorance of both lesbian oppression and the nature of heterosexual prejudice' (Wilton, 1995: 89). In this section I illustrate the operation of this 'ignorance' in psychological writings and suggest that it is in some sense a deliberate exercise of power: heterosexual feminists do not believe they *need* to know about lesbians' oppression as lesbians in the same way that they believe they need to know about their own oppression as women; and in not knowing about lesbian oppression, they perpetuate it.

Knowledge is not the only form of power: ignorance competes with it as a means of defining what is important, and on what terms knowledge itself can be constructed. As Marilyn Frye (1983: 119) says, 'ignorance is not a simple lack, absence or emptiness, and it is not a passive state . . . To begin to appreciate this one need only hear the active verb "to ignore" in the word "ignorance".' Ignorance is something in which many people have vested interests, and consequently take care to maintain. For example, the laws governing rape encourage ignorance in so far as 'it matters not at all what the raped woman perceives or wants just so long as the man raping her can claim not to have noticed (ignorance in which male sexuality receives careful education)' (Sedgewick, 1993: 24). The lesbian philosopher Sarah Lucia Hoagland (1988) offers a discussion of the ethics of invoking ignorance as an 'excuse' for oppressive behaviour, and shows how, within lesbian communities, ignorance as an 'excuse' has been challenged around major issues such as classism, racism, anti-Semitism, able-bodyism and ageism. Nevertheless, heterosexual feminists in general, and heterosexual feminist psychologists in particular, continue to maintain an astonishing ignorance about lesbian issues.

Equally, of course (though less salient in the context of this chapter), it is true that gay men have (in general) wielded the power of their own ignorance about women's oppression and about feminist struggles to end it. Lesbians, both within and beyond psychology, have always been forced to choose between aligning ourselves with non-lesbian women as part of feminist campaigns, or aligning ourselves with male homosexuals as part of lesbian and gay campaigns. For lesbian feminists, the selective ignorance of both camps has made this choice fraught with difficulties, and it has certainly not been the case (despite the heterosexism of feminism) that we have always chosen the gay movement. For example, at a time when feminists were challenging traditional stereotyped notions of 'masculinity' and 'femininity', gay psychologists were busily proving that gay men were as 'masculine' and lesbians as 'feminine' as their heterosexual counterparts; and while feminists continue to challenge arguments based on biology or 'nature' as blatant political rhetoric, gay psychologists continue to produce evidence for the biological bases of homosexuality (cf. Kitzinger, 1987; 1995). Lesbian analyses of gay men's apparent 'ignorance' of feminist issues have focused upon the extent to which this ignorance has enabled them to pursue and promote their own interests as *men* and to continue oppressing lesbians.

Feminist psychology has constructed itself in careful ignorance of developments in lesbian and gay psychology, and often misrepresents psychological work in this area. For example, it is common for feminist psychologists – when they make any reference to lesbians at all – to explain that, as feminists, they, unlike mainstream psychologists, do not consider lesbianism to be a form of pathology. It sometimes seems to be the case that feminist psychologists consider that simply by *acknowledging* the existence of lesbians, and by affirming our 'normality', they are doing something truly radical – something very much at odds with mainstream psychology. For example, there is only one reference to lesbians in feminist psychologist Jane Ussher's (1989) book on *The Psychology of the Female Body*: this single reference (Ussher, 1989: 101) asserts that 'women who have chosen a lesbian way of life are seen as deviant', and goes on to cite psychiatric evidence that 'there is no evidence that children socialized in a lesbian relationship suffer from any ill effects'. In *Half the Human Experience* (Hyde, 1991) the section called 'the lesbian experience' is illustrated with a photograph of two women hugging, captioned: 'Lesbians can and do form satisfying long-term relationships'. In making such statements which reinforce the 'normality' of lesbians as mothers and as couples, these authors may well be addressing the assumed prejudices of their student readers, but they are doing nothing explicitly 'feminist', nothing to differentiate themselves from contemporary main-stream psychological theory and practice on lesbian issues. The view of homosexuality as pathology is not – and has not been for a long time – the official view of the discipline. In 1973 the American Psychiatric Associ-ation removed homosexuality *per se* as a category from its *Diagnostic and Statistical Manual*, and in 1975 the American Psychological Association (APA) adopted the official policy that homosexuality *per se* does not imply any kind of mental health impairment, urging mental health pro-fessionals to take the lead in removing the stigma of mental illness that had long been associated with gay male and lesbian sexual identities. It is now unusual for explicitly anti-lesbian and anti-gay comments to be made by representatives of psychological bodies, or by acknowledged experts in the field, and it is rare to find overt reference, within Anglo-American psychological writing, to homosexuality as pathology (Morin and Roth-blum, 1991). Of course there are odd exceptions, and individual psychologists have recently displayed absurdly anachronistic heter-osexist prejudices (see, for example, Davis, 1995; Hamilton, 1995), but in treating these ideas as the norm, feminist psychologists flatter themselves that they have developed a distinctive position on lesbian and gay issues, when in fact they are doing little more than reflecting what are now mainstream views. As Corinne Squire (1989: 39–40) points out, 'as conventional psychological studies of lesbians become more tolerant, and egalitarian-feminist psychological studies of these subjects become more psychological, it is increasingly difficult to distinguish between the two'.

Moreover, feminist psychologists sometimes engage in a carefully orchestrated display of ignorance about recent work in lesbian and gay psychology. Within this field (recent texts include Gonsiorek and Weinrich, 1991; Garnets and Kimmel, 1993a; Greene and Herek, 1994; D'Augelli and Patterson, 1995), research on lesbian issues has moved well beyond simply the repeated demonstration of our 'normality': key topics of current concern include, for example, the challenges of lesbian adolescence, mid-life, and old age; parenting issues; anti-lesbian discrimination; cultural diversity; bisexuality; and questions of 'choice', flexibility and flux in sexual identities. Feminist psychologists repeatedly assert that they are ignorant of this research. For example, in an edited collection of essays on *Motherhood* (published as part of a book series on 'Gender and Psychology', subtitled 'Feminist and Critical Perspectives') there is only one indexed reference to lesbians, which reads (implausibly enough!) 'there has been little research on lesbian mothers' (Phoenix *et al.*, 1991: 227). This simply is not true: even prior to 1990 (when the book would presumably have gone to press), entire books had been devoted to the topic (among them Pies, 1985; Bozett, 1987; Pollack and Vaughn, 1987) and articles on lesbian mothering were published in such key journals as *American Psychologist* (Falk, 1989), *Psychological Reports* and *Women and Therapy* (Gibbs, 1988; Rohrbaugh, 1988) as well as elsewhere in psychology (see the reference list in Patterson, 1995, for dozens of pre-1990 references).

Ignorance is a form of power which enables writers to 'leave out' lesbians on the grounds that nothing is known about us. Ignorance is not simply a passive innocence, and oppression is not ended simply by providing information – indeed, the demand that 'we' teach 'them' about our oppression may constitute one form of that oppression. Analyses of the ways in which this works have been developed within writing on issues of race and ethnicity. So, for example, Haideh Moghissi (1994: 228) describes the grievance procedure she filed against a Canadian university which had rejected her application for a post:

> It was quite astounding to see the degree of ignorance apparently held by these senior academics about basic concepts and facts relating to racism and ethnocentrism. So we had to spend much

time defining racism and explaining what constitutes racist perceptions and practices.

Similarly, Irene Klepfisz (1982: 46) says: 'I find I am preoccupied not with countering anti-Semitism, but with trying to prove that anti-Semitism exists'. The demand to 'explain' racism or anti-Semitism or anti-lesbianism, to prove that these exist, and to define their principles of operation, functions to keep attention focused on the agenda set by those 'in ignorance' of racism, or anti-Semitism, or anti-lesbianism. In sum, ignorance (as much as knowledge) is a form of power, and the mobilization of ignorance has been used to construct oppressive agendas and to 'ignore' the pressing concerns of 'knowledgeable' groups: feminist psychology is implicated in this process.

'Including' lesbians: Constructing heterosexual normality

The supposedly generic woman of most feminist psychological theorizing turns out, in fact, to be white, Western, middle-class, able-bodied and heterosexual: the rest of us are 'inessential' women (Spelman, 1988). In many feminist psychology books, lesbians are 'included' only as items in a list of 'inessential' identities, flagged up under headings such as 'Diversity' or 'Difference'. This, of course, serves only to illustrate the persistent assumption of heterosexuality from which lesbians 'differ'. For example, in a book on *Feminist Groupwork* (Butler and Wintram, 1991: 76) lesbians appear under the heading 'Differences between women' as part of a listing including 'age, disability, race and ethnicity', and in a book on *Motherhood* (Phoenix *et al.*, 1991: 226), lesbians are mentioned in a section headed 'Differing Family Circumstances'. As Spelman (1988: 182) points out, the so-called 'problem of difference' is actually a reflection of 'the problem of privilege':

> One group of women have taken their own situation to be that of 'women in general', and now, in order not to have an account of 'the condition of woman' that is as exclusionary as masculinist accounts of 'the situation of man', differences among women must be discussed.

Feminist psychology's repeated affirmations that we must take 'differences' in sexual identity between women into consideration, that we must hear the voices of many different women (including lesbians), and that we must include more of the experiences of lesbians, are all attempts by 'insiders' to bring in 'outsiders' by employing the language that reflects the outsiders' outside status. Lesbians are invited to join heterosexual feminist psychology in order to make it more 'inclusive', on the terms set by heterosexual feminist psychologists.

The terms on which lesbians are invited to join in heterosexual feminist psychology are also quite limiting. One of these terms is what Esther Rothblum (1992; following Spender, 1989) calls the '20 per cent rule'. It refers to 'the fact that whenever the contribution of a minority group begins to constitute more than 20 per cent of an organization's membership or actions, the organization is viewed as being "overrun" by that minority group'. Dale Spender (1989) uses the example of book review space devoted to books by female authors in mainstream newspapers. When this space approaches 20 per cent, book review editors estimate that more space is devoted to women than to men (that is, they erroneously believe that over 50 per cent of space is devoted to female authors), and that men are being denied their fair share of reviews.

The 20 per cent rule (or a variant of it) surfaces again in relation to lesbian issues in feminist psychology. While a token lesbian presence is considered very important, anything more than tokenism is construed as a 'takeover'. So, for example, the heterosexual feminist psychologist Lynne Segal (1994: 341) has criticized the journal *Feminism & Psychology* for what she sees as its 'consistent endorsement of political lesbianism and an attack upon heterosexual feminists and heterosexuality'. This is an extraordinary statement for a number of reasons, not least because Lynne Segal is herself a member of the International Advisory Group for the journal, and has been asked on many occasions from 1991 (when the journal first appeared) onwards to submit her own work on heterosexuality for publication in the journal. (She has failed to submit anything to date.) Furthermore, an analysis of the first 19 issues of *Feminism & Psychology* (all those available at the time of writing) does not bear out this charge. These include two Special Issues, one on heterosexuality (Kitzinger *et al.*, 1992) and one on 'race'/ethnicity (Bhavnani and Phoenix, 1994a); of the 237 pieces (excluding book reviews) published in the remaining 17 issues of the journal, 23 (10 per cent) explicitly address lesbian issues – and exactly the same number explicitly address issues of 'race'/ethnicity. If we add to the former those pieces which address heterosexuality as an explicit topic (as opposed to those which simply *assume* heterosexuality), the percentage rises to 14 per cent. (Although, contrary to Lynne Segal's claims, some of the pieces which constitute this 14 per cent are explicitly supportive of heterosexual feminism and heterosexuality, among them Hollway, 1993; Frith, 1994; Van Every, 1995).

In view of these figures, it is perhaps surprising that lesbians and black women are apparently satisfied with this level of coverage. Yet Kum-Kum Bhavnani and Ann Phoenix (1994b: 14) write in their introduction that, while 'focusing on these areas in one edition can seem to be a token gesture', they do not believe that *Feminism & Psychology* is engaged in tokenism. Instead, they say:

the sustained interrogation of a topic such as racism can also serve to highlight its importance and signal to readers and potential contributions the weight a journal gives to this area. We would suggest that this is the case for *Feminism & Psychology*.

Within psychology, then, both lesbians and black women seem to be satisfied with about 10 per cent of the available resources – indeed, there is a general consensus in British feminist psychology that lesbian issues are somehow *over*-represented in the journal, indicating that 14 per cent is definitely overdoing it (at least as far as heterosexual feminist psychologists are concerned). Perhaps, for lesbian issues at least, the 20 per cent rule can be amended to the 10 per cent rule.

The 'inclusion' of lesbians as representatives of 'diversity' among women has also led (at least in the context of British psychology) to accusations of 'divisiveness' when lesbians have wanted more than simply 'inclusion' in heterosexual women's groups. This issue recently surfaced in a particularly painful way in relation to a proposal from a group of lesbian psychologists for a Psychology of Lesbianism section within the British Psychological Society (BPS). (A BPS 'section' is equivalent to an APA 'division'). The American Psychological Association has a division for the study of Psychology of Women (Division 35), approved in 1973, and a division for the study of lesbian and gay issues (Division 44), approved in 1984. Characteristically, British psychology has lagged behind. The BPS did not approve the Psychology of Women Section (POWS) until 1987, and there is still no formal grouping within the BPS for the study of lesbian or gay issues. Ironically, an important reason why there is not (and probably now never will be) a Psychology of Lesbianism section, is because POWS refused to support the proposal for this section (see Ussher, 1991a).

Just as lesbians were always involved in feminist activism more generally, so lesbians were also part of the early leadership in both research and professional organizing in 'psychology of women'. Pioneers in the psychology of women fought long and hard for their perspective (which was initially ridiculed as 'unscientific' and as self-interested pleading) in order to gain an institutional foothold in their professional organizations (cf. Wilkinson and Burns, 1990). A focus on lesbian issues would not have been helpful in seeking acceptability within mainstream psychology, and any interest the early campaigners might have had in lesbian issues was subordinated to the 'broader' aim of presenting 'psychology of women' on terms acceptable to the BPS. This meant that some 'out' lesbians (among them Kitzinger, 1990) felt alienated from 'psychology of women' from the outset.

The proposal for a Psychology of Lesbianism section arose out of the recognition that the 'inclusion' of lesbian issues within 'psychology of women' would always be subject to tokenism: as one of the North American supporters of the section proposal said at the time, 'a separate section or organization on lesbian issues is necessary in order to avoid the "20 percent rule"; that lesbian issues will not be addressed more than occasionally by women's groups' (Rothblum, 1992: 271). Although at least two of the proposers for the Psychology of Lesbianism section (Celia Kitzinger and Sue Wilkinson) had served on the POWS committee and were active within feminist psychology, POWS initially refused its support for a Psychology of Lesbianism section. Those of us who acted as the official proposers for the Psychology of Lesbianism section were appalled that the POWS committee, as a group of women who had struggled hard to gain formal representation within the BPS, should have refused to support a group of lesbian psychologists seeking similar representation – particularly as much of mainstream psychology's opposition to our proposed section paralleled its earlier opposition to POWS. In addition to outright prejudice and clearly articulated religious objections, opponents argued that our proposal was 'political' not 'scientific', and that it focused on a small topic marginal to the discipline which could readily be subsumed by other sections (see, for example, BPS, 1990; Schwieso, 1991). As stated by the Chair of the BPS Special Group in Counselling Psychology (the only BPS subsystem formally to support our proposal): 'We are sorry that the Psychology of Women Section has seen fit to oppose the proposal using the very same arguments that were used to oppose its own establishment' (Taylor, 1991).

Feminist psychologists on the POWS committee argued that the proposed Psychology of Lesbianism section would damage their own section by diverting and dividing women's energies (see Ussher, 1991b). The committee argued that a Psychology of Lesbianism section was unnecessary, and that there was no need for a separate forum devoted to lesbian issues, because lesbian concerns could be 'included' within psychology of women generally. Jane Ussher, then Chair of the POWS Committee, wrote, in a letter to the BPS Scientific Affairs Board, that 'it would be desirable that the aims of the [proposed Psychology of Lesbianism] Section could be accommodated and facilitated within the present structure of the Psychology of Women Section' (Ussher, 1991a). The POWS refusal to support the Psychology of Lesbianism section proposal did not come just from particular individuals: as Janet Sayers (1992: 269), who succeeded Jane Ussher as Chair of POWS, points out, the decision was made as a result of 'due democratic process', following first a POWS Committee meeting (10 May 1991) and a subsequent AGM (13 July 1991) at which POWS members were asked whether they wanted the Committee to reconsider its decision: 'an overwhelming majority voted against this proposal' (Sayers, 1992: 269). At the following POWS

Committee meeting (7 September 1991), the Committee, still declining to support an autonomous Psychology of Lesbianism section, suggested as 'a possible way out of the present impasse' the formation of a lesbian 'subsystem within POWS' (Sayers, 1992: 270). In part as a consequence of the lack of support from POWS, the BPS subsequently turned down the section proposal at its meeting of 12 October 1991 (and POWS has never pursued the idea of a lesbian subsystem within its own section). The lesbian initiative in British psychology was effectively sabotaged (under the banner of 'including' us within psychology of women more generally), and feminist psychologists in general must accept some of the blame for their active collusion with anti-lesbianism.

Eventually, after persistent lesbian campaigning (including the disruption of a POWS annual conference) the POWS Committee, with Halla Beloff as the new Chair, reversed its earlier decision in a dramatic 'U-turn' (Beloff, 1993) and has since supported the Psychology of Lesbianism (and subsequent Lesbian and Gay Psychology) section proposals. What is illustrated by the early relationship between POWs and lesbian psychology, however, is the extent to which feminism (within as well as beyond psychology) is willing to subordinate the interests of lesbians to those of 'women' more generally, and to stand in explicit opposition to our proposals, preferring to 'include' us within their groups (on their terms) rather than offering us support in constructing our own.

Accusing lesbians: Rejecting lesbian theory

Feminist psychologists in the UK continue to ignore or to downplay lesbian issues, and to accuse lesbians of being 'divisive' whenever we organize separately from feminist psychology, whether in proposing an autonomous BPS section or in trying to develop specifically *lesbian* theory derived from lesbian perspectives. For example, as we have seen, feminist theory tends to assume heterosexuality as a given, developing analyses with women's (and men's) heterosexuality as a taken-for-granted, but never explicitly addressed, substrate. Lesbian and gay psychology, by contrast, points to 'the fallacy of assuming that everyone is heterosexual, or that all important research questions shall be defined from the point of view of heterosexuals' (Garnets and Kimmel, 1993b: 600). Yet attempts by lesbian feminist psychologists to theorize heterosexuality have met with fear, hostility and defensiveness. Within feminist psychology, as within feminism more generally, feminists have reacted with particular 'anger and vituperation' (Jeffreys, 1994: 307) to any attempt to theorize or to problematize heterosexuality.

After publication of a book on *Heterosexuality* (Wilkinson and Kitzinger, 1993a), my co-editor and I were routinely attacked for being 'divisive' and for 'excluding' or 'silencing' heterosexual women: two common complaints were that we should have ensured the collaboration of a *heterosexual* co-editor for the book, and that the questions we suggested in our Call for Contributions should have been less 'confrontational'. These charges were made repeatedly by feminists who attended our conference presentations on heterosexuality, especially at the annual conference of the BPS Psychology of Women Section in 1993 (Wilkinson and Kitzinger, 1993b; subsequently published as Kitzinger and Wilkinson, 1994), where we were literally shouted down in the question period by women asserting that they had been silenced.

Initially, we reacted to the charge of 'silencing' with incredulity, and pointed to the fact that (despite the lesbianism of the editors) the book we had edited included contributions by well over 20 heterosexual feminists, who, far from being *silenced*, had thereby been given the opportunity to *speak*. Later, we began to understand that the accusation of 'silencing' cannot, of course, be taken literally but rather reflects heterosexual feminists' assumption of their right not just to speak as heterosexuals, but to speak on their own terms, and in relation to their own agenda as heterosexuals. In preparing the Call for Contributions from our perspective as radical lesbian feminists, and in editorializing the book, we had required heterosexual feminist writers (and readers) to engage with heterosexuality from the perspective of an agenda not of their own choosing – and it is from this unaccustomed sense of having to address a set of questions drawn from a *lesbian* rather than a *heterosexual* perspective that the experience of being 'silenced' derives. The feminist psychologist Mary Gergen (1993: 62), for example, describes her 'fear' at receiving an invitation from me to write on this topic:

> We are aware of Celia Kitzinger's writings, her public statements, and have some notions of her views on the oppressiveness of the heterosexual world. Is this a witch trial, or a trial by witches? Are we being rounded up for confessions in a public forum? For well-rounded feminist 'heterosexuals' this route may be open to us; confess our culpabilities; open our chapters of crime; commit ourselves to reform. . . . Yet, this path does not go very far. Only the judges and the prisoners have changed places. The oppressed become oppressors; the oppressors are oppressed.

Heterosexual feminism's resistance to and anxiety about theorizing heterosexuality is partly explained by Maia Ettinger's (1994) cogent analysis. As she says, 'an interesting thing often happens when people of color or queers speak up in class: everyone else feels silenced'. She describes how, after a lecture by Barbara Smith at Yale's Afro-American Cultural Centre, many members of the audience raised their hands to explain how excluded they felt because Smith's lecture, while broad in scope, was addressed first and foremost to the women of colour in the room. White people are, of course, accustomed to being the ones who set the agenda, and for whose benefit books are written and lectures delivered. The same is true of heterosexuals: the outrage, and the sense of exclusion and silencing derive from an unassailable sense of entitlement, the legacy of social privilege.

Ettinger (1994) explores this sense of entitlement with reference to the 'Pocahontas Paradigm', derived from the romantic myth of John Smith, who ventures into uncharted territory populated by an unfamiliar Other, and is rescued by 'a girl in braids whose spontaneous, unsolicited love transcends his foreignness and his whiteness and drives her to protect him from the more threatening elements among her own people'. As Ettinger (1994: 52–3) points out, the myth of Pocahontas is also the myth of John Smith's entitlement to protection:

> The crux of the Pocahontas Paradigm is the promise of aid and comfort from the Other: cultural and racial harmony are accomplished not because John Smith makes any effort to redefine his own position in a new and unknown world, but because Pocahontas volunteers to bridge the gap with love.

This saga is re-enacted whenever academics set sail into the uncharted waters that lie beyond the dominant (white, middle-class, heterosexual, able-bodied) discourse. Heterosexual feminist psychologists feel *entitled* not to our 'love' exactly, but to the sisterly support, attention and protection of lesbian feminists, and they expect to be able to set the agenda within which we are benevolently 'included'. Consequently, it is not surprising that they 'get sulky and petulant' (Ettinger, 1994: 51) when, instead, lesbian feminists set the agenda to which heterosexual women are asked to contribute. As Ettinger (1994: 51) says: 'What a remarkable sense of entitlement must drive their willingness to assert their experience of exclusion!'

The Pocahontas Paradigm is helpful in understanding some of the wilder excesses of heterosexual feminist writing, in which heterosexual feminists parade their own feelings of exclusion and hurt, blaming lesbians for everything they consider to be wrong with feminism today. For example, a young British feminist psychologist, writing in a book entitled (ironically enough!) *Challenging Women: Psychology's Exclusions, Feminist Possibilities*, accuses lesbians of alienating women and driving them away from feminism:

> Heterosexual and bisexual women, and many lesbians who have strong relationships with men, have been alienated by a prescriptive type of feminism which implicitly or explicitly says 'men are bad'

> . . . and by implication, that lesbianism (but only of a certain sort) is
> more aligned with feminist principles.
>
> (Catherine Bewley, 1996: 164)

She goes on to quote from the revolutionary lesbian theorist, Sheila
Jeffreys, and blames 'views such as these' for 'many women, including
lesbians, turning their backs on feminist organisations' (Bewley,
1996: 165). The specific targeting of lesbian theorists and lesbian theory as
the source of divisiveness among feminists is familiar. Among the
'different and self-defined identities (and lifestyles)' which cause divisions among us are the identities and lifestyles based on racism, classism,
ageism and anti-Semitism – and, of course, untheorized and unreflective
heterosexual lifestyles and their accompanying heterosexism. And yet it is
radical *lesbian* theory and practice which are singled out by Catherine
Bewley as 'alienating' for many women.

This 'accusatory' mode is mirrored in the extraordinary comment made
by the established feminist psychologist Jane Ussher (1991c: 231), that 'we
cannot replace one restrictive discourse (that of compulsory heterosexuality) with another (that of compulsory lesbianism)'. The reference to
'compulsory heterosexuality' draws, of course, on Adrienne Rich's (1980)
analysis of the overt and covert violence with which heterosexuality is
enforced upon women, including rape, pornography, seizure of children
from lesbian mothers in the courts, enforced economic dependence of
wives and the erasure of lesbian existence from history and culture. It is,
of course, ludicrous to suggest that lesbian feminist analyses of heterosexuality, or lesbian advocates of political lesbianism (however 'prescriptive' or 'restrictive') can begin even remotely to approach the totalizing
hegemonic power of compulsory heterosexuality. The heterosexual
feminist fantasy of 'compulsory lesbianism' is born rather of an anxious
sense that they are being asked to address questions derived from a
lesbian perspective, and to develop some kind of theory (of their own
heterosexuality) which threatens their own taken-for-granted identity.
Their sense of exclusion or alienation in the face of lesbian theory comes
from the unaccustomed experience of not having their own concerns at
centre stage.

Finally, at its most extreme, heterosexual feminism accuses lesbian
feminism of 'oppressing' heterosexual women. This accusation reveals a
wilful refusal to engage with the realities of lesbian oppression: the
critiques of lesbian feminists may, on occasion, lead heterosexual
feminists to feel guilty, excluded, vulnerable or unhappy – but that is not
the same thing as oppression.

> Oppression isn't simply the same as misery. Oppression has clearly
> defined boundaries measured by such things as discriminatory
> laws, physical attacks, verbal insults, threats, cultural invisibility

and stereotypes, deletion from historical records, discrimination in housing and work, and ostracism by family and other hetero-sexuals.

(Jo *et al.*, 1990: 72)

The continued refusal of heterosexual feminists to engage with agendas set by lesbians – particularly when those agendas include critiques of heterosexuality as institution or practice – illustrates the extent to which feminist psychology is threatened by lesbian issues.

Reading feminist psychology – especially (though not exclusively) *British* feminist psychology – from the perspective of a radical lesbian feminist, I am acutely aware of the extent to which lesbian viewpoints are merely tolerated, as long as what we say can be relegated to the token lesbian chapter, as long as there aren't 'too many' of us, and as long as we do not make heterosexual feminists too uncomfortable. Writing about the problem of exclusion in feminist theory, Elizabeth Spelman (1988: 183) says:

as long as I am simply tolerating your viewpoint, not actively seek-ing it out and taking seriously how it represents a critique of my own – indeed not wondering what it means to you apart from its rep-resenting a critique of me – I have not given any indication that I might be prepared to change my privileged position. This is es-pecially clear if on examination of what I am now 'allowing' you to say, it turns out that there are limits on what I will allow you to talk about or how I allow you to talk about it. For example, I might only let you speak or continue listening to you as long as you don't make me too uncomfortable.

In conclusion, I have illustrated in this chapter the ways in which un-examined heterocentricity is perpetuated in feminist psychology today. In part, as I have shown, this is a legacy of the historical relationship be-tween lesbian feminism and heterosexual feminism in the women's movement more generally. Feminist psychology demonstrates a privi-leged ignorance of lesbian theory and research; it 'includes' lesbians (but not too many of us) as part of its own agenda, while accusing us of being 'divisive' and 'alienating' if we propose our own agendas or develop sep-arate theory from lesbian perspectives. The token lesbian chapter is not good enough. A key future development for feminist psychology must lie in a more sustained and serious focus on lesbian issues.

References

Abbott, S. and Love, B. (1972) *Sappho was a Right-On Woman: A Liberated View of Lesbianism*. New York: Stein and Day.

Abraham, K. (1907) 'The female castration complex', in *Selected Papers of Karl Abraham MD*. London: Hogarth Press.

Alder, B. (1994) 'Postnatal sexuality', in P.Y.L. Choi and P. Nicolson (eds), *Female Sexuality: Psychology, Biology and Social Context*. London: Harvester Wheatsheaf.

Alderson, L. (1981) 'Statements from individual members of the collective', in Onlywomen Press (ed.), *Love Your Enemy? The Debate between Heterosexual Feminism and Political Lesbianism*. London: Onlywomen Press.

Bart, P. (1977) '"The mermaid and the minotaur": A fishy story that's part bull', *Contemporary Psychology*, 22(11): 834–5.

Bart, P. (1983) Review of Chodorow's *The Reproduction of Mothering*, in J. Trebilcot (ed.), *Mothering: Essays in Feminist Theory*. New York: Rowman and Allanheld.

Basow, S. (1992) *Gender, Stereotypes and Roles*, 3rd edn. Pacific Grove, CA: Brooks/Cole Publishing Co.

Beckett, H. (1986) 'Cognitive developmental theory in the study of adolescent identity development', in S. Wilkinson (ed.), *Feminist Social Psychology: Developing Theory and Practice*. Milton Keynes: Open University Press.

Begum, N. (1992) 'Disabled women and the feminist agenda', in H. Hinds, A. Phoenix and J. Stacey (eds), *Working Out: New Directions for Women's Studies*. London: Falmer Press.

Beloff, H. (1993) 'Progress on the BPS psychology of lesbianism front', *Feminism & Psychology*, 3(2): 282–3.

Bernay, T. and Cantor, D. W. (1986) *The Psychology of Today's Woman: New Psychoanalytic Visions*. Cambridge, MA: Harvard University Press.

Bewley, C. (1996) 'Power in feminist organisations', in E. Burman, P. Alldred, C. Bewley, B. Goldberg, C. Heenan, D. Marks, J. Marshall, K. Taylor, R. Ullah and S. Warner, *Challenging Women: Psychology's Exclusions, Feminist Possibilities*. Buckingham: Open University Press.

Bhavnani, K.-K. and Phoenix, A. (1994a) 'Shifting identities shifting racisms: An introduction', in K.-K. Bhavnani and A. Phoenix (eds), 'Shifting identities shifting racisms': A Special Issue of *Feminism & Psychology*, 4(1).

Bhavnani, K.-K. and Phoenix, A. (1994b) 'Shifting identities shifting racisms', in K.-K. Bhavnani and A. Phoenix (eds), *Shifting Identities Shifting Racisms: A 'Feminism & Psychology' Reader*. London: Sage.

Bozett, F. W. (ed.) (1987) *Gay and Lesbian Parents*. New York: Praeger.

Brown, L. (1990) 'The meaning of a multicultural perspective for theory-building in feminist therapy', in L. Brown and M. Root (eds), *Diversity and Complexity in Feminist Therapy, Part 1*. Special Issue of *Women and Therapy*, 9(1–2): 1–21.

BPS (1990) Letter to proposers of Psychology of Lesbianism Section, 6 December.

Bunch, C. (1975) 'Not for lesbians only', *Quest: A Feminist Quarterly*, 2(2): 50–6.

Butler, S. and Wintram, C. (1991) *Feminist Groupwork*. London: Sage.

Carby, H. (1987) 'Black feminism and the boundaries of sisterhood', in M. Arnot and G. Weiner (eds), *Gender and the Politics of Schooling*. London: Hutchinson.

Chaplin, J. (1988) *Feminist Counselling in Action*. London: Sage.

Chodorow, N. (1978) *The Reproduction of Mothering*. Berkeley: University of California Press.

Choi, P. Y. L. and Nicolson, P. (eds) (1994) *Female Sexuality: Psychology, Biology and Social Context*. London: Harvester Wheatsheaf.

Claudie, Graziella, Irene, Matine and Françoise (1981) 'Feminism and radical lesbianism', in S. L. Hoagland and J. Penelope (eds), *For Lesbians Only – A Separatist Anthropology*. London: Onlywomen Press.

D'Augelli, A. R. and Patterson, C. J. (eds) (1995) *Lesbian, Gay, and Bisexual Identities over the Lifespan: Psychological Perspectives*. New York: Oxford University Press.

Davis, M. (1995) Letter, *The Psychologist*, 8(4): 151–2.

Dinnerstein, D. (1976) *The Rocking of the Cradle and the Ruling of the World*. London: The Women's Press.

Douglas, C. A. (1990) *Love and Politics: Radical Feminist and Lesbian Theories*. San Francisco; ism Press.

Doyle, J. A. and Paludi, M. A. (1991) *Sex and Gender: The Human Experience*. New York: William C. Brown.

Ehrenreich, B. and English, D. (1978) *For Her Own Good: 150 Years of the Experts' Advice to Women*. New York: Anchor/Doubleday.

Ettinger, M. (1994) 'The Pocahontas paradigm, or will the subaltern please shut up?', in L. Garber (ed.), *Tilting the Tower: Lesbians Teaching Queer Subjects*. New York: Routledge.

Falk, P. J. (1989) 'Lesbian mothers: Psychosocial assumptions in family law', *American Psychologist*, 44: 491–7.

Frieze, I. H., Parsons, J. E., Johnson, P. B., Ruble, P. B. and Zellman, G. L. (1978) *Women and Sex Roles: A Social Psychological Perspective*. New York: Norton.

Frith, H. (1994) 'Turning us off', *Feminism & Psychology*, 4(2): 315–16.

Frye, M. (1983) 'On being white: Toward a feminist understanding of race and race supremacy', in *The Politics of Reality: Essays in Feminist Theory*. Freedom, CA: The Crossing Press.

Gannon, L. (1994) 'Sexuality and menopause', in P. Y. L. Choi and P. Nicolson (eds), *Female Sexuality: Psychology, Biology and Social Context*. London: Harvester Wheatsheaf.

Garnets, L. D. and Kimmel, D. C. (eds) (1993a) *Psychological Perspectives on Lesbian and Gay Experiences*. New York: Columbia University Press.

Garnets, L. D. and Kimmel, D. C. (1993b) 'Conclusion: Implications for practice, research and public policy', in L. D. Garnets and D. C. Kimmel (eds), *Psychological Perspectives on Lesbian and Gay Experiences*. New York: Columbia University Press.

Gergen, M. (1993) 'Unbundling our binaries – gender, sexualities, desires', in S. Wilkinson and C. Kitzinger (eds), *Heterosexuality: A 'Feminism & Psychology' Reader*. London: Sage.

Gibbs, E. D. (1988) 'Psychosocial development of children raised by lesbian mothers: A review of research', *Women and Therapy*, 8: 55–75.

Gonsiorek, J. C. and Weinrich, J. D. (eds) *Homosexuality: Research Implications for Public Policy*. London: Sage.

Greene, B. and Herek, G. M. (eds) (1994) *Psychological Perspectives on Lesbian and Gay Issues Vol. 1. Lesbian and Gay Psychology: Theory, Research and Clinical Applications*. Thousand Oaks, CA: Sage.

Griffin, C. (1986) 'Qualitative methods and female experience: Young women from school to the job market', in S. Wilkinson (ed.), *Feminist Social Psychology: Developing Theory and Practice*. Milton Keynes: Open University Press.

Hall, M., Kitzinger, C., Loulan, J. and Perkins, R. (1992) 'Lesbian psychology, lesbian politics', *Feminism & Psychology*, 2(1): 7–26.

Hamilton, V. (1995) Letter, *The Psychologist*, 8(4): 151.

Hartnett, O., Boden, G. and Fuller, M. (1979) *Women: Sex Role Stereotyping*. London: Tavistock Publications.

Hoagland, S. L. (1988) *Lesbian Ethics: Toward New Values*. Palo Alto, CA: Institute of Lesbian Studies.

Hollway, W. (1993) 'Theorizing heterosexuality: A response', *Feminism & Psychology*, 3(3): 412–17.

Hyde, J. (1991) *Half the Human Experience. The Psychology of Women*, 4th edn. Lexington, MA: D. C. Heath and Co.

Itzin, C. (1986) 'Media images of women: The social construction of ageism and sexism', in S. Wilkinson (ed.), *Feminist Social Psychology: Developing Theory and Practice*. Milton Keynes: Open University Press.

Jeffreys, S. (1985) *The Spinster and her Enemies: Feminism and Sexuality 1880–1930*. London: Pandora.

Jeffreys, S. (1990) *Anticlimax: A Feminist Perspective on the Sexual Revolution*. London: The Women's Press.

Jeffreys, S. (1994) 'Heterosexuality: A "Feminism & Psychology" Reader', *Feminism & Psychology*, 4(2): 307–9.

Jo, B., Ruston and Strega, L. (1990) *Dykes-Loving-Dykes: Dyke Separatist Politics for Lesbians Only*. Oakland, CA: Battleaxe.

Kashak, E. (1992) *Engendered Lives: A New Psychology of Women's Experience*. New York: Basic Books.

Kitzinger, C. (1986) 'Introducing and developing Q as a feminist methodology: A study of accounts of lesbianism', in S. Wilkinson (ed.), *Feminist Social Psychology: Developing Theory and Practice*. Milton Keynes: Open University Press.

Kitzinger, C. (1987) *The Social Construction of Lesbianism*. London: Sage.

Kitzinger, C. (1990) 'Resisting the discipline', in E. Burman (ed.), *Feminists and Psychological Practice*. London: Sage.

Kitzinger, C. (1995) 'Social constructionism: Implications for lesbian and gay psychology', in A. R. D'Augelli and C. J. Patterson (eds), *Lesbian, Gay and Bisexual Identities over the Lifespan: Psychological Perspectives*. New York: Oxford University Press.

Kitzinger, C. and Wilkinson, S. (1994) 'Virgins and queers: Rehabilitating heterosexuality?', *Gender and Society*, 8(3): 444–63.

Kitzinger, C., Wilkinson, S. and Perkins, R. (eds) (1992) 'Heterosexuality': A Special Issue of *Feminism & Psychology*, 2(3).

Klepfisz, I. (1982) 'Anti-semitism in the lesbian/feminist movement', in E. T. Beck (ed.), *Nice Jewish Girls: A Lesbian Anthology*. Watertown, MA: Persephone Press.

Krafft-Ebing, R. (1965) *Psychopathia Sexualis* (trans. M. E. Wedneck). New York: Putnams.

Lauritsen, J. and Thorstad, D. (1974) *The Early Homosexual Rights Movement*. New York: Times Change Press.

Llewelyn, S. and Osborne, K. (1990) *Women's Lives*. London: Routledge.

Mary (1970) *A Letter from Mary*. (Pamphlet) Somerville, MA: New England Free

Press. Reprinted in K. Jay and A. Young (eds) (1975) *Out of the Closets: Voices of Gay Liberation*. New York: Harcourt Brace Jovanovich.

Matlin, M. W. (1987) *The Psychology of Women*. New York: Holt, Rinehart and Winston.

Midgely, M. and Hughes, J. (1983) *Women's Choices: Philosophical Problems Facing Feminism*. London: Weidenfeld and Nicolson.

Miller, J. B. (1976) *Toward a New Psychology of Women*. London: Penguin.

Moghissi, H. (1994) 'Racism and sexism in academic practice: A case study', in H. Afshar and M. Maynard (eds), *The Dynamics of 'Race' and Gender: Some Feminist Interventions*. London: Taylor & Francis.

Morin, S. F. and Rothblum, E. (1991) 'Removing the stigma: Fifteen years of progress', *American Psychologist*, 46: 947–9.

Myron, N. and Bunch, C. (eds) (1975) *Lesbianism and the Women's Movement*. Baltimore: Diana Press.

Oakley, A. (1981) *Subject Woman*. Oxford: Martin Robertson.

Onlywomen Press (ed.) (1981) *Love Your Enemy? The Debate between Heterosexual Feminism and Political Lesbianism*. London: Onlywomen Press.

Patterson, C. J. (1995) 'Lesbian mothers, gay fathers and their children', in A. R. D'Augelli and C. J. Patterson (eds), *Lesbian, Gay, and Bisexual Identities over the Lifespan: Psychological Perspectives*. New York: Oxford University Press.

Perkins, R. (1991) 'Oppression, inequality and invisible lesbians', *Feminism & Psychology*, 1(3): 427–8.

Phillips, A. (1987) *Divided Loyalties: Dilemmas of Sex and Class*. London: Virago.

Phoenix, A., Woollett, A. and Lloyd, E. (eds) (1991) *Motherhood: Meanings, Practices and Ideologies*. London: Sage.

Pies, C. (1985) *Considering Parenthood*. San Francisco: Spinsters/Aunt Lute.

Pollack, S. and Vaughn, J. (1987) *Politics of the Heart: A Lesbian Parenting Anthology*. Ithaca, NY: Firebrand Books.

Radicalesbians (1969) *Woman-Identified Woman*. Somerville, MA: New England Free Press.

Rich, A. (1980) 'Compulsory heterosexuality and lesbian existence', *Signs*, 5(4): 631–60.

Rich, A. (1989) 'Foreword to "Compulsory heterosexuality and lesbian existence"', in L. Richardson and V. Taylor (eds), *Feminist Frontiers II: Rethinking Sex, Gender and Society*, 2nd edn. New York: Random House.

Rohrbaugh, J. B. (1981) *Women: Psychology's Puzzle*. New York: Abacus.

Rohrbaugh, J. B. (1988) 'Choosing children: Psychological issues in lesbian parenting', *Women and Therapy*, 8: 51–63.

Rothblum, E. (1992) 'We may be your worst nightmare, but we are also your future', *Feminism & Psychology*, 2(2): 271–4.

Sayers, J. (1992) 'A POWS Reply', *Feminism & Psychology*, 2(2): 269–70.

Sedgwick, E. K. (1993) *Tendencies*. London: Routledge.

Segal, L. (1994) *Straight Sex*. London: Virago.

Schwieso, J. (1991) 'Morally opposed to -isms' (letter), *The Psychologist*, 4(1): 19–20.

Spelman, E. V. (1988) *Inessential Woman: Problems of Exclusion in Feminist Thought*. London: The Women's Press.

Spender, D. (1989) *The Writing or the Sex? Or, Why You Don't Have to Read Women's Writing to Know It's No Good*. New York: Pergamon Press.

Squire, C. (1989) *Significant Differences: Feminism in Psychology*. London: Routledge.

Tavris, C. (1992) *The Mismeasure of Woman*. New York: Simon & Schuster.

Taylor, M. (1991) Letter to the BPS Scientific Affairs Board, 14 August.

Thompson, D. (1993) 'Against the dividing of women: Lesbian feminism and heterosexuality', in Sue Wilkinson and Celia Kitzinger (eds), *Heterosexuality: A 'Feminism & Psychology' Reader*. London: Sage.

Ussher, J. (1989) *The Psychology of the Female Body*. London: Routledge.

Ussher, J. (1991a) (Chair, BPS Psychology of Women Section) Letter to the BPS Scientific Affairs Board, 21 May, reprinted in *British Psychological Society Psychology of Women Section Newsletter*, 8: 66.

Ussher, J. (1991b) (Chair, BPS Psychology of Women Section), Letter to Rachel Perkins, member of Working Party to form a BPS Psychology of Lesbianism Section, 18 June, reprinted in *British Psychological Society Psychology of Women Section Newsletter*, 8: 67–8.

Ussher, J. (1991c) *Women and Madness*. London: Harvester Wheatsheaf.

Ussher, J. and Nicolson, P. (1992) *Gender Issues in Clinical Psychology*. London: Routledge.

Van Every, J. (1995) 'Heterosexuality, heterosex and heterosexual privilege', *Feminism & Psychology*, 5(1): 140–4.

Walsh, M. R. (ed.) (1987) *The Psychology of Women: Ongoing Debates*. New Haven, CT: Yale University Press.

Ward, C. (1995) *Attitudes toward Rape: Feminist and Social Psychological Perspectives*. London: Sage.

Watson, G. and Williams, J. (1992) 'Feminist practice in therapy', in J. M. Ussher and P. Nicolson (eds), *Gender Issues in Clinical Psychology*. London: Routledge.

Watt, S. and Cook, J. (1991) 'Racism: Whose liberation? Implications for women's studies', in J. Aaron and S. Walby (eds), *Out of the Margins: Women's Studies in the Nineties*. London: Falmer Press.

Wetherell, M. (1986) 'Linguistic repertoires and literary criticism: New directions for a social psychology of gender', in S. Wilkinson (ed.), *Feminist Social Psychology: Developing Theory and Practice*. Milton Keynes: Open University Press.

Whitelegg, E. *et al.* (eds) (1982) *The Changing Experience of Women*. Oxford: Basil Blackwell, in association with Open University.

Wilkinson, S. (ed.) (1986) *Feminist Social Psychology: Developing Theory and Practice*. Milton Keynes: Open University Press.

Wilkinson, S. and Burns, J. (1990) 'Women organizing with psychology', in E. Burman (ed.), *Feminists and Psychological Practice*. London: Sage.

Wilkinson, S. and Kitzinger, C. (eds) (1993a) *Heterosexuality: A 'Feminism & Psychology' Reader*. London: Sage.

Wilkinson, S. and Kitzinger, C. (1993b) 'Virgins and queers: Rehabilitating heterosexuality?', *Annual Conference of the British Psychological Society Psychology of Women Section*, University of Sussex, July.

Williams, J. and Watson, G. (eds) (1991) 'Clinical psychology: Training in oppression?', *Feminism & Psychology*, 1(1): 55–109.

Williams, J. H. (1987) *Psychology of Women: Behavior in a Biosocial Context*, 3rd edn. New York: W. W. Norton.

Wilton, T. (1995) *Lesbian Studies: Setting an Agenda*. London: Routledge.

7

Working-class women: psychological and social aspects of survival

————• VALERIE WALKERDINE

In this chapter I want to examine certain aspects of the discursive construction of working-class women within psychological and sociological literature. In the light of this I will examine the survival strategies open to working-class women in the present historical period. I want to do so for several reasons. In Left and feminist politics in Britain at least, it has been increasingly difficult to talk about class. This has meant that class politics has been associated with outdated and monolithic theories of social change and revolution, with the working class variously being seen as a reactionary class which has succumbed to embourgeoisement and the politics of the Right, or as having ceased to become a viable group altogether (see Walkerdine and Lucey, 1989, for a review). I have argued elsewhere (Walkerdine, 1991a) that such analyses contain within them a set of fantasies about 'the working class' as a fictional object, an object which is either overvalued in a romantic vision of 'the revolutionary class' or is maligned as 'the authoritarian and reactionary class', who failed to bring the revolution and who were responsible (single-handed) for the return of a reactionary government. Such extremes of love and hate are, I will argue, invested in the discourses through which 'claims to truth' (Foucault, 1979) are made about the class. In Foucault's terms, then, there is a will to truth about the working class, but I am adding here the importance of the fantasies which sweep through the truths which are produced and which are so central to the regulation and subjectification of members of that class in the present.

The black British literary critic, Homi Bhabha (1984) has utilized the work of Franz Fanon (1969) to discuss similar issues in relation to the development of colonial government and the regulation of the colonial subject. He posits a mixture of 'fear, phobia and fetish'. Such a mixture is clearly present in the discourses and practices through which the working class is constituted as an object and through which members of that class are identified and governed. In these discourses the working-class woman has a prominent place. She is present quite simply and exclusively as a mother: a mother who must be watched and monitored at all times through the available medical, educational, social work and legal apparatuses because she is seen as the relay point in the production of the democratic citizen. It is she, above all others, who will obey the moral and political order and not rebel. It is she who guards social democracy, and her fitness to ensure that the erstwhile masses become proper democratic citizens must be watched at all times.

My purpose here is to understand the effectivity for the present of the emergence of a mode of regulation through psychology, which designates and targets a group of women as pathological, understands their place as crucial in the production of a social pathology and fails entirely to engage with the psychological effects of oppression. I am choosing the group of women designated as working class in Britain during the postwar period, because this is the group in which I grew up and know best and because I feel strongly that a certain grand narrative about the object called the working class is obscuring important issues about how a particular group lives under oppression.

Social regulation of the working class

My argument is, following Foucault, that the bourgeois democratic order is to be assured through the production of the bourgeois individual. The threat of this order is the possibility that not all the subjects will be 'normal individuals'. In this analysis, the working-class subject is potentially a threat to the order and must be designated as potentially pathological. The apparatuses of normalization are those medical, social work, legal and educational technologies through which normality is defined and regulated. Since the individual, within this discourse, is produced through proper child-rearing by the mother, it is the working-class mother whose fitness to mother and whose actual practices of mothering must be the object of surveillance. Two things follow from this: first, the working-class woman becomes the object of surveillance in terms of her perceived fitness to mother; second, not only are her practices monitored, but her faulty practices and inadequacies become understood as the cause of a wide range of social problems, such as criminality, delinquency, and so forth. This means that oppression as an issue in the understanding of the position of working-class women has disappeared from the agenda (that is, if it was ever there) and is replaced by the targeting of such women (though only when they mother) as the psychopathological cause of the threat to the bourgeois political order itself.

I want to examine this with respect to the emergence in Britain in the postwar period of a bourgeois democratic hegemony in which certain liberal discourses about working-class families and education appeared within sociology, psychology and psychiatry, such that their incorporation in apparatuses of social regulation (Foucault, 1979) and forms of government of the individual helped both to define and regulate the production of class relations and forms of domination and subordination.

My reading of this moment will be at odds with a common understanding of this as a moment of increased opportunity for working-class people, in which, for the first time, certain educational opportunities were made available, in the context of increased possibility of relative wealth and property ownership, for example. Yet, it is precisely at this moment that the Left accuses the working class of selling out, of becoming wealthy and bourgeois – in short of ceasing to become a proper 'revolutionary class' – while at the same time the new technologies of the social celebrate that which the Left is derogating. In the middle of all this, working people are left to be defined and subjected.

Rather than talking of a class which has failed in its revolutionary job, I want to discuss how that class was defined and shaped in order to be the target of bourgeois practices. I want also to suggest that it is impossible to define the subjectification and subjectivity of working-class people without taking into account the specificity of their location. To accuse working-class people of having 'sold out' is to misrecognize the issue of subjectification itself, and it is clouded by the assumption that what has happened can be described in terms of the effects of ideology, especially with respect to the concept of 'false consciousness'. I shall argue not only that we cannot understand consciousness in these terms, but also that the idea is often presented as though middle-class intellectuals had a true consciousness, while the labouring working classes wallowed in self-delusion. This view in itself denies important aspects of the fantasies of the Other which have long formed a strong component of middle-class radical politics (see, for example, Steedman, 1990), as well as being an inadequate conceptualization of consciousness.

Social regulation of working-class women

I shall argue, following work which I have undertaken elsewhere (Walkerdine and Lucey, 1989), that the regulation of working-class women is central to the new forms of population management which were produced. The regulation depends upon a set of technologies, practices in which working-class women as mothers are systematically positioned as the basis for the transformation of the social order into a bourgeois liberal democracy. It is the working-class woman as mother who is to be held responsible for the future of democracy by the adequacy of her rearing of its future citizens. On the one hand, she may be the basis of her child's success in school and therefore upward mobility, and on the other, her very inadequacy may produce the very anti-social and criminal behaviour which poses the greatest threat to the liberal order.

In *Democracy in the Kitchen* (1989), Helen Lucey and I argued that modern ideas about mothering, like those of primary school teaching, depended upon what Foucault called soft forms of regulation. In other words, apparently benign strategies, designed to increase happy child development and successful mothering, should be understood as deeply regulative – in that subjectivity is understood in these models only as normal or as pathological.

What is important is the long history of the targeting of working-class women in terms of strategies of prevention and control that were aimed at the normalization of their children. It is in the child guidance clinics and the social work offices that psychoanalysis gradually became incorporated into the practices of the regulation of these women, with the aim of monitoring their own regulation of their children. I think that it is not overstating the case to say that almost all current developmental psychology, for example, has as an implicit base, theories and practices which relate to the concerns that I have outlined, even if the exponents of that work have been understood as radical.

This means that working-class women are likely to understand the effectivity of oppression upon them in individualized terms and yet, at the same time, to have few resources upon which to draw to understand the psychic effects of that oppression, itself experienced as an inadequacy or private pathology. I wish to challenge these two poles and also to begin to demonstrate how inextricably interlinked they are.

Working-class women in Marxism, psychoanalysis and feminism

What discourses are available for talking about the formation of working-class subjects and subjectivities in Marxism, psychoanalysis and feminism? The most commonly available discourses from within Marxism are those which refer to Marx's concept of ideology. The two metaphors used by Marx were those of the camera obscura and false consciousness. In the former, there is a sense of distorted perception, while in the second the sense of a true or revolutionary consciousness is juxtaposed with the false one. This idea has been developed in various kinds of Freudo-Marxism, from the Frankfurt School, through to Louis Althusser's use of Jacques Lacan's psychoanalysis. In the latter, the concept of false consciousness is reworked to fit in with Lacan's scheme of the Imaginary order. Thus, 'the working class' has a consciousness defined by the 'imaginary relations' and not the 'real relation' of production. In particular, this suggests that working-class people are tied to infantile wish fulfilment produced through their insertion into a bourgeois order in which commodity consumption relates to attempts to gain satisfaction for desire, in which the fetish objects which replace the mother are tied into the signs which structure the unconscious itself. While this theory has a certain elegance and appears more sophisticated than models of false consciousness which do not engage with the unconscious, nevertheless, since Lacan has ruled the 'real' out of order, any reference to materiality is unthinkable. The working class, in this analysis, remains duped and mystified again. I shall argue later in this chapter that it is precisely with materiality, and with ways of dealing with and defending against the pain of oppression that we should be concerned. The idea of a true as opposed to a false consciousness simply assumes a seeing or a not seeing. What if a working-class person sees and yet has myriad conscious and unconscious ways of dealing with or defending against the pains and contradictions produced out of her/his social and historical location?

In order to investigate this issue fully, I believe that it is necessary to examine the constitution of the masses within the emergent human and social scientific discourses of the nineteenth century, if not before. I suggest that all accounts of this mass, of whatever political persuasion, present the mind of the masses as a problem in one way or another. The issue of an easily swayed mass, which has to be individuated, recurs in discourses from Le Bon, through Freud, to the Frankfurt School. For Marx, too, the mass only becomes the working class through a transform-ation, and one effected through a change in consciousness. Unpoliticized working-class subjects, therefore, are presented as a problem until and unless they become something else through the transformation of their mental states. I want, therefore, to point out that the mass psyche is a heavily contested space, about which much ink has been spilled. But, despite this extensive attention, the discursive constitution of this mass is such that it is always the matter of psychic transformation in relation to a set of political objectives which is the issue and very little attention has been paid to the ways in which the masses have been produced and have coped psychically with the conditions of their existence.

Work within a feminist tradition has got us little further. While feminist appropriation of psychoanalysis has been useful in defining questions of unconscious femininity and issues of sexuality, feminism has remained totally silent about how working-class femininity is lived, except through models of pathologization, as we shall see. In addition, many struggles have concentrated on the relative importance of capitalism and patriarchy as sources of oppression. For example, Anne Philips (1988) writes exclusively about the way in which the loyalties of feminists are divided between analyses of class and of gender. She nowhere considers the possibility of lived subjectivity as both classed and gendered. She speaks, in the end, as a woman from the middle class, who sees and understands class intellectually, but somehow fails really to apply it to her own situation. But, as black British and American women have been saying for some time, 'difference' is lived daily by oppressed peoples. Working-class women, for example, must live the way that they are classed quite differently and more obviously than their middle-class sisters. It is perhaps important to ask why middle-class women find it so difficult to write about themselves as classed. In order to understand that, we have to examine how the bourgeois individual has become synonymous with normality and working-class subject with pathology. By psychologizing class, middle-class women are left somehow with the feeling that they are simply women, rather than women of a particular class. But when class is lived, the theoretical struggle between patriarchy and capitalism as cause of oppression becomes viewed very differently.

In order to understand how working-class women have become subjected, it is necessary to examine the specific conjuncture in which certain psychoanalytic ideas were taken together with a liberal concern for the 'facilitating environment' of child development, such that 'poor mothering' might be excused or explained in relation to poverty and exploitation, but in which oppression was never taken seriously for understanding the production of forms of life, except by recourse to an explanation which would put it on the agenda as one of the causes of inadequate mothering. There are no discourses which speak of the living of oppression, nor are there ways to understand working-class women who do not mother. In this chapter I want to make particular reference to working-class women who gained access through state education to the professions, some of them becoming members of those professions whose job it is to regulate working-class mothers, in this case social workers and teachers. This set them up as arbiters of the normal, pathologizing the very practices through which they were mothered and presenting them with a version of their own history which centres on an understanding of their situation through a discourse of deprivation, deprived and depriving mothering. Some of these women themselves become mothers, while others did not.

Psychical reality and environmentalism

I can only begin to sketch out some of the issues at stake here. For Freud, the subject was taken to be formed in relation to the inevitable separation from the mother's body. Freud proposed a theory of phantasy in which the trauma of recognition that the body which supplied food and warmth and comfort could not always be there, produced in the infant an inevitable distress. Freud proposed that the infant 'hallucinated' the absent breast and in so doing created a phantasy of satisfaction which served to protect itself against the trauma of loss. For Freud this was the basis of psychic life and all subsequent interactions in the 'real world' were lived through the 'psychical reality' that resulted from the production of the unconscious. The importance of Freud's early work was, however, that it was not possible to read off a cause and effect in any simple sense. Psychic distress, while related to events in childhood, was not simply produced by events in the 'real world' because that world was mediated by 'psychical reality'.[1]

From the 1930s onwards in Britain, psychoanalytic practices joined forces with, and were shaped by and in turn shaped, the concerns about the actual presence of the mother in the production of the bourgeois democratic citizen. Where the 'social hygiene' movement of the 1920s had concentrated on the mother at home, away from the streets, from drink and depravity (Bland, 1982), and on keeping the home clean and free from excess and degeneracy (Rose, 1985), the later practices extended the idea of the importance of the mother in the home by positing the production of considerable trauma by her absence and also highlighting that it was not simply her presence which was important (providing warmth and food) but her actual behaviours with her children: her sensitivity to their needs. Thus it came to be argued that 'deprivation' was something which could result not simply from absence itself but from inappropriate and inadequate mothering practices (cf. Bowlby, 1971).

Furthermore, such inadequate practices were said to relate directly to the production of delinquency in adolescence and to juvenile crime (cf. Winnicott, 1957). Thus the future of anti-social behaviour and uprising (of the masses) was implicitly laid at the door of the mother. This led to the surveillance of the adequacy of mothering through the various welfare, medical, legal and educational practices which came more and more to monitor working-class life for signs of 'maladjustment'. Freud's notion of psychical reality may have been preserved in some of the work (e.g. Winnicott) but it got hopelessly mixed up with ideas about what the mother actually did. Thus, an apparent concern for social welfare, injustice and inequality was created within psychotherapeutic discourses and practices, but it could only be understood in terms of a psychopathology of mothering which might have resulted in a 'poor environment'.

Fantasies of the Other

Earlier I quoted Homi Bhabha's (1984) contention that the regulation of the colonial subject is saturated with 'fear, phobia and fetish'. What fantasies underlie the regulation of the working-class subject as Other, in this case particularly the working-class woman? In order to understand this we have to examine the ways in which the working class has been both constituted as an object of romantic fulfilment and maligned as a 'bad object'. We need to examine the way in which regulation and surveillance of the working class depends upon the 'will to truth' (Foucault, 1979) understood both as a desire to know in order to control and as a vicarious desire ('What are they like?'; 'What is it like to be like that?') (Walkerdine, 1985; 1991a) – the fetishized object of so many fantasies that this class has something which the others lack: exotic sexuality, animal passions, closeness to the earth, to name only a few of the fantasies. These very characteristics are also simultaneously pre-sented as dangers to the social and moral body which must be kept in check and which the upper classes and bourgeoisie project into the proletariat: degeneracy, the threat of uprising, etc. Working-class women may thus simultaneously hold out a threat and a promise: the threat of their sexuality together with the promise of its Otherness, the closeness to the earth of their mothering as something both wonderful and terrible, and so on.

Subjectivity and survival

I want to examine some of these issues as raised in a discussion with a group of working-class women in two ways. First, I want to argue that their subjectivity is formed within those practices in which they are subjected. Thus, the anxieties and projections on to them which are entailed in their regulation will be present in their views of themselves and their own insecurities (for example, stupidity, promiscuous sexu-ality, inadequate mothering). In addition, I want to argue that the psychoanalytic discourse which claims to know them itself fails to come to terms with and deal with the psychic and social aspects of their oppression, which cannot be spoken or articulated within the psycho-analytic discourse itself. Thus, they struggle to find a story, a narrative or a way of talking about and bringing to consciousness the deep pain of the oppression that they have suffered. A traditional psychoanalytic nar-rative does not deal easily with such oppression. Although issues around parenting and sexuality are clearly woven through what these women are trying to talk about, nevertheless, existing theories (e.g. Lacan, Bourdieu, 1976) only add them as secondary phenomena.[2] I will argue that psychic aspects of oppression can only be understood in relation to the truths through which the oppressed are governed, the fantasies which are projected on to them as well as the way in which such fantasies form a defence against the threat posed by the Other and the potential uprising of that Other. In addition to this, the oppressed live in certain relations of exploitation and domination which are material. Oppressed peoples develop over long periods of time practices of survival for dealing both with material conditions and the truths and fantasies of the oppressor. These practices form the culture of the oppressed and can be understood on a symbolic level, but they contain within them complex psychic patterns of defence against oppression which allow the possibility of survival in dangerous conditions.

Educated working-class women

I will write here about a particular group of women, with whom I recorded five hours of discussion at the Women's Therapy Centre in London in 1989, part of which is now available as a film (Walkerdine, 1991b). These women all, like me, grew up working class and went on at some point in their lives to higher education. Although such women do not form part of what would normally be included in 'the working class', I want to write about them because they demonstrate important aspects of the specificity of what it means to talk about class today. In this context I want to mention developments in sociology in the postwar period. At the same time as Marxist sociologists were charting the demise of the working class, liberal British sociologists were studying the effectiveness of the new social democratic order with its stress on equality of opportunity. It is this new order which more than before solidified its targeting of the working-class woman as mother. It was she who, in the literature, became responsible for the success or failure of her children at school and hence the success of social democracy itself. In this way social class became understood as part of a discourse of social mobility in which to be working class gradually became a pathology. While previous discourses of hereditary intelligence were still in play, these had been augmented by an environmentalism which stressed what the mother could do. In short, to be working class became the fault of one's family, by turns stupid or pathological, unable to provide the necessary support to get its children out of the ghetto.

The Registrar-General's Classification of Occupations was the most commonly utilized tool of designation of class in social and psychological research from this time. This system of classification mapped father's employment in five categories from unskilled worker to professional and managerial. By this method it became common to understand classes 1 and 2 as middle class and 4 and 5 as working class, with class 3 being seen as a marginal category. The whole system of classification itself redefined class along the lines necessary to study class in terms of social and occupational mobility, with more and more frequent studies comparing children and families from categories 4 and 5 with those from 1 and 2, increasingly with an emphasis on the normality of the professional group and practices and the pathology of the manual working ones. This emphasis, then, was on how the familial, and increasingly, mothering, practices of classes 4 and 5 could be changed to make them more like those of classes 1 and 2 whose children were successful at school. The literature here is voluminous, but includes the work of, for example, Goldthorpe (1980), Halsey *et al.* (1980) and Douglas (1964).

It was the tripartite system of British secondary education, with its selection examination at the age of 11 (the 11-plus) which was crucial in supporting the idea that bright working-class children could be identified on the basis of mental measurement and then educated for entry into the professions. Finding working-class children therefore meant finding intelligent children in a stupid class and then, increasingly, as 'environmentalism' took hold, suggesting 'environmental' reasons why working-class children should fail in an education system which apparently offered them equality of opportunity.

It is the working-class woman as mother, then, who is increasingly targeted within modern apparatuses of social regulation. Such explanations had a huge impact on accounts of working-class child-rearing and the raising of daughters (Walkerdine and Lucey, 1989). What particularly interests me here is the way in which working-class subjectification and subjectivity is lived in this particular period. What are the effects of the truths through which working-class women are regulated on a group of working-class women who gain access to higher education? My subtext here is to understand what it means to be the target of these truths and their attendant fantasies and to have no place in which to speak of the psychic effects of oppression except through a discourse that implicitly or explicitly blames one's own family, or particularly one's mother, for one's pain.

The aim of the Women's Therapy Centre group was to begin to do what its leader, Pam Trevithick (a working-class woman, trained in counselling and now a lecturer in social work) has described as 'unconscious raising' (Trevethick, 1989). What I want to do here is to discuss some of the issues that the women raised, moving towards an approach that might be able to deal with the psychic effects of living under oppression.

Of the five women in this group, one was a primary school teacher, one taught in further education, one in higher education, one was a social worker and the fifth was a well-known photographer. All had completed university degrees and one was just finishing her PhD. They ranged in age from 25 to 55; some had gone to university at 18, whereas others were mature students, the oldest having obtained her degree at the age of 49. Two of the women had children of their own.

All of the women expressed difficulties in defining their identity. They felt working class but also felt that, as women who had now entered the professions, they were supposed to have made a successful and unproblematic transition into the middle class. None of the group felt that she had. Indeed, they struggled with the feeling of belonging nowhere, and with feelings of immense guilt for having left their people.

Several women raised the issue of stupidity. One of the 'truths' through which the working class is regulated is the discourse of intelligence. The class is where it is, so the story goes, because of its low intelligence, fitting it only for menial work. These women therefore represent exceptions because each of them was allowed entry into higher education on the basis of academic performance which suggested 'intelligence' and therefore set them apart from the majority of their class. This produces great pain and anxiety, the main one being the fear that their intelligence is a chimera, a fraud, which will be discovered and then they will be exposed, 'unmasked', as one woman puts it, and the basis of their life, the life they have gained through their intellectual labour, challenged. The facilitator asks Fiona what is 'her biggest struggle', 'the one that always gets to you'; 'what is the most important thing about you in relationship to your class that you want us to know?'. Fiona says:

> It's not being good enough, really, basically, not being good enough, but believing that, coupled with a sense of terror really of what I may or may not achieve, because I'm not sure what I can achieve. I think I try, but even if I try and think I've managed something, it's like disbelieving that it ever happened. I'm not sure how I get round that one really, knowing that it's very much part of my pattern. And then what, because I believe it, but that's quite an essential part of me really, an essential loss.

She goes on to say that she really has no sense of who she is, but only of who she is and is supposed to be in different places. She has no strong central sense of herself. The workshop leader asks her where she accumulated her feelings of inferiority, who told her that she was not good enough. She replies: 'I don't know, my mother was always telling me that she was never good enough, she still tells me that she's not good enough.' Fiona goes on to add that her mother was giving her a conflicting message. On the one hand, Fiona could be better than she, and on the other, since she was her daughter, she may be like her. She adds that her father also had a very unclear sense of himself. He wanted in his fantasy to be a giant, but felt that really he was a dwarf. No wonder, then, that Fiona, who like her parents has taken on board the 'truth' of the stupidity of her people, fears that, even though she has been chosen and educated as clever within the education system, she must underneath be the stupid woman, or like the dwarf-like father, who can barely see himself as a man (that is, since he cannot conquer his own oppression in the guise of giant, he must become that subhuman failure, the dwarf).

Her father more or less drank himself to death. If her father failed to survive oppression, Fiona fears desperately that she too might not survive, even though she has taken on all the trappings of a successful middle-class woman. Every one of the women in the group feels that she is really not clever and will be found out and also that, like Fiona, she lacks any kind of unifying centre.

Diane speaks of the way in which her fears about her stupidity and her sexuality as a working-class woman came together in her experience of secondary and university education. She explains that university was the place where she felt most fraudulent and lived in terror of being discovered. When the workshop leader asks her what she was afraid of being discovered as, she tells of several experiences of going to dances and being pursued by middle-class men who thought that she was a local working-class woman who had managed to get into the dance and not a student. Her fear was that if men felt her to be working class that would give them licence to mistreat her sexually since the assumption was that working-class women had 'looser morals'. She went on to recount how she and her sister, when living at home, and given a lift back from a dance, would always ask to be let out at a private estate of houses and not the public housing where they lived, again because middle-class young men would mistreat them if they found that they were 'common'. Her fear about her sexuality was extreme enough for her to find a middle-class boyfriend to protect her after three weeks at university. She stayed with him throughout her university career and ended up marrying him. She sees that now as a coping strategy that ensured her survival in relation to the interrelation of her objectification and the resultant problems with her own sexuality, that led her to seek protection. This form of survival strategy had serious and difficult consequences for her because the marriage did not work and it prevented her from coming to terms with aspects of her sexuality. However, in some important aspects it probably saved her life and certainly her career at university. On the other hand, Jo discusses the way in which her sexuality was a way out of the working class, through relationships with middle-class men who introduced her to 'Culture' (with a capital C). She feels, however, that all the time she was attempting to escape from the position she saw her mother in, she entered that position, that of a servant, in another way, sexually, through the sexual servicing of middle-class men, seen as her only escape route.

Both Diane and Francesca, the only mothers in the group, talk about their own mothering of their children as pathological: they perceive that they do not do the kind of things that they know, from their training in the caring professions, that mothers are supposed to do. Diane remembers that her own mother, who had eight children, never seemed to sit down except when she was feeding a baby. She quite simply never rested, and Diane fantasizes going to the sink and stopping her doing the washing up so that she could have time to talk and get close to her. Diane fears that she, too, like her mother, cannot stop working. Her deep fear is that she will fall apart if she stops, because the only way she has learnt to survive and cope is to keep on going. Indeed, this is likely to have been a significant coping and survival strategy, since in a life of routine and systematic oppression, where working was a necessary aspect of survival, stopping may have at the very least meant a breakdown and working therefore probably produced the very survival that routine just about held together, defending against the fear of falling apart.

Identification with fathers is also a very strong and important theme. Fathers are presented as being in the world outside the home and therefore, for some of the women, provide a way of identifying with something in the public sphere, since most of the mothers did not work outside the home. But also, more than anything else, they seemed to represent people who have been most clearly and graphically oppressed. They could see that their mothers were oppressed but they were also seen as conservative, as tied to the sink, when these women wanted desperately not to be in the same situation as them. As Jo says, she wanted not to be in the servant position, like her mother, but yet she entered that position in another way (in her case she meant she felt like a sexual servant in her relationships with middle-class men). However, the conscious identification with their fathers presented many difficulties, pain and guilt. The fathers had, for the most part, suffered terribly at work. They are not presented here as strong fathers (the all-powerful fathers of patriarchy theory) but as fathers who tried desperately to be strong, but actually felt weak and useless (which they experienced as emasculating, and which some of them violently took out on their families as the only beings weaker and more oppressed than they). Fathers who struggle and fathers who suffer, as in Fiona's giant and dwarf story.

It is a difficult struggle because, in the end, it cannot be won, as Diane graphically points out by discussing the time when her father took industrial action on his own, a move which she describes as 'very self-defeating'. He also lost an eye in a mining accident. Christine's father was told by his doctor: 'I'm sorry, Ernest, there is nothing I can do for you; you are worn out'. He died early, worn out by ceaseless overwork: he worked six days every week and on the seventh he slept. Although one might fondly imagine that such work conditions no longer exist, it is abundantly clear that indeed they do. How frightening, then, to watch these men battling against gigantic odds and then finally being injured or killed in the process, with only their fantasies of giant masculinity to defend themselves, fantasies directly projected on to them in all those discourses of the Left and Right which simultaneously see workers' power as the way forward and condemn them for being macho.

The effect of all this is to make this group of women feel guilty for having survived when their fathers have suffered and died. And yet at the same time they feel very protective to the extent that they are not really able to talk of feeling anger towards their fathers' violence. What they feel more is that this violence will be misunderstood as just one more working-class pathology by middle-class people, and thus they feel more that their fathers, who have suffered enough, must be defended against this. Instead, like them, they feel that they may not be strong enough to survive. Christine talks of having felt that she could not see clearly the division between herself and her father, where he ended and she began. Fiona said that she did not know whether she was a giant or a dwarf and had doubts about her ability to survive in a world in which he failed to survive. The world is presented as hostile and frightening, where survival is shakily achieved, a terrifying and oppressive place in which there is scarcely a sense of being in control. The world can be conquered, but desperately. Everything seems frightening but, more than that, to succeed in an alien world, the intellectual world of the bourgeoisie, represents a sentiment of disloyalty. To feel in control is to feel as though one has abandoned the oppressed, the world where one does not control. Yet, not to feel in control is at least not to have joined the other side: them. To feel defeated is also to feel safe, secure, whereas to succeed and to survive is to be bourgeois, to be one of the enemies. Of course, all of the families on the surface want their daughters to succeed, and yet, the struggle without winning is somehow safe: you know where you are.

The experience is of leaving one terrible place for another equally, though differently, terrifying. Yet this second place is without the security, as Diane says, of knowing the rules, rules which are different from home. Diane lived this as terrified of being found out as working class. They dreamed of leaving this 'expanse of deprivation', this 'horrible little postwar council estate', but for what? Fiona said that she had to be at least 500 miles from her home town out of a mixture of guilt and desire to get away from the horror. How, therefore, to feel hatred of one's location, vulnerability, and yet, at the same time, not to get away easily because it represents the most secure place that there is?

Towards another story

I have argued that the discursive frameworks presented by the apparatuses of social regulation provide a way in which the working-class women whose stories are outlined above are able to understand themselves, with the effect that it is easy to understand the pain that they suffer as an aspect of individual pathology. It could, of course, be argued that this constitutes an example of ideological obfuscation, which produces a false consciousness, which prevents these women from understanding the oppressive causes of their pain. However, I think that this would be quite mistaken. I have tried to demonstrate that the psychopathological discourses target working-class women as mothers and offer an understanding of pain as a result of poor mothering in difficult environmental conditions. While the masses, and in this case mothers, form the target of strategies of intervention and political transformation, there are plenty of accounts about these processes. But, as I have been at pains to point out, there is virtually nothing written about the psychic effectivity of the pain of class oppression. The model we are left with is of universalized patterns of psychic development, which can be affected by so-called environmental or social conditions. But what if social and historical processes produce certain psychic relations as defences, rather than central psychic processes simply being affected by them? The latter position leaves the working class as always pathological to the middle-class norm. But if we were to operate instead with a model in which there were no norm, but only patterns which resulted from the living of certain conditions of existence, then each class would have to be explained in relation to those conditions and not in relation to a universal normative model at all.

I want to begin to explore this idea in relation to the psychoanalytic literature on trauma, with particular reference to work on holocaust survivors. It was this literature which first brought to light the notion that an actual material event could necessitate defences, which in ordinary circumstances might seem pathological, but in the context of concentration camps could be understood as life-saving. Bruno Bettelheim's (1986) account of concentration camp survivors mentions the defence of splitting, in which the person acts as though what is happening is happening to somebody else, so that s/he, disembodied, watches it happening. This allows her/him to cope with extreme circumstances. Bettelheim notes three different coping strategies among holocaust survivors: the first is to be psychologically destroyed; the second is outward normality but deep inner denial; and the third is a lifelong struggle to cope with what has happened.

While it would not be appropriate to suggest that working-class people are like holocaust survivors, there are some important similarities on which I wish to draw. As discussed earlier, all of the women in the therapy group expressed what could be described as 'survival guilt', that is to say, they felt that it was not OK to be a well-paid professional when their parents had struggled all of their lives and had, in some cases, been injured or died as a result of back-breaking and dangerous work. To have moved out, therefore, was both a tremendous relief, to be away from the source of that pain and that danger, but also a terrible loss: a loss of family, community, identity. All of this was replaced by isolation in a professional, middle-class elite, in which they felt frightened and alien. In these circumstances, different members of the group had a variety of coping strategies. Christine was unable to sustain a full-time academic job because it made her feel too much of a traitor. Living in what she called 'genteel poverty' at least assured herself that she had not totally escaped from the world of her parents. Fiona worried that, like her father, who did not survive and coped with life by fantasizing being a giant among men but feared he was really a dwarf, she would not survive, even though her life as a social worker was not life-threatening in the direct way that his life had been.

Work with the children of holocaust survivors has indicated the way in which certain defences against coping with trauma may be passed on to children, even though the trauma itself is not spoken about. I strongly suggest that this literature helps to shed light on what has happened to these women.

This literature, and the associated literature on trauma, potentially allows the possibility of an account which engages with the specificity of the difficult, and sometimes dangerous, circumstances of the lives of oppressed peoples and the psychic effects of such conditions. Indeed, as Gail Pheterson (1993: 2) has suggested:

> early experiences of submission and domination in intra-familial and extra-familial contexts foster reality-distorting psychic defences for persons in both oppressed and dominant positions. Those defences, whose function is to avoid anxiety, resist change despite the dangers and inhumanities of the status-quo.

As Pheterson (1993: 13) also points out with respect to the holocaust literature and its applicability to other oppressions, 'genocidal persecution is not required to elicit psychic defence; daily mundane humiliation will do'. Indeed, Bergmann and Jucovy (1982: 52), who have written extensively on holocaust survival, maintain that responses to natural disasters or arbitrary war attacks do not cause the same psychic damage as 'continuous, systematic and organised assault [on] a people . . . singled out as a group that is less than human'. I would argue that the history of the discursive construction of the masses, the working class, tells us precisely this story and continues to tell it today, even, indeed, through stories which tell us that the working class no longer exists.

I wish to argue, therefore, that the approach that I am advocating will potentially allow us to understand the deep and cross-generational effectivity of social class as it is lived socially and psychologically by different generations today. I believe that it is possible to analyse social, cultural and domestic practices as practices of survival, containing elaborate defences against pain, be it in this or previous generations. It is the ability of this pain to transmit across generations which also tells potentially quite a different story of class transformation and upward mobility in the postwar years. I believe that most of that story remains to be told. It has been a long time coming.

Notes

1 In the final section of this chapter I will criticize this reading, which is usually considered to be the more radical and non-normalizing one, in which Freud is saved from normalizing accounts of psychical development, which are taken to misuse his concepts.
2 Lacan's adherence to Lévi-Strauss's account of kinship structures fails to come to grips with the practices through which psychical relations are lived (see Adams and Cowie, 1990). Bourdieu, while he talks about practices as rituals through which oppression is reproduced, fails to get to grips with the ways in which such rituals may form psychical coping strategies and a set of conscious and unconscious defences, which may be both positive and negative in their effectivity.

References

Adams, P. and Cowie, E. (1990) The Woman in Question. Cambridge, MA: MIT Press.

Bergmann, M. S. and Jucovy, M. E. (eds) (1982) Generations of the Holocaust. New York: Basic Books.

Bettelheim, B. (1986) The Informed Heart. Harmondsworth: Penguin.

Bhabha, H. (1984) 'The Other question: The stereotype and colonial discourse', Screen, 24.

Bland, L. (1982) 'Vampires on the race or guardians of the nation's health', in E. Whitelegg et al., The Changing Experience of Women. Oxford: Basil Blackwell in association with Open University.

Bourdieu, P. (1976) Outline for a Theory of Practice. London: Macmillan.

Bowlby, J. (1971) Attachment and Loss, Vol. 1. Harmondsworth: Penguin.

Douglas, J. W. B. (1964) The Home and the School. Glasgow: McGibbon and Kee.

Fanon, F. (1969) Black Skin, White Masks. Harmondsworth: Penguin.

Foucault, M. (1979) Discipline and Punish. Harmondsworth: Penguin.

Goldthorpe, J. H. (1980) Social Mobility and Class Structure in Modern Britain. Oxford: Clarendon Press.

Halsey, A. H. et al. (1980) Origins and Destinations: Family, Class and Education in Modern Britain. Oxford: Clarendon Press.

Pheterson, G. (1993) 'Historical and material determinants of psychodynamic development', in J. Adleman and G. Enguidanos (eds), Racism in the Lives of Women. New York: Haworth Press.

Phillips, A. (1988) Divided Loyalties. London: Virago.

Rose, N. (1985) The Psychological Complex. London: Routledge.

Steedman, C. (1990) Childhood, Culture and Class in Britain. London: Virago.

Trevithick, P. (1989) *Unconsciousness Raising with Working Class Women.* Women's Therapy Centre: London.

Walkerdine, V., Burgin, V. and Donald, J. (1985) 'Video replay: Families, films and fantasy', in K. Caplan (ed.), *Formations of Fantasy*. London: Routledge.

Walkerdine, V. (1991a) *Schoolgirl Fictions*. London: Verso.

Walkerdine, V. (1991b) *Didn't She Do Well?* London: Metro Pictures (film).

Walkerdine, V. and Lucey, H. (1989) *Democracy in the Kitchen: Regulating Mothers and Socialising Daughters*. London: Virago.

Winnicott, D. (1957) *Mother and Child*. New York: Basic Books.

. . . and interrogating method

———• 8

Using the master's tools:
Epistemology and empiricism

———• RHODA K. UNGER

Experimental social psychology has been under attack by feminists since the beginning of second-wave feminism in the late 1960s. At first we criticized its methods (see Weisstein, 1968; Sherif, 1979; Unger, 1979; Wallston, 1981). Our critiques ranged from biases in subject selection and the construction of research questions to biases in definition and interpretation. Some feminist scholars have even despaired about the usefulness of experimental methodology because of the problems of context stripping and lack of adequate controls for comparisons of populations of women and men (Parlee, 1979).

More recently, psychology has been attacked on more theoretical grounds (Hare-Mustin and Marecek, 1990; Riger, 1992; Unger, 1989b; 1990; 1995). For example, one of the challenges posed by postmodernist theory is how to deal with the proposition that a stable self does not exist, but is continually constructed as a function of social forces. This theory would seem to say that there is no such thing as stable personality or individuality. If this view is correct, then we cannot generalize – either about any one woman or about groups of women. We are left with the individual's life experiences and the meaning she extracts from them. But these meanings, too, are transient. They are subject to constant reconstruction by the individual as her circumstances change.

Postmodernist theory (Gavey, 1989; Morawski, 1994; Kimball, 1995) poses great problems for feminist empiricists who, unlike clinical psychologists, prefer nomothetic to idiographic analysis. There are two major dilemmas here. How can we reconcile using methodologies which strip individuals of their historical and situational context with feminist theory? And why would we want to do so? The second question is particularly problematic since these tools have frequently been used to devaluate socially powerless groups and to defend the status quo. Can feminist empiricism respond to Audre Lorde's challenging assertion that 'The master's tools will never dismantle the master's house' (Lorde, 1984: 112)?

I do not wish to suggest a theoretical defence of empiricism at this time. I believe, however, that feminist psychologists should not willingly discard one of the most powerful tools at our disposal. I propose that one of the 'jobs' of feminist psychology is to determine which aspects of identity are transient and/or unique to the individual and which are generalizable across different groups. We need both innovative theory and innovative methodology to do so.

The challenge for feminist social psychologists is to find variables that are related to differences in the construction of meaning across groups. Much of my own empirical research has been in this area. For much of this chapter I will summarize that research and discuss how it relates to feminist theory and practice. I believe, however, that this kind of historical/conceptual review is clarified by reflexivity. I will begin, therefore, by presenting some autobiographical information about my own epistemological roots.

> Once upon a time I was a confirmed behaviorist. In principle, this meant that I believed that effects derived from orderly determinist causes, that the subjective aspects of behavior were irrelevant, and that the best studies required maximal distance between experimenter and subject. In practice, this meant that my first major research, my doctoral dissertation, involved making lesions in the caudate nucleus of rats and examining their effects upon temporal and spatial alternation by means of operant conditioning procedures. If I thought of sex professionally at all, I saw it as a variable which could neither be manipulated nor controlled and therefore of very little scientific interest. Even the rats were male.
>
> (Unger, 1989a: 15)

In common with most psychologists, I would have been labelled a 'positivist', if that term had been in popular usage at the time (the early 1960s).

Unexamined positivism had/has many advantages for researchers. Behavioural observations were easy because I limited the rats' situational possibilities (there was not much they could do but push or not push the lever of a 'Skinner box'). The studies were replicable (there was not much different experimenters could do to change the rat subjects' behaviour in such a limited setting except, perhaps, drop them). One could argue for a lack of bias in the procedures (if one did not notice that all the rats were white and male and their environments highly controlled). And, most important for a positivist scientific model, one could argue for deterministic cause and effect relationships. Brain lesions appeared to 'cause' deficient behaviours. They probably did, but I was unaware that such findings did little to explain the complex nature of these relationships.

I came of academic age during the political turmoil of the late 1960s and early 1970s. I shifted my field of research from physiological to social psychology, which resulted in a shift from rats to human beings as my subject population of choice. At first, my new studies did not appear to require any sort of epistemological shift. They mostly involved changing the external characteristics of people so as to change their cue properties for other people's social behaviours (see Raymond and Unger, 1972; Unger *et al.*, 1974). These studies were similar to those of other early feminist empiricists. We were interested in documenting the existence of sex discrimination using experimental methodology. We believed it was important to demonstrate that women fared less well than men under identical circumstances.

It is easy to see why such studies were popular. Women researchers were trying to explain discrimination against people like themselves. One of the earliest studies in this area, for example, compared the identical curricula vitae of female and male psychologists and found that women were discriminated against in terms of hiring preferences, academic rank if they were hired, and recommended salary (Fidell, 1970). Another early study (Goldberg, 1968) found that women evaluated the work of other women as less good than the identical work of men. This study was consistent with other early studies showing that both women and men held similar beliefs about the characteristics of each sex (Broverman *et al.*, 1972). Few of these studies on gender stereotypes found significant differences between the sexes. In fact, men and women were remarkably similar in agreeing about their own differences (Unger and Siiter, 1974).

From the personal to the professional

These findings led me to ask two questions. First, when so much evidence exists that stereotypes are inaccurate and that prejudice is unfair, why are the stereotypes maintained? Second, why do people acquiesce in beliefs about their own groups that can lead to derogation of themselves as individuals? Since I was still a positivist, I conceived of the answers to these questions in terms of a failure of information transmission, akin to Deborah Tannen's (1990) view that the two sexes 'just don't understand' each other. I soon came to realize, however, that a more sophisticated question was required. What leads some people to reject evidence that is readily accepted by others with a different ideological orientation?

This question reflected a move away from positivism because it focused on the subjective underpinnings of attitudes and behaviours. 'Reality' became fluid and malleable – a product of both individual and cultural construction. But, the existence of such constructive processes also suggested that bias is inevitable. People with different epistemological positions will seek evidence to support their different explanations about the way the world works. And these explanations will influence their solutions for various social dilemmas (Unger, 1983).

Because I believed that empirical evidence might be more persuasive than theory, I decided to use positivist methodology to demonstrate the existence of pervasive subjective biases. We devised a method to measure whether differences in personal epistemology underlie the way information is legitimated and acted upon (Unger *et al.*, 1986). The measure was designed to look at people's covert metatheories. We believed that what we termed 'personal epistemology' provides a foundation for more specific attitudes and that it connects them. We wished to show that views about a variety of loosely related issues such as sexism and racism, as well as attitudes about the social and political world, share a deep epistemic connection. We were acutely aware of the irony of using positivist techniques to deconstruct the positivist view that there is such a thing as objective scrutiny of ideas!

We constructed a 40-item 'Attitudes about Reality Scale', which was designed to measure views about how the world works on a continuum ranging from (logical) positivism to (social) constructionism (Unger *et al.*, 1986). This scale differed from usual psychological inventories because it attempted to measure covert ideology. Responses to the same question could vary depending upon the way people interpret certain key words involving causality and the basis for what can be known. For example, how one might respond on an item such as 'The facts of science change over time' may depend on how one defines a fact – as a proximal position or as an enduring truth. In later studies we have shown that people who score at the extreme ends of the scale do, indeed, prefer different synonyms for some of the words used (Smith-Brinton and Unger, 1993).

The framework for the scale was derived from a theory about paradigm shifts within psychology (Buss, 1978). Buss argued that psychological theory has shifted back and forth between two fundamental paradigms – either 'reality constructs the person' or 'the person constructs reality'. We reasoned that individuals might also take a position within these two epistemological poles.

We defined positivism (represented in psychology by psychoanalysis as well as by behaviourism) as belief in some form of universal truth, in the importance and validity of external authority, in the existence and value of objectivity, and in the possibility of determining material causal relationships. We also suggested that positivist individuals would tend to support the societal status quo and believe that science works well and can solve society's problems.

We defined constructionism (represented in psychology by the gestalt movement and, perhaps, by the new cognitivism; see Sampson, 1993) as belief in the relative nature of truths, concern for subjectivity, focus on the individual as a source of authenticity and authority, and acknowledgement of the role played by chance in the determination of events. (As I will discuss later in this chapter, the latter two aspects of a constructionist epistemology may be paradoxical for some individuals.) We also suggested that constructionist individuals would prefer environmental explanations over biological ones and be sympathetic towards efforts to create social change.

Although the scale contains few items which focus explicitly on sex or gender, I believe that studies using it have important implications for feminist scholarship for the following reasons. First, we can explore questions about sex-related differences in comparison to the many other ways in which people may vary. Second, we can distinguish between aspects of gender which are often confounded. For example, which is the more important determinant of a person's world-view: her sex or her feminist ideology? Third, we can deal with accusations of bias against feminist scholars. Using positivist methodology, it is possible to demonstrate that everyone has ideological biases that influence the way she thinks about the world (Unger, 1992).

Some 'objective' research on subjectivity

How does one validate a philosophical construct such as epistemological world-view? Attitudes about reality can be shown to be associated meaningfully with demographic or background characteristics. In other words, personal epistemology reflects an individual's experiences as a member of certain social groups. But this relationship is not as simple as we once supposed.

We expected that members of groups which had experienced a relatively problem-free relationship with society would be more likely to have a positivist viewpoint. In contrast, members of groups which have encountered problems with society should be more likely to hold a constructionist point of view. For these individuals, the lack of relationship between their actions and their outcomes should lead them to question socially normative beliefs about how the world works. Thus, we predicted that women, members of minority ethnic groups, and those of working-class background would be more likely to have a constructionist epistemology than would men, white people, and those from the middle class.

Our first studies were conducted with college students at a large state university in the north-eastern United States. Contrary to our expectations, there were no significant differences in epistemology between women and men, nor any significant correlation with parental occupation (Unger *et al.*, 1986). A later study at the same university also failed to find any epistemological difference between black and white students (Unger and Jones, 1988). We did, however, find a significant relationship between positivism and political and religious conservatism among the white students. This connection has been replicated by several different researchers in various parts of the United States (Jackson and Jeffers, 1989; Harrison and Atherton, 1990).

Can demographic variables ever be meaningful psychological variables? Feminist scholars have long been aware that sex and gender are hopelessly confounded (Deaux, 1993; Unger and Crawford, 1993; Kimball, 1995). Similarly, so-called objective descriptors such as race or class may also be confounded with the subjective meaning of these labels for the individual and the degree to which he or she identifies with them. These subjective categories may be a more meaningful predictor of the individual's worldview than demographic labels.

In our original study of personal epistemology we had included two indicators of women's identification with the social category 'women' – whether or not they were enrolled in feminist courses and/or whether they considered themselves to be actively involved in feminist groups. We found that students enrolled in feminist courses had significantly more constructionist viewpoints at the beginning of such courses than did those enrolled in more traditional psychology courses at the same level. We also found that those few women who indicated that they were active feminists had extremely constructionist epistemologies as compared to other students.

And although the sample was much smaller, we later found that those African-American students who identified with black consciousness were more constructionist than their peers who did not possess this kind of racial awareness (Unger and Jones, 1988). These findings provide empirical support for the feminist position that sex and race are not simple 'difference' categories. They also offer a positivist argument for the value of studying subjectivity.

Statements about universal sex differences tend to ignore the fact that gender is both subjective and culturally situated. For example, the most parsimonious explanation for a unique feminist epistemology involves the definition of women as a social rather than biological category. Identification of oneself as a member of that category may be less important since feminist males appear to share the worldview of their feminist female counterparts.

(Unger, 1992: 234)

Such studies do not, however, address the question of whether a constructionist epistemology can also produce a form of cognitive bias. Studies in Canada and the USA have indicated that self-identified feminists have a constructionist world-view (Ricketts, 1989; 1992). In one study I conducted, self-identified feminist psychologists who were leaders of Division 35 (Psychology of Women) of the American Psychological Association (APA) had the most constructionist epistemology I have ever measured (Unger, 1984–5). Their scores were significantly more constructionist than either students enrolled in women's studies courses or a sample of faculty members in psychology.

Feminist leaders diverged most from other groups on statements that involved biological causality and the value of science for solving human problems. For example, they were significantly more likely than other groups to disagree with the following statements:

- Science has underestimated the extent to which genes affect human behaviour.
- Most sex differences have an evolutionary purpose.
- Most social problems are solved by a few very qualified individuals.

They were also more likely than their students to agree that:

- The way scientists choose to investigate problems is influenced by the values of their society.
- The facts of science change over time.

It is important, however, to look at the similarities between groups as well as the differences between them. All the groups studied concurred on items that related to people's ability to deal effectively with their circumstances. Feminist leaders agreed with other faculty members and students on statements such as:

- If one works hard at solving a problem, one can usually find the answer.
- Effort can often make up for an absence of talent in an area.
- Some non-conformity is necessary for social change to occur.

Their pattern of agreement and disagreement with these statements suggest a problematic area for feminists. On the one hand, we understand that outcomes are *not* always the product of individual competence and merit. On the other hand, we are committed to social change and share with others, particularly in the USA, a belief in the power of our own efforts to produce such change. These contradictory beliefs may contribute to feminist 'burnout', as well as to rather paradoxical findings such as a recent one of Crosby *et al.* (1994), indicating that feminist academics who identified feminism with activism were more dissatisfied with their teaching than other members of APA Division 35. Nevertheless, this kind of contradictory epistemology may be necessary for social activism. Activist individuals must be able to understand that the world is unfair, but also believe that their actions will make it fairer. Feminist activism may require a contradictory epistemology in order effectively to deal with a contradictory reality (Unger, 1988).

Differences in covert beliefs point out potentially valuable areas of dialogue between feminist faculty and our students. Students enrolled in women's studies courses appear to be aware of the political and economic nature of inequality, but are less aware of the underlying assumptions that provide the ideological foundation for these inequalities. Biology and the nature of science are less likely to be discussed in the classroom than are social and economic sexism. This omission is particularly dangerous when one considers the nature of the 'feminist backlash' in the USA (Faludi, 1991) and elsewhere. It is certainly no accident that beliefs about objectivity, biological determinism, and political religious conservatism are associated (see Unger, 1985; Ricketts, 1992).

The use of cultural comparison

One of the problems with doing studies at any single university is the relatively limited range of variability within the population studied. This issue was raised early on in terms of the sex composition of subject populations in most psychological studies in the USA and has been raised more recently in terms of race and class biases (Reid, 1988; Graham, 1992). Other sampling biases may also be present, but are less readily noticeable. We found, for example, that religiosity was associated with epistemological positivism among our students (Unger *et al.*, 1986). In our university's population, however, religiosity was confounded with belief in a particular religion – Roman Catholicism. We could not be sure, therefore, whether the connection was due to belief in a particular religion or to religious belief in general.

Obviously, the way one looks at the world is influenced by ideological beliefs other than feminism. Because of the ahistorical and acultural emphasis of psychology in the USA (Sampson, 1993; Morawski, 1994), however, there has been little systematic attention to many potentially important variables. Variables such as religion or culture have an even weaker theoretical underpinning than sex as an explanation of individual differences in behaviour.

I believe that questions about the situated context of sex may be resolved by examining gender as a variable in different cultural settings. The relative importance of gender as a predictor of how one sees the world may be explored by contrasting it with other ideological markers. In the USA, religion/religiosity appears to be a more important predictor of personal epistemology than sex. There is, however, no basis to predict whether sex or religion would be more important in a society where both variables have a different meaning.

In order to eliminate the confounding of religion and religiosity and to examine the relative importance of sex versus religion, it is necessary to do studies similar to those conducted in the USA in other cultural contexts. I conducted a series of studies in Israel – a country with a broad range of views about the roles of women and men as well as a variety of religions whose adherents range from secular to ultra-orthodox in their beliefs about these religions. These studies were part of a larger study involving political as well as epistemological attitudes (Unger and Safir, 1990).

We translated the Attitudes about Reality Scale into Hebrew and administered it to a large sample of university students enrolled at several Israeli institutions. Most of the students were enrolled at secular institutions. However, a sizeable subsample were enrolled in a single-sex component of the only university in Israel with an orthodox Jewish affiliation. Males and females studied in separate classes as enjoined by traditional religious ideology.

A comparison of the similarities and differences found US and Israeli students proved to be useful. As expected, religious students in Israel had significantly more positivist views about how the world works than did secular students. They were especially likely to prefer biologically determinist explanations for group differences and had more persono-logical views than less religious respondents. They were also less supportive of efforts for social change.

These views were more similar to those found among religious Christian students in the USA than to secular Jewish students in Israel. Religious Moslem, Christian and Druse students also had positivist world-views. These findings suggest that it is religiosity rather than the particular content of Western religions that is associated with epistemo-logical conservatism.

The more unexpected findings involved students' sex. Unlike the USA, women and men in Israel differed in their world-view, and sex interacted with religiosity among the Jewish students (we had too small a sample of non-Jewish students to examine these effects). Among secular students, men had a significantly more positivist world-view than did women. Among religious students, women had a more positivist world-view than men, although the difference was not statistically significant. The major effect was produced by the difference between the epistemology of secular women in Israel and that of everyone else. These women hold a world-view that is significantly more constructionist than that of secular men as well as that of their more religious female counterparts.

These findings suggest that we cannot look at sex-related differences in a social and cultural vacuum.

Which of these findings shows the *real* sex difference? If we limited our studies to the US, we would be able to assert there are no differences. If we had first conducted the study at a secular institution in Israel, we would have said that males see the world in more positivist terms than females. And if we had investigated a religious population first, we might have noted a tendency for females to be more positivistic than males.

(Unger, 1992: 235)

All of these sex differences argue that none is of particular value as a universal descriptor of human beings. Instead, sex operates as a marker variable to alert us to differences in the way people with different experiences construct reality. What we have to decide is why one marker variable is deemed more important than another. Why should sex be more important to feminist psychologists than other indicators of social identity such as race/ethnicity, class, or religion?

The relationship between epistemology and other attitudes

I noted earlier in this chapter that feminist women (and men) are more likely to have a constructionist epistemology than women (and men) who do not identify themselves as feminists. Conversely, constructionists are more likely to favour social, political and economic equality between women and men (Draper, 1990; Addelston, 1995). They are also less likely to believe in a 'just world'. More specifically, they are less likely to believe that individuals are personally responsible for their illnesses than are positivists (Ariely-Kagan, 1991).

These findings would appear to suggest that constructionists are more generally tolerant of others than are positivists. We tested this possibility in Israel using a method in which people were asked to choose which of ten groups they disliked the most and to indicate on a number of items the degree of personal and political tolerance they would accord members of their most disliked group (Shamir and Sullivan, 1983). As expected, constructionists and positivists chose different groups as their most disliked target (Unger and Safir, 1990). Constructionists were more likely to choose a right-wing militant group whereas positivists were more likely to choose left-wing Israeli supporters of the Palestine Liberation Organization. Once they had chosen their targets, however, epistemology predicted little about the degree of tolerance offered members of the target group. In other words, people were equally intolerant of whatever group they most disliked.

Neither sex nor religiosity influenced tolerance scores. In fact, on virtually every item, all groups scored above the mean in an intolerant direction. These students were alike in strongly agreeing that:

- Nothing can be gained by talking to members of one's most disliked group.
- Members of one's disliked group are dangerous.
- Members of one's disliked group should not be allowed to teach in the public schools.

Such findings show why reduction in intergroup conflict is not easy. Such findings also demonstrate why one should be cautious in making statements about differences in morality between women and men (see Kohlberg, 1981).

Constructionists differ from positivists in their attitudes about more global conflicts as well. Positivists in the USA were more likely to support the Gulf War and to assume that Saddam Hussein was primarily responsible for it (Unger and Lemay, 1991). Constructionists were more likely to attribute blame more broadly. Interestingly, personal epistemology significantly predicted students' attitudes about the war, although neither their sex nor their stated political affiliation did so.

Personal epistemology also appears to be related to attitudes about nuclear war. For example, Columbus (1993) has found that positivists believe more than constructionists that people with sufficient protection can survive a nuclear war and will be able to receive medical treatment afterwards. These views may be related to their greater belief in the efficacy of science. Constructionists, on the other hand, are more likely to endorse the idea of a nuclear freeze. There was no relationship between epistemology and nuclear anxiety. Columbus also found no sex differences in these views.

Epistemology and contradiction

Some of these views appear to be contradictory. One might expect a relationship between anxiety and fear for one's survival. I noted another contradiction earlier in this chapter. US feminists believe at the same time that situational and historical forces play a major role in creating social change and that their own efforts to transform society will be effective.

Epistemological contradictions can also be demonstrated in the way people process information about discrimination against members of their own social group compared to discrimination directed against themselves. For example, comparable groups of women differed greatly in their responses to items from the Attitudes about Reality Scale that were worded in either the first person singular or more generically (Unger and Sussman, 1986). They were much more aware of discrimination against others than against themselves.

The item that showed the most impressive differences when worded objectively rather than subjectively was the only item that looked directly at discrimination. Worded in the third person, the item read: 'At the present time, people are recognized for their achievements regardless of race, sex, and social class.' On a scale from 1 to 7, with 1 indicating extreme disagreement and 7 indicating extreme agreement, the mean score was 2.24. Worded in the first person, the item read: 'At the present time, I am recognized for my achievement regardless of race, sex, and social class.' The mean score for this statement was 6.37.

(Unger and Sussman, 1986: 633)

These women were also more likely to attribute personal efficacy and control to themselves than to others. However, their perceptions about personal control appeared unrelated to their beliefs about social causality in general.

Cognitive patterns that lead people to see themselves as more in control of circumstances than other individuals under the same conditions may cause them to ignore evidence of sociostructural biases. Such belief patterns may also lead to blaming the victim – assuming that he or she is more responsible for the negative consequences of behaviour than one would be oneself. These findings also indicate that there is no reason to believe that there is a strong connection between personal change and social change. Divergence between epistemology about the self and about the world in general permits the use of different 'yardsticks' when evaluating personally relevant or irrelevant information. Thus, people can come to share societal assumptions that are oppressive to themselves (Unger and Sussman, 1986).

This kind of splitting of consciousness about the 'self' and the 'other' may also lead people to disregard information about socially devalued groups. We have found recently, for example, that both males and females made differential judgements about the traits and employability of attractive and unattractive stimulus persons 'at first glance' (Locher *et al.*, 1993). We also found that women, when given unlimited time to make decisions, examined much more information about these individuals than men did. Nevertheless, their judgements did not differ from those of men or of women who were less informed about the stimulus persons because of time pressure.

The empirical verification of cognitive bias

Many of the studies summarized earlier in this chapter demonstrate that cognitive biases appear to be both universal and quite resistant to disconfirmation. Of course, feminist scholars have known this all along. These studies may be seen as elaborate techniques for 'proving the obvious'.

These studies can also be seen, however, as a way of providing support for one aspect of feminist theory rather than another. For example, these studies provide support for a so-called 'minimalist' position on sex-related differences. Men and women with a particular epistemological position are more like each other than they are like members of their own sexual categories with a differing epistemology. The studies also cast doubts on gynocentrist positions which argue that women are more caring than men.

Black feminist theorists recognized the need to explore differences among women quite a while ago (see hooks, 1984; Lorde, 1984; Collins, 1991). Recently, white feminist psychologists have begun to acknowledge their need to look at differences among women as well as women's differences from men (see various chapters in Landrine, 1995). No one has, as yet, provided a theoretical rationale as to why any aspect of difference is any more important than any other. I have argued elsewhere (Unger, 1992) that the examination of a variety of different groups can serve a feminist agenda by decreasing the relative importance of sex and gender as intrapsychic variables and by decreasing the probability that sex differences will be reified as universal aspects of human behaviour. However, these effects will not occur unless we can provide non-demographic sources of variability for analysis.

Studies on personal epistemology (and other related variables) can help us to recognize that aspects of subjectivity other than gender have important effects upon the way people think about themselves, other people, and the world. Experimental methodology allows us to make predictions about the relative importance of various forms of subjectivity for particular attitudes and forms of behaviour. Furthermore, an examination of when alternative variables do or do not predict behaviour in similar contexts may lead to a theoretical understanding of what such variables have in common.

It is possible that this is the next step in the development of feminist psychology. It involves a recognition that feminism is not just about the empowerment of women, but that we need to involve ourselves in coalitions concerned with social change. Such coalitions move us beyond the recognition that groups of women of differing race, ethnicity, sexuality, disability, or class have differing experiences.

There is no doubt that the recognition that a variety of factors operate simultaneously will make our theories more complex. Diversity will also make our theoretical perspectives less essentialist. What may not be as clear is that diversity will make our methodological perspectives more eclectic as well.

Empirical methodology is simply one tool among many. The use to which it is put depends upon the values of the user. The questions people ask are more important than the methods they use to evaluate the answers because questions betray epistemology. Epistemology, in turn, predicts what answers one wants to find and what answers one will believe.

What constructionism should teach us is to be wary about certainty. Feminists do not have any more unique access to 'truth' than any other group. We may be unaware of some aspects of reality. We can, however, continue to interrogate ourselves as well as others about epistemological bias and to recognize its role in both question formulation and claims to truth. If they can get you to ask the wrong questions, then they don't have to worry about the answers.

References

Addleston, J. (1995) 'Exploring masculinities: Gender enactments in preparatory high schools'. Unpublished doctoral dissertation, City University of New York.

Ariely-Kagan, K. (1991) 'How do psychology, social work and medical students' attitudes, knowledge and personal epistemology relate to AIDS versus polio victims?' Unpublished master's dissertation, University of Haifa.

Broverman, I. K., Vogel, S. R., Broverman, D. M., Clarkson, F. E. and Rosenkrantz, P. S. (1972) 'Sex-role stereotypes: A current appraisal', *Journal of Social Issues*, 28: 59–78.

Buss, A. R. (1978) 'The structure of psychological revolutions', *Journal of the History of the Behavioral Sciences*, 14: 57–64.

Collins, P. H. (1991) *Black Feminist Thought: Knowledge, Consciousness, and the Politics of Empowerment*. New York: Routledge.

Columbus, P. J. (1993) 'Attitudes about reality and college students' opinions about nuclear war', *Psychological Reports*, 73: 249–50.

Crosby, F. J., Todd, J. and Worell, J. (1994) 'Have feminists abandoned social activism? Voices from the Academy'. Paper presented at the annual meeting of the Association for Women in Psychology, Oakland, CA, March.

Deaux, K. K. (1993) 'Commentary: Sorry wrong number – a reply to Gentile's call', *Psychological Science*, 4: 125–6.

Draper, R. D. (1990) 'Discriminant and convergent validity of the Attitudes about Reality Scale'. Paper presented at the meeting of the American Psychological Association, Boston, MA.

Faludi, S. (1991) *Backlash: The Undeclared War against American Women*. New York: Doubleday.

Fidell, L. S. (1970) 'Empirical verification of sex discrimination in hiring practices in psychology', *American Psychologist*, 25: 1094–8.

Gavey, N. (1989) 'Feminist poststructuralism and discourse analysis: Contributions to a feminist psychology', *Psychology of Women Quarterly*, 13: 459–76.

Goldberg, P. A. (1968) 'Are women prejudiced against women?', *Transaction*, April: 28–30.

Graham, S. (1992) 'Most of the subjects were white and middle class', *American Psychologist*, 47: 629–39.

Hare-Mustin, R. T. and Marecek, J. (eds) (1990) *Making a Difference: Psychology and the Construction of Gender*. New Haven, CT: Yale University Press.

Harrison, W. D. and Atherton, C. R. (1990) 'Cognitive maturity and the "one foundation" controversy in social work education', *Journal of Social Work Education*, 26: 87–95.

hooks, b. (1984) *From Margin to Center*. Boston: South End Press.

Jackson, L. A. and Jeffers, D. L. (1989) 'The Attitudes about Reality Scale: A new measure of personal epistemology', *Journal of Personality Assessment*, 53: 353–65.

Kimball, M. M. (1995) *Feminist Visions of Gender: Similarities and Differences*. Binghamton, NY: Haworth Press.

Kohlberg, L. (1981) *The Philosophy of Moral Development: Moral Stages and the Idea of Justice*. San Francisco: Harper & Row.

Landrine, H. (ed.) (1995) *Bringing Cultural Diversity to Feminist Psychology: Theory, Research, and Practice*. Washington, DC: American Psychological Association.

Locher, P., Unger, R. K., Sociedade, P. and Wahl, J. (1993) 'At first glance: Accessibility of the physical attractiveness stereotype', *Sex Roles*, 28: 729–43.

Lorde, A. (1984) *Sister Outsider*. Trumansberg, NY: The Crossing Press.

Morawski, J. G. (1994) *Practicing Feminisms, Reconstructing Psychology: Notes on a Liminal Science*. Ann Arbor: University of Michigan Press.

Parlee, M. B. (1979) 'Psychology and women', *Signs: Journal of Women in Culture and Society*, 5: 121–33.

Raymond, B. J. and Unger, R. K. (1972) '"The apparel oft proclaims the man": Cooperation with deviant and conventional youths', *Journal of Social Psychology*, 87: 75–82.

Reid, P. T. (1988) 'Racism and sexism: Comparisons and conflicts', in P. A. Katz and D. A. Taylor (eds), *Eliminating Racism: Profiles in Controversy*. New York: Plenum, pp. 203–21.

Ricketts, M. (1989) 'Epistemological values of feminists in psychology', *Psychology of Women Quarterly*, 13: 401–15.

Ricketts, M. (1992) 'The feminist graduate student in psychology: Stranger in a strange land?', in J. C. Chrisler and D. Howard (eds), *New Directions in Feminist Psychology: Practice, Theory, and Research*. New York: Springer-Verlag, pp. 116–29.

Riger, S. (1992) 'Epistemological debates, feminist voices: Science, social values, and the study of women', *American Psychologist*, 47: 730–40.

Sampson, E. E. (1993) *Celebrating the Other: A Dialogic Account of Human Nature*. Boulder, CO: Westview Press.

Shamir, M. and Sullivan, J. (1983) 'The political context of tolerance: The United States and Israel', *American Political Science Review*, 77: 911–28.

Sherif, C. W. (1979) 'Bias in psychology', in J. A. Sherman and E. T. Beck (eds), *The Prism of Sex: Essays in the Sociology of Knowledge*. Madison: University of Wisconsin Press, pp. 93–133.

Smith-Brinton, M. and Unger, R. K. (1993) 'Ideological differences in the construction of meaning', *Imagination, Cognition, and Personality*, 12: 395–412.

Tannen, D. (1990) *You Just Don't Understand: Women and Men in Conversation.* New York: Morrow.

Unger, R. K. (1979) 'Toward a redefinition of sex and gender', *American Psychologist*, 34: 1085–94.

Unger, R. K. (1983) 'Through the looking glass: No Wonderland yet! (The reciprocal relationship between methodology and models of reality)', *Psychology of Women Quarterly*, 8: 9–32.

Unger, R. K. (1984–5) 'Explorations in feminist ideology: Surprising consistencies and unexamined conflicts', *Imagination, Cognition, and Personality*, 4: 387–405.

Unger, R. K. (1985) 'Epistemological consistency and its scientific implications', *American Psychologist*, 40: 1413–14.

Unger, R. K. (1988) 'Psychological, feminist, and personal epistemology: Transcending contradiction', in M. Gergen (ed.), *Feminist Thought and the Structure of Knowledge*. New York: New York University Press, pp. 124–41.

Unger, R. K. (ed.) (1989a) *Representations: Social Constructions of Reality*. Amityville, NY: Baywood Press.

Unger, R. K. (1989b) 'Sex, gender, and epistemology', in M. Crawford and M. Gentry (eds), *Gender and Thought*. New York: Springer-Verlag, pp. 17–35.

Unger, R. K. (1990) 'Imperfect reflections of reality: Psychology and the construction of gender', in R. Hare-Mustin and J. Marecek (eds), *Making a Difference: Representations of Gender in Psychology*. New Haven, CT: Yale University Press, pp. 102–49.

Unger, R. K. (1992) 'Will the real sex difference please stand up?', *Feminism & Psychology*, 2: 231–8.

Unger, R. K. (1995) 'Cultural diversity and the future of feminist psychology', in H. Landrine (ed.), *Bringing Cultural Diversity to Feminist Psychology: Theory, Research, Practice*. Washington, DC: American Psychological Association, pp. 413–31.

Unger, R. K. and Crawford, M. (1993) 'Commentary: Sex and gender: The troubled relationship between terms and concepts', *Psychological Science*, 4: 122–4.

Unger, R. K. and Jones, J. (1988) 'Personal epistemology and its correlates: The subjective nature of sex and race'. Paper presented at the meeting of the International Society of Political Psychology, Meadowlands, N.J., 4 July.

Unger, R. K. and Lemay, M. (1991) 'Who's to blame? The relationship between political attributions and assumptions about reality', *Contemporary Social Psychology*, 15: 144–9.

Unger, R. K. and Safir, M. (1990) 'Cross cultural aspects of the Attitudes about Reality Scale'. Paper presented at the annual meeting of the American Psychological Association, Boston, MA, 13 August.

Unger, R. K. and Siiter, S. (1974) 'Sex role stereotypes: The weight of a "grain of truth"'. Paper presented at the annual meeting of the Eastern Psychological Association, Philadelphia.

Unger, R. K. and Sussman, L. E. (1986) '"I and thou": Another barrier to societal change?', *Sex Roles*, 14: 629–36.

Unger, R. K., Raymond, B. J. and Levine, S. (1974) 'Are women discriminated against? Sometimes!', *International Journal of Group Tensions*, 4: 71–81.

Unger, R. K., Draper, R. D. and Pendergrass, M. L. (1986) 'Personal epistemology and personal experience', *Journal of Social Issues*, 42(2): 67–79.

Wallston, B. S. (1981) 'What are the questions in the psychology of women? A feminist approach to research', *Psychology of Women Quarterly*, 5: 597–617.

Weisstein, N. (1968) *Kinder, Kirche, Kuche as Scientific Law: Psychology Constructs the Female*. Boston: New England Free Press. (Reprinted – with commentaries – in *Feminism & Psychology* (1993), 3(2): 189–245.)

9

You and I and she: Memory-work and the construction of self

──────● NIAMH STEPHENSON, SUSAN KIPPAX
AND JUNE CRAWFORD

Introduction

This chapter describes a feminist method for psychology and sociology, history and cultural studies: memory-work. It focuses, in particular, on the way in which the method and the theory informing memory-work are inseparable and how the process of memory-work affords a number of subject positions to those who take part in it: researchers and research participants alike. Our project is to understand intersubjectivity as it underlies the construction of sexed selves.

We have chosen the topic 'moral dilemmas' to illustrate memory-work in action and also to show how the social relations between 'I'/'me' and 'she'/'her' and 'you'/'you' are implicated in the construction of self. Following Mead (1909), we are drawing on the active/passive distinction. In remembering, it is 'I' who remembers what happens to 'me', and 'she' who reflects on what happens to 'her'. Mead argues that the self needs to be understood as both subject and object – 'me' being the object to the subject 'I'. In this chapter, we characterize memory-work as a process through which researchers move between active and passive, subject and object positions. We are indebted to Haug (1987) and Shotter (1984; 1986; 1993) and to J. Onyx, U. Gault and P. Benton, our co-authors in early work on emotion (Kippax *et al.*, 1988; Crawford *et al.*, 1992).

The theory informing memory-work holds that the self is a social product and arises out of interactions with others (Harré, 1983; 1986). People construct their 'selves' via their attempts to make their actions intelligible to themselves and others: their attempts to 'make sense'.

Subjectively significant events or episodes are remembered and reflected on in the search for intelligibility. Remembering and reflecting on experience are thus intimately bound up with the construction of self. As Haug (1987: 50) argues: 'Our basic premise was that anything and everything remembered constitutes a relevant trace – precisely because it is remembered – for the formation of identity.'

Without an understanding of experience, feminist theory and research have 'no grounds from which to dispute patriarchal norms' (Grosz, 1994: 94). Memory-work is a feminist epistemology; it takes women's experience as its object without assuming an unproblematic, causal link between experience and subjectivity. Within Cartesian epistemologies the subject of knowledge is rational, unitary and masculine (Henriques et al., 1984; Hodge, 1988). By comparison, in memory-work we assume, like Scott (1993: 409) that '[s]ubjects are constituted discursively, but there are conflicts among discursive systems, contradictions within any one of them, multiple meanings possible for the concepts they deploy. And subjects do have agency.' Memory-work provides a basis for theorizing women's experience, and the relationships between experience and subjectivity, experience and knowledge. We do not take experience as the 'authoritative (because seen or felt) evidence that grounds what is known, but rather that which we seek to explain, that about which knowledge is produced' (Scott, 1993: 401). Accounting for subjectivity, then, involves an examination of the ways in which subjects are discursively constituted. The written memories produced in memory-work provide snapshots of subjectivities as they arise within and out of discursive contradictions.

Although reflection on experience appears to be a truly individual endeavour, the social is implicated in at least two ways. First, reflection requires an ability to view oneself as others view one. Reflection is premised on the ability to attribute meaning to self as other, to engage in signification. To remember requires the ability to engage in a specific practice, social in origin: namely, the production and interpretation of narrative forms (Vygotsky, in Wertsch, 1985). Such narratives, and discourses which they articulate, are produced and captured in memory-work. Because reflection lies at the heart of memory-work it is a powerful way to examine the process of self-construction. Second, the stuff of reflection is social. What is remembered is remembered because it is problematic or unfamiliar. What renders something unfamiliar, enigmatic, problematic, complex or contradictory is its difference from the taken-for-granted, the everyday. The problematic or unfamiliar is not a 'natural' given but is socially defined. In memory-work, co-researchers can reflect on the discursive practices in which the 'natural' and the 'problematic' are constructed.

The strength of memory-work is that, in taking experience as problematic, it captures individual appropriations of the social, i.e.

memory-work addresses both the process of appropriation and the social nature of what is appropriated. Appropriation occurs as subjects are positioned by and position themselves within conflicting discourses. Discursive subject positions, Gavey (1992: 326) argues, 'offer us ways of being and behaving, and of understanding ourselves and events in our world . . . positionings will always be to some extent partial as they are contested and interrupted by other discursive possibilities'. Memory-work emphasizes this partiality of subject positions. It does this through an analysis of the tensions between the subject positions of 'I'/'me' and 'we'/'us' and 'she'/'her' and 'they'/'them'. By foregrounding the gaps and tensions between subject positions, in memory-work we explore the shared ways in which we come to make sense of the fragmented and conflicting nature of experience. Like Davies and Harré (1990) we use notions of dialogue, language, narrative and conversation in their broadest sense. We are concerned with subject positions and positioning because they provide a means for discussing the process of intersubjectivity.

In memory-work the written memories are read as narratives of the process of appropriation of the social. In a manner reminiscent of Vygotsky, Le Guin (1992: 39) argues that narrative 'is a fundamental operation of the normal mind functioning in society. To learn to speak is to learn to tell a story.' The ways in which we talk to others are the same as the ways in which we reflect on ourselves. The understanding that human communication is the basis of the social character of consciousness (Mead, 1909) demands a consideration of intersubjectivity. To communicate requires recognition of the other as both similar and different. Shotter (1993), drawing on Billig (1987) and MacIntyre (1981), stresses the role of difference and argumentation in participation in a culture, where culture is viewed as a 'living tradition' rather than a set of givens. A living tradition consists of dilemmas which afford different subject positions. Participation in a tradition entails communication about the ongoing debates which characterize the tradition. Conflict or argumentation is vital to both the social construction of selves and the reproduction and transformation of society. Conflict is played out both interpersonally and intrapersonally between the different subject positions constituted in cultural dilemmas.

In this chapter, we draw on the work of Taylor (1977) and Gadamer (1986) to characterize the process of a living tradition in terms of dialogue. These writers, like Shotter (1993), recognize the dialogic nature of self: the self as constituted in conversation or talk between persons. Gadamer (1986: 106) argues that conversation is about 'placing our own aspirations and knowledge into a broader and richer horizon through dialogue with the other'. Conversation is inherently relational, involving both the 'I' and the 'you'. The self (as an 'I'–'you' dialogue) although fluid and dynamic, is embodied in a living tradition, and constructed in the dilemmas of that tradition.

Memory-work is a collective process in which memories are written and produced collectively. In writing memories, the self is translated into a 's/he'–'other' dialogue. The process of self-construction can be seen in the appraisal of self-as-other – a process which involves conflict and contradiction between competing subject positions. The dilemmas of living traditions are the stuff of memory-work. Sarah's memory of 'telling lies' illustrates the way in which we are subjected to and actively take up subject positions within living traditions:

> She was young, maybe nine or ten. She hated how hairy her legs were, so one night she sat in bed and shaved her legs with a razor blade of her mother's that she had sneaked off her mother's dressing table. Because it was just a blade it was hard to handle so she ended up having cuts on her legs. For some reason she showed her mother the cuts and made up some story that she had been cutting her nails with the blade (she did this in order to authenticate her story) and it had dropped into her bed and she had slept on it and that is how the cuts got there. It must have been so obvious what she had been doing, but her mother was more concerned about the cuts. She felt afraid that she would be found out.

The dilemma in Sarah's memory can be understood as arising from a conflict within the discourse of femininity. Women (and girls) are supposed to be naturally beautiful, yet because our bodies aren't good enough we are required to work on them (for example, shave them) (Bartky, 1990). The work that goes into the production of 'natural' feminine beauty is secretive and shameful because it is testimony to the inherent flaws in women's bodies. In Sarah's memory, the 9- or 10-year-old girl actively appropriates the discourse of natural feminine beauty; she secretively sets to work on herself to produce hairlessness. The memory illustrates how young girls appropriate the subject position of flawed girl/woman; how other women can be complicit in this process in their failure to challenge our subject positions (in this memory, Sarah's mother's seeming acceptance of her lie implies her acceptance of Sarah's subject position within the discourse of femininity). Because Sarah's lie is not challenged the range of subject positions afforded to Sarah, on this occasion, is limited. This memory (like others, below) illustrates the role of *inter*subjectivity in the appropriation of discursive positions.

Before turning to the issue of moral dilemmas to illustrate memory-work, we discuss the method and process of memory-work.

Method

Here we give a brief summary and urge those who wish to know more to read Haug (1987) and Crawford *et al.* (1992). There are at least three phases to memory-work, which involves a collective of co-researchers who meet on a number of occasions. These phases are: first, the writing of memories by the group of participants (co-researchers) according to certain rules; second, the sharing and collective analysis of the written memories by the same group or collective of co-researchers or co-workers; finally, a recursive process whereby the researchers collectively reflect back on their own memories and the memories of others (Phase 1) and on the collective theorizing of them by reading and listening to the group discussions (Phase 2) and critically examine the themes and common understandings reached.

In Phase 1 the rules, which are essentially the same as those recommended by Haug (1987) are as follows:

1 Write a memory to a cue or trigger
2 of a particular event or episode
3 in the third person
4 in as much detail as is possible, including 'inconsequential' or apparently trivial detail
5 but without importing interpretation, explanation or biography.

The force of these rules is to ensure that each participant or co-researcher writes a description of a particular event or episode (such as Sarah's lie about her attempt to shave her legs) rather than an account of a general abstracted description. An abstracted event is likely to be 'typical' of a number of similar events, and thus to contain interpretation, justifications, or warranting.

The process begins with the co-researchers choosing a topic or cue related to the group's research interest. Some of the cues used in past projects have been 'hair', 'holidays', 'saying you are sorry', 'being praised', a 'moral dilemma', 'telling lies', 'not believing someone', 'touching', 'initiating', 'secret' and 'danger'. Each participant writes a memory which is triggered by the cue. Remembering a particular incident may take some time – a week or more – but once triggered the memories are usually detailed. Detail is important because it reveals the constraints placed on understanding by notions of relevance. The so-called irrelevant aspects of events and episodes often point to the hidden moral and normative characteristics of actions. For example, in Sarah's memory, the mention of mother's dressing table lead the group to a consideration of ways in which the modes of feminine production are concealed, rendering them simultaneously mysterious and shameful.

Writing in the third person enables the memory-work participant to take a 'bird's-eye' view of the scene, to observe her/himself from the outside, to picture the detail, and to describe rather than warrant. Autobiography and biography are avoided because biography brings a spurious coherence that conceals the social: the coherence of the reinterpretation of past events as antecedents of what follows (Haug,

1987). If (auto)biography can be understood as 'the linguistic embodiment of the self' (Hooton, 1992: 31), writing in the third person is a process which challenges the notion that the self exists prior to its production in writing (see below).

Writing rather than 'talking' the memories is also important. Writing imposes a narrative form and the writing 'involves making public the events of our lives, wriggling free from the constraints of purely private and individual experience' (Haug, 1987: 36). Writing also helps to avoid justification and warranting; it is difficult not to get caught up in justification when one is identified as the speaker.

In Phase 2 the co-researchers meet to read each other's memories and to analyse them. The guidelines are as follows:

1 Each memory-work participant expresses views and ideas about each of the memories,
2 looks for similarities among and differences between the memories . . . members should question particularly those aspects of the events which do not appear amenable to comparison;
3 each participant should identify clichés, generalizations, contradictions, metaphors, cultural imperatives . . .
4 and discuss theories, popular conceptions, sayings and so on about the topic
5 and examine what is not written (but might be expected to be written) in the memories
6 and finally, each participant should rewrite the memory.

The analysis aims to uncover the 'common' sense (in the sense of common to the group), the shared understandings contained in the memories. Intersubjectivity is the key to this second phase. The memories are theorized as a cross-sectional example of social and shared experience.

Co-researchers discuss the memories in terms of shared understandings of the social rather than the individual circumstances of the actors. What is of interest is not why Sarah shaved her legs but why young girls like Sarah shave their legs. In this way, autobiography and self-justification are avoided. At this stage, each memory is also examined for clichés, metaphors, and cultural imperatives – the figures of speech that hide the normative aspects of action. For example, in Sarah's memory the formulaic expression 'For some reason' stands in for a description of what Sarah experienced when her secret leg-shaving exercise resulted in cuts and blood. This covers over what may have been an experience of horror and distress, experiences we 'forget' as we appropriate the modes of feminine production as natural.

The theorizing of the episodes exposes the processes involved in making sense of the actions and episodes described in the memories. The taken-for-granted and everyday aspects of an absences in the memories are uncovered. Further, the processes involved in the ways the co-researchers understand themselves and others are revealed. In attempting to resolve conflicts both in the memories and between readings of the memories co-researchers occupy a range of subject positions afforded by the dilemmas of their shared living tradition (Shotter, 1993). The tension between these subject positions is played out in the intersubjective negotiation which occurs in the memory-work group; in such negotiations meanings are transformed and new subject positions are taken up.

Phase 3 involves the reappraisal of the understandings reached in Phase 2 and a return to the initial memories equipped with these insights. The writing of this chapter is part of this recursive process. It involves the co-researchers in looking at the processes of memory-work itself. Memory-work is a self-reflexive methodology; its essentially collective nature provides appropriate checks, balances, criticism and challenge in a situation which may be compared with everyday social interaction.

It is important, however, to note that the three phases of memory-work described above feed into and off each other. We have written about them as though they were separate but in practice the three phases of the process are not so easily or neatly distinguished.

We now focus on an aspect of memory-work which has particular relevance for the construction of self (and, as we shall see later, the moral order). That is, we are concerned with the nature of and tensions between subject positions, as they arise in the written memories and in the group discussions.

Positioning in memory-work

Biography

Memory-work is the 'I' writing about the 's/he', whereas autobiography is the 'I' writing about the 'me'. Autobiography is writing about self from the position of self; it entails a description in terms of individual circumstances and personal history. Autobiography serves to justify and explain experience. Although the rules of memory-work enjoin participants to avoid (auto)biography, co-researchers often find this puzzling and difficult to maintain. Writing in the third person is sometimes characterized as contributing to the objectification of women and the lack of cultural representation of women as subjects. We hold, on the contrary, that self-consciousness is inherently social (Mead, 1909). In taking up the subject position of 'she' we do not deny subjectivity, rather we attempt to shift the focus of our research from the subject – as existing independently of positioning in living traditions – to the social practices in which subjectivity is constituted. In this sense memory-work also differs from the kind of interviews and analysis undertaken by the Harvard Project on Women's Psychology and Girls' Development. Gilligan (in Kitzinger and Gilligan, 1994: 415) stresses the importance of isolating distinct voices by 'pull[ing] those first-person voice statements out of women's interview texts, and really try[ing] to listen for how a woman speaks for herself', whereas, in memory-work, by examining the tensions produced between different subject positions our research is self-consciously disruptive of the coherence produced by speaking in the first-person.

The felt need to biographize is strong. ('Biographize', in this chapter, refers to a process of giving autobiographical detail and explanation during group discussions.) As one group member put it: 'I'm allowed five minutes of biographizing to explain that story'. In biographizing the author of the memory marks herself as different from the other co-researchers – biographizing functions to retain an authority over the interpretation of the memory which the process of memory-work, as laid out in the rules, challenges. The rule to avoid biography does not in practice exclude it but rather produces a useful tension between subject positions. The tension both enables and contrains thought and change (Shotter, 1993), and in memory-work is played out in both the writing of memories and in discussion of them. Previous descriptions of memory-work have glossed over or failed to theorize one pole of this tension, i.e. the biographizing that takes place within the memory-work group. In earlier work (Crawford et al., 1992), biographizing tended to be regarded by the group as a necessary but largely irrelevant preliminary to the serious business of collective theorizing.

Biographizing serves the important function of providing a first-person perspective on the memory that has just been read in its third-person version: a perspective sometimes in conflict with or in contradiction to that provided by the written memory. It is from this tension that the collective theorizing takes off. Some of the details and particularities of the biographizing can be set aside as irrelevant. Other aspects of the biographical discussion, including further memories triggered off by the discussion, lead into the constructive theorizing which then takes place. In this theorizing, the tension between analysing the memories at the collective level and using biographical information sometimes reappears.

The following description of the group discussion of a memory exemplifies the tension between biography and the written memory. The memory was written by Veronica in response to the cue or trigger 'initiating' (in a heterosexual encounter).

Veronica and Bob had travelled to New York on the same plane, although Bob had travelled first class and she economy. They had met in London and had discovered they would be in New York at about the same time. They were staying in different hotels and Bob agreed to pick Veronica up for dinner after they had both settled in and caught up on some sleep. Bob failed to ring Veronica, so she rang him and woke him up. He suggested that she come and pick him up and they go out for a meal. Veronica walked up to his hotel . . . She had decided she would like to go to bed with him and as they were walking out of the restaurant after a pleasant meal, suggested as much. He was surprised and pleased. They went back to his hotel – it was bigger and better. They made love and went to sleep. During the night, Veronica woke him and they made love again.

In the group discussion surrounding this and other memories of 'initiating', the group noted that most of the memories involving initiating sex were on holiday or in some way removed from the everyday. The discussion examined notions of the 'shipboard romance', the freedom of such encounters from normal constraints involving considerations of commitment. Note that in this memory there is little evidence of moral conflict, though the man's surprise at Veronica's suggestion is indicative of a breaking of convention – even though it is a pleasurable surprise.

The group discussion contrasted situations of freedom, holiday and transience with the codes of fidelity, trust and commitment underlying sexual relationships of other kinds. In this discussion, Veronica introduced biographical material regarding how later she and Bob, back in Australia, had an ongoing relationship in which Bob's involvement with his wife and his reluctance to tell his wife about Veronica became very problematic. Any reference to these ensuing problems is entirely absent from the written memory.

It was in the group discussion which contrasted the relationship in this memory with relationships involving commitment, that Veronica's biographizing emerged. Veronica's 'she' and 'I' subject positions simultaneously uphold and challenge the cultural imperative that women's sexual advances are contained in shipboard romances. In this instance, Veronica's biographizing highlights the partiality of subject positions (Gavey, 1992). To make sense of the 'she' subject position readers draw on their shared understanding of the nature of 'shipboard romances'; these kinds of relationship afford freedom from social restraints, such as the taken-for-granted assumptions of women's passivity in committed relationships. Yet in adopting the 'I' subject position, in biographizing, Veronica offers a narrative which resists this dichotomy between proper realms for women's sexual activity. What Veronica began in New York was not a mere holiday romance but developed into an ongoing relationship, and the shipboard romance discourse of women's sexuality only makes partial sense of Veronica's experience.

As well as the first-person positions of 'I' and 'me', memory-work also affords its participants the second- and third-person positions of 'you', 's/he' and 'her'/'him', as discussed in more detail later. It is these tensions between subject positions which provide fertile ground from which to theorize. We now turn to an analysis of memories of 'a moral dilemma' to show how memory-work exposes processes of self-construction, and the dialogic nature of the self.

An illustration: Moral selves

Self-understanding is 'the backdrop against which our tastes and desires and opinions and aspirations make sense' (Taylor, 1992: 33–4). Agency resides in the ability to reflect on this background in order to articulate strong evaluations.[1] While selves can be understood as subjects of a moral order, the self is not simply subjected to a moral order. Outside of the moral order one would not be who one is. When confronted with moral dilemmas, and in making strong evaluations, persons appropriate aspects of the social and in so doing engage in the process of self-construction. Being selves is something people *do*.

Being moral selves involves the intersubjective negotiation of subject positions rather than the application of distinct codes of ethics – for example, Gilligan's (1982) articulation of the masculine ethic of justice and the feminine ethic of care. Gilligan (1986: 327) argues that women's 'care perspective . . . is neither biologically determined nor unique to women', rather it develops out of women's more connected under-standing of self. Yet, the notion of self remains unproblematized. Like Tronto (1987) and Lykes (1985), we question the role of gendered selves in Gilligan's argument; a focus on identities (i.e. of women and men) as opposed to social practices and institutions obscures the possibility that an ethic of care has been 'created in modern society by the condition of subordination' (Tronto, 1987: 647). In the process of memory-work on moral dilemmas, the tension produced between the 'I' and the 'she' subject positions directs attention to appropriation of morality rather than subjection to it, that is, to the self in process rather than the self as given.

The memories we use here to illustrate the production of selves were produced in response to the cue 'a moral dilemma'. We draw on two of these memories only, one from childhood and one from adult life. The authors of these memories are attempting to evaluate different self-interpretations. Denise's and Jill's memories give accounts of confusion and uncertainty arising from conflicting subject positions.

Denise was sitting at her desk in her fifth class classroom. They had all been given two pieces of paper on which they had to write their votes for school prefects for the next year – one girl and one boy. They had been told to write who they thought would do the job best. Denise quite quickly wrote the name of a boy she thought would be good – he was the smartest boy in the class and pretty daggy, but nice. The room was in silence and everyone was hiding their pieces of paper from each other. Denise could not decide which girl to vote for – she wanted very much to be a prefect herself, but she couldn't vote for herself. Everyone else was writing and the teacher was calling out that they only had a few minutes. Denise thought through the girls she could vote for. She didn't want to vote for any of them – the ones she liked and admired she felt upset about for other reasons – and she didn't want any of them to get the reward of being a prefect. She still couldn't decide. She became increasingly anxious and could not bring herself to write her own name on the paper, although she wanted to. Her held felt buzzy and she was scared that someone would see if she wrote her own name. The teacher then said that everyone had to put in their pieces of paper now and Denise felt very panicky. She quickly wrote her own name on the piece of paper, folded it so no one could see and handed it in. She felt frightened and anxious, but there was nothing she could do about it now – she had voted for herself.

(Denise)

Jill was in her late 20s. She was living with a very nice man who she liked. However, their sex life was no longer very interesting.

One night she was at a work dinner. There was a man there, Robert, who lived near her place so they shared a taxi home. Jill and he were attracted to each other. He suggested they stop at a pub for a drink before going home, so they did.

Pretty soon they were kissing and fondling each other. They left the pub and went back to his place where this continued. They were both, at this stage, a bit drunk.

Robert's live-in girlfriend was overseas for three months. While they were kissing and fondling, Robert wanted them to go to bed. The bedroom door was open and faced out towards the lounge room where they were sitting. His bedroom seemed very feminine, with lacy white bedspreads and curtains; Jill felt it was full of his girlfriend. There was a big bed in the middle of the room and the floorboards were polished.

Jill began to have doubts about what she was doing and told Robert that she thought it was wrong both to his girlfriend and Jill's boyfriend. Robert disagreed with her, saying it was all right for them to have sex, nobody would know.

They had a long talk about it. Jill was a bit distressed and felt she wasn't thinking clearly. She can remember her thoughts were confused and she didn't really know what to do. They were sitting on the couch very close together and were still touching each other, so she was still sexually aroused. This maintained her confused state.

Jill kept eyeing the bedroom; it was hard not to as it was right in front of them. She eventually decided she ought to go home so Robert rang a taxi for her. He said if she decided to change her mind he was always available (or something along those lines).

When she got home, Fred was still awake. Jill was very upset. She ran in and hugged him and told him that she'd almost slept with someone. She was crying now.

(Jill)

In voting for herself Denise has to consider the value of being a prefect and the implications of taking care of herself (not exactly the kind of thing a prefect should do). Jill treads the line between being a faithful girlfriend with a boring sex life and an unfaithful girlfriend who might damage another couple's relationship as well as her own.

In Denise's memory, choosing a boy to vote for is easy; he's clever and nice, so being 'daggy' (i.e. not trendy) does not go against him. The boy can still do a good job. But making the right decision about which girl should be prefect involves a consideration of whether the girls Denise is 'upset' with should be 'rewarded' with the job. It is not just a matter of capability, Denise doubts these girls' worthiness of the position. This added consideration highlights the moral dimension of voting. In the memory, voting for boys is characterized as a moral choice, while voting for girls becomes a moral problem. This dichotomy makes sense against the backdrop of the separate spheres discourse (Welter, 1966), in which it is understood that men's place is in the public realm and women are relegated to the private realm. By virtue of his sex, the boy Denise votes for is already worthy of being a prefect, whereas she and her girlfriends are inherently unworthy. Denise is guilty of judging herself worthy of being a prefect, of aspiring to move beyond the confines of the private realm. The conclusion to her memory ('she had voted for herself') offers a moral perspective on Denise as a guilty child giving into the temptation to blow her own trumpet. The finality of 'there was nothing she could do about it now' suggests that in acting on her desire she is somehow doomed.

Jill's memory about near-infidelity can be understood against two paradoxical backdrops of women's sexuality – as inherently moral and inherently amoral. Women's morality is understood as pertaining, not just to the private realm, but to sexuality in particular (Haug, 1992). Yet women's sexuality is also characterized as wanton, out of control and hence intrinsically problematic and threatening to the social order (Bersani, 1988). From the 'she' subject position Jill's memory is about negotiating sexual boredom within the constraints of monogamous heterosexual coupledom. The prospect of neglecting her feminine duty to uphold the social order by controlling her sexual desires is characterized as 'distress[ing]', 'sexually arous[ing]', 'confus[ing]' and tear-inducing. Jill's final sentence, 'She was crying now', offers the moral conclusion that while a woman's job in upholding moral values in the private, sexual realms may be a difficult cross to bear, her tears are the just reward for her near-infidelity.

From the 'she' subject position, the moral of Denise's and Jill's memories can be read as about the shame and anxiety of succumbing, or nearly succumbing, to the temptations of transgressing or neglecting their duties to uphold the public–private distinction.

Tensions between the 'I' and the 'she' positions

In the group discussion (Phase 2), when co-researchers shift into the 'I' subject position they resist the moral of the 'she' stories (as we saw in the discussion of Veronica's memory, above). In the 'I' subject position they begin to biographize. Part of talking to each other (the 'I'–'you' of the co-researchers' dialogue) is an attempt to resist being subsumed into the common meanings. This is an element of memory-work which breaks up the narrative of the memory and counters the moral of the story. The tension between the 'I' and the 'she' subject positions serves to challenge the notion of the unitary individual entering into and resolving moral dilemmas.

Denise's decision to vote for herself is an articulation of her desire to be prefect; she would like to be seen as capable and worthy of holding 'public office'. What is not said is the 'other reasons' why Denise won't vote for the girls she admires. In biographizing Denise adds that at the time of the vote a new girl has taken Denise's best friend. The new girl is highly popular and Denise sees the voting as a popularity contest. She explains: 'I wanted to beat her to get my friend back'. From the 'I' subject position, Denise doesn't see a position in the public realm as an end in itself. Rather, getting voted prefect is a way of resolving dilemmas in the private realm.

From the 'she' subject position Jill's memory is about the difficulties of upholding monogamous heterosexual coupledom. But in the end this is what she decides to do and she confesses her thoughts of transgression to her partner. Jill's tears suggest that she feels remorse for flirting with the option of invoking chaos. In biographizing Jill added that she and Fred broke up later, and that she did have sex with Robert after this, when he was still in a relationship with the same girlfriend. As the memory stands, Jill's story is about remorse for being tempted to disrupt the social order; her biographizing disrupts this moral conclusion.

The authors of stories of moral dilemmas invite particular understandings of their experiences and their resolutions. But, as critics of the written memories, the authors resist the meanings of the stories by giving information which serves to question the moral conclusion of the story, and thereby the construction of the narrative. In questioning the moral conclusion authors question the fixity of that narrative, and the coherence of subjectivity.

First-, second- and third-person positions

In the group discussion, in Phase 2, the imperative to search for similarities means that the co-researchers seek a common understanding of the memories. In all phases of memory-work, but particularly in Phase 2, there is a sense in which 'I' becomes 'we', 'me' becomes 'us' and 's/he' becomes 'they'. The collectivities in which actions unfold are implicated in the construction of selves. Biographizing represents not only a breaking away from 's/he' into 'I', but also from the social analysis of experience (that is, from 'we', 'women' and 'cultural imperatives' into 'I'). In Phases 2 and 3 of memory-work co-researchers reflect on these distinctions between subject positions; the resistance of 'I' to the subject positions of 's/he' and 'we' is reconsidered in terms of shared experiences of discursive positioning. For example, when Veronica takes up the subject position of 'I' and adds that the sexual relationship she initiated was an ongoing one as opposed to a shipboard romance, co-researchers continue to theorize her experience in terms of the social practices which afford and limit women's initiation of sexual encounters. The fact that there was a natural conclusion to the episode in the written memory (that is, it was a shipboard romance) explains not only Veronica's action in initiating sex, but the circumstances which enable women in general to do so.

As well as first- and third-person positions, memory-work also enables co-researchers to take up the second-person position 'you'. In Phase 2, in particular, the common understandings and meanings sought by the co-researchers involve each of the participants in sharing each other's subject positions. The meaning which a speaker attributes to an utterance is bound up with his or her relationship to the addressee. Thus the tension between the speakers' 'I' and 's/he' positions can be characterized as a tension between 'I'–'you' and 's/he'–'other' dialogues.

Tensions between 'I'–'you' and 'she'–'other' dialogues

In Phase 2 the 'I'–'you' relationship takes two different forms. That is, co-researchers can reflect on the dialogue between themselves in the group discussion, and on the intersubjective relations between the actors in the memories. Following Hollway (1984: 227), in memory-work the 'approach to subjectivity is through the meanings and incorporated values which attach to a person's practices and provide the powers through which he or she can position him- or herself *in relation to others*' (emphasis added). Memories reflect the self in dialogue. In writing moral dilemma memories, authors describe how they attempt to resolve differences between subject positions and to position themselves in relation to others in the memory. In the written memory, the dialogue in question occurs between 'she' and 'other'; and in discussing the written memory co-researchers take up both the subject positions of 'she' and 'other'. In Phase 2 of memory-work, there is a different audience for the memories and a different dialogue occurs between subject positions. In the 'I'–'you' dialogue, the author of the memory resists the moral of the written memories by justifying herself. This serves to challenge 'you' the co-researchers *not* to read the memory in terms of the sense it makes to 'them' the others in the memory.

Denise's moral dilemma occurs as she attempts to make sense of her experience of losing her friend to the 'new girl'. The person whom she would normally vote for, and call on to ratify her decisions, is no longer available to her. The 'she'–'other' dialogue of the written memory can be read as a justification for Denise's actions addressed to her friend, and co-researchers are positioned as her friend. As such, the memory reads 'I wanted to be prefect but I only voted for myself because I couldn't vote for you, and it wasn't something I was happy about'. Yet in biographizing, the 'I'–'you' dialogue of Phase 2, Denise acquaints co-researchers with her desire to beat the new girl in a popularity contest. In occuping the subject position of 'you', co-researchers reflect on the role of popularity in girls' and women's experiences of the boundaries between public and private realms. Popularity is a public realm phenomenon, it marks a sanctioned form of success for women in the public realm. The boy Denise votes for is described as 'nice', not popular. The requirement of popularity for girls in order for them to be prefects shores up women's inherent unworthiness to occupy positions in the public realm. In this way, when co-researchers occupy the 'you' subject position they subsume Denise's biographizing in a further analysis of discursive positioning.

Jill's memory explains her dilemma in terms of her relationship difficulties with her partner. Like Denise, her dilemma occurs as she tries to make a decision which will affect her relationship without having discussed her predicament with her partner (a detail Jill gave in biographizing). When reading the 'she'–'other' dialogue in the memory as addressed to Fred the narrative positions Jill as ultimately willing to uphold heterosexual monogamy. Yet in the 'I'–'you' dialogue of the collective discussion, Jill offers a perspective on the memory which challenges the discursive positioning of women as sexual gatekeepers. Co-researchers are offered the discursive position of the now single woman who is no longer dissuaded from challenging heterosexual monogamy by thoughts of the other woman's 'lacy white bedspreads'. This subject position is constituted in the discourse of women's sexuality as essentially uncontrollable and dangerous.

So co-researchers position each other in two ways: they invite each other to take up the subject positions of the others in the written memories, and in introducing biography into the discussion of the memories they provide the co-researchers with first-person ('I') subject positions. It is in this process of interposing the 'you' (each other) between the 'I' and the 's/he' which takes place during the group discussion that memory-work exposes how individuals share ways of appropriating the social, by engaging in the arguments of a living tradition.

The subject positions negotiated in memories of 'a moral dilemma' are not simply afforded by a care ethic; rather they arise within specific discursive practices such as heterosexual monogamy, having and keeping best friends, and popularity. What memory-work highlights is that not only do these discourses give rise to moral dilemmas, but also, and more importantly, moral dilemmas arise in the intersubjective negotiation of conflicting and partial subject positions, such as the positions of a faithful girlfriend in a sexually unsatisfying relationship, of being an unfaithful girlfriend, of having sex with another woman's partner, of being a popular prefect and winning back a friend, of being left out.

Conclusion

Rather than taking experience as a given, in memory-work experience is understood in terms of the process of appropriation of conflicting discourses. Memory-work operates at two levels: it exposes the processes involved in the social construction of self as well as providing a research tool for studying the points of argument which constitute a living tradition.

This chapter has concentrated on describing the way in which memory-work enables analysis of the process of intersubjectivity, through the consideration of the tensions produced between first-, second- and third-person positions. By engaging co-researchers in dialogic relationships such as exist between 'I' and 'you', 's/he' and 'other', memory-work highlights the partiality and conflicting nature of discursive positions. For example, in Western culture, women as sexual beings are understood to be both morally responsible and morally irresponsible. To understand how people negotiate conflicting subject positions we look to intersubjectivity. 'Moral dilemma' memories can be understood as constructed in the tensions between subject positions, both interpersonally and intrapersonally. Attempts to reconcile subject positions, which are only partly successful and hence the dilemma, reveal the intersubjective self in process.

Memory-work reveals and further implicates co-researchers in the ongoing debates which constitute a living tradition. It is in resisting being positioned within these debates, and in taking up subject positions, that the self is constructed.

Acknowledgement

The authors would like to thank Madeline Oliver for her insightful comments on an earlier draft of this chapter.

Note

1 We make strong evaluations when we question the quality of our motivation to do something. Making strong evaluations is different from making simple choices based on the expected outcomes of actions. Strong evaluation involves reflection on a plurality of backdrops, each with a different meaning for self and social interpretation. We choose moral dilemmas to illustrate the processes of intersubjectivity because moral dilemmas involve strong evaluation and are thus peculiarly suited to a discussion of the processes of self construction (Taylor, 1977).

References

Bartky, S. L. (1990) *Femininity and Domination: Studies in the Phenomenology of Oppression*. New York and London: Routledge.
Bersani, L. (1988) 'Is the rectum a grave?', in D. Crimp (ed.), *AIDS: Cultural Analysis, Cultural Activism*. Cambridge, MA: MIT Press.
Billig, M. (1987) *Arguing and Thinking: A Rhetorical Approach to Social Psychology*. Cambridge: Cambridge University Press.

Crawford, J., Kippax, S., Onyx, J., Gault, U. and Benton, P. (1992) *Emotion and Gender: Constructing Meaning from Memory*. London: Sage.

Davies, Bronwyn and Harré, Rom (1990) 'Positioning: the discursive production of selves', *Journal for the Theory of Social Behaviour*, 20(1): 43–63.

Gadamer, H.-G. (1986) *The Relevance of the Beautiful and Other Essays* (translated by Nicholas Walker). Cambridge and New York: Cambridge University Press.

Gavey, N. (1992) 'Technologies and effects of heterosexual coercion', *Feminism & Psychology*, 2: 325–51.

Gilligan, C. (1982) *In a Different Voice: Psychological Theory and Women's Development*. Cambridge, MA: Harvard University Press.

Gilligan, C. (1986) 'On *In a different voice*: An interdisciplinary forum. Reply', *Signs*, 11: 324–33.

Grosz, E. (1994) *Volatile Bodies: Toward a Corporeal Feminism*. Sydney: Allen & Unwin.

Harré, R. (1983) *Personal Being: A Theory for Individual Psychology*. Oxford: Blackwell.

Harré, R. (1986) 'The social construction of selves', in K. Yardley and T. Honess (eds), *Self and Identity*. Chichester: John Wiley.

Haug, F. in collaboration with others (1987) *Female Sexualisation: A Collective Work of Memory* (translated by Erica Carter). London: Verso.

Haug, F. (1992) *Beyond Female Masochism: Memory-Work and Politics* (translated by Rodney Livingstone). London: Verso.

Henriques, J., Hollway, W., Urwin, C., Venn, C. and Walkerdine, V. (1984) *Changing the Subject: Pyschology, Social Regulation and Subjectivity*. London and New York: Methuen.

Hodge, J. (1988) 'Subject, body and the exclusion of women from philosophy', in M. Griffiths and M. Whitford (eds), *Feminist Perspectives in Philosophy*. Bloomington: Indiana University Press.

Hollway, W. (1984) 'Gender differences and the production of subjectivity', in J. Henriques, W. Hollway, C. Urwin, C. Venn and V. Walkerdine (eds), *Changing the Subject: Psychology, Social Regulation and Subjectivity*. London and New York: Methuen.

Hooton, J. (1992) 'Autobiography and gender', *Australian Feminist Studies*, 16: 25–40.

Kippax, S., Crawford, J., Benton, P., Gault, U. and Noesjirwan, J. (1988) 'Constructing emotions: weaving meaning from memories', *British Journal of Social Psychology*, 27: 19–33.

Kitzinger, C. and Gilligan, C. (1994) 'Listening to a different voice', *Feminism & Psychology*, 4: 408–19.

Le Guin, U. (1992) *Dancing at the Edge of the World*. London: Paladin.

Lykes, M. B. (1985) 'Gender and individualistic vs. collectivist bases for notions about the self', *Journal of Personality*, 53: 356–83.

MacIntyre, A. (1981) *After Virtue*. London: Duckworth.

Mead, G. H. (1909) 'Social psychology as counterpart in physiological psychology', *Psychological Bulletin*, 6: 401–8.

Scott, J. (1993) 'The evidence of experience', in H. Abelove, M. A. Barale and D. M. Halperin (eds), *The Lesbian and Gay Studies Reader*. New York: Routledge.

Shotter, J. (1984) *Social Accountability and Selfhood*. Oxford: Blackwell.

Shotter, J. (1986) 'A sense of place: Vico and the social production of social identities', *British Journal of Social Psychology*, 25: 199–211.

Shotter, J. (1993) *Cultural Politics of Everyday Life: Social Constructionism, Rhetoric and Knowing of the Third Kind*. Buckingham: Open University Press.

Taylor, C. (1977) 'What is human agency?', in T. Mischel (ed.), *The Self*. Oxford: Blackwell.

Taylor, C. (1992) *Multiculturalism and 'The Politics of Recognition': An Essay*. Princeton, NJ: Princeton University Press.

Tronto, J. C. (1987) 'Beyond gender difference to a theory of care', *Signs*, 12: 644–63.

Welter, B. (1966) 'The cult of true womanhood: 1820–1860', *American Quarterly*, 18: 151–74.

Wertsch, J. (1985) *Vygotsky and the Social Formation of Mind*. London: Harvard University Press.

10

Q-methodology as feminist methodology: Women's views and experiences of pornography

CHARLENE Y. SENN

Shulamit Reinharz (1992) has suggested that while few methods have been invented specifically by feminist researchers, a large range of methods designed by non-feminists have been used productively by feminist researchers across the social science disciplines. While almost any method can be used dynamically and inventively by feminists (see Reinharz, 1992, for examples), some methods require fewer contortions of feminist researchers than do others. This chapter briefly chronicles my methodological passage in research on women's experiences with pornography: from an experimental approach which required too much distortion for my comfort to a Q-methodological approach which provided a much better fit with my philosophical and political goals. I then explain Q-methodology as a feminist research tool, using my pornography research as an exemplar. I will not be suggesting that this approach is uniformly applicable, nor that more 'traditional' methods are never useful. In fact, I use a variety of methods in my ongoing research programme. I am suggesting, however, that in terms of its ability to capture the views and experiences of women in their everyday lives, the research I conducted for my dissertation went much further and was more personally rewarding than other methods I had used up until that time.

In the last year of my BSc in psychology I began the journey of 'becoming a feminist' by taking women's studies courses and by becoming active in my community. But at that stage, I didn't think my training in psychology had anything to offer my feminism. It wasn't until I returned to university following a year of front-line work that I began to think that my experimental psychology training could be useful if it were applied to topics of relevance to women and used to advance feminist goals. The result was my MSc thesis, which was an experimental investigation of the effects of pornography on women (Senn, 1985; 1993; Senn and Radtke, 1990). I did not, on the whole, feel restricted by the experimental method. We do what we know and I had never been exposed to alternatives. The study was interesting and ended up supporting my hypotheses regarding the harms of pornography to women. However, I became increasingly disillusioned with the method itself. My changing values and beliefs increasingly collided with those inherent in my experimental work.

The change in my research methods was preceded by a change in my theoretical perspective. While my earlier approach was not a rigidly positivist view, it was for the most part based on such a view of the world. It embodied a single truth: 'pornography either harms (or does not harm) women'. I operationally defined the construct 'pornography', breaking sexually explicit materials into three categories: erotica, non-violent pornography, and violent pornography. I hypothesized that exposure to pornography (violent and non-violent) would harm women in particular – and measurable – ways, and I designed an experimental manipulation to assess whether my hypothesis was 'true' or 'false'. The answer to the question, posed in this way, was that pornography harms women, specifically by making them depressed, anxious, angry and fatigued. I was able to be even more specific in my understanding of the particular features of the images that caused the harm, because the sexually explicit images that contained no sexism, dehumanization or violence (i.e. the erotica) had no ill effects.

But while the data suggested that such generalizations were defensible, it was also clear that there was more complexity in the world than these 'answers' suggested. For example, in response to the violent images, women were fairly consistent in their evaluations: their ratings were all negative. However, this was not true of the women's evaluations of the erotic images: women did not uniformly like them. The comments of two of the women in the erotic exposure condition illustrate the range of responses. One woman left the session saying, 'If I had known the slides were like this, I would have brought my vibrator!', while another asked me why I had included 'those disgusting pictures of two women together'. The violent and dehumanizing images depicted similar sexual activities, but women uniformly responded to the degradation and violence in the pornographic images, rather than assessing the sexual acts themselves. In the erotic condition which contained no violence, women responded to the sexual content and they differed substantially in their attitudes, beliefs and feelings about it.

Differences among women had been previously identified in the literature in this field (see, for example, Stock, 1983; Mayerson and Taylor, 1987) and I was aware of this. From my readings in the feminist literature, and my own life experience, I also knew that women are not a monolithic category who all respond the same way in a given situation. I knew that women do not share the same life experiences, they are privileged or not in different ways, they make different choices, and they change their minds over time. But the focus in experimental investigations is on those experimentally created group differences (e.g., differences among exposure conditions) rather than on differences in experience and perspective. Experimental studies are not generally designed to explore these differences. Moreover, I became convinced that in investigations of women's experiences of pornography, as in other areas, research on women as a unitary category is probably not as productive as the investigation of differences and similarities among women.

I came to identify with certain aspects of a constructionist theoretical approach (see, for example, Gergen, 1985). Using that framework, individuals' perspectives on issues and on their own experiences are seen to be shaped by the culture and historical time in which people live, and by their position and privilege in that culture, along with the factors that are often focused on by social psychologists such as the context of the specific situation, their socialization, etc.

But I didn't know how to investigate issues in a manner that would explicate both similarities and differences within a constructionist framework. When I read an article entitled 'A Q-methodological Study of Lesbian Identities' (Kitzinger and Stainton Rogers, 1985) I realized I had found a method that could address this problem. Elsewhere, Celia Kitzinger (1986: 153) described Q-methodology as an important methodological tool for feminist research:

> [t]he theoretical basis on which Q methodology is founded relies on the axiom that researchers should acknowledge and present the reality constructions of different women and men without prejudging or discrediting them, and without insisting on the superior (more 'objective') status of the researcher's own construction of reality.

While Q-methodology is not appropriate for all topics or research investigations, it is particularly useful in fields where questions of difference are important. Therefore, it is particularly well suited for feminist research agendas.

Q-methodology was invented in the 1930s by William Stephenson, an American researcher and theorist. His subsequent book, *The Study of Behavior* (1953) is still an important resource. However, the practical aspects of the process are best described in Steven Brown's *Political Subjectivity* (1980).

Q-methodology involves the use of a particular philosophy and technique for gathering data (a participant-centred, social construction approach) by means of a research instrument, the Q-sort. The Q-sort is a collection of items that represent the broadest possible variety of attitudes, perspectives, experiences, and/or beliefs on a topic. Participants in a Q-study read each Q-sort item and position it along a continuum, ranging from those they feel most accurately represent their experience or view to those they feel least accurately represent their experience or view. In effect, then, they are modelling their own construction of the topic in question.

To explain how Q-methodology differs from the more typical 'R'-type analysis, it is useful to contrast their theoretical and statistical assumptions. With an R-type analysis ('R being a generalized reference to the application of Pearson's product-moment correlation, r, to the study of trait relationships' (Brown, 1980: 9)), psychologists put the data gathered from the participants into a matrix, the rows of which are the participants and the columns of which are their responses to the items (the variables of interest). Then a factor analysis is used to collapse across rows (people) to answer the question of 'which items hang together', that is, which items seem to represent the same or similar constructs. The participants are simply a means of collecting multiple responses to the items. Q-analysis, by contrast, transposes the traditional matrix to consider the items of the Q-sort as the rows and the individuals who complete the Q-sort as the columns, making individuals, rather than items, the focus of the analysis. Factor analysis of this matrix answers the question 'which individuals cluster together because they have similarly modelled their experience/ views' so a factor, in a Q-analysis, represents a cluster of *people* (or their Q-sorts) not a cluster of *items*. These statistical procedures permit the researcher to identify groups of participants whose beliefs and experiences are similar and examine their differences from participants having other views/experiences. These perspectives can then be interpreted on the basis of prior research and theory, and in the context of the participants' own lives.

What follows here is an abbreviated description of my dissertation research on women's experiences of pornography to illustrate the use of Q-methodology.

Method

Phase one: Development of Q-sort

To design a Q-sort deck, it is necessary to sample as widely as possible the domain 'relevant to the problem under consideration' (Brown, 1980: 192).

Items can be derived from interviews or from other sources, such as the relevant literature or mass media constructions. I chose to use interviews.

The participants in my study were 30 women recruited and specifically selected for their varying backgrounds, views and experiences with pornography. The interview was semi-structured, covering issues and topics identified in the feminist and psychological literature on pornography, with opportunities for women to add anything relevant to their experience that had been missed. The interviews were audio-taped and varied between 25 and 90 minutes, with most being less than one hour.

The interview responses for all participants were transcribed. Three women who had some knowledge of the issue of pornography or women's issues (having written theses or dissertations on the topic or related topics) were given detailed instructions regarding how to write and select Q-sort items. The final result was a Q-sort deck with 98 items.[1] The items were randomly numbered from 1 to 98, typed on to decks of 3 × 5 inch index cards, and each deck was shuffled to ensure random presentation of items.

Phase two: Q-sorting

Participants were recruited on a non-random basis from two distinct groups of women living in a large Canadian city and the surrounding regions. One group of women (mature students and their female professors) was recruited from classes in a variety of disciplines at a university college specializing in returning students.

The second group of women was recruited from the interview sample, since it is important to have Q-sorts from some women who have also been interviewed. Sixteen of these women completed the Q-sort.

All participants were given detailed written instructions on how to complete the sorting task. To summarize, they were asked to read each item and place it on a continuum from +5 (strongly agree) to −5 (strongly disagree) (a physical template was provided). A forced quasi-normal distribution was requested;[2] however, any woman who had difficulty with this requirement was encouraged to do a free sort.

Results of the Q-sort

Technical details

The 59 Q-sorts were analysed using principal components analysis with varimax rotation (SAS Institute, 1985). A five-factor solution accounted for 60 per cent of the variance. The factor loadings for each participant are presented in Table 10.1. The participants whose accounts were pure representations of each factor (i.e., showing no significant loadings on

Table 10.1 Rotated factor loadings: four-factor solution

ID	Factor 1	Factor 2	Factor 3	Factor 4
Laura	0.89	0.07	−0.09	0.00
Bobby	0.85	0.04	0.19	−0.03
023	0.83	0.20	−0.02	0.05
Molly	0.79	0.11	0.17	0.07
016	0.76	0.33	0.21	0.13
020	0.75	0.10	0.12	0.22
009	0.74	0.19	0.17	−0.19
Sydney	0.72	0.04	0.12	−0.08
003	0.71	0.31	0.34	0.10
Clementine	0.70	−0.14	0.17	0.24
039	0.68	0.32	0.15	0.15
033	0.67	0.23	0.34	0.06
Esther	0.60	0.17	−0.04	0.06
Lisa	0.57	0.37	0.22	0.32
024	0.54	0.21	0.25	0.08
Clare	0.50	−0.18	0.21	0.31
007	0.44	0.21	0.32	0.39
Martha	0.13	0.80	0.08	0.11
044	0.13	0.75	−0.02	0.20
030	0.04	0.74	0.35	0.15
Erica	0.32	0.67	0.25	0.08
031	0.30	0.61	0.32	0.21
032	0.35	0.61	0.31	0.18
022	0.06	0.56	0.38	0.14
019	−0.02	0.13	0.74	0.15
004	0.18	0.36	0.66	0.15
001	0.05	0.09	0.60	0.21
Melissa	0.09	0.31	0.58	0.34
014	0.34	0.25	0.58	0.02
040	0.16	−0.04	0.57	−0.11
015	0.07	0.37	0.53	0.14
041	0.39	0.35	0.50	0.24
Sara	0.06	0.23	0.48	0.12
036	0.19	0.37	0.47	0.08
034	−0.13	0.05	0.02	0.73
042	0.10	0.25	0.16	0.69
008	0.09	0.14	0.18	0.56
037	0.30	0.12	0.35	0.42
Andy	0.33	0.12	0.35	0.03
005	0.55	0.52	0.13	−0.01
006	0.53	0.44	0.28	−0.12
027	0.45	0.57	0.21	0.06

Table 10.1 Continued

ID	Factor 1	Factor 2	Factor 3	Factor 4
010	0.52	0.53	0.12	0.41
Catherine	0.46	0.53	0.35	0.07
029	0.37	0.52	0.42	−0.11
025	0.47	0.52	0.38	0.01
026	0.31	0.51	0.47	0.25
002	0.46	0.48	0.13	−0.14
012	0.42	0.46	0.44	0.11
Amelia	0.59	0.26	0.05	−0.01
028	0.31	0.54	0.28	0.48
011	−0.19	0.50	0.30	0.21
017	−0.04	0.48	0.35	0.41
038	0.29	0.48	0.52	0.20
021	−0.05	0.37	0.51	0.41
043	0.06	0.41	0.51	0.16
018	0.29	−0.02	0.17	0.56
013	−0.04	0.14	0.48	0.53
035	0.26	0.36	0.26	0.42

other factors[3]) were selected. Following Brown's (1980) instructions, the scores of these subsets of participants were merged (weighting them according to factor loadings), converted to Z scores, and then re-numbered to reapply the template features (in the +5 to −5 pattern), to arrive at a representative sort for each factor. The representative sorts illustrate the common information between women who load purely on the factor. Within any factor, idiosyncratic responses or responses not held in common with the other women drop out into the neutral zone (Z scores of approximately 0) of the sort.

Basic interpretation of factors

The representative sort for each factor constituted the principal data for the first stage of interpretation. Representative scores match the positions on the original template, from +5 (strongly agree) to −5 (strongly disagree) with 0 as a neutral (does not apply) category. The second stage of interpretation was to turn for substantiation and clarification to the interview data provided by women who held each perspective. Only one factor (factor 4) did not have an interview participant loading purely on it. In that case, the interviews of women who loaded significantly on that factor, even though these were not pure loadings, were used to assist in the second phase of interpretation.

The results for the first four factors are presented in abbreviated form here. Example Q-sort items defining each factor will be presented and illustrated briefly by quotations from the interviews. A more detailed interpretation of the factors can be found elsewhere (Senn, 1991; 1993).

Factor 1: The 'radical feminist' perspective   The first of these perspectives was the most strongly represented by the women in the sample. It exemplifies the view put forward by radical feminist theorists (see, for example, Brownmiller, 1975; Dworkin, 1981; MacKinnon, 1987) and the experiences identified by radical feminist theories and researchers alike (Stock, 1983; Russell, 1984; Senn, 1985). Some of the women in this group actually identify as radical feminists (e.g., Sydney, Bobby, Laura). For others, the description of 'radical feminist' may not be part of their self-identity. However, for all of the women who loaded purely on this factor, feminism or a feminist perspective has been important to their perceptions of pornography. In this perspective the personal and political come together.

75.[4] Pornography has led me to a greater awareness of women's issues.   +3
65. My feelings about pornography have been influenced by feminism.   +2

Factor 1 women have had a lot of exposure to pornography and have difficultly avoiding it in their daily lives. They dislike pornography immensely. They dislike it because they believe that it presents very negative images of women as a group at the same time as it puts forward a highly unrealistic standard of physical attractiveness that individual women cannot achieve. They see much violence and victimization of women in pornography.

71. Pornography gives a negative impression of women.   +5
42. I have no strong feelings about pornography.   −4
43. I have not seen a lot of pornography in my life.   −2

They do not believe that all sexually explicit images are pornographic. However, the positive aspects of sexual imagery are not stressed, and they do not, on the whole, enjoy viewing sexual imagery. The interview data suggest that this may be because few of the women had seen any sexual materials which they did not consider pornographic (i.e., the positive sexual imagery).

60. Materials that are designed to cause sexual arousal are pornographic.   −2
20. I enjoy looking at sexually explicit materials.   −2

One of the most interesting components of women who hold this perspective is that they do not separate themselves from the women in the pornographic images. They often think of themselves in relation to the women in pornography (even though most of the factor 1 women had never been filmed or photographed themslves).

10. Actresses and models in pornography are doing a job like any other job.   −3
49. I rarely think about myself in comparison to the women in pornography.   −2
51. I see myself as different from the women in pornography.   0

The negative effects of pornography on the women's own lives are described as involving harms to specific relationships and more general harms involving the woman in her ongoing sense of self. In terms of relationships, the harms described ranged from arguments with male partners revolving around pornography to negative effects on the whole relationship. In more general terms, pornography is described as having negatively affected women's views of men, views of their own body, their sexuality, and their whole life.

8. A partner's use of pornography affected our whole relationship.   +2
67. My life would have been different without pornography.   +3

The women in Factor 1 do not accept these harms passively. As such, while they have experienced many harms of pornography in the past, these harms are counteracted by an active stance against further harm. This is not a 'victim' stance. These women would never again knowingly become involved with a male consumer, they would mind if a male partner used pornography, they would let their views be heard, and they would not knowingly let pornography into their homes. Some women have left events or public places because of the presence of pornography. Others have become anti-pornography activists.

This perspective could best be characterized as pro-control rather than pro-censorship as the women are not unambivalently supporting government controls. They support government restrictions on pornography but they do not agree with the way these are currently being carried out.

19. I don't think there should be legal limits on the availability of pornography.   −4
91. The government does not do enough about pornography.   +4
92. The government takes the wrong approach on pornography.   +2

Factor 2: The 'conservative' perspective The perspective of factor 2 women is also a commonly discussed perspective in the literature on pornography. It is best described in this case as a conservative perspective, although similar perspectives have been called 'fundamentalist' (Cowan et al., 1989) in other studies. It is not labelled fundamentalist in this case because it represents not only religious conservatism but also secular conservatism (e.g., Erica).

Similar to the findings of Cowan *et al.* (1989) for fundamentalist women, the women who held a conservative perspective had very little exposure to pornography and had no difficulty avoiding it. They have unambivalent negative feelings about pornography that are moderately strong. They believe that all sexually explicit materials are pornographic.

61. Materials that describe/show explicit sex scenes are pornographic.   +2

As Erica expresses it:

> What is it? [pornography] I just see pornography as explicit doings, . . . things just that reveal lots of, say, the person's body, doing acts which should only be kept in private or not even done at all.

Factor 2 women's sorts represent a view that is not based substantially on personal experience. In addition, the conservative women distance themselves from the women in pornography, they see themselves as different and they rarely think about themselves in relation to those women. They have also never been photographed or filmed themselves.

51. I see myself as different from the women in pornography.   +3

Factor 2 women believe that pornography is harmful and that it is related to violence against women. However, unlike the radical feminist perspective, there is an emphasis on men also being victims of the pornographic images. Their negative views about the men in pornography do not carry over to the men they know. In some ways, this could be construed as an extension of the distancing these women feel personally from the women in pornography. There is support from the interview transcripts to suggest that factor 2 women believe that the men they know are very different from the men in pornography. As Martha says:

> I don't think that it has really changed my view [of men] because I take a lot of what I see with a grain of salt, I don't, I say so okay, there it is but that is not really the way it is. And so I don't think it has made any difference.

41. I have never been involved with a man who used pornography regularly.   +4

Pornography is not perceived to be harmful to these women. However, it is believed to be harmful to others.

13. Exposure to pornography does not have an effect on people.   −2
17. I do not think pornography is related to violence against women.   −4

The focus about harm caused to others may be the result of the religious (e.g., Christian) and political (e.g., conservative) orientation of the women whose sorts loaded on factor 2. Factor 2 women's views about pornography have been profoundly affected by their religious and/or political beliefs. They have also been somewhat influenced by feminist views of pornography. This is particularly evident in their definitions of pornography and the messages they believe it gives about women and men.

Factor 2 women act out their beliefs about pornography by taking very strong personal stands. They refuse to have it in their homes and will not become involved with male consumers.

59.   In the future, I would get involved with someone who used pornography.   −5
57.   I wouldn't mind if my partner used pornography.   −5

This perspective also presents a pro-control view but with less critique of government action than seen among factor 1 women.

Factor 3: The 'humanist, child-centred' perspective   Factor 3 represents a perspective in which women are concerned with the harms of pornography to men and women, but with special emphasis on the harm to children. The emphasis on children is more profound than for the other factors. All but five of the women in the entire sample sorted item 85, 'Pornography using children is the worst kind of pornography', at the affirmative end of the sorting (i.e., they agreed with the item). However, factor 3 women placed special emphasis on all of the items relating to children. They are more worried about the effects of exposure to pornography on children than on adult women.

Women who load on this factor have not seen a lot of pornography, nor do they find it difficult to avoid. In the views of factor 3 women, pornography gives a very bad impression of women, presenting them as only existing for male pleasure. They do not believe that men understand how women feel about pornography.

80.   Pornography involves material or acts that degrade, demean, or exploit.   +5
62.   Men understand how women feel about pornography.   −3

It appears that factor 3 women have been involved with men who have used pornography but they do not consider them to be 'consumers'. This contradiction is illustrated by this extract from Sara's interview:

Q: Has pornography played any part in your adult relationships with men?

A: Well, I have only had one relationship. And if it is that horrible stuff that I wouldn't even touch or anything, no. But as I said, my husband likes to buy *Playboy* and *Penthouse* . . . I still would not want my daughters in those kinds of magazines but as I say they are not around in the house where the children can find them.

Q: What percentage of men that you have been involved with would you say were consumers?

A: One hundred per cent! (laughs) No, he's not a consumer.

Q: So you wouldn't consider him a consumer?

A: No.

Factor 3 women agreed with items suggesting that their partner's use of pornography had not affected their whole relationship or had a bad effect on them, and that it had not affected the children of the relationship. They also agreed strongly that what happens in sexual activity spills over into other parts of the relationship. When these responses are viewed together it becomes clear that the male partners of factor 3 women have not brought their consumption into the bedroom in an overt or coercive or violent manner and/or that the women have been able to overlook it. This appears to be a difference between factor 1 and factor 3 women.

Similar to factor 2 women, factor 3 women do not identify with women in pornography and feel they are quite different. Not surprisingly, then, factor 3 women do not feel they have been directly harmed by pornography in any way, even though they dislike it.

76.   Pornography has not had much of an effect on my life.   +3

In direct contrast with their views on the effects of pornography on themselves, the women who hold this perspective are very concerned about the possibility of children viewing pornography. Their refusal to have pornography in their own homes may be due more to their feelings about their children seeing it than to their own preferences. They support legal limits on pornography, and the interviews suggested that they place special emphasis on trying to keep pornography out of the reach and view of children.

56.   I would not want children to see pornography.   +5

Asked whether pornography has had a positive, negative or neutral impact on her life, Sara said:

Neutral. Now if it was involving one of my children that would be different!

Factor 4: The 'ambivalent but mildly pro-pornography' perspective   None of the women interviewed loaded above 0.39 on factor 4. This would suggest that this factor is not adequately represented in the interview sample. Factor 4 represents quite a different perspective from the others discussed so far. Women who load on this factor have not seen a lot of pornography and they haven't thought about it much. There is some evidence to suggest that the types of material viewed by these women are different from those seen by women holding the perspectives discussed so far. These women have some mildly positive attitudes towards pornography (e.g., its OK for my partner to use it), but they also have some very mixed feelings about specific sexual materials.

40.	I have mixed feelings about pornography.	+5
52.	I think there are different types of pornography.	+5
21.	I feel differently about different types of pornography.	+4

Factor 4 women were mostly positive about their exposure to pornography. While the age of exposure varied, the viewing was always self-directed, they were usually alone, and they experienced high levels of enjoyment and sexual arousal. They also learned things about sex from these materials. Use of pornography with a partner may have been less positive.

98.	When I first saw pornography I was curious about it.	+5
20.	I enjoy looking at sexually explicit materials.	+3
30.	I have been sexually aroused by pornography.	+4
7.	A partner's use of pornography has affected the way I feel about myself.	+2

Factor 4 women show some striking differences in the perception of pornography from the women whose perspectives have been presented so far. First, factor 4 women disagreed that most pornography shows violence and victimization. They also disagreed that pornography is related to violence against women. This is the only perspective in which these views are held. It is possible that factor 4 women have seen different types of pornography than other women – perhaps only the milder versions of that which is commonly available. Another possibility is that factor 4 women simply do not see violence or victimization where other women do.

While factor 4 women agree with others that pornography presents women as sex objects for male pleasure, they do not necessarily think this is a bad thing. In fact, they do *not* believe that pornography gives a negative impression of women. They do, however, believe that people might become addicted to pornography.

Given these differences in the description of pornographic materials, it is not surprising that factor 4 women see the harms of pornography in a different way, too. After all, if the materials are not seen as violent, one would not expect them to incite violence. Factor 4 women describe the effects of pornography specifically as creating an unrealistic standard of physical attractiveness and body size and shape. They feel that the only way that they have ever been harmed by pornography personally is that it has increased their negative feelings about their own bodies.

58. Images of women in pornography set unreal standards for how a woman's body should look.   +4
79. Pornography hasn't had that much effect on how I feel about my body.   −3

Another obvious difference between the perspective of women who load on factor 4 and the other women was in their perceptions of women in pornography. Factor 4 women supported the view that participation in pornography is a job like any other job and did not view the models/ actresses as 'victims'. They then strongly dissociated themselves from these 'workers'. Women could place an item in the neutral category if it did not apply to them and they could only place three items in each of the 'extreme' positions on the template. Factor 4 women chose these items as two of their three 'strongly disagree' items. Interestingly, this distancing exceeded or matched the distancing done by the most conservative women in the sample (factor 2).

28. I have been paid to appear in sexual photographs or films.   −5
29. I have been photographed or filmed in a sexual context by a partner.   −5
51. I see myself as different from the women in pornography.   +2
10. Actresses and models in pornography are doing a job like any other job.   +2

Factor 4 women believe in legal limits for pornography, but they do not believe that the government takes the right approach on the issue. While they agree that the world would be a better place without pornography, they do not worry about the current availability of materials. They themselves do not find it hard to avoid pornography. Since they also indicated that the government does enough about pornography, they may favour less restrictive censorship laws.

Discussion

A feminist inquiry using Q-methodology is a multi-phase project. Each phase makes unique contributions to feminist understandings of issues and experiences. In the research described here, Q-methodology was used to describe and explore women's varied experiences with pornography. The interview methodology of the first phase of the research resulted in extremely rich and detailed descriptions of women's reality. These interviews could, of course, have been treated as an end in themselves, analysing them as discourse, or for their content (for examples, see Reinharz, 1992). Instead, the interviews in the current study provided the basis for writing Q-sort items representing a wide diversity of views and experiences. These items were then used to elicit

an even larger group of women's experiences and perspectives. Moreover, the interviews were useful anchors for the interpretation of the
factors in the Q-sort portion of the study.

The Q-sort technique resulted in very powerful interpretations of
women's experiences. The statistical procedures allow the most important features of women's perceptions to be highlighted (those which are
shared with some women and differentiate them from others) while the
idiosyncratic responses fall into shadow.

Analysis of the Q-sorts in this study led to the identification of different
combinations of life experiences, exposure patterns, individual coping
styles, and cognitive frameworks, all of which are likely to have influenced the construction of the four perspectives represented by the
factors. This does not mean, of course, that there are only four perspectives: using a different sample, the same Q-sort items would be likely to
generate additional perspectives.[5]

I have come away from this project convinced that Q-methodology is a
valauble tool for feminist inquiry. However, there were some difficulties
that I encountered which should be addressed in the future. One of the
problems was the result of my decision to use a forced sort. A few of the
participants felt unduly restricted by this requirement. While there are
good statistical and theoretical reasons for requiring the quasi-normal
distribution (such as reducing the influence of response tendencies on the
factors), I would, in the future, suggest rather than require a forced
distribution. In addition, the complexity of the sorting task may have
discouraged some women from completing it. While this is not a universal problem of Q-studies, sorting of 98 items took women a considerable
length of time, and involved a metre-wide template and 98 index cards
scattered around. This may prove to be an unwieldy task for some
women, such as those with small children and some with disabilities. It
also requires a considerable length of time during which the woman is
concentrating on the task. For women whose interest in the topic of
pornography was limited, this may have been simply too long to sustain
the interest in completing the task. Simplifications in the instructions,
free sorting specifications, and fewer items could reduce these problems.

In future Q-studies, I would also add a third phase to the study. My
student status at the time (and its corresponding financial and time
restraints) prevented the addition of a phase in which the interviewed
women were given the results and interpretations of the factors. The
purpose of such an addition would be to assess the participants' satisfaction with the representation of their experience, and to provide a certain
kind of validity to the findings.

Overall, this methodology's strengths far outweigh its weaknesses.
Q-methodology was extremely powerful in describing how various
groups of women experience pornography in the context of their lives. It

allowed women's voices to emerge beyond the statistical analyses in a way that factorial and correlational designs normally do not. The sampling procedure and methodology combined enabled perspectives to emerge which had not been previously identified in the research or feminist literatures.

Q-methodology has also been applied successfully and inventively by other feminist researchers to a variety of topics including lesbian identities (Kitzinger, 1987), feminist identities (Snelling, 1993) and humour (Gallivan, 1993). As we continue to make this methodology work for us, making changes and refining procedures, I believe it will add much to our knowledge of the diversity and complexity of women's experiences and views.

Notes

1 Other researchers (among them Stephenson, 1953; Brown, 1980; Kitzinger, 1986) have written all Q-sort items themselves. The instructions for the raters were designed from descriptions of Kitzinger's procedure for writing the items. The instructions on writing items given to the raters can be obtained from the author. The Q-sort items are also available from the author.

2

+5	+4	+3	+2	+1	0	−1	−2	−3	−4	−5
3	5	8	11	14	16	14	11	8	5	3

A debate exists over the benefits and drawbacks of a forced distribution sort over a free sort with no such structure (Block, 1956; Gaito, 1962). The forced method was selected for statistical ease and to reduce the effects of response bias.

3 Several 'pure' loadings on a factor are necessary for factor interpretation. By using 0.27 as the significance cut-off ($p<0.01$), several factors had only one pure loading. By using a more stringent cut-off of 0.39, all factors had multiple pure loadings.

4 The number on the left of each Q-sort item is its reference number; the number on the right is its position on the template (ranging from +5 to −5) as calculated from the factor scores.

5 Other perspectives were suggested from the transcripts of women who did not participate in phase two. These perspectives are based on one or two participants' experiences and as such are discussed elsewhere. They were: the effects of a male partner's massive consumption of pornography when the woman refuses to participate; and the perspectives of women who have been involved in the production of pornography.

References

Block, J. (1956) 'A comparison of forced and unforced sorting procedures', *Educational and Psychological Measurement*, 16: 481–93.

Brown, S. R. (1980) *Political Subjectivity: Applications of Q Methodology in Political Science*. New Haven, CT: Yale University Press.

Brownmiller, S. (1975) *Against Our Will: Men, Women and Rape*. New York: Simon & Schuster.

Cowan, G., Chase, C. J. and Stahly, G. B. (1989) 'Feminist and fundamentalist attitudes toward pornography control', *Psychology of Women Quarterly*, 13(1): 97–112.

Dworkin, A. (1981) *Pornography: Men Possessing Women*. London: Women's Press.

Gaito, J. (1962) 'Forced and free Q sorts', *Psychological Reports*, 10: 251–4.

Gallivan, J. (1993) 'Humor appreciation: A Q-methodological study'. Paper presented at the Canadian Psychological Association Annual Convention, Montreal.

Gergen, K. (1985) 'The social constructionist movement in modern psychology', *American Psychologist*, 40: 266–75.

Kitzinger, C. (1986) 'Introducing and developing Q as a feminist methodology', in S. Wilkinson (ed.), *Feminist Social Psychology*. Milton Keynes: Open University Press.

Kitzinger, C. (1987) *The Social Construction of Lesbianism*. London: Sage.

Kitzinger, C. and Stainton Rogers, R. (1985) 'A Q methodological study of lesbian identities', *European Journal of Social Psychology*, 15: 167–87.

MacKinnon, C. A. (1987) *Feminism Unmodified: Discourses on Life and Law*. Cambridge, MA: Harvard University Press.

Mayerson, S. F. and Taylor, D. A. (1987) 'The effects of rape myth pornography on women's attitudes and the mediating role of sex role stereotyping', *Sex Roles*, 17: 321–38.

Reinharz, S. (1992) *Feminist Methods in Social Research*. New York: Oxford University Press.

Russell, D. E. H. (1984) *Sexual Exploitation: Rape, Child Sexual Abuse, and Workplace Harassment*. Beverly Hills, CA: Sage.

SAS Institute Inc. (1985) *SAS User's Guide: Statistics Version 5*. Cary, NC: SAS.

Senn, C. Y. (1985) 'Women's reactions to violent pornography, nonviolent pornography and erotica'. Unpublished master's thesis, University of Calgary, Calgary, Alberta, Canada.

Senn, C. Y. (1991) 'The impact of pornography in women's lives'. Unpublished doctoral dissertation, York University, Toronto, Canada.

Senn, C. Y. (1993) 'Women's multiple perspectives and experiences with pornography', *Psychology of Women Quarterly*, 17: 319–41.

Senn, C. Y. and Radtke, H. L. (1990) 'Women's evaluations of and affective reactions to mainstream violent pornography, nonviolent pornography, and erotica', *Violence and Victims*, 5: 143–55.

Snelling, S. J. (1993) 'Perspectives on feminism: A Q-methodological investigation'. Paper presented at the Canadian Psychological Association Annual Convention, Montreal.

Stephenson, W. (1953) *The Study of Behavior: Q-technique and Its Methodology*. Chicago: University of Chicago Press.

Stock, W. (1983) 'The effects of violent pornography on the sexual responsiveness and attitudes of women'. Unpublished doctoral dissertation, State University of New York at Stony Brook, Stony Brook, NY.

11

Appropriating questionnaires and rating scales for a feminist psychology: A multi-method approach to gender and emotion

STEPHANIE A. SHIELDS AND
JILL J. CROWLEY

One of the hallmarks of a feminist approach to research is a deliberate and self-conscious acknowledgement of the subjective, value-based nature of the research enterprise. If anything associated with the research process can be accepted as 'fact', it is that from identification of the research problem (i.e., considering what constitutes a legitimate question for study), through development of strategies for investigation, to the interpretation and social application of research results, how we do research does not exist independently of who we are as individuals and the values that we hold (see also the chapter by Rhoda Unger in this volume). The way in which this fact is incorporated into the conduct of feminist research is more visible in the implementation of some methods than of others. For example, it has become accepted practice for ethnographers to write themselves and informants' responses to them into their ethnographies. And, of course, discourse analysis is a method that takes its very *raison d'être* from a critical stance towards meaning in linguistic representation.

In experimental social psychology, the more quantitative the measure, the more it apparently resists being employed within a feminist frame-work. Formats that pre-specify response categories, such as Likert-type scales, may foreclose the opportunity for dialogue between investigator and research participant. According to many researchers, this type of dialogue is one of the hallmarks of a feminist investigation. A dialogue opens up the research process to an acknowledgement of the personal and social values that inform all phases of the investigatory process. Feminist work recognizes that values are not only an inevitable component of all research, but also, when explicitly acknowledged, can affirm and incorporate the voices of researcher-as-collaborator and participant-as-collaborator. Rather than being ignored (as in conventional research) or dismissed as a nuisance variable, 'value' plays an acknowledged role in shaping truth claims.

The goal of this chapter is to show how questionnaires and rating scales, research tools usually associated with the most regressive of positivistic approaches to psychological research, can be useful in feminist research. To accomplish what to sceptics may seem an impossible challenge, we will draw on our own experiences in examining the relation between gender and emotion.

It is not surprising that the topic of emotion has long been problematic for feminists. In the United States feminist scholars who endeavour to reconcile the uneasy relationship between gender and emotion face a precarious situation. Stereotypic representations of the emotional female/unemotional male are so prominent in North American culture that these stereotypes reinforce the notion that the starting point for any gender-based analysis of emotion should be gender *differences* in emotion. Challenging stereotypic visions of emotional women and unemotional men catches the challenger in a no-win situation. To deny the existence of difference fails to address the power and prevalence of emotion stereotypes. On the other hand, to accept gender difference leaves two alternatives: one either asserts defensively that 'Female emotionality is healthy', or adopts a kind of feminist revisionism, as in 'It's really men who are hobbled by emotion because they don't know how to do it correctly'. Neither of these positions, however, explains the frequent devaluation of emotion, especially 'female' emotion (Shields, 1987; Fischer, 1993).

Social psychology lags behind anthropology and sociology in turning the lens of feminist theory towards an appraisal of emotion. The limited attention paid to emotion as a topic of feminist analysis attests to the strength of the androcentric model of 'objective' science to which experimental social psychology aspires. Some feminist psychologists have elected to eschew conventional methods in favour of developing new methods, such as 'memory work' (Crawford *et al.*, 1992; see also Stephenson *et al.*, this volume, for the application of memory work to another topic). However, a small but growing number of feminist psychologists have begun to apply conventional experimental psychological techniques in innovative ways to the study of emotion and gender (see, for example, Brody *et al.*, 1990; LaFrance and Banaji, 1992; Fischer, 1993; Grossman and Wood, 1993; Stoppard, 1993; Stoppard and Gunn Gruchy, 1993).

Classic views and feminist appropriations of questionnaires

Before going further, we need to define what our discussion of scales and questionnaires will encompass. Although standardized tests that aim to measure dimensions of personality or intelligence (such as the Bem Sex Role Inventory or Minnesota Multiphasic Personality Inventory (MMPI)) fall under this rubric, we focus on investigator-developed measures, specific to a particular research question. These consist of closed-ended response items, which vary from simple requests for categorical demographic information such as age, sex, and the like, through questions that ask the research participant to mark or rank items for their applicability to herself or himself, to questions whose response options, via Likert-type items, yield numbers that claim to translate experience into an interval scale.

Conventionally, the development of a quantifiable rating instrument, whether self-report or behavioural assessment of another, is viewed as marking a transition from the messy phase of research (in which a long list of potential variables is tamed to operationalization) to the production of the final, relatively 'clean' research design. The point of using a scale (or other closed-ended response) is to enable some degree of pre-processing of research participants' response options: the resulting product of the study is not a narrative to be sifted and sorted, but tidy numbers, numbers which can lull the researcher into believing that questions have been adequately asked and answers completely and accurately given. This activity is not entirely misdirected in that the goal is to reduce the investigator's influence on the participants by placing some distance between the task itself and responses to it. However, feminist critiques of science and the experimental method have demonstrated that efforts to remove oneself from this process are not only unsuccessful, but misguided (see Reinharz, 1992, for a review). Further, across the range of closed-ended response items, the investigator must seriously consider the implications of pre-defining the content and scope of possible responses. Even simple self-descriptive categories may be problematic in feminist research because they may ask research participants to apply self-descriptions that do not necessarily bear meaning for them. For example, in multicultural California we cannot accommodate all racial or ethnic self-descriptions in a brief list of generic categories such as 'Asian' or 'Hispanic'. As a result the selection of 'Other' from such a list may encompass a significant and varied minority proportion of our respondents, collapsing the specificity of their experiences and identities.

Do questionnaires and rating scales therefore have no place within a feminist approach? We believe that these research tools neither (necessarily) rob the research participant of her or his voice nor (inevitably) foreclose the direction of research results to conform to investigator expectations. Indeed, we contend that feminist research can benefit from using closed-ended questionnaires and rating scales in three contexts: first, as part of a larger package of research strategies (a multi-method approach); second, as a tool for refining the research question (i.e., when the rating scale is deployed as a work-in-progress rather than, as is more typical, a final, precise quantitative expression of a broad construct); and third, when the investigator uses the rating scale as a deliberate strategy to disrupt the research frame and, thereby, her or his own subjective investment in the inquiry. Anyone familiar with experimental social psychology will recognize these contexts as quite different from standard operating procedures.

In this chapter, we outline how we use questionnaires and rating scales within these three contexts to inform our research as feminist psychologists. One of the ways in which our approach reflects a change from experimental social psychology business-as-usual is in the selection of the research question itself. We have found that taken-for-granted psychological constructs and everyday notions of gender and emotion are areas in which a feminist approach has been particularly useful (Shields, 1994). Through an analysis of our research on gender and emotion, we show how questionnaires, when used as part of a multi-method approach to refine the research question, and to disrupt the research frame, can both enrich the development of psychological theory and be consistent with the aim of a feminist project.

One of us (SAS) has been studying the connections between gender and emotion since the early 1980s and has collaborated with several graduate students and a large and diverse group of undergraduates. The other (JJC) much more recently has brought her professional background in advertising and her research experience in media influence to bear on the topic of emotion. Both of us identify as feminist psychologists and want to appropriate conventional psychological research methods for investigations informed by feminist theory. The terrain of feminist social psychology includes examining how the beliefs about emotion are implicated in the maintenance of social identity and the individual's lived experience. As feminist experimental psychologists, we draw on a wide array of methods from within psychology and from the wider community of feminist research and theory.[1] We have used a variety of research strategies to address problems in gender and emotion – from content analysis and an examination of popular culture, to conventional experimental social psychology techniques employing both closed and open-ended questionnaires. Each method enables us to address the problem area from a different angle, giving us a rich and nuanced picture of the interplay between beliefs about emotion and beliefs about gender.

Questionnaires as one component of a multi-method approach

Our research on gender and emotion focuses not on the cognitive or social processes that elicit or maintain emotional states, but rather on the social meaning of emotion. Because we begin from the observation that emotion labels have social currency, much of our work is aimed at identifying the understanding emotion beliefs. Such beliefs include the representation of emotion in language; beliefs about what constitutes 'good' or 'bad' emotion; beliefs about emotion and the body; beliefs about the relationship of emotion to behaviours such as sex and aggression; and so on. People can name many of the beliefs they have about emotion, but not all such beliefs are easily or readily articulated.

We began our research by identifying the circumstances in which one's own or someone else's behaviour is acknowledged as 'emotional', and this work branched out into a concern with the consequences of naming emotion. It will be a surprise to no one that we have found that explicit acknowledgement of emotion is very frequently a value-based assessment of the relationship between feeling and behaviour. That is, the statement that one is 'angry' (or 'scared' or 'jealous') is a statement about the appropriateness of that condition for the person in that situation. The very act of labelling emotion is a value judgement. It will be a surprise to no one that emotion is also a gendered construct (Shields, 1991; 1995).

Questionnaire studies have been particularly useful in understanding how notions of emotionality and gender are intertwined. For example, although the term 'emotional' can define a specific emotional state, it clearly also defines characteristics of the person (Shields, 1986). People use the phrase 'being emotional' to refer to what a person is doing in a particular situation (as in 'Stop being so emotional!') and they also use it to describe an enduring personality trait (as in 'She's the emotional type'). In other words, people seem to make a distinction between someone who *gets* emotional in a particular situation and someone who *is* emotional across situations. Open-ended questionnaires show that the concept of 'emotional' evokes different images when applied to oneself or another. When people are asked to use the word 'emotional' to describe another person, they usually describe a woman, who (in their view) tends to overreact to situations (Shields, 1987). When asked to describe a time when they themselves felt 'emotional', people discuss feeling sad or depressed more often than feeling happy (Parrott, 1995). Many report weeping during an emotional episode, and feeling confusion as well as experiencing conflicting or 'mixed' emotions. Both men and women discuss feeling out of control and irrational when emotional, but do not invoke the concept of overreaction to describe themselves.

So, if 'being emotional' is read in others as 'being *too* emotional', what influences the observer's evaluation of the appropriateness of the emotional display? What guides the observer to see another's emotional display as too much, not enough, or appropriate to the situation (especially at moderate levels of expressiveness, where violation of expressive norms may be less flagrant)? We found the most useful strategy to address such questions was to conduct a laboratory experiment using rating scales. In other words, we have focused specifically on how an observer's values and attitudes affect her or his perceptions of another's emotional behaviour. In one study, for example, research participants viewed a video-taped debate between two speakers on opposing sides of a controversial issue. After viewing the tape they rated each debater on the 'appropriateness' of the emotions and the personal attributes exhibited during the debate. (The participant rated each emotion on a scale that ranged from 1 = not enough of this emotion to 7 = too much of this emotion. 'Appropriateness' was calculated as the absolute value of the difference between the rating and the scale mid-point, 4 = the right amount of this emotion.[2]) We were interested in finding out whether observer values, as expressed in their position on the topic of the debate, would influence the assessment of another person's emotional appropriateness. Participants who were familiar with, and had an opinion about, the topic of the debate, felt that the video-taped speaker who shared their opinion expressed more appropriate emotions than the speaker whose argument ran counter to their own beliefs (Shields *et al.*, 1988). This study tells us about the filters through which observers interpret the emotional behaviour of others. Combining the questionnaire and laboratory studies, our work shows that just as values influence the inferences that observers make about general personal attributes (the 'halo effect'), they also colour interpretation of another's visible emotional behaviour. In these studies we concentrated on values and beliefs that people are aware they possess. Observers were readily able to express their own values on the topic that was debated and could easily report their beliefs about the debaters on each side of the issue. But what about the values and beliefs that individuals cannot so readily express?

'Bedrock beliefs' that are widely shared within a culture may be more difficult to articulate. In so far as they are foundational to our understanding of emotion, we may not even recognize them as beliefs, but rather revere them as reality. A questionnaire approach to this problem is much more difficult to employ effectively than are other methods that lend themselves to revealing subtle yet persistent themes in language and imagery. To pursue the question of bedrock beliefs, we looked at representations of gendered emotion in popular culture, in this case advice literature. Although advice literature cannot tell us what people actually *do*, it can tell us what people *believe* they ought to do. For example, we found a striking difference in the way the emotions of mothers and fathers are represented in parent advice books published since 1915

(Shields and Koster, 1989). Maternal emotion is represented as a barely controllable tendency to 'overreact' emotionally. Numerous warnings concerning maternal emotion suggest that a mother really doesn't know what constitutes the 'appropriate' amount of emotional experience or display and, further, that this is the normative condition. Fathers are also warned about the negative consequences on children of losing emotional control; however, unlike the mother, the problem is not perceived to be within the father, but instigated by some external agent – his wife, his job, or the children themselves. The same pattern of representation occurs in parenting manuals directed to stepparents, single parents (both custodial and non-custodial), and adoptive parents (Shields *et al.*, 1995). Gender-specific descriptions of emotion are especially striking in manuals directed towards single parents. One extended example will be used to illustrate this. Ex-spouses are portrayed very differently depending on whether husband or wife is described. His bitterness is noted in passing. She, on the other hand, is described as 'a bitch on wheels' (Ferrar, 1985: 12), and the single father is caused great emotional 'torment' by 'the thought of leaving the children to the mercies of a woman whom the acid of divorce has stripped of human form and revealed as a man-eating piranha' (Atkin and Rubin, 1977: 20). Both parents are advised not to speak negatively about the other in front of the children. But whereas the father's possible negative reaction to his ex-spouse is underplayed, the mother is described as, for example:

> So mad at you and life in general that she is like the old proverb – cutting off her nose to spite her face. This woman is going to do whatever she can to get back at you for her unhappiness . . . She's like a two-year-old in the middle of a tantrum. You cannot get through to her, and everything you say will only stir her up more . . . if you do try to reason with her, she will distort your words and accuse you of saying things you didn't.
>
> (Dodson, 1987: 76)

In addition to their flagrant mother-bashing, these advice books clearly reveal a friction between the ideology of nurturance and standards of 'appropriate' emotional experience and expression. Emotional expressiveness is a significant constituent of the care-giving script, particularly for mothers. Yet, for the woman in a care-giving role, the very expressiveness that is the defining feature of 'appropriate' maternal behaviour is believed inevitably to jeopardize the child's healthy development. More important, it is not simply expressiveness, but the female care-giver's emotion *itself* that is represented as destructive.

In summary, our multiple modes of exploring who is identified as 'emotional', and beliefs about the source and consequences of 'being emotional', reveal that emotion terms are mediated by observer judge-ments of the appropriateness of the emotional response. They also reveal that the meaning of specific emotion terms shifts when applied to one sex or the other. The qualitative examination of texts has been most useful in moving us past the initial stages of problematizing found-ational constructs and making explicit bedrock beliefs about emotion. Our questionnaire studies have been particularly successful in revealing how the constituents of emotion beliefs (those beliefs for which people have certain expectations about gender) articulate with one another and function as a coherent gender belief system.

Using scales and questionnaires to refine our questions

Reading gender-specific emotion motifs in mass-market media testifies to the pervasiveness of beliefs about the emotional 'nature' of women and men. To understand how the individual interprets and evaluates these culturally shared beliefs, we need to focus our attention on *individual* beliefs. In the USA, explicit references to emotion are fairly infrequent in everyday conversation (even though felt emotion and non-verbal or paraverbal emotion expression are part of the very fabric of interpersonal interaction). A more direct way to explore the individ-ual's understanding of emotion ideology, and the importance she or he places on it, is to use a questionnaire format.

Since the term 'emotional' is stereotypically identified with females and specific emotion labels (e.g., sad, happy, angry) are associated more with one sex or the other (Fabes and Martin, 1991; Fischer, 1994), we wanted to know how people would interpret scenarios in which counter-stereotypical information was conveyed. To see if people evalu-ate the 'emotional' responses of men and women differently, we developed a questionnaire which contained scenarios that portrayed positive and negative forms of both stereotypical and counter-stereotypical gendered emotion. When respondents read a scenario in which a 'feminine' emotion label is attached to a man, do they interpret his emotion in the same way as when a 'feminine' emotion label is attached to a woman?

Each questionnaire contained one scenario depicting a male (Brian) or female (Karen) actor responding to an emotionally provoking situation. The actor's responses were described generally as 'emotional', or specifically as 'sad', 'angry', 'happy', or 'enthusiastic', depending on the situation. In selecting the scenarios, we attempted to provide re-spondents with situations that were close enough to their own daily experiences to be personally meaningful, and to ensure that each specific emotion response would be evaluated similarly. For example, we included the scenario 'Karen/Brian was happy when s/he had received the highest grade', because the emotional response was appropriate for both Brian and Karen, and close enough to the daily experience of our research participants to be meaningful to them. The selection process itself provided us with a better understanding of the social meaning of emotion and its special place within a feminist inquiry. For example, we were unable to generate a scenario in which being afraid would seem equally appropriate for Karen or Brian. Our own subjective position as women and as feminists made us cognizant of the many ways in which fear informs women's daily experiences and that these experiences simply could not be expressed in universal or generic terms.

The questionnaire consisted of both closed- (Likert-type) and open-ended questions. The closed-ended questions assessed respondents' attitudes about the person in the scenario on several dimensions. These included judgements about the appropriateness, control and intensity of the response and the degree to which the response was caused by personality or situational factors. For example, after reading the scenario, respondents were asked the question 'How appropriate was the response?'. They then made their evaluation using a five-point scale (1 = not appropriate at all; 5 = very appropriate). Respondents were free to describe their impressions of the person in the scenario using an open-ended question at the end of the questionnaire. The open-ended question asked the participant if she or he had created a picture of the scenario in her or his imagination, and if so, to describe the picture. Both male and female college students participated in the study.

Responses to the questions about perceived appropriateness showed that participants felt that general 'emotional' responses were less appropriate than responses described by specific emotion terms. In addition, people considered general 'emotional' responses to be less controlled and more intense than responses described by specific emotion terms. This corroborated what we had found concerning people's assessments of 'emotional' behaviour in earlier studies. The combination of closed-ended and open-ended responses enabled us to pin down the gender specificity of emotionality. For example, in one scenario, 'Karen/Brian was emotional when s/he found out that her/his car had been stolen', respondents judged that being 'emotional' meant something different for Brian and Karen. Karen's reaction was interpreted as being caused more by her personality than by the situation. Respondents' beliefs seemed to parallel what we found in parent advice literature: he *gets* emotional (if provoked); she *is* emotional (whenever). The open-ended responses corroborated this interpretation of the questionnaire items. When Karen's reaction was described as 'emotional', respondents described her irrational and excessive behaviour in detail:

[I imagined] Karen at a parking lot crying hysterically because her car had been stolen. She lacked control and was too emotional for that particular situation.

[I imagined] a woman (Karen) standing in the parking lot crying, looking around for her car, clutching the keys in her hand.

Karen's car got ripped off and she flipped!! Started screaming and crying no one could calm her down.

Responses to Brian's emotional behaviour were markedly different. When writing about their impressions of the scenario, people seemed to make excuses for Brian's emotional behaviour and attributed his reaction to the situation. Respondents tended to put themselves into the situation more often and downplay or rationalize Brian's emotional response:

I just imagined any average reaction (i.e. my own) if I found out that my car was stolen. I just imagined that he probably worked pretty hard for his car, and that he had taken care of it, so of course it would be upsetting.

I assume Brian's initial response was shock but then weigh[ing] out the consequences he realized life goes on. There is probably disappointment but he can live with it.

I thought about how upset I would be if someone stole my car. I imagined Brian as being shocked and upset and confused about what to do next.

Instead of making counter-stereotypical attributions, our participants maintained their stereotypic beliefs by changing the meaning of the emotional response so that it was consistent with gender expectations. In other words, when Brian was emotional, it meant something different than when Karen was emotional. Instead of applying the stereotypical feminine definition of 'emotional' to Brian, people redefined the word when applying it to a man. Similar to our analysis of masculine inexpressivity in popular literature, and to the tendency of young children to recall counter-gender-stereotypical emotional displays in still cartoons as if they were gender-'correct' (Martin et al., 1990), we found that emotion knowledge depends on gender knowledge.

A qualitative analysis of the open-ended responses to other scenarios indicated that people not only changed the meaning of emotion terms to fit beliefs about gender, but also manipulated gender to fit beliefs about emotion. For example, in the male version of the scenario in which sadness was the specific emotion response ('Brian was sad when he found out that his dog had died'), people adjusted Brian's age to reconcile their conception of maleness with the emotion, often referring to him as a boy. We interpreted this as an important expression of beliefs about gendered emotionality. The implication here seems clear: Brian is not exhibiting 'manly' emotion, so he must not be a man. In other words, when people were confronted with counter-stereotypical emotion re-actions, they either redefined these emotions to fit stereotypical beliefs about gender or redefined gender to fit stereotypical beliefs about emotion.

Questionnaires as a deliberate disruption of the research frame

Throughout the last forty years, psychology in the United States has been heavily influenced by the hypothetico-deductive model (Cattell, 1966) of scientific inquiry. Researchers using this model rely on an iterative process of theory development and data collection continually to refine and to improve theoretical constructs. Our way of using questionnaires is very different: we use responses ('data') to problematize not only our theory but also our subject position, as researchers, relative to the respondents. In this way, we are able to use a questionnaire in a critical analysis of our own epistemic position *vis-à-vis* the respondents as well as in the pursuit of 'objective' discovery.

Things don't always turn out the way we (the researchers) think they should. The empiricist's conventional wisdom is that 'numbers don't lie'. Our feminist experimentalist version of this is that numbers themselves have no special claim on truth, but that they can be effective in revealing our own and our research participants' tacit assumptions. For example, in the questionnaire study described above, we selected certain scenarios and emotions which we felt would enable us to examine how people interpret counter-stereotypical information about gender and emotion. To a large extent, we were able to do this. However, even though an experimental check demonstrated that there were no differences in the way in which people evaluated the reactions of Karen and Brian using the specific emotion terms, we found that the scenarios themselves were evaluated differently. In particular, the pattern of responses to the 'angry' scenario ('Karen/Brian was emotional/angry when s/he found out that her/his car had been stolen') differed from the pattern evident in the other scenarios. In this scenario, people felt the actor's response was more intense, less controlled, yet more appropriate than the actor's response in other scenarios. In planning the study we had aimed to contrast the general 'emotional' label with a set of specific emotion labels; what our numbers told us is that we could not treat the specific emotion labels as equivalent. Specifically, there seems to be something 'special' about anger (Shields, 1987). In addition, a quick perusal of some of the open-ended responses to the Karen/Brian questionnaire items revealed again that our research participants did not read the scenarios or the actors in a uniform way. In their responses, some people assigned Karen to a racial category (while they did not do this for Brian). Even though the names used in the questionnaire were matched on ratings of intelligence, age and attractiveness (Kasof, 1993), they clearly also conveyed information about the ethnicity of the actor. Sometimes we have been caught out in assumptions which we were unaware we had been using to frame our inquiry.

Because scales and questionnaires are inserted as an intermediate step in the dialogue between investigator and research participant, they can turn the tables on the investigator. Anyone who has conducted quantitative research has, at one time or another, obtained numbers which do not follow the anticipated patterns. One's first reaction, almost inevitably, is 'these numbers *can't* be right!'. The conventional empiricist and the feminist researcher alike may first assume that there is something amiss with the research 'design' or execution, a flaw that must be identified and corrected so that the 'true story' can be revealed. For the feminist researcher, though, that initial reaction must be an occasion to consider not only the adequacy of the questionnaire but also the presumptions which frame the approach to the research problem. Recalcitrant numbers can reveal implicit biases in one's own thinking as well as unwarranted assumptions about the research process itself.

Knowing that women's emotions are devalued tells us little about how and why such devaluing occurs. In particular, the persistant stereotype that 'she is more emotional' by itself provides us with very little information about how certain emotion terms develop and maintain their gendered meanings. For us, a feminist analysis of emotion and gender *requires* a critical stance towards foundational, taken-for-granted constructs. When the pre-selection of response alternatives in questionnaire and rating scales is used to open up inquiry rather than to limit discussion or to foreclose interpretive options, quantitative results can quickly reveal promising leads as well as culs-de-sac. The numbers generated by individual respondents are not themselves the end point of the project, but a component of the exchange between investigator and research participant. Carefully constructed rating scales may enable respondents to express beliefs, preferences or perceptions that they may be unable to articulate spontaneously without such a framework. By 'carefully constructed' we mean not only employing the usual criteria for a 'good' scale (e.g., no leading questions; clearly worded questions that are readily understood), but also adding provisos that fit the scale for a feminist programme of research. It is also important that the investigator be attentive to the ways in which questions and available answers can deny the experience of some research participants (as, for example, in a researcher's presumption of a heterosexual point of view in a questionnaire dealing with close relationships).

Conscientious scientists, and feminist scholars in particular, have addressed these criticisms by making their own discipline the object of study. By problematizing psychological constructs and addressing issues of subjectivity, historicity and ontology, feminist psychologists have attempted to appropriate psychology from its andro-, Anglo- and heterospecificity. Consistent with this aim, we have attempted to create a space for a feminist psychology by feminist psychologists which, from the very onset of the project, does psychology differently. The project is simultaneously positivist and situated, quantitative and qualitative, conventional and radical. Using conventional methods within a feminist project is one way of rejecting these binaries.

One final word. In this chapter, we have given what appears to be a chronological account of the progress of our programme. It is, of course, not that clear-cut. Also, we have been able to discuss only one of the major strands of our group's work on gender and emotion. We have left out not only projects that are incomplete or somewhat tangential to the work described in this paper, but also the various culs-de-sac, red herrings, and garden paths which have devoured – and which continue to devour – much of our individual and collective time and without which innovation would be impossible.

Acknowledgements

The authors would like to thank Sue Wilkinson for helpful comments on an earlier draft of this chapter. They would also like to thank the graduate and undergraduate researchers at the Center for Interdisciplinary Social Psychology of the University of California at Davis for their assistance with many of the studies cited and for their helpful comments on early drafts of this chapter.

Notes

1 We accept the label 'feminist empiricist' but do not equate that position with the assertion that feminist science is simply good science without the bias (Harding, 1986). Rather, we, like a number of others (such as Lott and Maluso, 1993; Unger, 1995) fit the profile of feminist psychologists described by Jill Morawski (1994: 69) who opt for ambiguity and plurality as a strategy for moving towards transformative science.
2 The tapes had been edited to produce an evenly matched debate (that is, a group of undergraduate raters unfamiliar with the aims of the study did not consistently identify one of the two speakers as the winner of the debate).

References

Atkin, E. and Rubin, E. (1977) *Part-time Father*. New York: Signet.

Brody, L. R., Hay, D. H. and Vandewater, E. (1990) 'Gender, gender role identity, and children's reported feelings toward the same and opposite sex', *Sex Roles*, 7/8: 363–87.

Brody, L. R., Lovas, G. S. and Hay, D. H. (1995) 'Sex differences in anger and fear as a function of situational context', *Sex Roles*, 32: 47–78.

Cattell, R. B. (1966) 'Psychological theory and scientific method', in R. B. Cattell (ed.), *Handbook of Multivariate Experimental Psychology*. Chicago: Rand McNally.

Crawford, J., Kippax, S., Onyx, J., Gault, U. and Benton, P. (1992) *Emotion and Gender: Constructing Meaning from Memory*. Newbury Park, CA and London: Sage.

Dodson, F. (1987) *How to Single Parent*. New York: Harper & Row.

Fabes, R. A. and Martin, C. L. (1991) 'Gender and age stereotypes of emotionality', *Personality and Social Psychology Bulletin*, 17(5): 532–40.

Ferrar, F. (1985) *On Being a Father*. Garden City, NY: Dolphin.

Fischer, A. H. (1993) 'Sex differences in emotionality: Fact or stereotype', *Feminism & Psychology*, 3: 303–18.

Fischer, A. H. (1994) 'Deconstructing the stereotype of the emotional woman in four steps'. Paper presented at the meeting of the International Society for Research on Emotion, Cambridge.

Grossman, M. and Wood, W. (1993) 'Sex differences in intensity of emotional experience: A social role interpretation', *Journal of Personality and Social Psychology*, 65(5): 1010–22.

Harding, S. (1986) *The Science Question in Feminism*. Ithaca, NY: Cornell University Press.

Kasof, J. (1993) 'Sex bias in the naming of stimulus persons', *Psychological Bulletin*, 113(1): 140–63.

LaFrance, M. and Banaji, M. (1992) 'Towards a reconsideration of the gender–emotion relationship', in M. Clark (ed.), *Review of Personality and Social Psychology: Volume 14*. Beverly Hills, CA: Sage.

Lott, B. and Maluso, D. (1993) 'The social learning of gender', in A. E. Beall and R. J. Sternberg (eds), *The Psychology of Gender*. New York: Guilford.

Martin, C. L., Fabes, R. A., Eisenbud, L., Karbon, M. M. and Rose, H. A. (1990) 'Boys don't cry: Children's distortions of others' emotions'. Paper presented at the Southwestern Society for Research in Human Development, Tempe, AZ.

Morawski, J. G. (1994) *Practicing Feminisms, Reconstructing Psychology: Notes on a Liminal Science*. Ann Arbor: University of Michigan Press.

Parrott, W. G. (1995) 'The heart and the head: Everyday conceptions of being emotional', in J. A. Russell, J. Wellenkamp, A. S. R. Manstead, J. M. Fernandez Dols (eds), *Everyday Conceptions of Emotions*. Dordrecht: Kluwer.

Reinharz, S. (1992) *Feminist Methods in Social Research*. New York: Oxford University Press.

Shields, S. A. (1986) 'Are women "emotional?"', in C. Tavris (ed.), *Everywoman's Emotional Well-being*. New York: Doubleday, pp. 131–47.

Shields, S. A. (1987) 'Women, men, and the dilemma of emotion', in P. Shaver and C. Hendrick (eds), *Sex and Gender: Review of Personality and Social Psychology: Volume 7*. Newbury Park, CA: Sage, pp. 229–50.

Shields, S. A. (1991) 'Gender in the psychology of emotion: A selective research review', in K. T. Strongman (ed.), *International Review of Studies on Emotion: Volume 1*. Chichester: Wiley, pp. 227–46.

Shields, S. A. (1994) 'Practicing social constructionism: Confessions of a feminist empiricist'. Paper presented at the symposium 'Taking Social Constructionism Seriously: Feminist Theory and Feminist Psychology', American Psychological Association, Los Angeles.

Shields, S. A. (1995) 'The role of emotion beliefs and values in gender development', in N. Eisenberg (ed.), *Review of Personality and Social Psychology: Volume 15*. Thousand Oaks, CA: Sage, pp. 212–32.

Shields, S. A. and Koster, B. A. (1989) 'Emotional stereotyping of parents in child rearing manuals, 1915–1980', *Social Psychology Quarterly*, 52: 44–55.

Shields, S. A., Simon, A. and Sands, R. (1988) 'The effect of observer values on judgments of the appropriateness of others' emotions'. Unpublished manuscript.

Shields, S. A., Steinke, P. and Koster, B. A. (1995) 'The double bind of caregiving: Representation of emotion in American advice literature', *Sex Roles*, 33: 467–88.

Stoppard, J. M. (1993) 'Beyond gender stereotypes: Putting the gender–emotion relationship into context'. Paper presented at the meeting of the American Psychological Society, Chicago.

Stoppard, J. M. and Gunn Gruchy, C. D. (1993) 'Gender, context, and expression of positive emotion', *Personality and Social Psychology Bulletin*, 19: 143–50.

Unger, R. K. (1995) 'How I looked at the psychology of women literature and what I didn't find there'. Invited address for the meeting of the Association for Women in Psychology, Indianapolis, IN.

——————• 12

Missing voices, changing meanings: Developing a voice-centred, relational method and creating an interpretive community

——————• JILL McLEAN TAYLOR, CAROL GILLIGAN
AND AMY M. SULLIVAN

Anita, a 14-year-old African-American girl in the eighth grade, sits at a table in a small, sunny room off the library in her elementary school, talking about her life in and out of school. She twists her hair and speaks animatedly, laughing often with Jill,[1] a white New Zealand woman from a university, someone whom Anita seems to think of as a teacher, or like a teacher. Information about Anita's life emerges during the interview: she lives in a housing project with her mother, stepfather, a younger sister, and two of her three brothers, and she continues to see her father frequently. Anita seems an adolescent with a great deal of energy and curiosity as well as a complicated relational world.

After Anita responds to what makes her feel good about herself at school, Jill then asks: *'Can you tell me about a time you felt bad about yourself in school?'* Anita replies:

> Well, last year me and another teacher in this school didn't get along so well, so we had like our ups and downs. And so one time we got into an argument and I said something very bad about her, or very rude, which I shouldn't have said, and I felt kind of bad because I was thinking, how would I feel if I was in that predicament and, you know, like how would I feel if that was me, if I would feel sad or angry, not angry, but what would I do, what would my actions be? And then from here on, we get along great.

Jill continues: '*So what happened at that time when you felt really badly with the teacher and you said something rude?*' Anita explains:

> Well, after school I went up to the teacher and I sat down with her for about 45 minutes and I was talking to [her and other teachers] about what happened, and they understood why I said, why we got into an argument. Sometimes people say things or things slip out, like not what you want to say, but it just comes out because you probably wanted to say it for a long time. So they understood why I said it and they said they were angry but at the same time they wasn't.

Asked again, '*Can you tell what it was about that situation that made you feel bad about yourself?*', Anita responds:

> Because I never said – well, it wasn't a crude racial comment, it wasn't racial either, a crude comment to a teacher, because all my teachers, I really liked them a lot and they gave me a lot of respect, but just that one teacher, I don't know. I don't know. We just, and she didn't say anything bad, and I was wondering why she didn't say anything back and she just walked away.

Asked once more, '*Do you think it made you feel bad because she didn't say anything back?*', Anita says:

> It made me feel bad because I was talking to a grownup, like I don't usually say bad things to a grownup, I respect all my grownups and adults and stuff, and I never disrespected an adult before, so I disrespected an adult and I really felt bad over that, and I was just thinking why did I say that, but I knew why I said it, but at the same time I didn't, and I was kind of confused why I said it . . . Because you are supposed to give everybody respect, that's what I think . . . Respect is like, oh God, not talking behind their back, you know, saying racial comments behind them and you give them respect, do what they tell you to do, you know, don't get an attitude with them.

Anita alludes to 'a racial comment' three times and each time Jill does not ask Anita specifically about the comment or what led up to it, focusing instead on why the incident made Anita feel bad about herself. Because of differences in power and authority that inhere in Jill's age, race, social class and position, her failure to pick up the issue of race when it is introduced may have silenced a discussion of race and racism, or the accompanying confusion and anger voiced by Anita. Yet Anita does not immediately comply with a tacit code of silence around race, continuing to raise the issue of 'a racial comment'.

The interaction between interviewer and participant and the role taken by both in constructing a narrative account are relatively new areas for exploration. Elliot Mishler (1992:2), for example, points out that although in clinical and research interviews there is a 'dynamic process through which a story takes on its specific shape and meaning', in many forms of analysis this dynamic is lost:

> The dialectic of speaking and listening, the essential reciprocity between conversational partners is removed from the analysis and is absent in the interpretation of the story. Further, there is a tendency to treat the particular story expressed in a specific situation as 'the' story, rather than as one of a number of possible 'retellings'.

Increasingly, in the Harvard Project on Women's Psychology and Girls Development we made it a critical factor in our research to attend to and examine the responsiveness and the resonances in the relationship between interviewee and interviewer (Gilligan, 1982; 1990a; Gilligan *et al.*, 1990a; 1991; 1992; Taylor, 1991; Brown and Gilligan, 1992). Who is listening, as well as who is speaking, becomes an essential consideration, as through this relationship a narrative account is produced interactively, depending not only on the questions of the interviewer and the experiences of the narrator, but also on the 'social location'[2] of both. Hence any telling or hearing of 'a story' may be affected by race, ethnicity, gender, class, age, sexual orientation, religious background, personal history, character – an infinite list of possible factors that form the scaffolding of relationships between people. Anita's negation, 'it wasn't racial', may have cued Jill not to pick up on this thread in the conversation, which also went unnoticed later by the interpretive community comprised at that time of four white women and a white man. Janie Ward, an African-American woman who was a consultant to the project,[3] immediately observed that Anita had attempted on three occasions to introduce the topic of race into her responses.

The question of difference is at the centre of the present work: the Understanding Adolescence Study, and the Women and Race retreats.[4] The former is a three-year longitudinal study with girls considered to be 'at risk' for school drop-out and/or early motherhood, and the latter a series of weekend retreats with black, white and Latina women. These two projects were designed to address directly questions of cultural, class and racial difference among girls and women. The notion of difference initially came into our construction of development through questioning the equation of difference with deficiency in previous representations of women's psychological development (Gilligan, 1977; 1982). Challenging this equation of gender difference with women's deficiency in the work of Freud, Erikson, Piaget, and Kohlberg led us to conceptualize difference as central to an understanding of relationship and to the construction of a relational psychology (see also Miller, 1976). In our explorations of difference, voice is central and a concern with maintaining or voicing differences in our work is at the heart of our voice-centred relational method.

Within psychology, cultural, class and racial differences have also often been conceived and represented as deficiency (Spencer and Markstrom-Adams, 1990). Once again, we challenge this equation of difference with deficiency, joining the many others who have seen in this representation of difference an implicit endorsement of the status quo and who have found in psychological theories and methods ways of rationalizing, jus-tifying or rediscovering the existing social order (Freire, 1970; Miller, 1976; hooks, 1984; 1989; 1990; 1994; Fine, 1988; 1991; 1992; Spelman, 1988; Martin-Baro, 1994).

The voice-centred relational method described in this chapter seeks to break through the negative dynamics in the declaration of difference – whether in culture, race or gender – and an assumption of conformity or an ideal type (*the* mother–daughter relationship, *the* child, *the* adolescent, *the* family). Our approach offers a way of attending to difference in the encounters of interviewer and interviewee using a guided method for listening to interview narrative, the *Listening Guide* (Brown *et al.*, 1988; Brown and Gilligan, 1992; 1993; Taylor *et al.*, 1995), and conducting analysis and interpretation in the context of a diverse interpretive com-munity. By maintaining different voices rather than assimilating people's voices to an absent third-person narrative, our method explores connec-tion through the representation of differences in relationships. This allows us also to reflect on the interviewer's voice and the dynamic process of relationship.

The purpose of the Understanding Adolescence Study was to listen to and understand voices like Anita's that have been missing from or inade-quately represented in theories of adolescent development and women's psychology. The adolescents attended school in a large urban area, came from diverse racial and ethnic backgrounds, and were economically dis-advantaged. Students were chosen for the study by means of a survey administered to seventh and eighth graders and designed to identify students who were considered to be 'at risk' for school drop-out and/or early parenthood. Because the at-risk predictors in themselves provide only limited information about a student's life, teachers with whom these students had relationships were then called on to help prune the list. The teachers supplied information that enabled us to exclude some students who met the standard 'at-risk' criteria, such as chronic tardiness or frequent absence combined with being from a minority racial or ethnic group and having come from a single-parent family (generally mother only), but who nevertheless showed competence, say, by doing well in school, or caring for younger family members while their mothers worked. The final list for the study included 48 adolescents – 33 girls and 15 boys.[5] We concentrate here on what we learned from just one of the adolescent girls in the study: Anita.

The urban public school system that these adolescents attended has an extremely diverse student population, with over 60 nationalities represented and 20 languages spoken. In our group of 'at-risk' adolescent girls there were eight African Americans, four Hispanics, eight Portuguese and six European Americans, all from poor or working-class families. A simple naming of these students in terms of their race and ethnicity obscures important differences within each group. Among black students, some girls are immigrants from Jamaica, some girls' parents are from Haiti, and others describe themselves as African-American. There is a wide cultural variation among these students, as some of their families are recent immigrants to the USA, others are new to the Northeast, and still others have lived here all their lives. These differences are important for this study because they affect how children and adults assimilate and are acculturated into American society (Ogbu, 1987; Gibson and Ogbu, 1991; Suarez-Orozco and Suarez-Orozco, 1995).

Reassessing risk

What unifies this particular group of girls is that they all have been identified as 'at risk', yet precisely what they are at risk for – and, of equal importance, what strengths, skills and strategies develop alongside these risks – became key questions in our research. Traditional notions of risk generated the funding for this study and defined the selection of girls who participated. These are primarily material dimensions of risk, rooted in the social realities of unequal opportunity and unequal outcome in the educational and economic spheres which are largely structured by race, class and ethnicity. The risks of high-school drop-out and adolescent motherhood are defined largely in terms of physical and material consequences – low-paying jobs or unemployment, health problems, high infant mortality, inadequate education – with their attendant social and personal costs. While the risks are real, the label of risk is one to be used with caution.

A primary danger of the at-risk label is its tendency to shift attention away from the social conditions that place adolescents at risk by locating the risk within the adolescents themselves. This shift places the burden of change on the adolescent and frees the larger society of responsibility for addressing the inequities of race, class and sex that create the conditions of risk. It also creates a 'within-child' deficit model which attributes failure in school to 'deficits the child brings to school', and fails to account for the larger context within which the child or adolescent lives (Trueba *et al.*, 1989: 3; see also Fine and Rosenberg, 1983; Fine, 1992).

Working from a notion of deficit also tends to diminish the value placed on the adolescents' perspective. This consequence is demonstrated by the absence of the voices of adolescents themselves from most studies of students who are considered at risk, a point made with respect to women's voices as well (Gilligan, 1977; 1982). As social psychologist Klaus Hurrelmann (1989: 109) argues, we need to take account of the at-risk 'adolescent's own perceptions, expectations, goals, and capacities . . . in a much more fundamental way than has been done before'. Listening to the voices of adolescents – to their concerns, their experience, their insights – and listening for their strengths and resources as well as their weaknesses and liabilities, not only reveals a range of competencies that would not be evident within prevailing assumptions of risk and deficit, but also makes many current interpretations and conclusions of deficit or deviance untenable.

Finally, as is the danger with most labels, the 'at-risk' label obscures the differences between those in the labelled group and suggests that those who are likely to suffer the material consequences of risk are a homogeneous group. Material risks, however – whether economic, educational or social – all too often differ according to race, ethnicity and economic class. Data on school retention and completion in the USA show that black and Hispanic students are less likely to persist than are white and Asian students (National Center for Education Statistics (NCES), 1993).[6] Variability in school performance and retention between different racial and ethnic groups continues to be a central issue in public education (Rothstein, 1993),[7] one in which the subtext is race and social class (Fine, 1988; 1991; Weis, 1990). Psychological and developmental risks may also vary by race, ethnicity and class. Any attempt to attenuate either the material or the psychological risks needs to be informed by an understanding and appreciation of this diversity of experience.

Fortunately, not all studies of risk have located it within the children and adolescents involved. Research on 'resilience', the avoidance of negative outcomes in spite of adverse social or economic conditions, has countered a deficit approach by focusing on the psychological and relational resources of children or adolescents deemed at risk. This work has contributed to our understanding of the internal and external resources that serve to protect children and adolescents, by documenting the role of supportive, confiding relationships in mitigating the effects of stress (Rutter, 1980; Garmezy and Rutter, 1983; Anthony and Cohler, 1987; Takesheni, 1992). A recognition of resilience does not minimize the very real risks that children and adolescents may face, but it provides a more realistic, balanced and hopeful portrait of psychological responses to trauma and loss.

The research of the Harvard Project offers a different approach to understanding the psychology of risk by tracing the development of girls coming of age in a patriarchal culture. Focusing on the crossroad between childhood and adolescence and the evidence of heightened risk for girls at this time, Gilligan *et al.* (1990a) analysed the psychological dynamics of girls' resilience and resistance. The Laurel School Study, a five-year longitudinal and cross-sectional study at a girls' independent school in Cleveland, Ohio, made it possible to hear the psychological dynamics of this crisis for girls as they move into adolescence. Prior to adolescence, many young girls show a strong sense of self, based on an ability to know and voice their feelings and thoughts and on a trust in the authority of their own experience (Gilligan, 1987; 1990a; 1990b; Brown, 1989; 1991a; 1991b; Brown and Gilligan, 1990; 1992; Gilligan *et al.*, 1990a; Rogers, 1993). Girls at this time often speak with an unsettling directness that reveals a clear perception of the complex, often conflictive experience of being in relationship. The richness and immediacy of their experience and knowledge constitute the grounds for a healthy opposition or a resilience based on a resistance to disconnection and an eye for false relationship.

At adolescence, however, a disturbing shift takes place for many girls when they experience a relational impasse and a developmental crisis that is part of a cultural initiation. To be in relationship at this juncture often means to shape themselves in accordance with the dominant cultural ideals of femininity and womanhood, or the ideals of maturity and adulthood. This poses a relational crisis because the middle-class ideals of womanhood and femininity are ideals of 'selflessness', and the ideals of maturity and adulthood are ideals of separation and independence (Gilligan, 1982). Girls, experiencing this initiation into dominant cultural ideals and values, often perceive that either way they will lose their relationships. Either they will give up their voices to others, learning to think, feel and say what others want and think, or they will give up their relationships with others and learn to be self-sufficient, entire unto themselves (see Gilligan, 1982; 1990a; Gilligan *et al.*, 1990a; Gilligan *et al.*, 1990b). Girls' pre-adolescent resilience may then begin to give way to an increasing uncertainty, a hesitancy in speaking, a tendency to doubt themselves, questioning the accuracy of their feelings and dismissing the validity and importance of their experience (Brown, 1989; 1991a; 1991b; Brown and Gilligan, 1990; 1992).

In our previous research, we found that women and girls who were working-class or from non-dominant cultures often saw more clearly the limitations of this choice between 'selfless' and 'selfish' roads to follow and resisted, fighting sometimes very carefully and effectively for their voices and their relationships. Signithia Fordham also explicates and complicates the interaction of voice, silence, and race in her work with black adolescent girls in a high school in Washington, DC, presenting a cultural-specific route to womanhood among African-American women, something Fordham sees as inevitable in the United States stratified by gender, social class, culture and race. 'Those loud black girls' is a metaphor, Fordham (1993:11) notes, 'proclaiming African-American women's existence, their collective denial of, and resistance to their socially proclaimed powerlessness, or "nothingness"'. Recognized as not achieving what standardized test scores show they are capable of, these girls are well known in the school for their refusal to become silent, like (most) white, middle-class girls at school. In contrast, the high-achieving girls in Fordham's study have adopted 'a deliberate silence, a controlled response to their evolving, ambiguous status as academically successful students' (Fordham, 1993:12).

Girls' political resistance to the patriarchal social order can take two forms. Political resistance can be overt as for 'the loud black girls', where a girl speaks out or acts against relationships that feel false, or against conventions that require self-sacrifice or silence, or against conventions that equate separation from relationships as maturity and success. The primary danger in this kind of resistance lies in the reactions it may elicit from other people or systems that are threatened by such protest. Or, it can be covert, where a girl goes underground with her feelings and knowledge (like the high-achieving girls in Fordham's study, who have adopted 'a deliberate silence'). That is, aware of the consequences of speaking out, she appears to comply with the conventions but does so as a strategy of self-protection. This strategy poses a danger, because the thoughts and feelings that are hidden or covered over may eventually be lost to the girl herself, and the act of compliance may shift to a genuine acceptance of harmful conventions of social behaviour. Clearly there are costs to both forms of political resistance and psychological dissociation. As Gilligan (1990a: 529) explains:

> If girls know what they know and bring themselves into relation-ships, they will be in conflict with prevailing authorities. If girls do not know what they know and take themselves out of relationship, they will be in trouble with themselves. The . . . difficult problem of relationship [is] how to stay connected with themselves and with others, how to keep in touch with themselves and with the world.

The developmental story of girls in adolescence is not simply a story of risk and loss, however, but one of strength and resilience as well. What Audre Lorde said of her own experience in 'the war against the tyrannies of silence' is true for girls in adolescence as well: 'I am not only a casualty', wrote Lorde (1984: 41), 'I am also a warrior'. Girls' active attempts to maintain connections both with others and with their own thoughts and feelings, although often resulting in psychological distress or landing girls in trouble with authorities, are acts of resistance. Thus, what puts girls at risk can also be their strength.

Tuning in

In the first two years of the study each student was interviewed once for 45–90 minutes.[8] In the third year, two separate interviews of 60–90 minutes were scheduled for each participant. In the elementary schools the interviews were conducted in cafeterias, libraries or classrooms. In the high school, space was provided in speech and physical therapy rooms. Every effort was made to have the same woman interviewer throughout the years. The interviews were taped and transcribed for later analysis.

We used two methods to carry out the interview analysis. The first entailed creating matrices to code and organize major aspects of the girls' descriptions of their experiences and to chart the progress of themes in these descriptions over time (Miles and Huberman, 1984). In speaking about their relationships with women other than their mothers, for example, categories included relational roles (aunt or neighbour), types of shared experience (such as being the oldest sibling, running away from home), duration of relationships, uniqueness of relationship, types of interaction (such as listening, talking) and content of communication (school problems, dating, future plans).

In contrast and complement to the first method's focus on breaking down and organizing narratives into summary descriptions of themes in relationships across girls, the second method – the *Listening Guide* – retains the coherence and integrity of individual narratives. This voice-centred, relational method consists of following the participant's line of thought, asking questions to flesh out a story, and following the associative logic of girls' psyches, and working as an interpretive community. In becoming an interpretive community we explicitly rejected the model of individual interpreters seeking to obtain reliability with other individual interpreters on the assumption that ideally every-one will hear or see the 'truth'. As an interpretive community we share values concerning development and also a method. Our differences are also crucial. In the Understanding Adolescence Study, we developed a more racially diverse community to analyse interviews in order to hear different voices. As we came to find through working in an interpretive community – closely and collaboratively, with the same texts – it was precisely those differences that led us to interpretations which took our understanding forward.

The method (see also Brown *et al.*, 1988; Gilligan *et al.*, 1991; Brown and Gilligan, 1992: Chapters 1 and 2; Taylor *et al.*, 1995) specifies reading through an interview at least four separate times, each time listening in a different way. The first listening attends to the overall shape of the narrative and the research relationship: to the questions asked, the story or stories being told, and the researchers' responses. Researchers note their first impressions, identify recurring themes, contradictions and images, and track their emotional responses to the person and the story, paying particular attention to how their own culture, race, ethnicity and social class affect their responses and understanding. A worksheet separates the evidence of the person's voice and silences from the interpretations of the researcher so as to leave a trail of evidence and make explicit the relationship between the interviewee's and the researcher's voice, silences and interpretation.

The second time through the interview, researchers listen for the spoken self or first-person voice. In listening to the 'I', investigators hear what a girl says about herself – how she thinks, what she feels and does – and also notice what she does not say that they might expect or wonder about, where she sounds sure of her words and where she sounds tentative or confused. They locate how she represents herself. Under-lining the 'I' statements, excerpting them and placing them in sequence enables us to gain a strong impression of how the person speaking experiences herself in relation to the world in which she lives. The following are Anita's 'I-statement' responses about what makes her feel good about herself in school when she is in eighth grade:

> I felt good . . . I made the basketball team . . . I made the honour roll . . . I was doing real good in school . . . and I really felt good about myself . . . I always wanted . . . I had thought very low of myself . . . I would make it or I wouldn't cheat . . . I wouldn't pass the test . . . I did and I was so happy . . .

As the narrator, the thinking, feeling, active 'I', Anita is at the centre of her explanation of what makes her feel good about herself, and in other narrative accounts of school, of making decisions, of resolving a hypothetical dilemma. The following year, however, when Anita is 15 and in the tenth grade in high school, she cannot think of anything that makes her feel good about herself:

> Oh, I'm never happy. I don't know . . . I don't know. I guess I can do great, I don't know, I don't know, I'm never happy . . . When I know . . . I don't know . . . I'm never feeling good, I don't know . . . I don't know.

Following the 'I' statements throughout the interview each year allows us to hear changes in how Anita speaks about herself. We also note that Anita responds 'I don't know'[9] six times in eighth grade, and that this has increased to 65 times in ninth grade in an interview of comparable length. In tenth grade when she is 16, Anita's unhappiness alternates with good feelings about her efforts to succeed at different activities at school ('I don't know' appears only 21 times in two long interviews). She begins by repeating the theme of her ninth-grade response:

> When I felt happy . . . I never felt happy . . . I don't know . . . when I, you know, try . . . I can . . . I feel happy . . . I may not succeed . . . I've tried . . . I feel this good, I feel this great confidence I mean . . . I can do it . . . I may not succeed . . . I mean . . . I give myself . . . I probably won't get it . . . I mean . . . I can't do . . . I think I can do . . . I try . . . I try to do . . . I can't swim for beans! . . . I try . . . I try . . . I try . . . I mean . . . I put in . . . I push myself . . . I mean, I may not always . . . I may not learn . . . I mean . . . I feel good 'cause I tried . . . I don't feel stupid . . . I have this good, I have good confidence for myself . . . I can do it . . . I mean, I don't really succeed all the time, you know.

The *Listening Guide* then specifies listening for relational voices. In this study, in the third reading, we listened for the voice of political resistance, looking for evidence of girls' healthy resistance to disconnection from their own thoughts and feelings. This could be a girl's resistance to unhealthy conventions of femininity and womanhood in the dominant culture or in the girl's culture; her struggle not to internalize or take into herself the negative messages about her value including gender, race and class, and to resist the idealization of relationships which then leads girls more readily into self-condemnation.

For example, when asked by her interviewer, 'What might it be good to know as a black girl in this school?', Anita, who begins to speak before the end of the question, says:

> = = = That we don't take no crap! We don't take no kind of b.s. from nobody! That's how we are. We, we don't care who you are, black girls don't take no kind of trash from nobody! I mean, I know a lot of girls, I mean, I know a lot of my girl friends that are white, they take a lot of trash from a lot of people, and I sit there like, hmm, what's your problem? What are you taking that for, you know what I mean, but I mean, we're very outspoken, you know, we're very blunt, OK, we would tell you, you know, what's on our minds, if we don't like you, or whatever, you know what I mean, cause we don't bite our tongues for anybody, you know.

Anita's joining of self and voice, being one of the 'loud black girls' that Fordham (1993) hears in high schools, is heard at first in our interpretive community of white researchers as healthy resistance to conventions of 'quiet' and 'polite'. Girls' healthy resistance becomes political when girls are standing up to, challenging and refusing to accept a voice of authority carrying messages that attempt to override and derogate what they feel and know. Political resistance can become dangerous when girls are punished for speaking up and out, and Anita is sent to mediation, an intervention that from her point of view 'doesn't work'.

On the fourth and last reading, we listened for evidence of psychological distress or loss. We listen for evidence of dissociation – girls' separation of themselves from their experience, their knowledge, their feelings, their needs, their desires. Evidence of psychological distress includes confusing stories, missing pieces of stories (such as no mention of sadness or anger when they seem merited), and language such as repeated 'I don't know' or 'I don't care'.

For example, over the three years of the study, when Anita is asked about a time she felt bad about herself out of school she returns each year to a fight with her mother that occurred when she was in eighth grade. In tenth grade Anita says that she remembers exactly when it started and what it was about. Later in the interview, when she was asked about her relationship with her mother, Anita portrays it in terms that are very different from her previous descriptions at the same time as the terms cover over their ongoing difficulties to which she refers throughout the interview:

> *What's your relationship with your mother like?* It's good. It's, it's better than what it was before, like I told you we was fighting and all that stuff? We don't fight like that no more, I mean, we're very good, we give each other a lot of respect, you know, we get, we give each other our space and what we need, you know. I mean, I mean, it's not just like she won't be there for me because she is, you know, but she still gives me my space, you know, whenever I tell her to leave me alone or whatever, it's cool, you know, she don't get the attitude . . . *Can you tell me about a time you and your mother felt particularly close, or having a good time together?* When um, I don't know. When I guess, we went out to dinner . . . and we were talking about, you know . . . we never brought up that we used to fight, and stuff. *Why do you think you didn't bring it up?* 'Cause we don't want to think about it, we don't want to think back on it when it happened, you know what I mean, 'cause I was foolish, I mean, I didn't mean to fight, it just happened that way, you know.

Issues of loyalty and respect for her mother may influence Anita's decision not to say more to her interviewer about her relationship with her mother in ways that would reveal what she has spoken about and alluded to over three years: that her mother, for a number of reasons, cannot be available for her in an emotional or psychological sense. Anita may be psychologically resisting knowledge that is difficult to accept, and at the same time, blaming herself for problems in their relationship. This in turn, may lead to psychological dissociation.

When psychological strengths and resilience lead girls into conflict with those in power, the attempt to maintain psychological health (a healthy resistance to psychological trouble) often turns into a political resistance or struggle. Frequently, political resistance leads to retaliation, which may take the form of isolation (ostracism, exclusion, not being listened to, not being heard) or may involve various forms of betrayal, violation and violence. In this case, the same portion of text may be marked as an example of psychological health *and* psychological distress.

The resonance of race

Because this method focuses on relationships, and thereby 'shifts the nature of psychological work from a profession of truth to a practice of relationship in which truths can emerge or become clear' (Brown and Gilligan, 1992: 22), the method also highlights who is listening as well as who is speaking. The Understanding Adolescence Study provided an opportunity to explore further and understand some of the ways in which differences such as race and social class between speaker and listener affect resonances between interviewer and interviewee. In answering a question of what it is like to be interviewed by a woman who is white, for example, Anita in tenth grade first responds breathlessly: 'Oh, no problem. No problem. I don't have a problem. I mean, I don't know. It's alright, no problem. I love it. It doesn't matter.' When asked if it would be different if she were interviewed by a black woman Anita replies:

Not really, but she'll, like, bug out, because everything I told you, you know, I think she'll laugh at everything I said, you know, because like, you know, this, we understand this stuff, you know what I mean? It doesn't really matter.

Anita taps into a central question in all psychological research. Can one understand another whose life experience is different? While Anita rejects the 'you can't understand anything' position, with respect to racial difference, she also suggests that the interviewer's understanding is limited because of her racial difference. 'This stuff' has a number of possible meanings, and as Anita elaborates further, many of these meanings are related to race and racism. Asked by the interviewer, 'Can you give me an example where you felt I didn't understand and someone else would have?', Anita refers to earlier part in the interview when the interviewer clearly did not 'get' what Anita was talking about: 'boys and things like that, in school, and you know, how we're dressing and stuff . . . because like you'll see us like on the streets if you were black, especially if you lived in [the city] or something, you'll understand how we dress.' The interviewer asks: 'Is there anything else that you think I'd understand if I were the same as you, the same background as you?' Anita draws on her knowledge of race and class differences, and what sociologist Patricia Hill Collins (1990) calls 'the controlling images' of black adolescents held by the dominant culture, to explain what she thinks a black interviewer would understand:

> What we want to achieve in life, yah. I mean, what I want to be, because there are a lot of us black kids that are like falling back and they're dropping out of school and getting into, you know, getting arrested and going to fail and all this stuff, but I guess, you'd probably understand where I'm coming from and what I want to do and what I want out of my life, you know what I mean? There's a lot of people that I know that don't want a black kid to be somebody . . . I know you understand, but.

The controlling images, or negative stereotypes, of black adolescents that Anita names – falling back, dropping out of school, getting arrested and going to jail – are those that dominate the nightly news and daily newspapers and prevail in the minds of many white people. Anita knows the images and assumes that her interviewer understands some but not all of what she is saying: 'But, if you lived where I lived, you'd probably, you know, see me, you know, you get what I'm trying to say, like, you'd probably understand what I'm trying to say.'

Advantages to being an outsider have been well elaborated by anthropologists, as this position may elicit some explanations that are assumed to be known by someone with insider status. But adolescents may chose not to speak about what they know and feel, particularly to interviewers who are seen as representing authorities who do not listen to them and unresponsive institutions are for the most part representative of a different race and culture than is dominant in the USA (Miller, 1976; Freire, 1984). The degree of Anita's protest that it is 'no problem' that her interviewer is white may indicate that she feels it would actually not be completely safe to say what she really thinks, given the amount of social distance between them. The distinction between political resist-ance and psychological dissociation becomes more difficult to hear in studies with girls who come from backgrounds unlike those of the researchers than in studies with girls who may feel that their researcher has a similar background and is someone with whom it is safe to speak openly and feely – someone who is a member of the underground (Gilligan, 1990a). This issue is something that is often negotiated or tested within the interview and is a key dynamic in our analysis of the relational process of our research.

Transforming our listening, transforming ourselves

Over the three years of the Understanding Adolescence Study, the group of investigators changed, with our changing life circumstances. As we began to do a systematic, layered reading of the interviews, the group consisted of four women (Jill McLean Taylor, Deborah Tolman, Amy Sullivan and Sarah Ingersoll) and one man (Mark Schernwetter). Carol Gilligan was the principal investigator of the study. Although there is diversity in our cultural, social, religious and family back-grounds, all of us are white and fall within the spectrum of the middle class.

As we began to read the interviews, taking in the adolescents' voices, noticing what they said and did not say, how they spoke about themselves, what they said about their feelings, and our responses, we all focused our attention on Anita as initial readings had shown evidence of marked changes between her interviews as a 14-year-old eighth grader and a year later, as a ninth grader. We brought our individual interpretations of her to the group in order to develop an understanding which resonated for us all. The relational voices we first began listening for, as in earlier studies, were those of separation and connection, and justice and care (Gilligan, 1977; 1982; Gilligan et al., 1988; 1990b). Conventions of femininity in the dominant culture are uncovered in these readings as 'I' changes to 'you', and 'should' signals recognition of, and resistance to, these conventions. Researchers work-ing on the Laurel School Project were, at the same time, hearing girls struggling against loss of voice and relationship, and finding that girls who were doing well by standard psychological measures often were also experiencing distress (Gilligan et al., 1990a). Replacing listening for relational voices of care and justice with considering what resistance might sound like (resistance to others, including interviewers; resistance to themselves, their own thoughts, perceptions, and desires; resistance to debilitating conventions of femininity), we drew on the ways that resistance had been articulated in the Laurel Study while at the same time we listened to other ways or things that these girls, labelled 'at risk', might resist.

In the spring of 1990, when the Understanding Adolescence Study was in its third and final year of interviews, we decided to revise and to expand our research questions in response to preliminary findings of the study and the analysis of the Laurel Study in which political and psychological resistances were heard and explored. Meeting with Michelle Fine, a white woman noted for her ethnographic work on the phenomenon of dropping out in urban public schools, and Janie Ward, who was at the time on the faculty of another college, we started with Anita. We concentrated on how Anita described herself, her relationship with her mother and others, the changes we heard in her words, her voice between eighth and ninth grades. We posed as our questions, 'What does resistance sound like for this African-American girl? What can Anita teach us about resistance that is healthy and about resistance that is debilitating?'

Janie Ward made a key point. She observed that Anita had attempted, on three separate occasions in the eighth-grade interview, to introduce the problem of race (alluding to her experience both in making and, indirectly suggested, in being on the receiving end of racial comments) and that none of us had noticed – neither during the interview itself, nor during the subsequent months of analysing the transcript. Anita's insistence in repeatedly bringing up the issue of race can be heard as a kind of a political resistance, but the failure of the interviewer to pick up this reference may have ultimately colluded in Anita's dismissal, her 'no problem'.

The meeting with Michelle Fine and Janie Ward marked a turning point in the Understanding Adolescence Study. As Ward had pointed out, despite our relational method, we had made Anita the focus of our attention, leaving out of our analysis what was occurring in the interview itself, how that interaction between the interviewer and Anita shaped her narrative accounts. Instead, we were working from the standpoint of a relationship between the reader/interpreter and the interviewee. If we asked girls of colour about their experience and did not speak about the racial or ethnic differences between us or inquire about the meaning of race in their lives, we were, in effect, continuing psychology's tradition of silencing and exclusion. We began to engage in a self-conscious process that bell hooks (1990: 53) sees as the 'serious need for immediate and persistent self-critique'. hooks adds:

> Committed cultural critics – whether white or black, scholars or artists – can produce work that opposes structures of domination, that presents possibilities for a transformed future by willingly interrogating their own work on aesthetic and political grounds. This interrogation itself becomes an act of critical intervention, fostering a fundamental attitude of vigilance rather than denial.

Moving towards an 'attitude of vigilance' by bringing race and class – the participants' and our own – to the centre of our method of inquiry and analysis was transformative in our understanding of the dynamic interaction of participants and researchers in an interpretive community.

We made changes in the interview protocol in what was now the third year of the study, when the adolescents were in the tenth grade. We began by asking interviewees what would be a good question to ask so that researchers could learn about what it is like to be a teenager at their school, eliciting what individual adolescents considered important. The discussion with Michelle Fine focused our attention on power dynamics in the interview situation, in which the onus was on us, as the white adults, to introduce the sometimes uncomfortable/dangerous topic of race, clarifying our willingness to listen and speak about race. We started to ask questions about race: about how an adolescent identifies herself, what she needs to know as an adolescent girl at the high school, and also about what it is like to be interviewed by someone who is from a different racial or ethnic group. As most interviews were conducted by white women, most frequently the question was what it was like to be interviewed by a white woman, as in the interview with Anita.

What we now began to note in these relationships was power and authority aligned with 'differences', tied both to social structures and individual status. We also noted the ways in which the girls may use their power in the interview relationships. Anita, for example, can resist, politically, by being silent, a survival strategy historically employed by African Americans (Jones, 1986; Williams, 1991; Higginbotham, 1992), by withdrawing from the study, or by responding in a way that does not allow us to learn anything about her life. Paradoxically, to the extent that adolescent girls comply with cultural images of 'good' and 'nice' girls and women, they might stay on in a study, even when wanting to leave. In the third year of the Understanding Adolescence Study, when the students were in tenth grade, several girls, although they had agreed to be interviewed and we had set up times, were always unavailable, but they were still reluctant to say an outright 'no'. This was in marked contrast to the boys, six of whom, having asked what the purpose of the study was and how it would affect them, stated clearly that they wished to withdraw from the study. Nevertheless, our studies with adolescents, both in educationally privileged schools and in the inner-city youth clubs, suggest that girls (and also boys) want to talk to someone who will listen to them and take seriously what they say (see also Way, 1994). Anita's repeated efforts to connect with the interviewer can be read as indicative of the strength of this desire, and underscore the importance of the interviewer's responding to her, hearing and picking up on what she says.

We made two key changes in our work to respond to the need for a more diverse interpretive community. While our previous method had attended to the resonance of gender, we now attended more closely to the resonances and interrelatedness of race, social class and gender. It was therefore essential for women of colour to be part of our 'interpretive community', analysing and interpreting texts. Drawing on the pool of women at the Harvard Program in Human Development and Psychology, we asked Pamela Pleasants, an African-American woman who had completed her work for a master's degree at Harvard Graduate School of Education, to join our interpretive community, and we continued to seek out Janie Ward as a consultant. Beverly Smith, an African-American teacher and graduate student, and Jamie Gardine, a Caribbean-American undergraduate, agreed to read interviews of the black adolescent girls in the study. On a more informal basis, we asked Latino and Portuguese women and men to discuss with us our interpretation of interview texts. Simultaneously, we began the Women and Race retreats.

By enlarging our interpretive community in these ways, we affirmed once again the central place that voice has for women – for our interviewees, and for us and others in the interpretive community. 'What does she say, show me, but how does she say it, where is the evidence? Couldn't that also be . . .? But listen to her voice as she's saying it!' In order to hear girls of colour we had to learn from and with women of colour, and in the process to discover and stay with our surprise, embarrassment, shame, guilt, anger, strong and painful feelings – about race, class and privilege.

Anita revisited

Throughout Anita's interviews over three years, voice is central as she describes speaking up and speaking out – activities that lead to trouble both in and out of school. Arguing with a teacher, describing black girls as 'very outspoken . . . not biting our tongues for anyone', Anita defines mainstream, white middle-class conventions of femininity or good womanhood as conventions of silence. In our interpretive community, Jill, who interviewed Anita, lauded her insistence on speaking up, on saying what she thinks and knows, despite concern about Anita's description of herself as a fighter accompanied by loss of connection to her mother and to other people.

For Jill, who grew up in New Zealand, attending a girls' school (whose motto translates 'So That We May Serve'), and for many years obediently following the conventions of femininity in a colonial culture, Anita's ability to resist being a 'nice', 'good' girl who keeps silent about things not usually spoken about (including sex[9]) seems a strength. Although Jill is aware of the possible costs in terms of an educational system that demands conformity in a society that is racist and sexist, she nevertheless idealizes or valorizes what she was not, but what Anita describes black girls as being: 'We're very outspoken, we're very blunt, OK, we would tell you, you know, what's on our minds, if we don't like you or whatever, you know what I mean, cause we don't bite our tongues for anybody.'

As Jill spoke about her interpretations of Anita's interview, she was interrupted by the two black women in our group who had very different responses. Pam Pleasants (who at the same time was working with adolescent girls in the Boston public school system) observed in her initial reading and response to Anita's eighth-grade interview:

> As I read Anita, I find myself becoming agitated by her attitude. She strikes me as probably being like the students that I least look forward to dealing with in the schools . . . brash, opinionated, cocky and just a pain because they constantly challenge you. Perhaps [this is] because she dared to say and do things I never would have done and only does things that I associated with the 'wild crowd' in my high school.

As a group, we talked about the interaction between race and class and how class differences between Pam and Janie, who came from middle-class backgrounds, and Anita, who was poor may have affected their interpretation. Both women were firm in their belief that it is not class that makes the difference here. To Janie, Anita's statements can be heard as excessively assertive, almost belligerent, and unyielding, an example of 'resistance for survival', a reaction against destructive elements in her social world and in the larger sociopolitical context of the USA (Robinson and Ward, 1991: 89). Janie and Pam pointed out something that may have been less obvious to the others in the interpretive community – that Anita may have carried her outspokenness too far, that she seems to have moved from an effective political resistance into a counterproductively aggressive manner of conducting herself that was getting her into trouble, damaging her relationships, and causing her confusion and distress.

The opportunities for discussion around interpretations from our different social locations in this particular interpretive community proved essential to developing rich or multilayered interpretations of the voices of the girls in this study. Constant 'vigilance' as to our own Eurocentrism or Afrocentrism, plus evidence from the text, allowed the interpretations to be broader, more complex, more finely tuned, more accurately voiced. The relationships between black, white and Latina women in the interpretive community and in the Women and Race retreats deepened the researchers' understanding and strengthened the interpretations of the meanings of the interviews with the girls in the study.

This research has led us to reiterate the complexity of human connection. We found that girls' voices resonated in different ways across all the cultural and race and class differences – women listening to girls were moved by and learned from them. What began as a study of a diverse group of adolescent girls and as an effort to expand our method of analysis has opened up into an ongoing conversation and exploration about race, class, power and privilege, and also about closeness, relationships and differences. As we listened to girls' voices in interviews and to women's voices in the Women and Race retreats, we were drawn to examine and to give words to what the inclusion of girls and women so different from and also similar to each other in many ways meant – not only for our relational, voice-sensitive method of study, and for an emerging theory of psychological development, but also for ourselves as women in a diverse and changing society.

Notes

1 Feminist methodology has begun to address power relations in research settings, attempting to make clear and correct the imbalances that exist. A seemingly minor point, for example, is the struggle to find ways to alter the usual custom of giving participants a pseudonym – usually first name only – and, after a full introduction, using the researcher's surname only. In this chapter we use first names for both interviewee and interviewer.

2 Social location or 'standpoint' has been an important discussion in feminist theory. See, for example, Collins (1986; 1990); Harding (1990); hooks (1984); Frankenberg (1993).

3 Janie Victoria Ward joined the Harvard Project in the early 1980s as a doctoral student and worked on the Emma Willard Study looking at the experiences of a small number of black girls in a predominantly white independent school. Now an associate professor at Simmons College, Janie was a consultant to this project and a member of the Women and Race retreats.

4 Started as a single, preparatory weekend for two retreats (Women Teaching Girls; Girls Teaching Women) with a culturally and racially diverse group of women teachers, counsellors, and principals from two Boston public middle schools, the Women and Race retreats expanded into six meetings over two years. The project overlapped with the final year of the Understanding Adolescence Study, and ultimately included 11 women: five black, five white, and one Latina. The retreats took their impetus from a question that was spurred by our attention to girls: will women – will we – perpetuate past divisions among women into the future, including the racial and class divisions that have been so psychologically and politically divisive and painful?

The participants in the Women and Race retreats were five white women, Lyn Mikel Brown, Judith Dorney, Carol Gilligan and Jill McLean Taylor (psychologists, educational researchers, and university teachers associated with the Harvard Project), and Kristin Linklater (a voice teacher and actor). The five black women were Katie Cannon (a theologian), Joyce Grant (an educator and administrator), Wendy Puriefoy (an administrator in a philanthropic foundation), Christine Robinson (a public health and policy analyst) and Janie Ward (a researcher and university teacher who was associated with the Harvard Project). Teresa Bernárdez, an Argentinian woman (a psychiatrist and a teacher), was also a member of the retreat group.

5 Fifteen boys were interviewed as part of the Understanding Adolescence Study. Our circumstances at the School of Education at Harvard University, a shortage of men of colour, led us to postpone analysis of these interviews, as we did not feel we could hear the complexity in these boys' voices without any men of colour in our community.

6 Statistics on school drop-out rates for students aged 16–24 are: white students, 7.7%; black students, 13.5%; Hispanic students, 29.7% – 11 % overall. The rates for students in low-income families are considerably higher: white students, 19%; black students, 24%; Hispanic students, 44.7% (NCES, 1993).

7 See, for example, Ogbu (1987; 1991), who argues that conventional explanations are lacking in three important ways as to why there is such variability between different minority groups in terms of school performance. First, according to Ogbu, 'the wider historical and societal forces that can encourage or discourage the minorities from striving for school success' have been ignored. Second, conventional explanations 'do not consider a group's collective orientation toward schooling and striving for success as a factor in academic achievement. They assume that school success is a matter of family background and individual ability and effort.' Third, according to Ogbu, 'theories fail to consider the minorities' own notions of the meaning and the "how-to" of schooling in the context of their own social reality' (Ogbu, 1991: 7). Required for a better understanding Ogbu believes, is a 'cultural model' that incorporates the perceptions and understanding that minority ethnic/racial groups have of the social realities of their lives and schooling.

8 Graduate students were trained as interviewers by the project director and assistant project director and joined other researchers from the Harvard Project on Women's Psychology and Girls' Development, who were experienced in the voice-centred, relational approach of the Harvard Project studies. Almost all of the interviewers were white, with one black woman interviewing, and one Hispanic man interviewing boys.

9 In the first year of the study, when students were 13–14 years of age and in the eighth grade, the school gave us permission to ask about decisions in a real-life dilemma that we had heard in a previous study. Students responded to a story about a girl whose boyfriend was pressuring her to have sex. The following two years, when the students were in high school, we asked questions about whether they had ever had to make a decision regarding sexual activity. There was a variety of responses that ranged from not having to make decisions until after marriage, to students in tenth grade speaking openly about their relationship with their boyfriends. Anita spoke openly during her tenth-grade interviews about being sexually active with her boyfriend. The following year, Anita had a baby, returned to school, then dropped out a few months later.

References

Anthony, E. James and Cohler, Bertram (eds) (1987) *The Invulnerable Child*. New York: Guilford Press.

Brown, Lyn Mikel (1989) 'Narratives of relationship: The development of a care voice in girls ages 7 to 16'. EdD dissertation, Harvard University Graduate School of Education, Cambridge, MA.

Brown, Lyn Mikel (1991a) 'A problem of vision: The development of voice and relational voice in girls ages 7 to 16', *Women's Studies Quarterly*, 19(1/2): 52–71.

Brown, Lyn Mikel (1991b) 'Telling a girl's life: Self-authorization as a form of resistance', *Women and Therapy*, 11(3/4): 71–86.

Brown, Lyn Mikel and Gilligan, Carol (1990) 'Listening for self and relational voices: A responsive/resisting reader's guide'. Paper presented to the Symposium on Literary Theory as a Guide to Psychological Analysis, held at the annual meeting of the American Psychological Association, Boston, MA.

Brown, Lyn Mikel and Gilligan, Carol (1992) *Meeting at the Crossroads: Women's Psychology and Girls' Development*. Cambridge, MA: Harvard University Press.

Brown, Lyn Mikel and Gilligan, Carol (1993) 'Meeting at the crossroads: Women's psychology of girls' development', *Feminism & Psychology*, 3(1): 11–35.

Brown, Lyn, Argyris, Dianne, Attanucci, Jane, Bardige, Betty, Gilligan, Carol, Johnston, Kay, Miller, Barbara, Osborne, Richard, Tappan, Mark, Ward, Janie, Wiggins, Grant and Wilcox, David (1988) *A Guide to Reading Narratives of Conflict and Choice for Self and Moral Voice* (Monograph No. 1). Cambridge, MA: Harvard Graduate School of Education, Project on Women's Psychology and Girls' Development.

Collins, Patricia Hill (1986) 'Learning from the outsider within', *Social Problems*, 33(6): 14–32.

Collins, Patricia Hill (1990) *Black Feminist Thought*. Boston: Beacon Press.

Fine, Michelle (1988) 'Sexuality, schooling and adolescent females: The missing discourse of desire', *Harvard Educational Review*, 58(1): 29–53.

Fine, Michelle (1991) *Framing Dropouts: Notes on the Politics of an Urban Public High School*. New York: State University of New York Press.

Fine, Michelle (1992) *Disruptive Voices: The Possibilities of Feminist Research*. Boston: Beacon Press.

Fine, Michelle and Rosenberg, Pearl (1983) 'Dropping out of high school: The ideology of school and work', *Journal of Education*, 165: 257–72.

Fordham, Signithia (1993) '"Those loud black girls": (Black) women, silence, and gender "passing" in the academy', *Anthropology and Education Quarterly*, 24(1): 3–32.

Frankenberg, Ruth (1993) *The Social Construction of Whiteness: White Women, Race Matters*. Minneapolis, MI: University of Minnesota Press.

Freire, Paulo (1970/1984) *The Pedagogy of the Oppressed*. New York: Seabury Press.

Garmezy, Norman and Rutter, Michael (eds) (1983) *Stress, Coping, and Development in Children*. New York: McGraw-Hill.

Gibson, Margaret and Ogbu, John (eds) (1991) *Minority Status and Schooling: A Comparative Study of Immigrant and Involuntary Minorities*. New York: Garland.

Gilligan, Carol (1977) 'In a different voice: Women's conceptions of self and of morality', *Harvard Educational Review*, 47: 481–517.

Gilligan, Carol (1982) *In a Different Voice: Psychological Theory and Women's Development*. Cambridge, MA: Harvard University Press.

Gilligan, Carol (1987) 'Adolescent development reconsidered', in C. Irwin (ed.), *New Directions for Child Development: No 37. Adolescent Social Behavior and Health*. San Francisco, CA: Jossey-Bass.

Gilligan, Carol (1990a) 'Joining the resistance: Psychology, politics, girls and
› women', *Michigan Quarterly Review*, 29(4): 501–36.

Gilligan, Carol (1990b) 'Teaching Shakespeare's sister: Notes from the underground of female adolescence', in C. Gilligan, N. Lyons and T. Hanmer (eds), *Making Connections: The Relational Worlds of Adolescent Girls at Emma Willard School*. Cambridge, MA: Harvard University Press, pp. 6–29.

Gilligan, Carol, Ward, J. and Taylor, J. (eds) (1988) *Mapping the Moral Domain: A Contribution of Women's Thinking to Psychological Theory and Education*. Cambridge, MA: Harvard University Press.

Gilligan, Carol, Brown, Lyn and Rogers, Annie (1990a) 'Psyche embedded: A place for body, relationships, and culture in personality theory', in A. Rabin, R. Zucker, R. Emmons and S. Frank (eds), *Studying Persons and Lives*. New York: Springer-Verlag, pp. 86–147.

Gilligan, Carol, Lyons, Nona and Hanmer, Trudi (1990b) *Making Connections: The Relational Worlds of Adolescent Girls at Emma Willard School*. Cambridge, MA: Harvard University Press.

Gilligan, Carol, Rogers, Annie and Tolman, Deborah (eds) (1991) *Women, Girls, and Psychotherapy: Reframing Resistance*. New York: Haworth Press.

Gilligan, Carol, Rogers, Annie and Noel, Normi (1992) Cartography of a lost time: Women, girls and relationships. Unpublished manuscript, Harvard University Graduate School of Education, Project on Women's Psychology and Girls' Development, Cambridge, MA.

Harding, Sandra (ed.) (1990) 'Feminism, science, and the anti-enlightenment critiques', in Linda Nicholson (ed.), *Feminism/Postmodernism*. New York: Routledge.

Higginbotham, Evelyn Brooks (1992) 'African-American women's history and the metalanguage of race', *Signs: Journal of Women on Culture and Society*, 17(2): 251–74.

hooks, bell (1984) *From Margin to Center*. Boston: South End Press.

hooks, bell (1989) *Talking Back: Thinking Feminist, Thinking Black*. Boston: South End Press.

hooks, bell (1990) *Yearning: Race, gender, and cultural politics*. Boston: South End Press.

hooks, bell (1994) *Outlaw Culture: Resisting Representations*. New York: Routledge.

Hurrelmann, Klaus (1989) 'Adolescents as productive processors of reality: Methodological perspectives', in K. Hurrelmann and U. Engel (eds), *The Social World of Adolescents: International Perspectives*. New York: Walter de Gruyter, pp. 107–18.

Jones, Jacqueline (1986) *Labor of Love, Labor of Sorrow: Black Women, Work and the Family, from Slavery to the Present*. New York: Vintage.

Lorde, Audre (1984) 'The transformation of silence into language and action', in *Sister outsider: Essays and speeches by Audre Lorde*. Freedom, CA: The Crossing Press, pp. 40–4.

Martin-Baro, Ignacio (1994) *Writings for a Liberation Psychology*, edited by A. Aron and S. Crone. Cambridge, MA: Harvard University Press.

Miller, Jean Baker (1976) *Toward a new psychology of women*. Boston: Beacon Press.

Miles, Matthew and Huberman, A. Michael (1984) *Qualitative Data Analysis*. London: Sage.

Mishler, Elliot (1992) 'Narrative accounts in clinical and research interviews'. Paper presented at the conference on Discourse and the Professions, Swedish Association for Applied Linguistics, Uppsala University, Sweden.

National Center for Education Statistics (NCES) (1993) *Dropout Rates in the United States: 1992*. NCES 93–464. Washington, DC: US Department of Education, Office of Educational Research and Improvement.

Ogbu, John (1987) 'Variability in minority responses to schooling: Nonimmigrants vs. immigrants', in G. Spindler and L. Spindler (eds), *Interpretive Ethnography of Education: At Home and Abroad*. Hillsdale, NJ: Lawrence Erlbaum, pp. 255–78.

Ogbu, John (1991) 'Immigrant and involuntary minorities in comparative perspective', in M. Gibson and J. Ogbu (eds), *Minority status and schooling*. New York: Garland.

Robinson, Tracey and Ward, Janie (1991) '"A belief in self far greater than anyone's disbelief": Cultivating resistance among African American female adolescents', *Women and Therapy*, 11(3/4): 87–103.

Rogers, Annie (1993) 'Voice, play, and a practice of ordinary courage in girls' and women's lives', *Harvard Educational Review*, 6: 265–95.

Rothstein, Stanley (ed.) (1993) *Handbook of Schooling in Urban America*. Westport, CT: Greenwood Press.

Rutter, Micheal (1980) *Changing Youth in a Changing Society: Patterns of Adolescent Development and Disorder*. Cambridge, MA: Harvard University Press.

Spelman, Elizabeth (1988) *Inessential Women: Problems of Exclusion in Feminist Thought*. Boston: Beacon Press.

Spencer, Margaret and Markstrom-Adams, Carol (1990) 'Identity processes among racial and ethnic minority children in America', *Child Development*, 61: 290–310.

Suarez-Orozco, Carola and Suarez-Orozco, Marcelo (1995) *Trans-formations*. San Francisco: Stanford University Press.

Takesheni, Ruby (ed.) (1992) *Adolescence in the 1990's: Risk and Opportunity*. New York: Teachers College Press.

Taylor, McLean Jill (1991) 'Breaking the silence: Questions about race'. Symposium paper presented at the Annual Meeting of the American Psychological Association, San Francisco.

Taylor, Jill McLean, Gilligan, Carol and Sullivan, Amy (1995) *Between Voice and Silence: Women and Girls, Race and Relationship*. Cambridge, MA: Harvard University Press.

Trueba, Henry, Spindler, George and Spindler, Louise (eds) (1989) *What Do Anthropologists Have to Say about Dropouts? A First Centennial Conference on Children at Risk*. New York: Falmer Press.

Way, Niobe (1994) '"Can't you see the courage, the strength that I have?" – Listening to urban adolescent girls speak about their relationships', *Psychology of Women Quarterly*, 19: 107–28.

Weis, Lois (1990) *Working Class without Work: High School Students in a De-industrializing Economy*. New York: Routledge.

Williams, Patricia (1991) *The Alchemy of Race and Rights*. Cambridge, MA: Harvard University Press.

—————• 13

Meta-analysis and feminist psychology

—————• KELLY SHAW-BARNES AND
ALICE H. EAGLY

When a body of research literature has accumulated on a given topic, researchers and other interested people often begin to wonder what all of the studies, taken together, have to say. Do they lead to the same conclusion? If not, why not? What explains the inconsistencies sometimes reported in the results of studies focused on the same hypothesis? Motivated by such questions, investigators often wish to review the existing literature and to draw conclusions based on the findings of all of the available studies. These concerns have become acute among feminist researchers who are often aware that very large numbers of studies have addressed the same hypotheses in the burgeoning research literatures on gender. Presumably conclusions would be more reliable and valid if they were based on more, rather than less, evidence from empirical research.

Until fairly recently, psychologists and other behavioural scientists used only very informal methods to locate relevant studies and to draw conclusions based on their findings. These traditional, informal methods of integrating research have become known as *narrative reviewing*. Starting in the late 1970s, some reviewers began to augment these existing techniques with the new methods of *quantitative synthesis* that are popularly known as *meta-analysis*. As we will explain, the quantitative synthesis of research features thorough and systematic techniques for locating relevant studies and has as its defining quality the implementation of quantitative methods for aggregating and integrating the findings reported in such studies. These new methods of synthesizing research findings constitute a very important addition to the battery of research methods available to feminist psychologists.

The quantitative synthesis of research makes use of a family of statistical techniques designed for integrating the results of research testing a specific hypothesis. This method of research integration uses individual studies in much the same way that primary research uses individual research participants. Thus, a research problem is formulated, relevant studies are gathered, and appropriate data are retrieved from the studies. Conclusions about the research literature are drawn based on the results of statistical tests on the set of findings taken from the individual studies.

The primary purpose of this chapter is to discuss the quantitative synthesis of research and to explore its role in feminist research. We will first compare the meta-analytic method with the more traditional mode of synthesizing research, the narrative review. We will then present an overview of the meta-analytic process, explaining the typical steps that are carried out. Following the overview, we will discuss the importance of meta-analysis to feminist social psychology.

To illustrate the importance of meta-analysis to feminist research in social psychology, we focus on the area of sex differences and similarities. Questions of similarity and difference have long been important in feminist discourse, and, to address these questions empirically, reviewers have increasingly turned to the methods of quantitative synthesis to guide them in interpreting the findings of studies that have compared female and male behaviour. These efforts have attracted considerable attention and remain a focus of debate, not only among feminist researchers but also in the larger community of psychological researchers (see Eagly, 1987b; 1994; 1995; Haug et al., 1993; Hyde, 1994).

Meta-analysis and the narrative review

Contrary to the practices of narrative reviewers, whose exact methods are generally left undefined for readers of the reviews (see Block, 1976), the techniques of meta-analysts entail explicit descriptions of the methods used to produce the review. Meta-analysts explain how the relevant studies were located and selected, define the variables of interest, and describe how their analyses were performed. They also explain how they arrived at their conclusions with guidance from statistical tests. In contrast, readers of narrative reviews generally have no access to the exact methods used by the reviewer. The methods used, for example, to locate relevant studies may in fact be quite unsystematic, based largely on the reviewer's personal knowledge of the relevant research.

After locating a number of studies, narrative reviewers usually proceed by presenting brief descriptions of the reviewed studies. They then arrive at a conclusion about the state of the literature, guided by their impression of the overall pattern of results. Often narrative reviewers use the flawed decision rule of voting with the majority of the studies in the sense that they claim support for a hypothesis only if the majority of studies have confirmed it at a statistically significant level.

Because meta-analysts use systematic methods for retrieving studies, implement quantitative methods for analysing their findings, and report these methods in detail, the statistical findings of quantitative syntheses can ordinarily be replicated. Just as the reporting of an individual study entails a reasonably exact description of its methods, the reporting of a quantitative synthesis entails providing information about the details of the synthesis, generally in a method section. If quantitative reviewers apply identical methods to synthesizing the same research literature, the findings of their reviews should prove to be quite similar. When meta-analysts have differed in the thoroughness of their searches for relevant studies or in the particular statistical methods they have used to analyse data, their reviews have, of course, produced different results. As long as meta-analysts have provided precise and detailed reports, the causes of differences in conclusions can usually be discerned.

Another major criticism of narrative reviewing pertains to its use of statistical significance as an indicator that the effect of interest is present in a study. Although statistical significance is useful for interpreting the results of an individual study in primary research, it is not a good metric for comparing and synthesizing research findings across studies. As we shall see, meta-analytic techniques permit the researcher to assess the magnitude of the difference between two groups, instead of merely noting whether a particular finding in a particular study reached statistical significance. Statistical significance, because it is strongly affected by the researchers' sample size, is only a rough indicator of the magnitude of an effect. Two studies may actually produce quite similar findings, with one, but not both, reaching significance based solely on the basis of sample size. Meta-analysis is not subject to this problem because the metric used to compare studies (i.e., effect sizes) is independent of their sample sizes. Meta-analytic techniques thereby allow researchers to place the results of studies on a continuum, rather than into groups based on the presence or absence of statistical significance.

Critics of quantitative synthesis sometimes misconstrue its methods by claiming that practitioners of meta-analysis naively believe that their methods are objective (see, for example, Marecek, 1995). On the contrary, these methods, like those of primary research, entail many subjective decisions – for example, about what criteria to use for including and excluding studies. However, these decisions are carefully explained, in order to communicate them to the readers of the review. Because the decisions of quantitative reviewers are made public, they are subject to methodological scrutiny and criticism – a hallmark of the scientific method.

The methods of quantitative synthesis

Formulating the hypothesis

Decisions made at the beginning of a synthesis guide the reviewer through the process of collecting studies, coding study features, and analysing effect sizes (Hall *et al.*, 1994). The first task is to define the topic of interest. The problem must be stated with sufficient clarity to enable relevant research to be identified and meta-analysed. Independent and dependent variables must be defined. The researcher must delineate the types of studies which will be included in the sample of studies that is subjected to analysis. Inclusionary and exclusionary critieria are ordinarily designed to include studies that provide clear tests of a hypothesis but to exclude studies that do not. These criteria guide the researcher in the quest for studies and may be modified as new types of studies are discovered and additional reasons are discerned for including and excluding studies from the meta-analysis.

These methods for collecting studies are far more rigorous than those ordinarily used in narrative reviews. The meta-analyst explicitly states the criteria used in selecting studies for the analysis. These criteria are consistently applied in determining each study's suitability for inclusion in the analysis. Careful meta-analysts generally keep a list of the studies they have rejected as unsuitable and may record the specific criterion (or criteria) that justified the elimination of each such study.

An appropriate balance should be achieved in formulating criteria for including and excluding studies from a synthesis. Criteria that are too narrowly defined may lead to the loss of studies that are relevant to the hypothesis being tested. More appropriate criteria would have allowed these studies to remain, and the methodological differences between these studies and others in the sample could have been represented in the coding scheme. Such coding would allow the reviewer to examine whether the different types of study in fact produced differing findings. At the same time, the sample must be defined narrowly enough to allow clear generalizations based on the studies included. Finally, limitations of time and resources may restrain reviewers from defining research literatures so broadly that they would encompass thousands of studies.

Locating studies

The next step is to retrieve studies relevant to the research problem (White, 1994). It is important to identify and retrieve as much of the relevant literature as possible – indeed, retrieving all studies should be the goal that reviewers keep in mind. Published literature is the easiest to identify and locate. Relevant doctoral dissertations from the USA and some other nations are also easily located. Although other types of unpublished literature can be more difficult to find, there are established techniques for accomplishing this task (Rosenthal, 1994). Using several techniques for identifying studies will ensure that the search is as complete as possible.

Computerized data bases are especially helpful for the task of locating studies (Reed and Baxter, 1994). There are many data bases available; the decision concerning which ones to use is based on the research topic of interest. A few of these data bases are essential for locating research on psychological topics. In particular, PsycINFO is the most widely used computer data base for accessing material from psychology and related fields. PsycLIT is the CD-ROM companion to the PsycINFO data base. Educational Resources Information Center (ERIC) provides access to a wider range of journals in the social and behavioural sciences as well as to unpublished reports and papers presented at meetings and conferences, while ASSIA is useful for applied research. Doctoral dissertations and master's theses can be located through Dissertation Abstracts Online. Social SciSearch, the computer data base that contains information from the Social Science Citation Index (available via BIDS in the UK), indexes an extremely wide range of journals in the social sciences. This data base can be used to carry out a search that retrieves all articles that have cited a particular article. In research literatures that emanate from an early core study that is ordinarily cited by later investigators, this technique is particularly useful for locating relevant studies.

A search strategy is developed using the terms and conventions of the particular database system. These strategies should be broad enough to locate the relevant studies. Using a search strategy that is too narrow may result in the loss of relevant studies. However, using a search strategy that is too broad may access thousands of irrelevant studies, and the time required to sort the 'hits' from the 'misses' may be prohibitive. Knowledge of the research area, combined with an understanding of types of search strategy that can be invoked within the data base, aids the researcher in the development of an adequate search strategy. Preliminary interaction with data bases in relation to a specific hypothesis allows an individual to fine-tune a single search strategy or to develop several cross-cutting search strategies that locate a particular research literature.

To achieve an adequate search, an investigator needs to possess some prior knowledge of the ways that relevant findings would probably be organized within a research area. Illustrating this necessity is the rather common situation in which tests of the hypothesis in question do not always appear as the focal (or primary) hypothesis of the studies in the research literature. The search strategy would have to take this consideration into account. For example, if the topic of interest were sex differences in attitudes towards homosexuality (see Whitley and Kite, 1995), many articles not primarily concerned with comparing the sexes may nevertheless contain the critical comparison between female and male respondents. Therefore, all documents that reported attitudes towards homosexuality should be located, and these documents would be examined to discover whether a comparison of the sexes was included. Using terms such as 'sex or gender differences' in the search would locate some studies but fail to locate many other studies that reported a sex comparison in an ancillary analysis whose presence in the document would not be apparent from its title or abstract.

In addition to utilizing computerized data bases, reviewers ordinarily invoke several other methods for searching the literature. Checking the reference lists of all located studies often uncovers reports that might otherwise go undetected. The reference lists of prior review articles can also yield many studies. Also, to locate recently published articles not yet indexed in computer data bases, reviewers may hand-search journals that publish work relevant to the topic. Hand-searching multiple volumes of key journals also provides a cross-check on the adequacy of computerized searches that the researcher has already carried out.

Many papers delivered at meetings and conferences are never indexed in any formal way. For this reason, examining paper titles and abstracts in conference programmes may uncover studies on the research topic that would not have been located by more formal methods. Finally, contacting authors who work in the field may provide access to their unpublished studies.

Coding and analysis

After all relevant studies have been located, the characteristics of each study are coded, and effect sizes are calculated to represent the magnitude and direction of the findings. The study characteristics that a reviewer desires to code will vary depending on the research problem being studied (Lipsey, 1994). For example, in a study of sex differences in spatial ability, one potentially interesting characteristic would be the type of spatial task used in the ability test (Voyer *et al.*, 1995). To enable such study characteristics to be recorded for later analyses, a researcher must develop a coding form for the particular research problem (Stock, 1994). Design of the coding system would be guided by reviewers' knowledge of the methodological features of the particular research literature and also by their theoretical understanding of the features of the studies that are likely to be consequential in influencing their outcome. The coding system should be carefully constructed to allow for the representation of all potentially interesting features of each study. Just as in coding for primary research, in coding for meta-analysis two (or more) individuals first learn the coding system, then code independently, and finally compare their coding and resolve any disagreements. The report of a quantitative synthesis ordinarily includes statistics on intercoder reliability.

In addition to coding the characteristics of each study, a reviewer calculates an effect size for every report. To reduce error, these calculations should be carried out by two individuals working independently. The two most commonly used effect sizes are d and r. The effect size d represents the difference between two means in standard deviation units and therefore can be interpreted as a type of standard score. In studies of sex differences, this effect size would represent the difference between men and women on the variable in question – for example, a difference in aggression or in spatial ability. A d of 0.5 indicates that there is a difference of 0.5 standard deviations between the average performance of men and women.

The calculation of an effect size in the d metric can be accomplished by taking the difference between the two means and dividing it by the within-group (or pooled) standard deviation. When the means and standard deviations for the two groups are not present in a research report but the groups have been statistically compared, the effect size can nevertheless be calculated in many instances from statistics such as t-tests, F-tests, or exact p-values, or from information provided in tables that report an analysis of variance.

Correlation coefficients can also serve as effect sizes – for example, a reviewer could obtain correlations between the participants' sex, treated as a dichotomous variable, and their performance on tests of verbal or quantitative ability. In practice, meta-analysts prefer r over d as their metric for a quantitative synthesis when the two variables that are related in tests of their hypothesis are ordinarily both continuous in research data. Examples are the relation between academic achievement and socioeconomic status (White, 1982) and the relation between psychological factors and heart disease (Booth-Kewley and Friedman, 1987). When the independent variable of interest is not a continuous variable but is dichotomous, as in the case of sex of research participants, quantitative reviewers generally prefer to use d as the effect size.

Readers of meta-analyses often wonder how large an effect size should be in order to be considered important. There has been considerable discussion of this issue (Rosenthal and Rubin, 1982; Abelson, 1985; Prentice and Miller, 1992). Judgements about effect magnitude should take into account not only the numerical value of an effect size, but also particular features of the research literature under consideration. For example, in an experimental literature with highly controlled stimuli, uncontrolled variability in responses should be less than in less controlled experiments or field studies, and effect sizes should be correspondingly larger. Although numerical guidelines have been offered for the interpretation of the magnitude of effect sizes (Cohen, 1977), these should be used only very cautiously because they do not take into account the specific methodological features of studies that would constrain or enlarge effect sizes. Therefore, rather than compare effect sizes to rather arbitrary numerical guidelines, reviewers should compare them to the sizes of other findings in related research areas, particularly in areas which share similar methodological features (see Eagly, 1995).

After effect sizes have been calculated for every study, they are examined for their homogeneity – that is, their consistency across the studies. This analysis reveals whether the effect sizes have essentially the same magnitude, or whether there are differences between effect sizes beyond those that would be expected on the basis of random error. If the effect sizes have the same magnitude (and direction), they can be considered to be sampled from the same population. If the effect sizes are found to vary, the magnitude of the aggregated effect sizes becomes less interesting, and the meta-analyst's next step is to investigate the extent to which features of the studies may contribute to the variability of the effect sizes. Further statistical analyses would be conducted to determine the relation between various study features and the effect sizes.

An investigator's theory associated with the particular topic might suggest some promising features to explore as predictors of the effect sizes. Guided by theory or other considerations, the meta-analyst identifies moderators, or study characteristics that might influence the effect sizes, and uses these to predict study outcomes (Hall and Rosenthal, 1991). For example, in a meta-analysis of gender-related helping behaviour, social role theory suggested that the social setting of the study might be an important moderating variable (Eagly and Crowley, 1986). Such moderators can exist within studies if, for example, different experimental conditions of a study established different social settings. Moderators can also exist between studies. Social settings would vary between studies, as would many other study characteristics such as the publication year or the sex(es) of the author(s) of the study.

There are a number of publications that cover the meta-analytic method in more detail (Cooper, 1989; Hunter and Schmidt, 1990; Rosenthal, 1991; Cooper and Hedges, 1994). Hedges and Becker (1986) present a discussion of statistical considerations in the meta-analysis of sex differences. In addition, software packages are available for computing and analysing effect sizes. DSTAT (Johnson, 1989) and BASIC (Mullen, 1989) are the two most widely used programs.

Contributions of meta-analysis

As already noted, until the late 1970s narrative reviewing was the sole method of integrating the results of research studies in a given domain. Glass (1976) first introduced the term 'meta-analysis', although precursors of meta-analysis can be identified in earlier periods. Bangert-Downs (1986) provided a brief review of early studies that used meta-analytic methods. The first published meta-analysis was that of Smith and Glass (1977), which examined the question of whether psychotherapy is effective. The number of researchers carrying out quantitative syntheses grew rapidly, and thousands of meta-analyses have been published not only in psychology but also in the social sciences and health sciences more generally.

Quantitative syntheses have become very influential in psychology because of the promise they offer of validly assessing hypotheses in research literatures and therefore establishing psychology as a science in which research has the potential to cumulate over time. In addition to overcoming many of the limitations of narrative reviewing that impeded cumulation, meta-analysis has provided other benefits. In particular, these new techniques have made it possible to go beyond the hypotheses tested in primary research (Hall *et al.*, 1994). For example, Eagly and Carli (1981) and other reviewers examined the sex of authors of research reports as a predictor of sex differences in the behaviours examined in these reports, and many meta-analysts have examined publication year as a correlate of study outcome.

Although some quantitative syntheses are relatively atheoretical, meta-analysis can also contribute to theoretical developments (Miller and Pollock, 1994). Just as in primary research where different theories may suggest contrasting predictions, in meta-analysis different theories may also suggest contrasting predictions, especially for the impact of moderator variables on effect sizes. These predictions can then be tested meta-analytically. Of particular relevance to feminist psychology is Eagly and Wood's (1991) discussion of theory-testing in meta-analyses of sex differences and similarities in social behaviour.

In addition, the outcomes of meta-analyses can provide important guides for designing research. Eagly and Wood (1994) discussed the different types of meta-analytic outcome and analysed the implications of these outcomes for future research. One of the main points of their discussion is that different levels of certainty are associated with the generalizations yielded by quantitative syntheses; low levels of certainty ordinarily indicate a need for more research in an area. An appropriately interpreted meta-analysis can guide researchers to the most important questions that remain unresolved by empirical research.

Meta-analysis and feminist psychology

Soon after the first meta-analysis was published, feminist researchers began to use meta-analytic techniques for the integration of research on gender and related topics. Meta-analysis has proved to be an important addition to the battery of techniques available to feminist psychologists, who have applied it to many research questions. These questions include: whether androgyny affects psychological well-being and social behaviour (Taylor and Hall, 1982); whether psychotherapy is biased against women (Smith, 1980); whether success and failure are attributed to different causes for women and men (Swim and Sanna, 1995); and whether people are prejudiced against women (Swim et al., 1989; Eagly et al., 1992).

Despite interest in numerous such hypotheses, the majority of the meta-analytic research by feminist psychologists has concerned the general question of whether the sexes are different or similar in their behaviour and psychological attributes. As in psychology as a whole, in this research area the integration of research findings was traditionally achieved through the use of narrative reviewing. The first reviews of research on sex differences (Woolley, 1910; Thorndike, 1914) appeared not long after systematic research on this issue began in the early part of the century (Thompson, 1903). Early feminist psychologists examining female and male behaviour often took the position that sex differences were absent or trivial in a variety of domains, and, following in this tradition, subsequent narrative reviewers often reported that few differences existed between women and men (see, for example, Maccoby and Jacklin, 1974). However, with the advent of meta-analytic techniques, a different picture began to emerge. Contrary to the views of narrative reviewers, the presence of a substantial proportion or even a majority of non-significant sex comparisons in a research literature is not ordinarily consistent with the conclusion that the sexes do not differ (see Hedges and Olkin, 1980). Statistical significance is a poor guide to conclusions because effect sizes of small to moderate magnitude often fail to attain statistical significance in small-scale studies. Relying on effect sizes rather than statistical significance and drawing conclusions guided by statistical inference rather than by intuitive reasoning, the evidence for sex differences now seems much more substantial in many domains of psychological research (Eagly, 1995). However, in some cases, the findings of meta-analyses have been used to discount narrative reviewers' claims in favour of sex differences. For example, Hyde (1981) retrieved studies that had been included in Maccoby and Jacklin's (1974) review of cognitive differences between men and women. She then meta-analysed their findings and reported that the sex differences were quite small, contrary to the impression conveyed by Maccoby and Jacklin.

Similarly, Frieze *et al.* (1982) reported that sex differences in causal attributions of success and failure were not as large or consistent as narrative reviewers had concluded.

There has been considerable discussion of the use of meta-analysis for the study of sex differences and similarities (see, for example, Hyde and Linn, 1986; Hyde, 1990; Eagly and Wood, 1991). Controversy has often surrounded these meta-analytic investigations and sex difference research more generally. Authors have expressed their concern that the practice of comparing the sexes in research data might perpetuate stereotypes or contribute to continued discrimination against women (McHugh *et al.*, 1986). Baumeister (1988) suggested that the reporting of sex comparisons is both politically and scientifically undesirable and called for a cessation in such reporting. Moreover, an informal survey indicated that many feminist psychologists look unfavourably on work that compares women and men (Mednick, 1991). However, others have argued in favour of comparing the sexes and have supported this position on both political and scientific grounds (Eagly, 1987a; 1990). In some cases, the condemnation of research on sex differences appears to be a reaction to much earlier times, when investigators not sympathetic to feminist goals used research findings to demonstrate the supposed inferiority of women (Hyde, 1990). The more balanced conclusions emerging from the contemporary meta-analytic phase of research suggest that each sex exceeds the other in some characteristics that are generally regarded as desirable (Eagly, 1995). Furthermore, the issues of whether reporting sex differences is on the whole beneficial or harmful to women, and, indeed, whether questions about sex differences are the 'right' ones to ask, are subjects for current debate (for some contrasting perspectives, see Kitzinger, 1994).

The first quantitative synthesis of sex differences and similarities integrated studies concerned with decoding non-verbal cues (Hall, 1978). Since that time, meta-analyses of sex differences have been conducted in a variety of domains, from mathematics performance (Hyde *et al.*, 1990) and verbal ability (Hyde and Linn, 1988) to aggressive behaviour (Eagly and Steffen, 1986) and leadership style (Eagly and Johnson, 1990). There are several reasons why meta-analysis is important for drawing conclusions about the differences between female and male psychology. First, there is an extremely large amount of comparative data to be integrated. Without quantitative techniques, the task of reviewing such large literatures would be overwhelming. It would be difficult accurately to summarize the findings of many studies, just as in primary research it would be difficult to summarize the behaviour of many research participants without quantification of their data. Also, when males and females are compared, the independent variable (sex of research participant) is more clearly defined and more stable in operationalization across studies than are most other independent variables of interest to psychologists. In addition, meta-analysis is less likely than narrative reviewing to be influenced by the researcher's prior expectations and preferences concerning similarity and difference. In an area as fraught with political meaning as female–male comparisons, researchers' biases need to be held in check as much as possible.

Another advantage of meta-analytic integrations of research is that they allow researchers to track sex differences over time. This objective is usually accomplished by examining the relation between study outcomes and the year the findings were published. Meta-analysis can thus be used to investigate whether differences between men and women have increased, decreased or remained stable over a given period of time. For example, Feingold (1988) reported that gender differences in cognitive ability had decreased from 1947 to 1980.

Meta-analysis has also contributed to a better understanding of the magnitude of the sex differences that have been found. In response to researchers who claimed that sex differences were so small as to be of no importance, Eagly (1995) suggested that meta-analyses had demonstrated effects of varying sizes and that the magnitudes of sex differences were probably representative of the magnitudes of effects found in many other areas of psychology.

Quantitative synthesis has fostered the development of theories of sex differences. Eagly (1995) has discussed the relative absence of new theoretical work in the years immediately following the influential Maccoby and Jacklin (1974) book on sex differences. This absence of theory development may have followed at least in part from Maccoby and Jacklin's conclusion that sex differences in all but a few behaviours were either small or non-existent. As meta-analysts began to demonstrate that there were indeed notable differences between the sexes, the development of theory once again became a focus of attention. In fact, even more interesting than their conclusions regarding sex differences, meta-analysts demonstrated that the magnitude of differences between the sexes often differed between studies and between experimental conditions within studies. Reviewers and theorists then set out to explain these complex findings.

Quantitative syntheses have also contributed to answering the question of whether people exaggerate the differences between men and women or imagine differences where these do not actually exist. Using meta-analytic findings, Swim (1994) failed to confirm the generalization that perceivers exaggerate and fabricate differences. Swim compared people's estimates of differences between the sexes with the meta-analytic results of sex difference studies. She found that not only were her research participants fairly accurate in their estimates of differences between the sexes, but also, when they were inaccurate, they tended to underestimate, not overestimate, these differences. Briton and Hall (1995) reported similar findings in their study of perceivers' beliefs about sex differences in non-verbal communication.

Conclusion

The techniques of quantitative synthesis have made important contributions to feminist psychology. Most important is the ability that these techniques give feminist psychologists to scrutinize long-standing conclusions about the presence and absence of sex differences. If meta-analytic methods have been properly utilized, the resulting findings allow psychologists to draw conclusions that validly represent a research literature. Questions of external validity – that is, of generalizing these findings to natural settings – remain to be explored. Yet, the conclusions of quantitative syntheses are more externally valid than those of individual studies because meta-analyses ordinarily investigate a variety of research participants and settings, whereas the typical primary study focuses on a particular group of research participants in a specific setting. However, although the meta-analytic conclusions may be more externally valid, the quality of their conclusions still depends on the quality of the research literature itself. Research literatures suffer from a variety of flaws and limitations which cannot be rectified by quantitative syntheses. Therefore, a meta-analytic investigation of a particular hypothesis does not necessarily provide the truth concerning that hypothesis. Rather, the investigation validly summarizes the studies that are available.

Meta-analytic results are important from a political perspective as well. As meta-analytic researchers continue to explore sex differences and similarities, they have the opportunity to use this knowledge to contribute to discussions concerning the status of women and to understand the origins and consequences of women's disadvantaged status in society. This knowledge may also be useful in formulating public policy on a variety of issues, including education. For example, Eagly (1990) has discussed the potential contributions of meta-analytic findings on sex differences in cognitive performance to the development of more effective educational programmes for both men and women.

Finally, more thorough investigations of female and male behaviour should facilitate a more complete understanding of the reasons underlying the differences and similarities. Instead of fearing that meta-analytic investigations may reveal sex differences, feminist researchers should welcome the opportunity to explore the reasons for differences and similarities. Surely more can be accomplished by researchers who are aware of the reasons why women and men sometimes differ and sometimes do not differ than by those who fail to examine this important area of research.

References

Abelson, R. P. (1985) 'A variance explanation paradox: When a little is a lot', *Psychological Bulletin*, 97: 129–33.

Bangert-Downs, R. L. (1986) 'Review of developments in meta-analytic method', *Psychological Bulletin*, 99: 388–99.

Baumeister, R. F. (1988) 'Should we stop studying sex differences altogether?', *American Psychologist*, 42: 1092–5.

Block, J. H. (1976) 'Issues, problems, and pitfalls in assessing sex differences: A critical review of "The Psychology of Sex Differences"', *Merrill-Palmer Quarterly*, 22: 283–308.

Booth-Kewley, S. and Friedman, H. S. (1987) 'Psychological predictors of heart disease: A quantitative review', *Psychological Bulletin*, 101: 343–62.

Briton, N. J. and Hall, J. A. (1995) 'Beliefs about female and male nonverbal communication', *Sex Roles*, 32: 79 90.

Cohen, J. (1977) *Statistical Power Analysis for the Behavioral Sciences* (rev. edn). San Diego, CA: Academic Press.

Cooper, H. M. (1989) *Integrating Research: A Guide for Literature Reviews* (2nd edn). Newbury Park, CA: Sage.

Cooper, H. and Hedges, L. V. (eds) (1994) *The Handbook of Research Synthesis*. New York: Russell Sage Foundation.

Eagly, A. H. (1987a) 'Reporting sex differences', *American Psychologist*, 42: 756–7.

Eagly, A. H. (1987b) *Sex Differences in Social Behavior: A Social-role Interpretation*. Hillsdale, NJ: Erlbaum.

Eagly, A. H. (1990) 'On the advantages of reporting sex comparisons', *American Psychologist*, 45: 560–2.

Eagly, A. H. (1994) 'On comparing women and men', in C. Kitzinger (ed.), Special Feature: 'Should psychologists study sex differences?', *Feminism & Psychology*, 4(4): 513–52.

Eagly, A. H. (1995) 'The science and politics of comparing women and men', *American Psychologist*, 50: 145–58.

Eagly, A. H. and Carli, L. L. (1981) 'Sex of researchers and sex-typed communications as determinants of sex differences in influenceability: A meta-analysis of social influence studies', *Psychological Bulletin*, 90: 1–20.

Eagly, A. H. and Crowley, M. (1986) 'Gender and helping behavior: A meta-analytic review of the social psychological literature', *Psychological Bulletin*, 100: 283–308.

Eagly, A. H. and Johnson, B. T. (1990) 'Gender and leadership style: A meta-analysis', *Psychological Bulletin*, 108: 233–56.

Eagly, A. H. and Steffen, V. J. (1986) 'Gender and aggressive behavior: A meta-analytic review of the social psychological literature', *Psychological Bulletin*, 100: 308–30.

Eagly, A. H. and Wood, W. (1991) 'Explaining sex differences in social behavior: A meta-analytic perspective', *Personality and Social Psychology Bulletin*, 17: 306–15.

Eagly, A. H. and Wood, W. (1994) 'Using research syntheses to plan future research', in H. Cooper and L. V. Hedges (eds), *The Handbook of Research Synthesis*. New York: Russell Sage Foundation.

Eagly, A. H., Makhijani, M. G. and Klonsky, B. G. (1992) 'Gender and the evaluation of leaders: A meta-analysis', *Psychological Bulletin*, 111: 3–22.

Feingold, A. (1988) 'Cognitive gender differences are disappearing', *American Psychologist*, 43: 95–103.

Frieze, I. H., Whitley, B. E., Hanusa, B. H. and McHugh, M. (1982) 'Assessing the theoretical models for sex differences in causal attributions for success and failure', *Sex Roles*, 8: 333–44.

Glass, G. V. (1976) 'Primary, secondary, and meta-analysis research', *Educational Researcher*, 5: 3–8.

Hall, J. A. (1978) 'Gender effects in decoding nonverbal cues', *Psychological Bulletin*, 85: 845–57.

Hall, J. A. and Rosenthal, R. (1991) 'Testing for moderator variables in meta-analysis: Issues and methods', *Communication Monographs*, 58: 437–48.

Hall, J. A., Rosenthal, R., Tickle-Degnen, L. and Mosteller, F. (1994) 'Hypotheses and problems in research synthesis', in H. Cooper and L. V. Hedges (eds), *The Handbook of Research Synthesis*. New York: Russell Sage Foundation.

Haug, M., Whalen, R. E., Aron, C. and Olsen, K. L. (eds) (1993) *The Development of Sex Differences and Similarities in Behaviour*. London: Kluwer Academic.

Hedges, L. V. and Becker, B. J. (1986) 'Statistical methods in the meta-analysis of research on gender differences', in J. S. Hyde and M. C. Linn (eds), *The Psychology of Gender: Advances through Meta-analysis*. Baltimore, MD: Johns Hopkins University Press.

Hedges, L. V. and Olkin, I. (1980) 'Vote-counting methods in research synthesis', *Psychological Bulletin*, 88: 359–69.

Hunter, J. E. and Schmidt, F. L. (1990) *Methods of Meta-analysis: Correcting Error and Bias in Research Findings*. Newbury Park, CA: Sage.

Hyde, J. S. (1981) 'How large are cognitive gender differences?', *American Psychologist*, 36: 892–901.

Hyde, J. S. (1990) 'Meta-analysis and the psychology of gender differences', *Signs: Journal of Women in Culture and Society*, 16: 55–73.

Hyde, J. S. (1994) 'Can meta-analysis make feminist transformations in psychology?', *Psychology of Women Quarterly*, 18: 451–62.

Hyde, J. S. and Linn, M. C. (eds) (1986) *The Psychology of Gender: Advances through Meta-analysis*. Baltimore, MD: Johns Hopkins University Press.

Hyde, J. S. and Linn, M. C. (1988) 'Gender differences in verbal ability: A meta-analysis', *Psychological Bulletin*, 104: 53–69.

Hyde, J. S., Fennema, E. and Lamon, S. J. (1990) 'Gender differences in mathematics performance: A meta-analysis', *Psychological Bulletin*, 107: 139–55.

Johnson, B. T. (1989) *DSTAT: Software for the Meta-analytic Review of Research Literatures*. Hillsdale, NJ: Erlbaum.

Kitzinger, C. (ed.) (1994) Special Feature: 'Should psychologists study sex differences?', *Feminism & Psychology*, 4(4): 501–46.

Lipsey, M. W. (1994) 'Identifying potentially interesting variables and analysis opportunities', in H. Cooper and L. V. Hedges (eds), *The Handbook of Research Synthesis*. New York: Russell Sage Foundation.

Maccoby, E. E. and Jacklin, C. N. (1974) *The Psychology of Sex Differences*. Stanford, CA: Stanford University Press.

Marecek, J. (1995) 'Gender, politics, and psychology's ways of knowing', *American Psychologist*, 50: 162–3.

McHugh, M. C., Koeske, R. D. and Frieze, I. H. (1986) 'Issues to consider in conducting nonsexist psychological research: A guide for researchers', *American Psychologist*, 41: 879–90.

Mednick, M. T. (1991) 'Currents and futures in American feminist psychology: State of the art revisited', *Psychology of Women Quarterly*, 15: 611–21.

Miller, N. and Pollock, V. E. (1994) 'Meta-analytic synthesis for theory development', in H. Cooper and L. V. Hedges (eds), *The Handbook of Research Synthesis*. New York: Russell Sage Foundation.

Mullen, B. (1989) *Advanced BASIC Meta-analysis*. Hillsdale, NJ: Erlbaum.

Prentice, D. A. and Miller, D. T. (1992) 'When small effects are impressive', *Psychological Bulletin*, 112: 160–4.

Reed, J. G. and Baxter, P. M. (1994) 'Using reference databases', in H. Cooper and L. V. Hedges (eds), *The Handbook of Research Synthesis*. New York: Russell Sage Foundation.

Rosenthal, M. C. (1994) 'The fugitive literature', in H. Cooper and L. V. Hedges (eds), *The Handbook of Research Synthesis*. New York: Russell Sage Foundation.

Rosenthal, R. (1991) *Meta-analytic Procedures for Social Research* (2nd edn). Newbury Park, CA: Sage.

Rosenthal, R. and Rubin, D. B. (1982) 'A simple, general purpose display of magnitude of experimental effect', *Journal of Educational Psychology*, 74: 166–9.

Smith, M. L. (1980) 'Sex bias in counseling and psychotherapy', *Psychological Bulletin*, 87: 392–407.

Smith, M. L. and Glass, G. V. (1977) 'Meta-analysis of psychotherapy outcome studies', *American Psychologist*, 32: 752–60.

Stock, W. A. (1994) 'Systematic coding for research synthesis', in H. Cooper and L. V. Hedges (eds), *The Handbook of Research Synthesis*. New York: Russell Sage Foundation.

Swim, J. K. (1994) 'Perceived versus meta-analytic effect sizes: An assessment of the accuracy of gender stereotypes', *Journal of Personality and Social Psychology*, 66: 21–36.

Swim, J., Borgida, E., Maruyama, G. and Myers, D. G. (1989) 'Joan McKay versus John McKay: Do gender stereotypes bias evaluations?', *Psychological Bulletin*, 105: 409–29.

Swim, J. K. and Sanna, L. J. (1995) 'He's skilled, she's lucky: A meta-analysis of observer-attributions for women's and men's successes and failures'. Manuscript submitted for publication.

Taylor, M. C. and Hall, J. A. (1982) 'Psychological androgyny: Theories, methods, and conclusions', *Psychological Bulletin*, 92: 347–66.

Thompson, H. B. (1903) *The Mental Traits of Sex: An Experimental Investigation of the Normal Mind in Men and Women*. Chicago: University of Chicago Press.

Thorndike, E. L. (1914) *Educational Psychology*, Vol. 3. New York: Teachers College.

Voyer, D., Voyer, S. and Bryden, M. P. (1995) 'Magnitude of sex differences in spatial abilities: A meta-analysis and consideration of critical variables', *Psychological Bulletin*, 117: 250–70.

White, H. D. (1994) 'Scientific communication and literature retrieval', in H. Cooper and L. V. Hedges (eds), *The Handbook of Research Synthesis*. New York: Russell Sage Foundation.

White, K. R. (1982) 'The relation between socioeconomic status and academic achievement', *Psychological Bulletin*, 91: 461–81.

Whitley, B. E. Jr and Kite, M. E. (1995) 'Sex differences in attitudes toward homosexuality: A Comment on Oliver and Hyde (1993)', *Psychological Bulletin*, 117: 146–54.

Woolley, H. T. (1910) 'A review of the recent literature on the psychology of sex', *Psychological Bulletin*, 7: 335–42.

Index

CHALLENGING WOMEN
PSYCHOLOGY'S EXCLUSIONS, FEMINIST POSSIBILITIES

Erica Burman, Pam Alldred, Catherine Bewley, Brenda Goldberg, Colleen Heenan, Deborah Marks, Jane Marshall, Karen Taylor, Robina Ullah and Sam Warner

Challenging Women builds upon feminist analyses of psychology to look critically at the assumptions which underlie both psychology and feminism. Drawing upon current feminist research and theory, the authors explore key professional issues in psychology and its related disciplines. While opening up questions rather than imposing answers, they develop practical feminist interventions and contributions to these issues.

Challenging Women examines a range of topics central to psychology as well as other clinical, educational and policy disciplines. These include sexual abuse, menstruation, feminist therapy, the regulation of mothering, the gendering of the 'caring' professions, and women's safety. Throughout, the authors explore themes of:

- difference, power and reflexivity;
- the politics of research;
- the 'cultural maleness' of psychological theory and teaching;
- the relations between 'race' and gender.

Challenging Women is the first book to provide a systematic and mutual critique of feminism and psychology, and to explore the practical implications they have for each other. It will be of interest to undergraduate and postgraduate students of psychology, gender, women's studies, and the health and caring professions.

Contents
Introduction: contexts, contests and interventions – Part 1: Theoretical challenges – Women, food and fat – Constructing femininity – In a bad humour . . . with psychology – Part 2: Reflecting on research – Heavy periods – Black parent governors – Keeping mum – Part 3: Institutions, interventions and difference – Gendered 'care' and the structuring of group relations – 'Fit to parent'? Developmental psychology and 'non-traditional' families – Power in feminist organisations – References – Index.

224pp   0 335 19510 5 (Paperback)   0 335 19511 3 (Hardback

THEORISING HETEROSEXUALITY
TELLING IT STRAIGHT

Diane Richardson (ed.)

Little attention has traditionally been given to theorising heterosexuality. Heterosexuality tends to be taken for granted, as something that is 'natural' and 'normal'. *Theorising Heterosexuality* questions this assumption and demonstrates how much of our understanding of ourselves and the social worlds we inhabit is based upon unquestioned assumptions about the nature of heterosexuality.

- In what ways does heterosexuality encode and structure everyday life?
- How does heterosexuality shape our sense of identity?
- What is the nature of heterosexual desire?
- What is the relationship between heterosexuality and feminism?

In addition to addressing these questions, the contributors to *Theorising Heterosexuality* provide a critical examination of recent debates about heterosexuality, in particular within postmodern, feminist and queer theory.

Well written in a clear and lively style, this book brings together leading authors in the field, who represent a variety of differing approaches and viewpoints. Heterosexuality is theorised in terms of its institutionalisation within society and culture, as practice and as identity. The result is an impressive and exciting collection, whose insights invite a radical rethinking of many of the concepts we use to theorise social relations.

Theorising Heterosexuality will be of interest to a wide range of students in the social sciences and humanities, especially in sociology, cultural studies, lesbian and gay studies, social psychology and women's studies.

Contents
Heterosexuality and social theory – Heterosexuality and feminist theory – Heterosexuality and domestic life – Heterosexuality and social policy – Heterosexuality and the desire for gender – Recognition and heterosexual desire – Heterosexuality and masculinity – Which one's the man? The heterosexualization of lesbian sex – In the same boat? The gendered (in)experience of first heterosex – Collusion, collaboration and confession – References – Index.

Contributors
Jean Carabine, Janet Holland, Wendy Hollway, Stevi Jackson, Sheila Jeffreys, Caroline Ramazanoglu, Diane Richardson, Victoria Robinson, Carol Smart, Rachel Thomson, Jo VanEvery, Tamsin Wilton

224pp   0 335 19503 2 (Paperback)   0 335 19504 0 (Hardback)